犬夜叉
INUYASHA™

ANI-MANGA™ Vol. 8

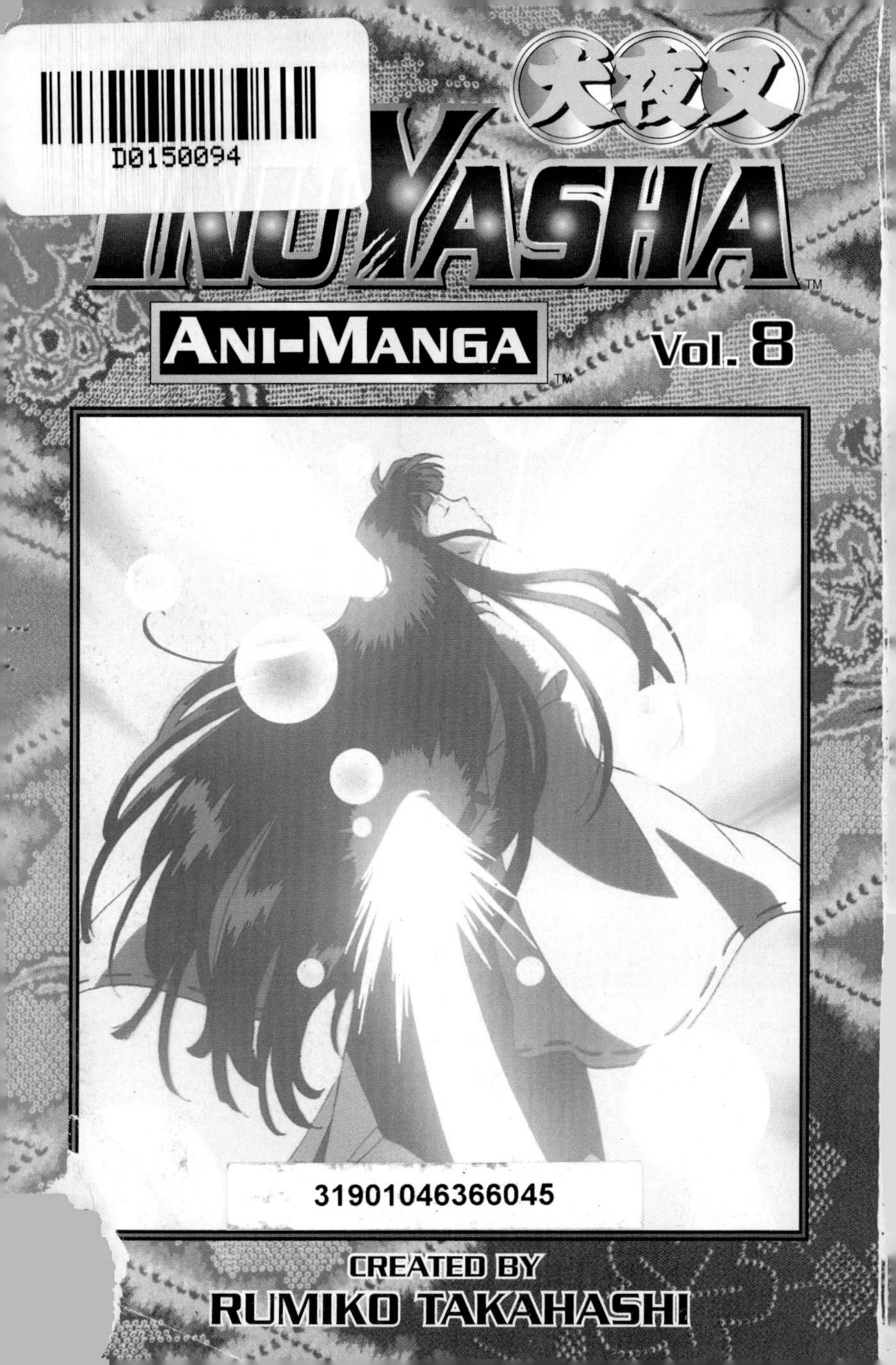

CREATED BY
RUMIKO TAKAHASHI

Inuyasha Ani-Manga™
Vol. #8

Created by
Rumiko Takahashi

Translation based on the VIZ anime TV series
Translation Assistance/Katy Bridges
Lettering/John Clark
Cover Design & Graphics/Hidemi Sahara
Editor/Frances E. Wall

Managing Editor/Annette Roman
Director of Production/Noboru Watanabe
Editorial Director/Alvin Lu
Sr. Director of Acquisitions/Rika Inouye
Vice President of Sales & Marketing/Liza Coppola
Executive Vice President/Hyoe Narita
Publisher/Seiji Horibuchi

© 2001 Rumiko Takahashi/Shogakukan, Inc.
© Rumiko Takahashi/Shogakukan, Yomiuri TV, Sunrise 2000.
First published by Shogakukan, Inc. in Japan as "TV Anime-ban Inuyasha."
Ani-Manga is a trademark of VIZ, LLC. New and adapted artwork and text © 2005 VIZ, LLC.
All rights reserved. The stories, characters, and incidents mentioned in this publication are entirely fictional.

Printed in the U.S.A.

Published by VIZ, LLC
P.O. Box 77010
San Francisco, CA 94107

10 9 8 7 6 5 4 3 2 1
First printing, March 2005

www.viz.com

Story thus far

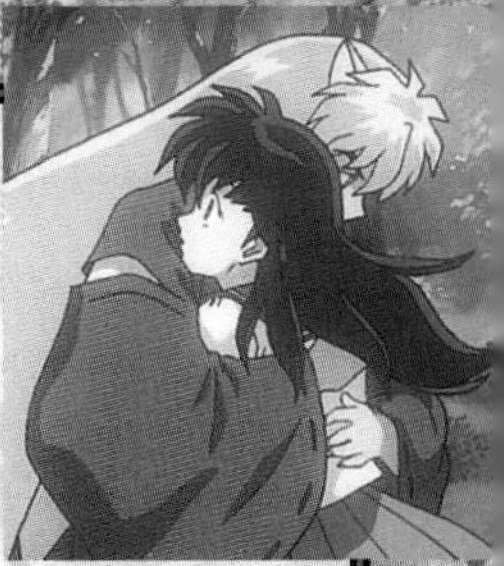

Kagome, a typical high school girl, has been transported into a mythical version of Japan's medieval past, a place filled with incredible magic and terrifying demons. Who would have guessed that the stories and legends Kagome's superstitious grandfather told her could really be true!?

It turns out that Kagome is the reincarnation of Lady Kikyo, a great warrior and the defender of the Shikon Jewel, or the Jewel of the Four Souls. In fact, the sacred jewel mysteriously emerges from Kagome's body during a battle with a horrible centipede-like monster. In her desperation to defeat the monster, Kagome frees Inuyasha, a dog-like half-demon who lusts for the power imparted by the jewel, and unwittingly releases him from the binding spell that was placed 50 years earlier by Lady Kikyo. To prevent Inuyasha from stealing the jewel, Kikyo's sister, Lady Kaede, puts a magical necklace around Inuyasha's neck that allows Kagome to make him "sit" on command.

In another skirmish for possession of the jewel, it accidentally shatters and is strewn across the land. Only Kagome has the power to find the jewel shards, and only Inuyasha has the strength to defeat the demons who now hold them, so the two unlikely partners are bound together in the quest to reclaim all the pieces of the Shikon Jewel.

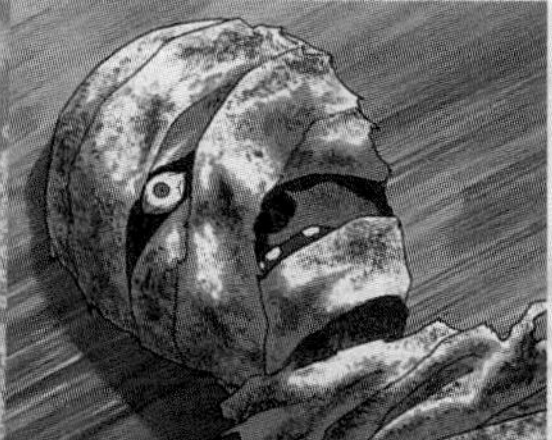

Inuyasha battles with Sesshomaru and wins back their father's powerful sword, the Tetsusaiga, but not before suffering terrible injury at the hands of his half-brother. Fearing for Kagome's safety, Inuyasha sends her back to the modern world—and steals the Shikon Jewel shards they had collected so that Kagome cannot return to the Warring States Era! Kaede, Shippo, and Miroku implore Inuyasha to rest and recover from his wounds, but Inuyasha is determined to find and fight Naraku, the nefarious shape-shifting demon who deceived Inuyasha and killed Kikyo 50 years ago. While Kagome manages to make her way back into the past, Inuyasha comes face-to-face with Naraku, and Naraku's true identity, as well as the distinctive spider-shaped burn mark on his back, is revealed. Naraku and Inuyasha come to blows, and Inuyasha's strength surprises Naraku, but nonetheless Naraku is able to escape!

InuYasha
ANI-MANGA™ Vol. 8

Contents

22
A Wicked Smile and Kikyo's Wandering Soul

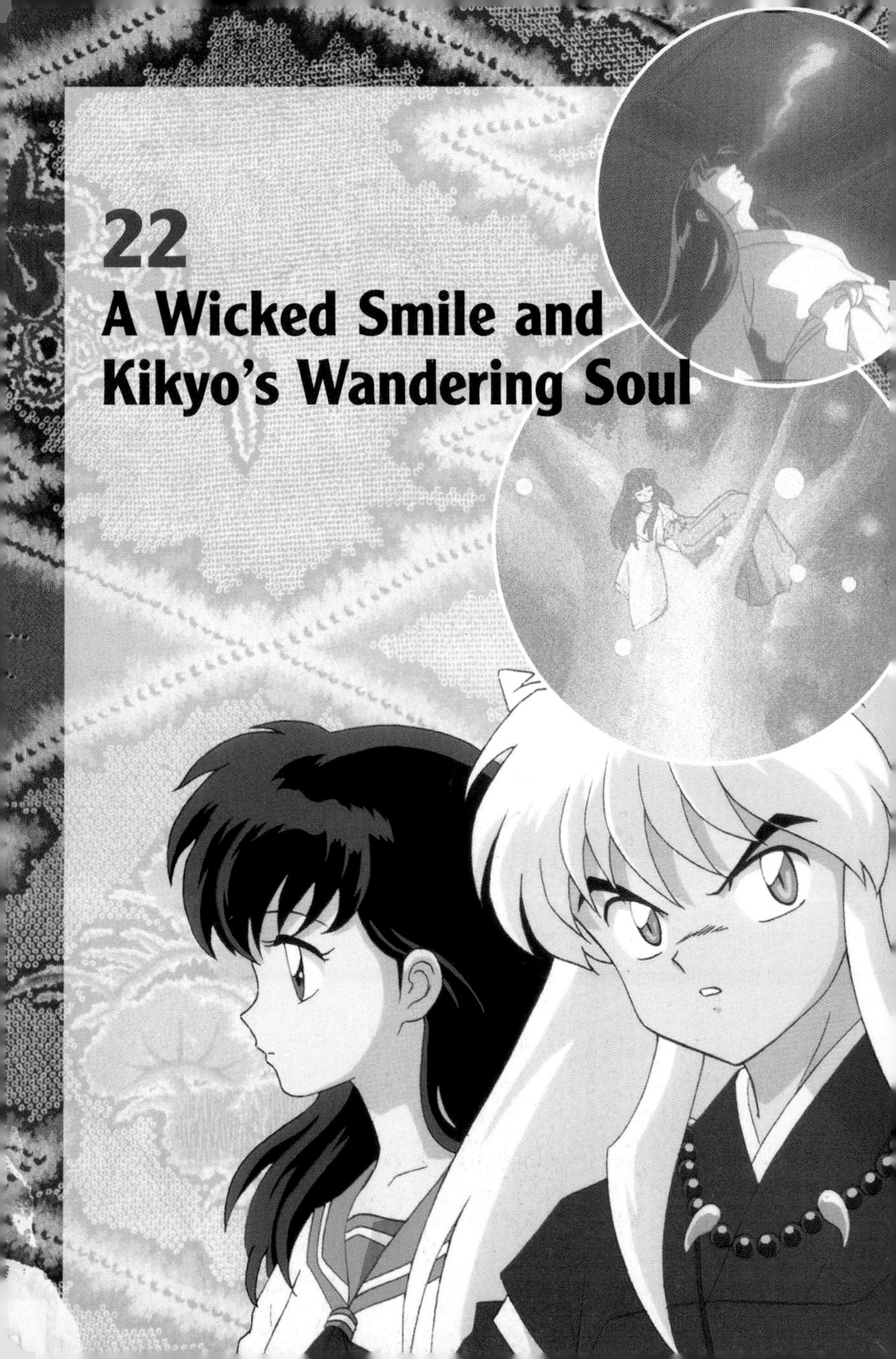

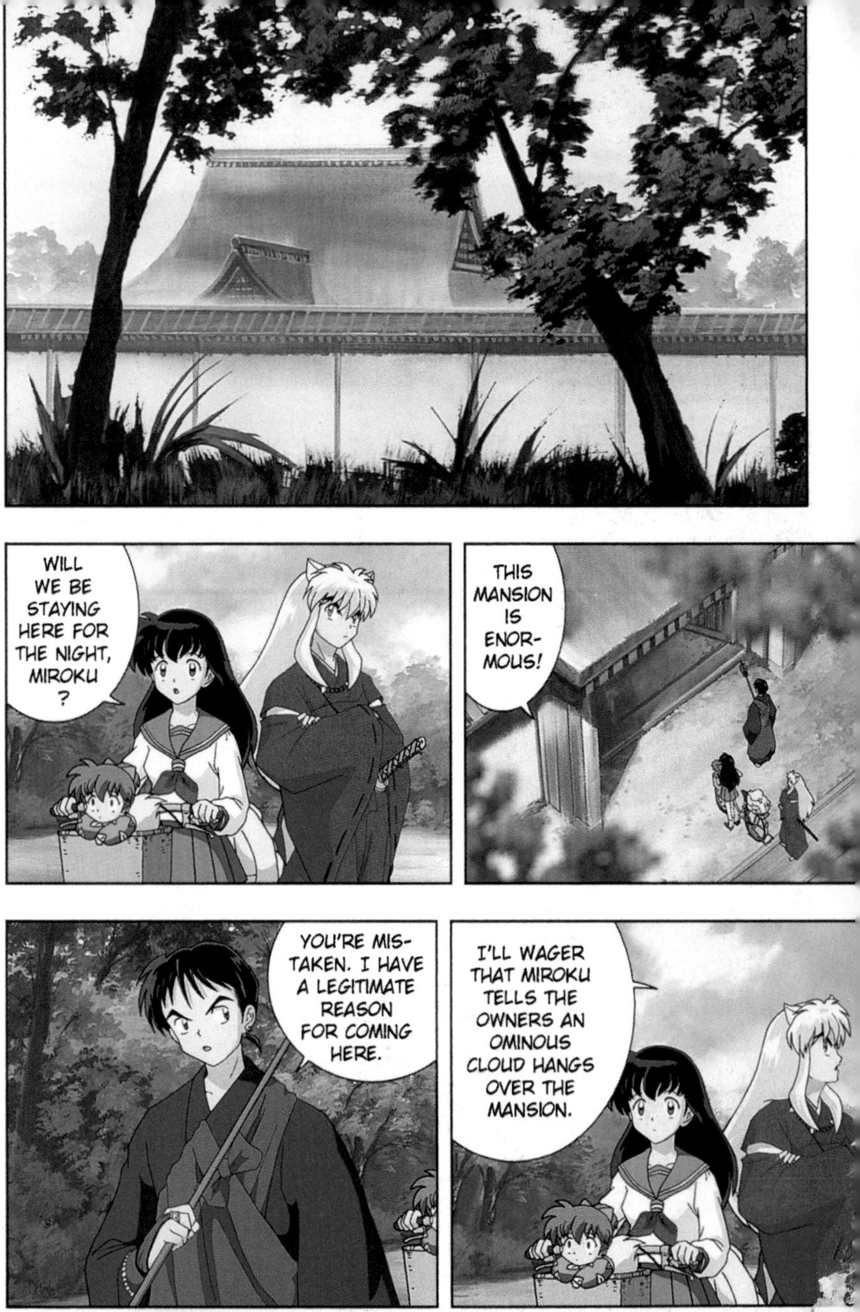
THIS MANSION IS ENOR-MOUS!
WILL WE BE STAYING HERE FOR THE NIGHT, MIROKU ?
I'LL WAGER THAT MIROKU TELLS THE OWNERS AN OMINOUS CLOUD HANGS OVER THE MANSION.
YOU'RE MIS-TAKEN. I HAVE A LEGITIMATE REASON FOR COMING HERE.

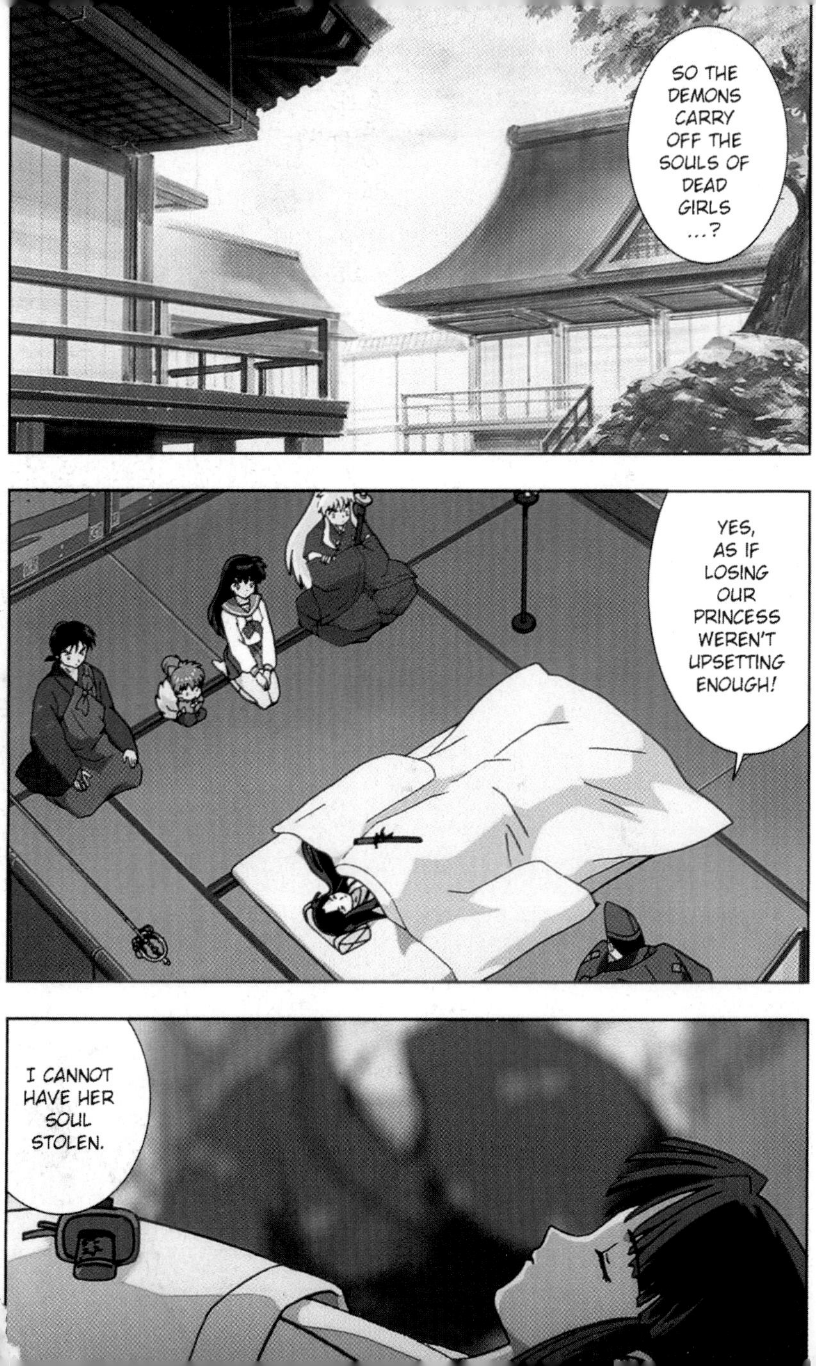
SO THE DEMONS CARRY OFF THE SOULS OF DEAD GIRLS ...?
YES, AS IF LOSING OUR PRINCESS WEREN'T UPSETTING ENOUGH!
I CANNOT HAVE HER SOUL STOLEN.

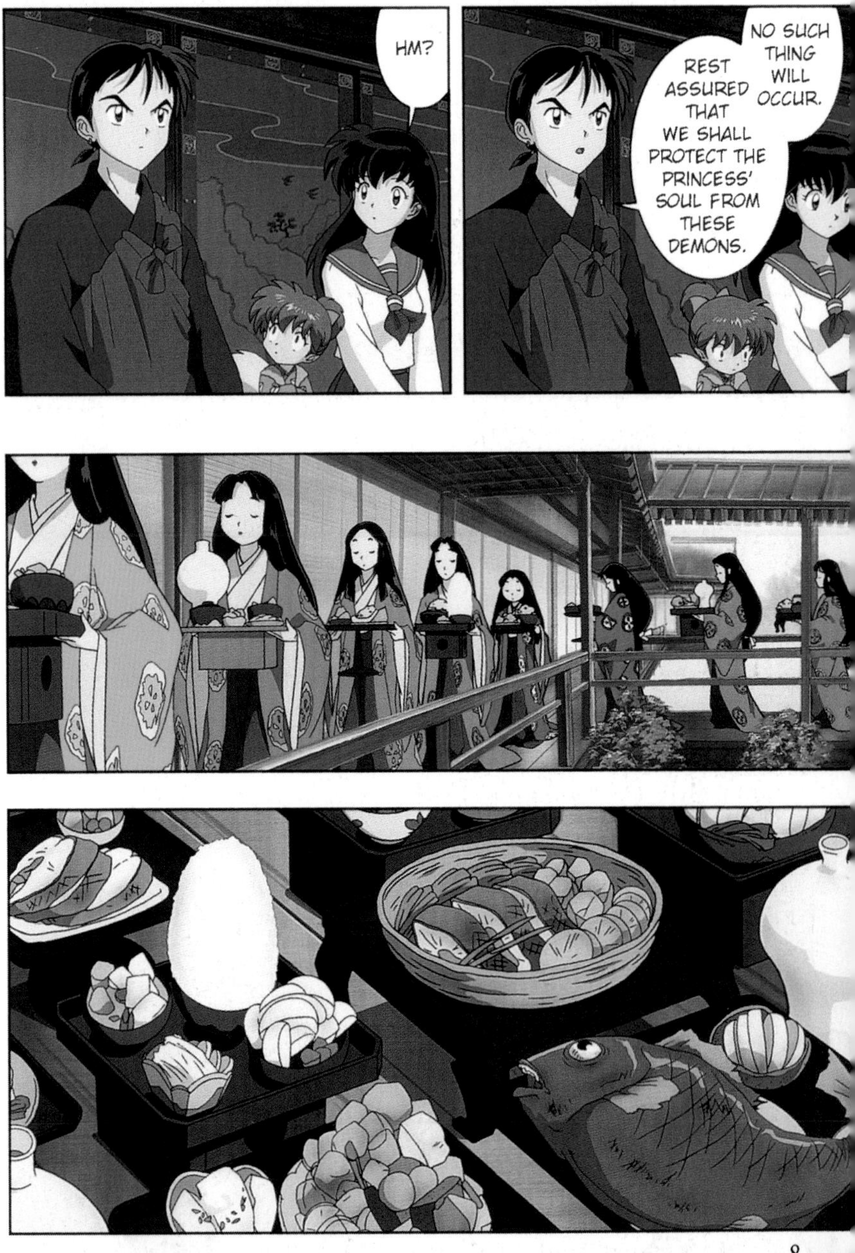
NO SUCH THING WILL OCCUR.
REST ASSURED THAT WE SHALL PROTECT THE PRINCESS' SOUL FROM THESE DEMONS.
HM?

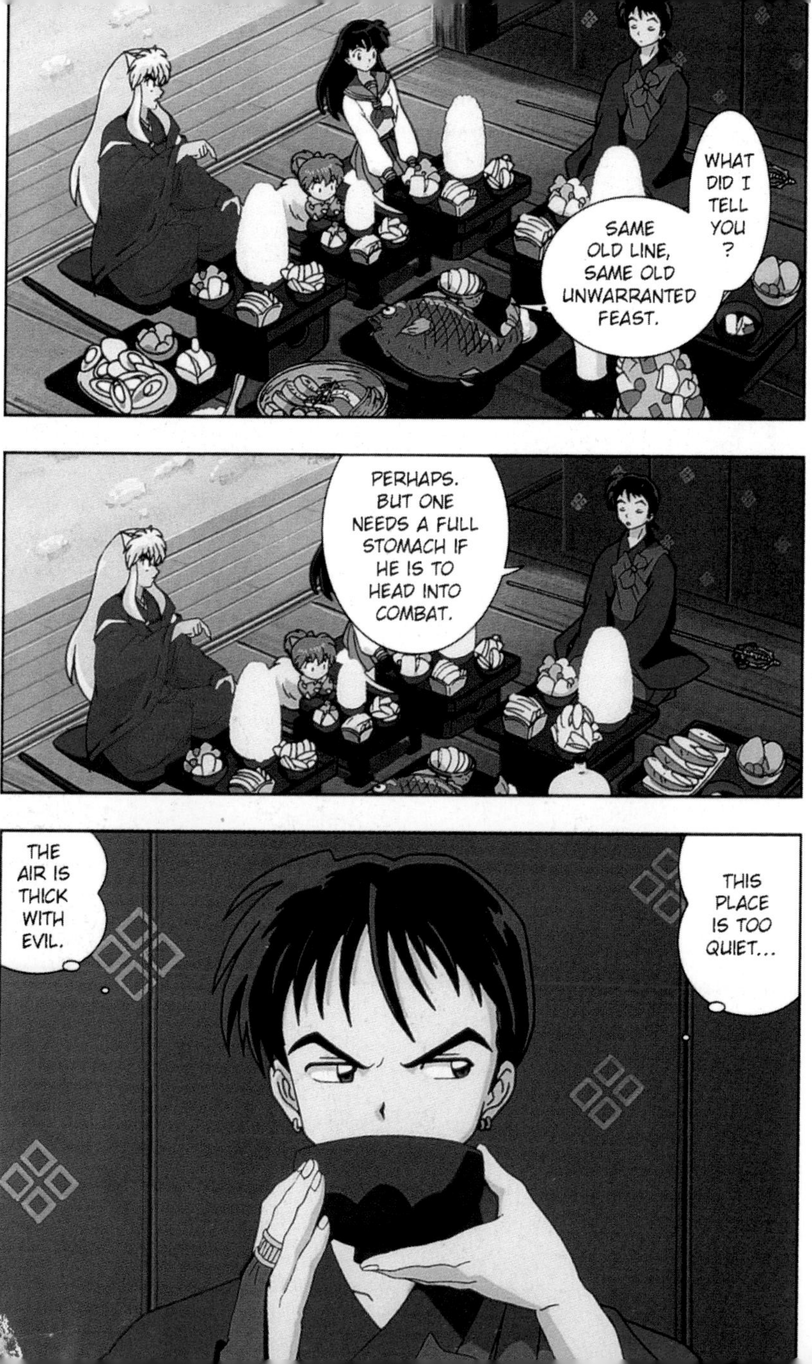
WHAT DID I TELL YOU?
SAME OLD LINE, SAME OLD UNWARRANTED FEAST.
PERHAPS. BUT ONE NEEDS A FULL STOMACH IF HE IS TO HEAD INTO COMBAT.
THIS PLACE IS TOO QUIET...
THE AIR IS THICK WITH EVIL.

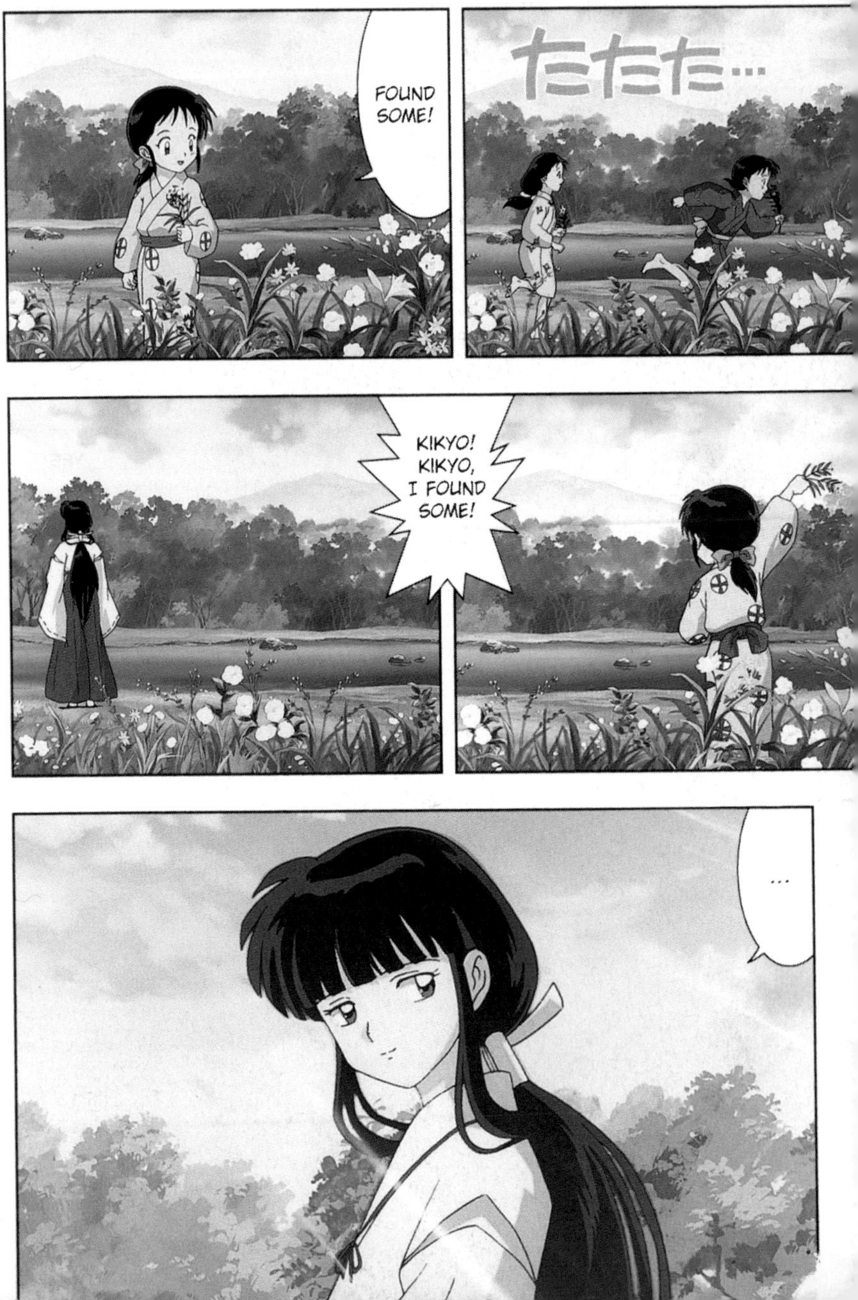
たたた…
FOUND SOME!
KIKYO! KIKYO, I FOUND SOME!
...

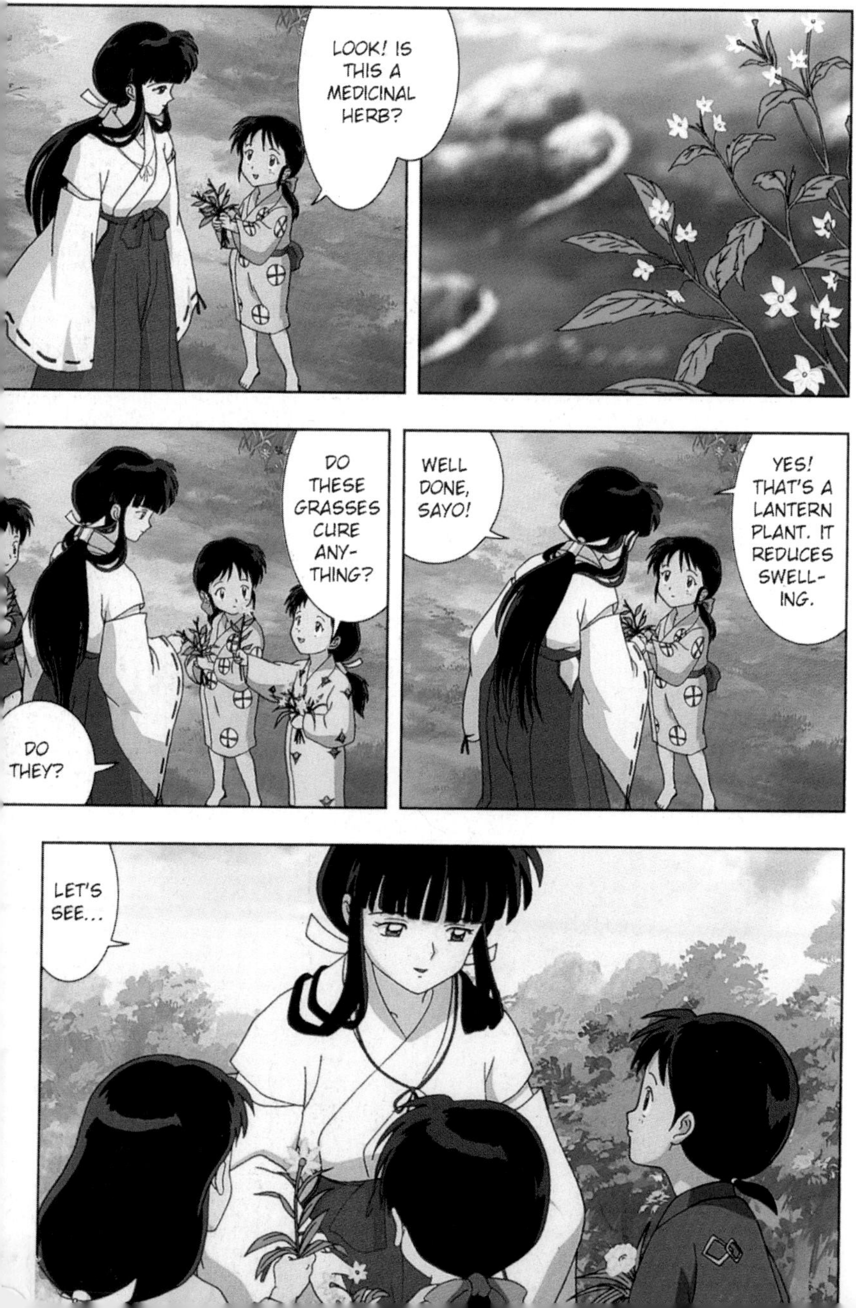
LOOK! IS THIS A MEDICINAL HERB?
YES! THAT'S A LANTERN PLANT. IT REDUCES SWELL-ING.
WELL DONE, SAYO!
DO THESE GRASSES CURE ANY-THING?
DO THEY?
LET'S SEE...

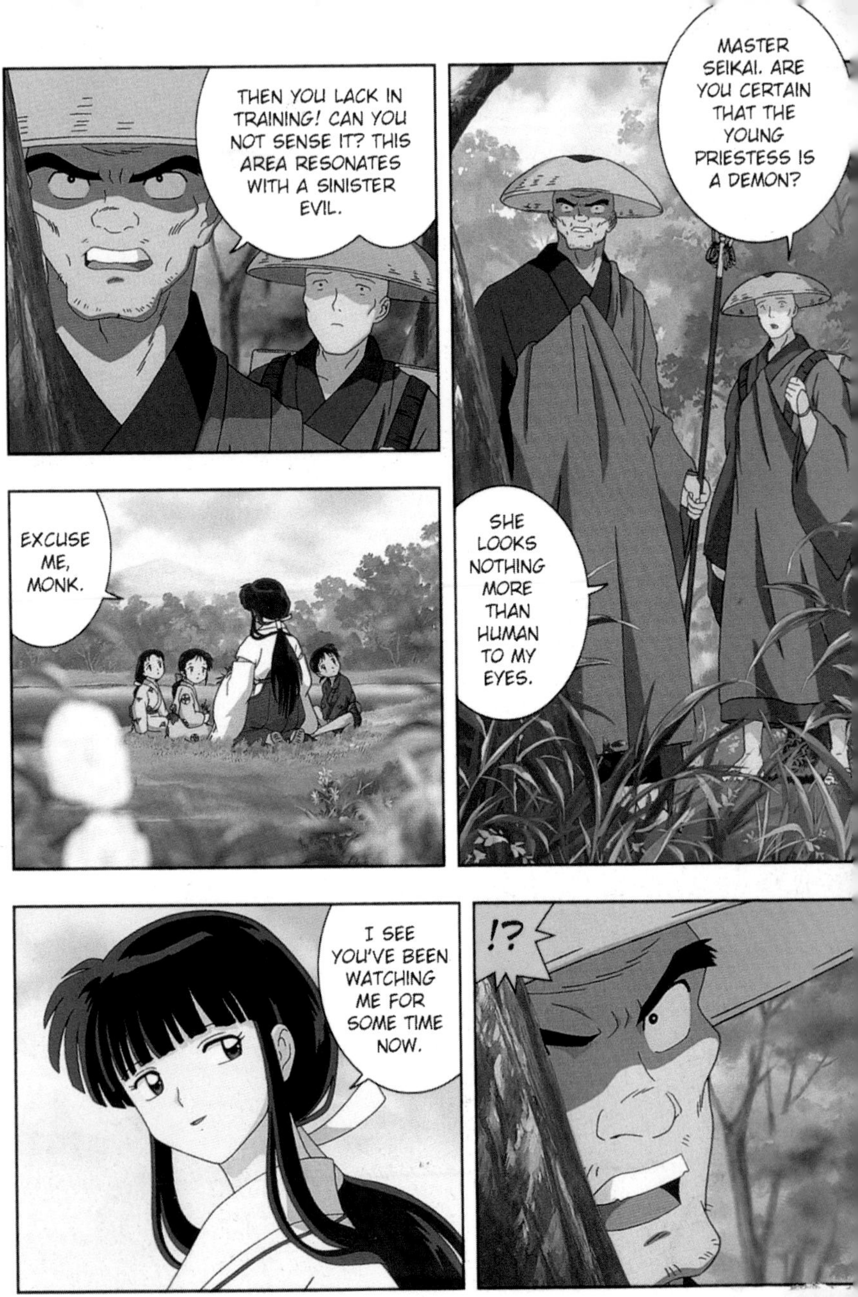
MASTER SEIKAI. ARE YOU CERTAIN THAT THE YOUNG PRIESTESS IS A DEMON?
SHE LOOKS NOTHING MORE THAN HUMAN TO MY EYES.
THEN YOU LACK IN TRAINING! CAN YOU NOT SENSE IT? THIS AREA RESONATES WITH A SINISTER EVIL.
EXCUSE ME, MONK.
!?
I SEE YOU'VE BEEN WATCHING ME FOR SOME TIME NOW.

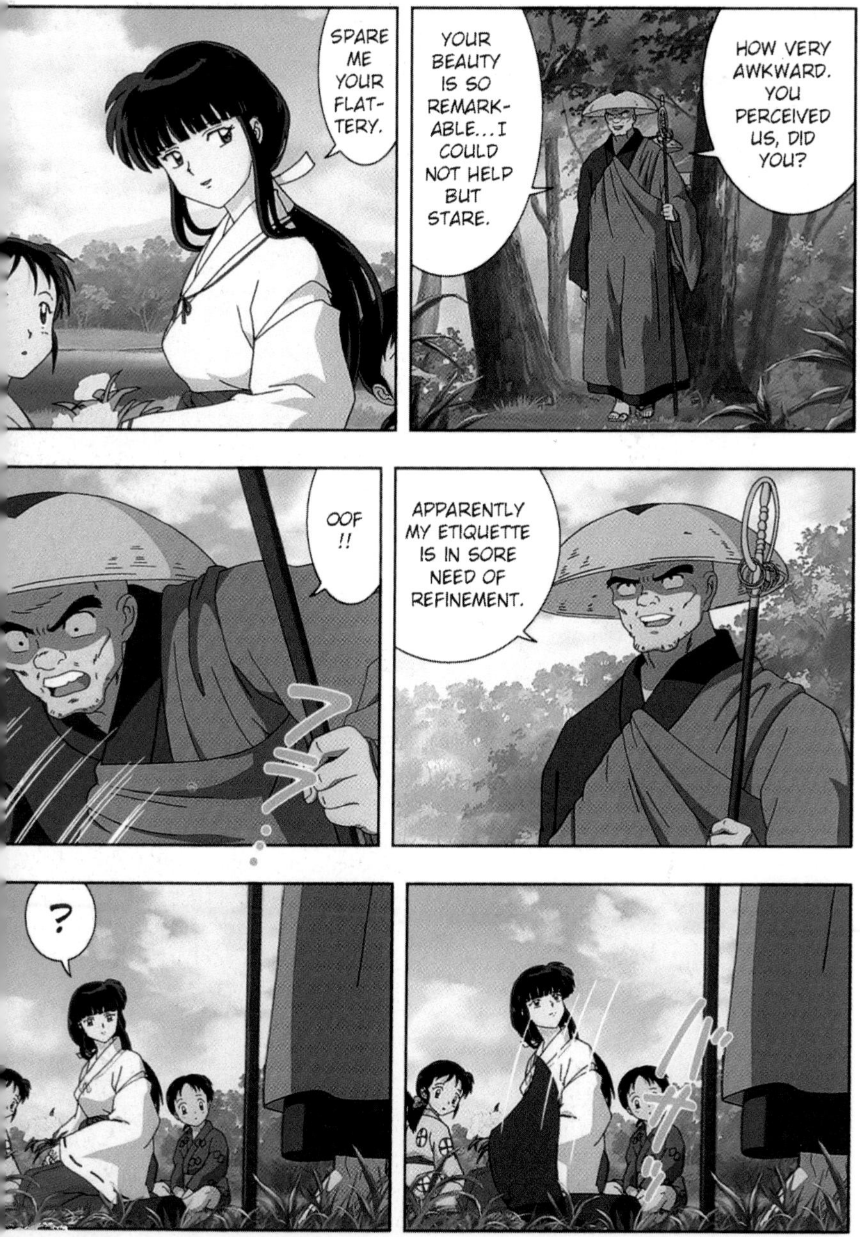
HOW VERY AWKWARD. YOU PERCEIVED US, DID YOU?
YOUR BEAUTY IS SO REMARKABLE...I COULD NOT HELP BUT STARE.
SPARE ME YOUR FLATTERY.
APPARENTLY MY ETIQUETTE IS IN SORE NEED OF REFINEMENT.
OOF !!
フラ
ザザッ
?

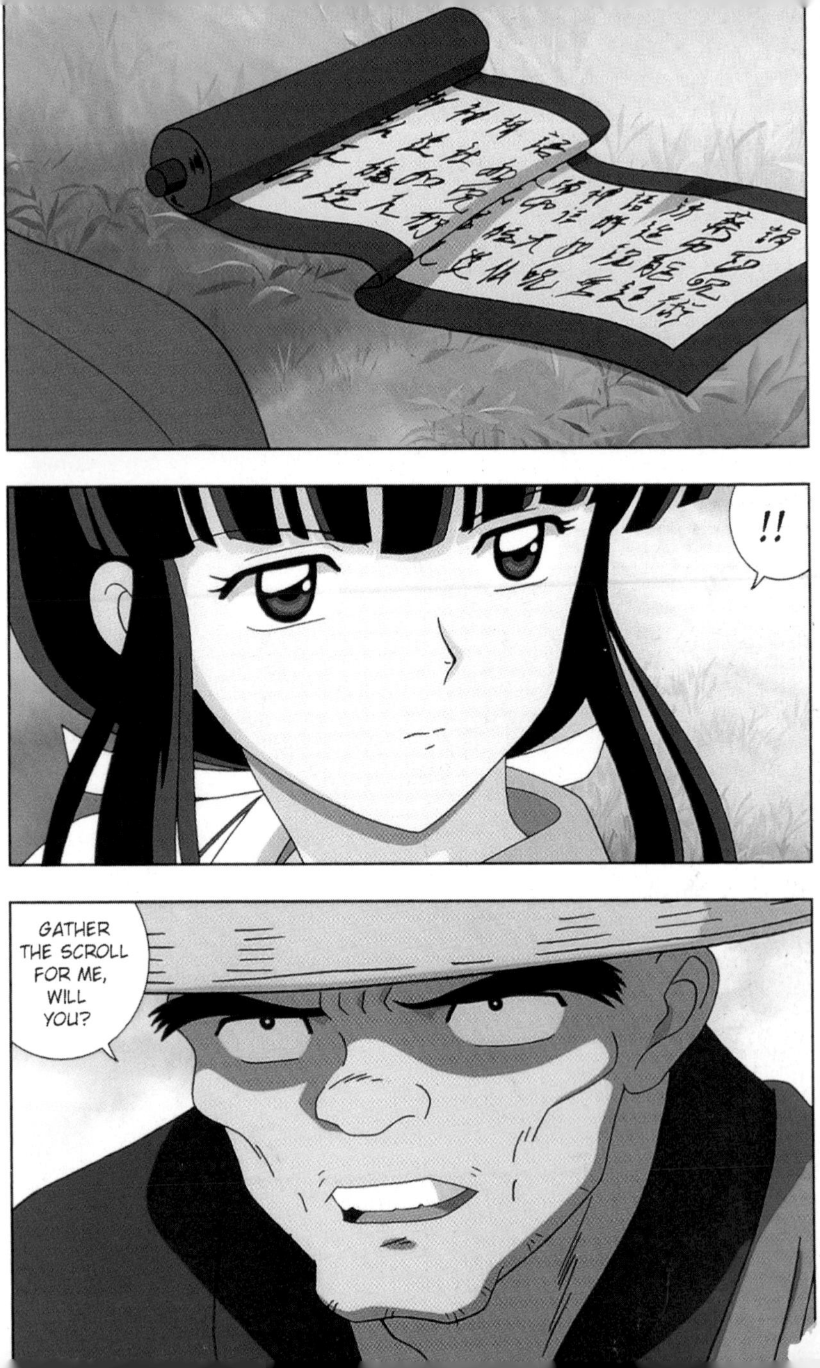
!!
GATHER THE SCROLL FOR ME, WILL YOU?

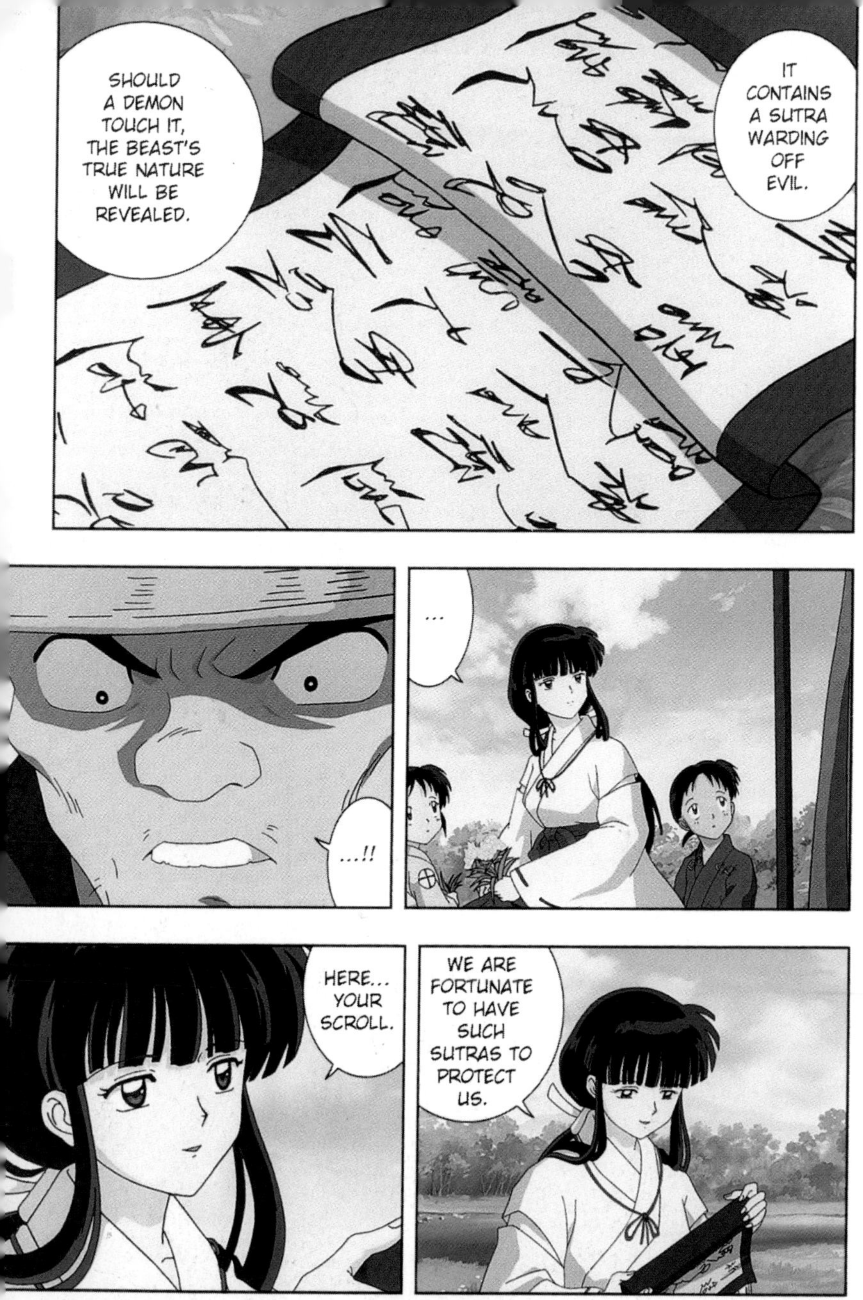
IT CONTAINS A SUTRA WARDING OFF EVIL.
SHOULD A DEMON TOUCH IT, THE BEAST'S TRUE NATURE WILL BE REVEALED.
...
...!!
WE ARE FORTUNATE TO HAVE SUCH SUTRAS TO PROTECT US.
HERE... YOUR SCROLL.

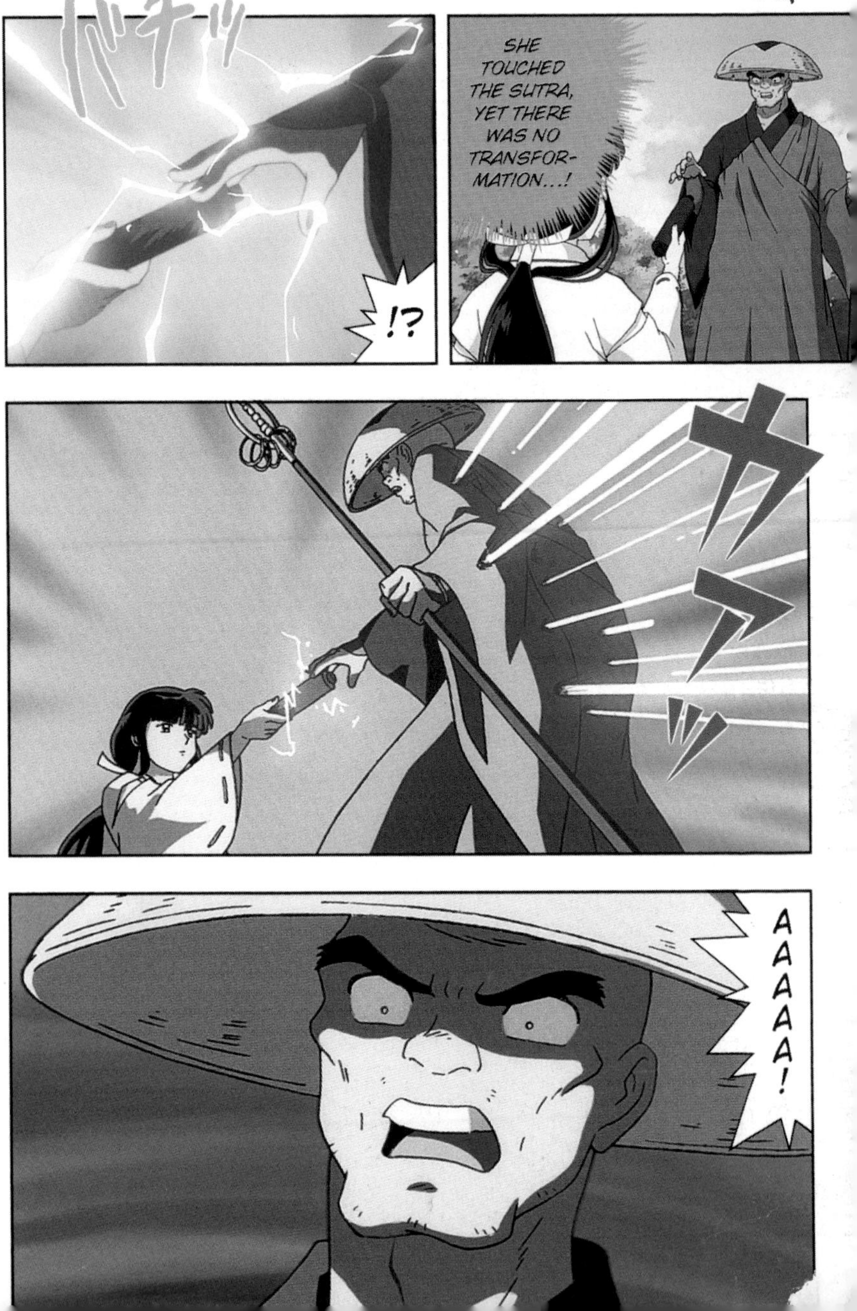
SHE TOUCHED THE SUTRA, YET THERE WAS NO TRANSFOR-MATION...!
バチッ
!?
AAAAAA!

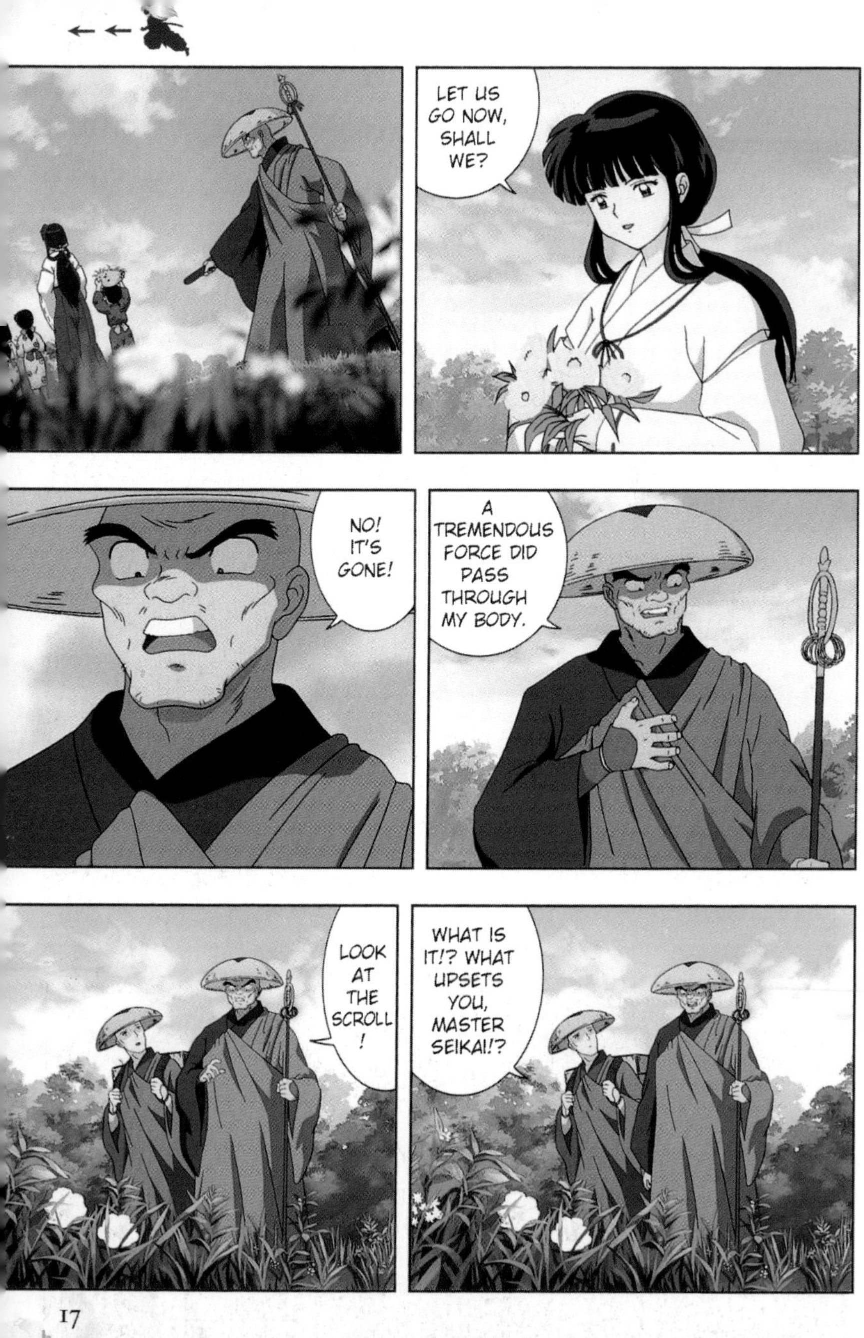

LET US GO NOW, SHALL WE?
A TREMENDOUS FORCE DID PASS THROUGH MY BODY.
NO! IT'S GONE!
WHAT IS IT!? WHAT UPSETS YOU, MASTER SEIKAI!?
LOOK AT THE SCROLL!

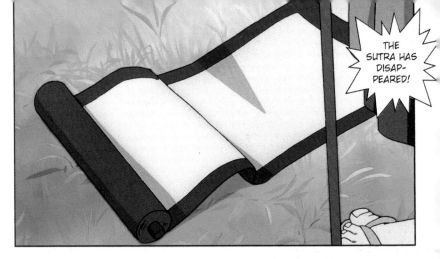

THE SUTRA HAS DISAP-PEARED!

PRIEST-ESS!

IT'S AS THOUGH IT HAS BEEN ERASED!

...?

...

18

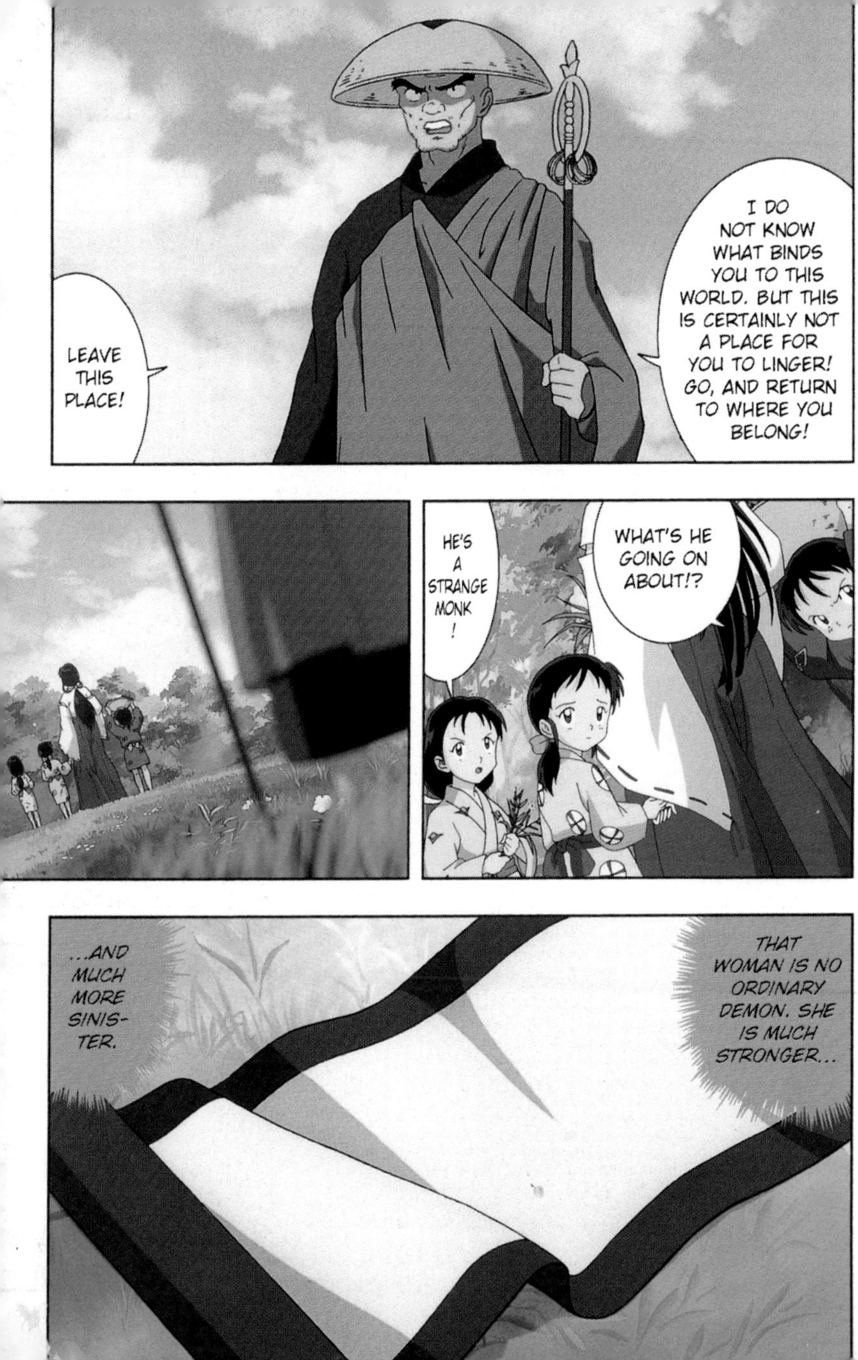
I DO NOT KNOW WHAT BINDS YOU TO THIS WORLD. BUT THIS IS CERTAINLY NOT A PLACE FOR YOU TO LINGER! GO, AND RETURN TO WHERE YOU BELONG!
LEAVE THIS PLACE!
WHAT'S HE GOING ON ABOUT!?
HE'S A STRANGE MONK!
THAT WOMAN IS NO ORDINARY DEMON. SHE IS MUCH STRONGER...
...AND MUCH MORE SINIS-TER.

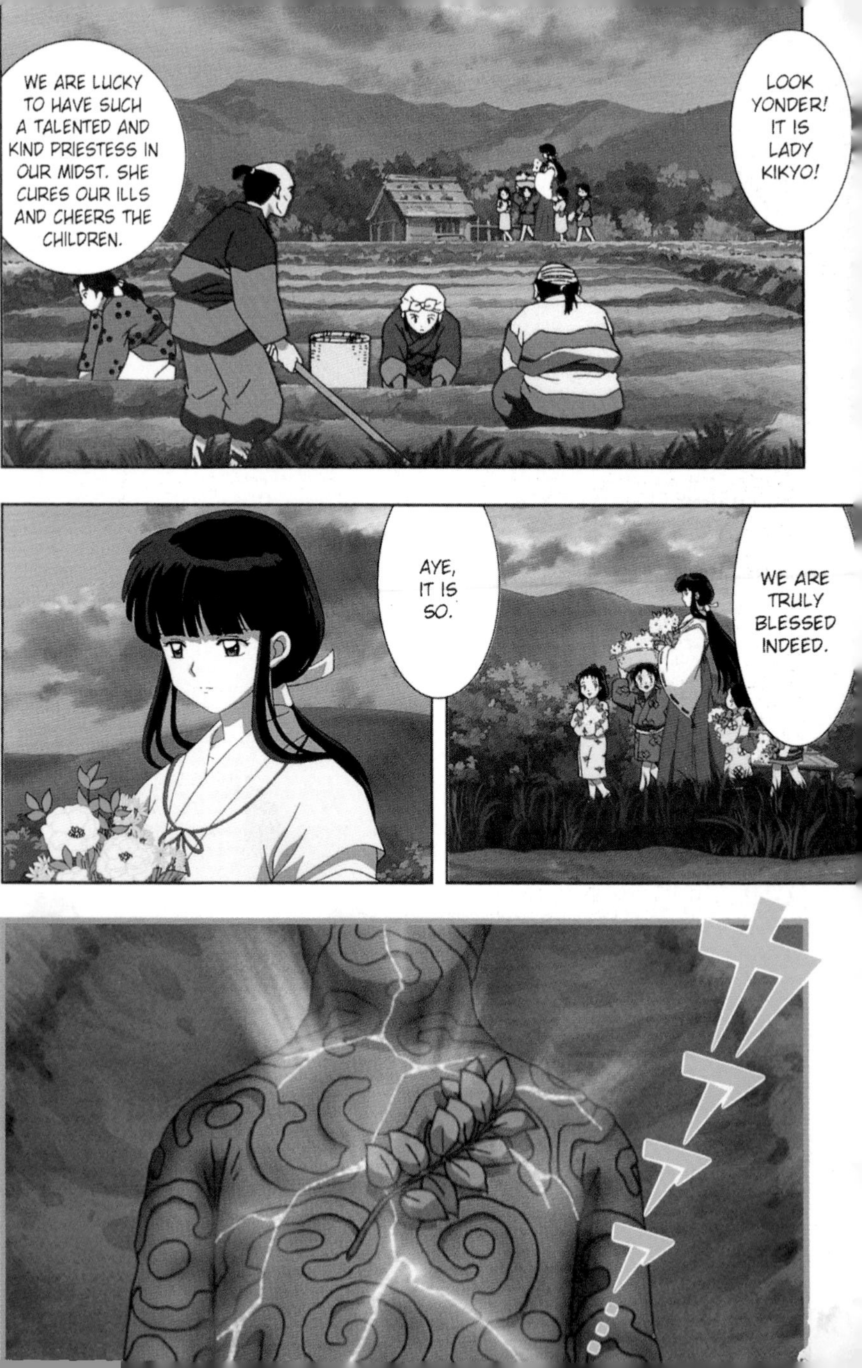
LOOK YONDER! IT IS LADY KIKYO!
WE ARE LUCKY TO HAVE SUCH A TALENTED AND KIND PRIESTESS IN OUR MIDST. SHE CURES OUR ILLS AND CHEERS THE CHILDREN.
WE ARE TRULY BLESSED INDEED.
AYE, IT IS SO.
カァァァ…

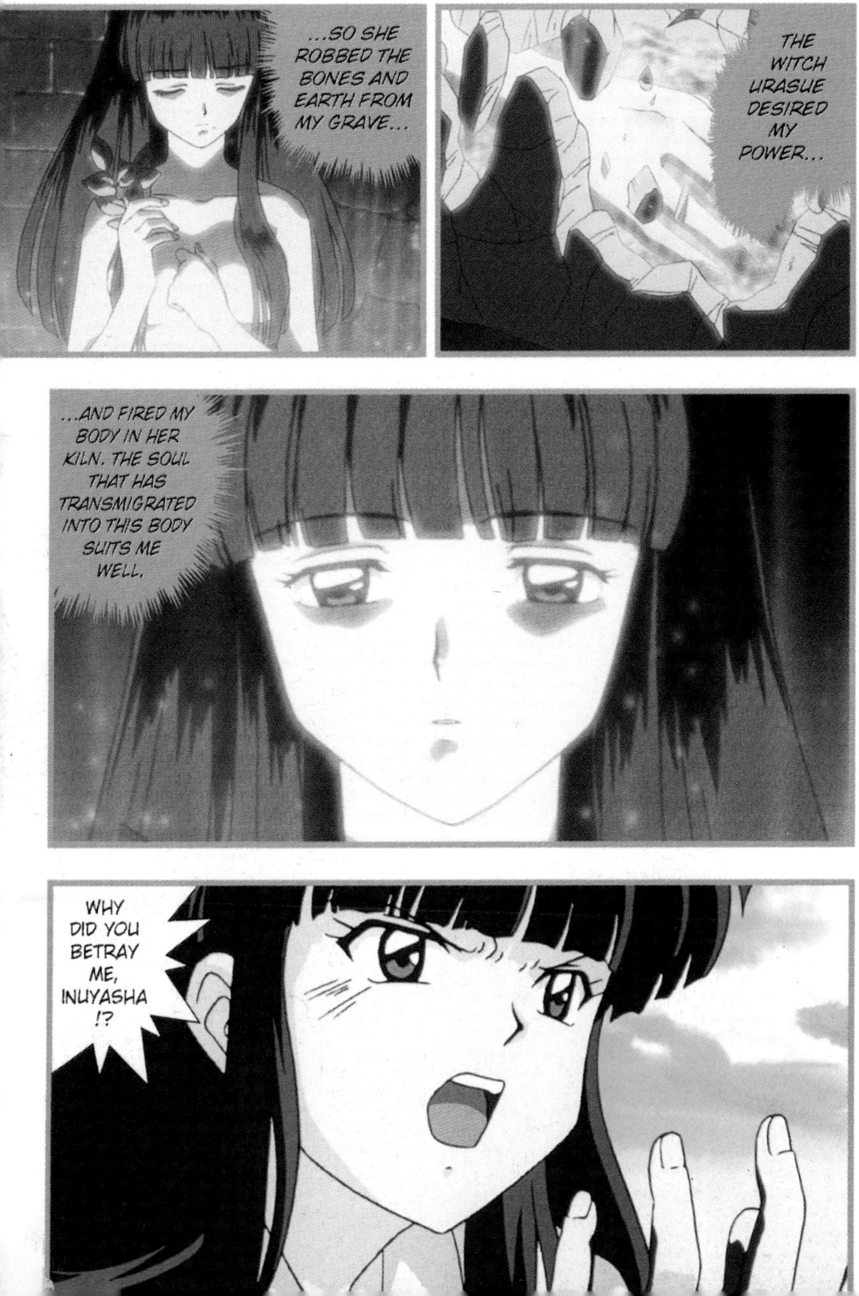
THE WITCH URASUE DESIRED MY POWER...
...SO SHE ROBBED THE BONES AND EARTH FROM MY GRAVE...
...AND FIRED MY BODY IN HER KILN. THE SOUL THAT HAS TRANSMIGRATED INTO THIS BODY SUITS ME WELL.
WHY DID YOU BETRAY ME, INUYASHA!?

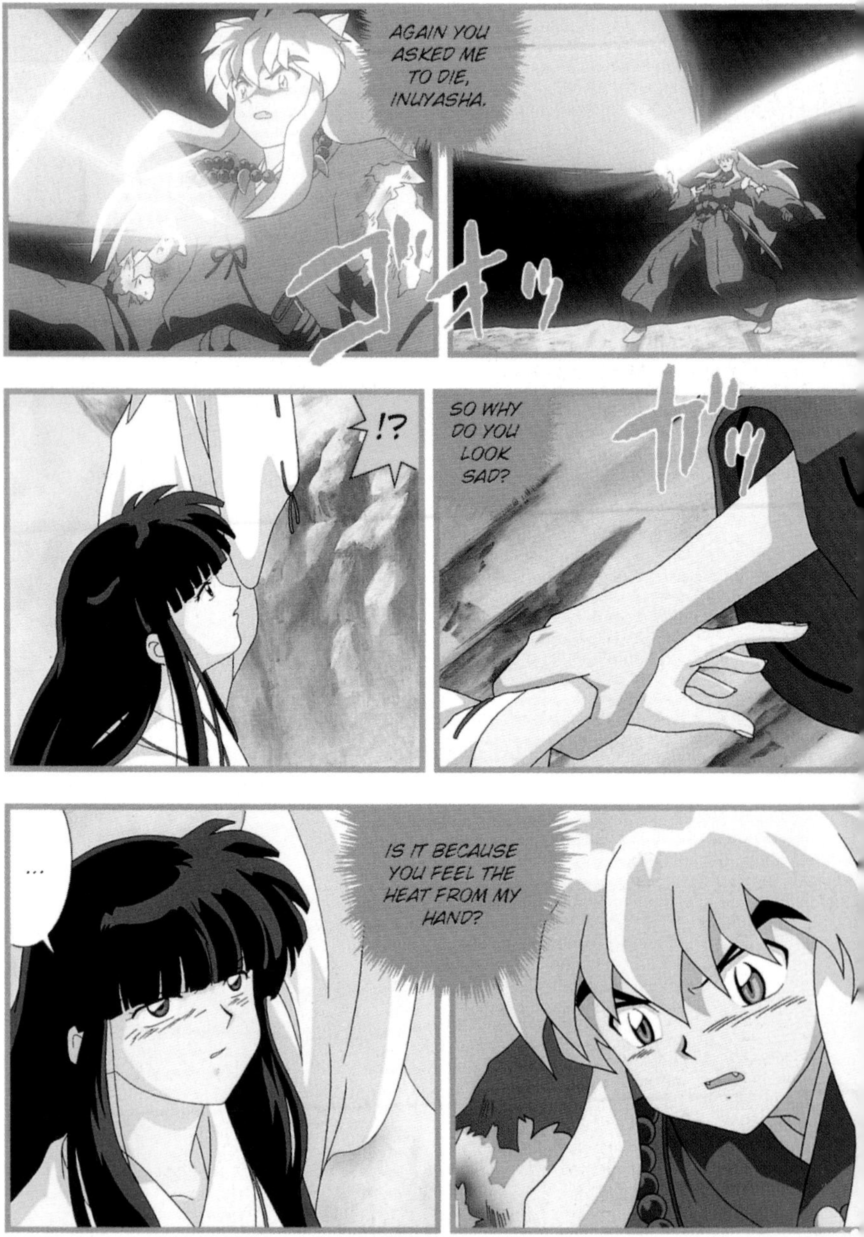
ゴオッ
AGAIN YOU ASKED ME TO DIE, INUYASHA.
ガッ
SO WHY DO YOU LOOK SAD?
!?
IS IT BECAUSE YOU FEEL THE HEAT FROM MY HAND?
...

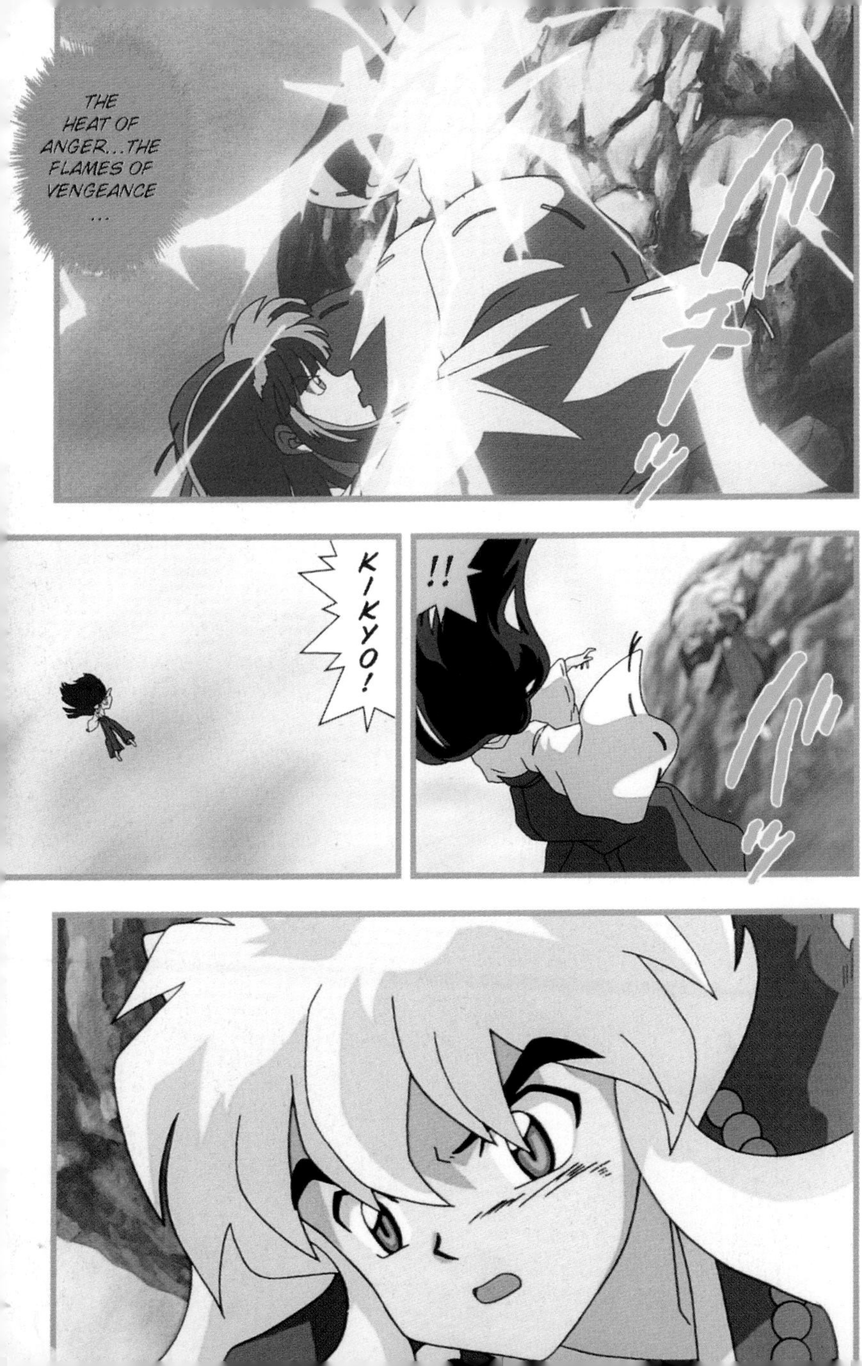
THE HEAT OF ANGER...THE FLAMES OF VENGEANCE ...
バチッ
!!
グッ
KIKYO!

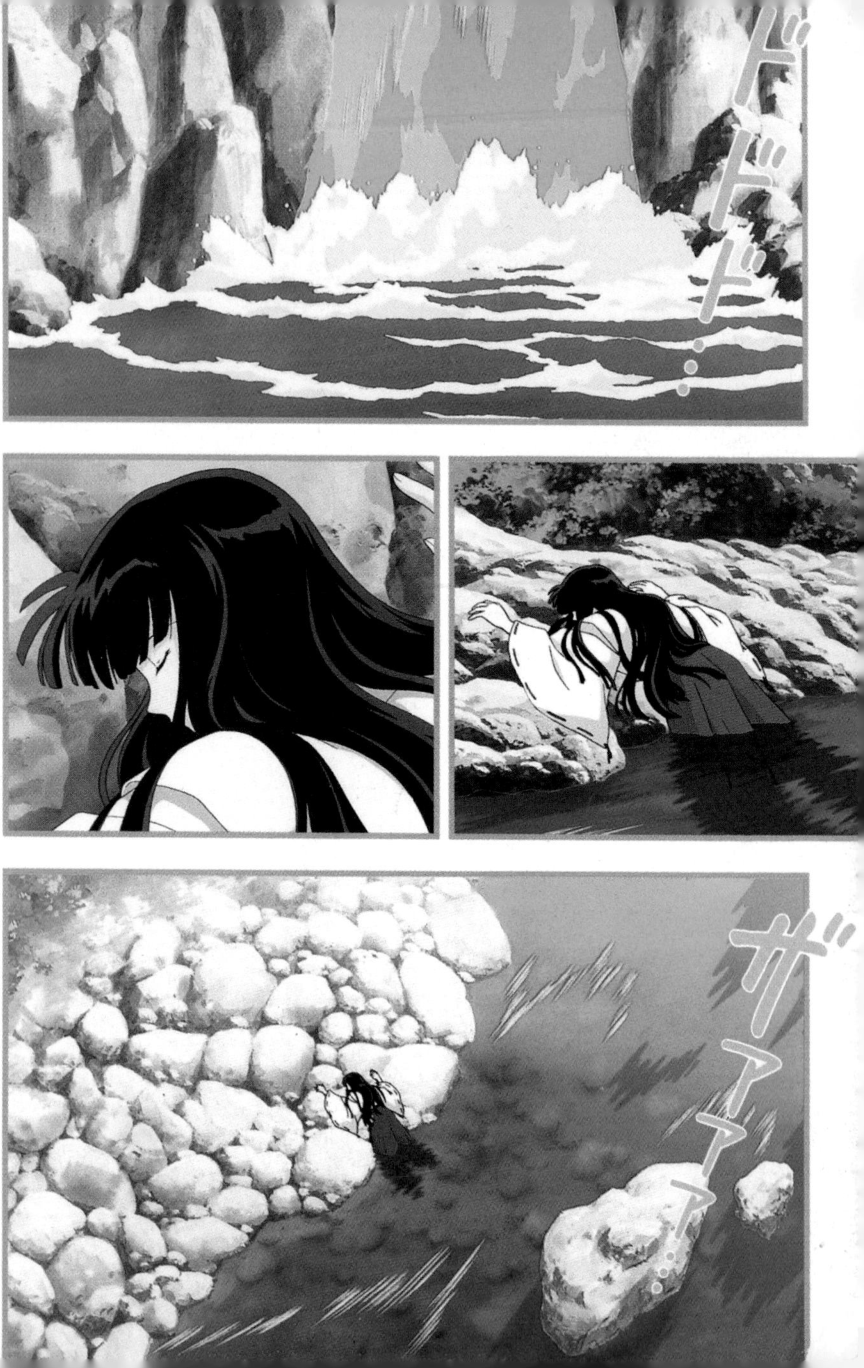
ドドド…
ザアアア…

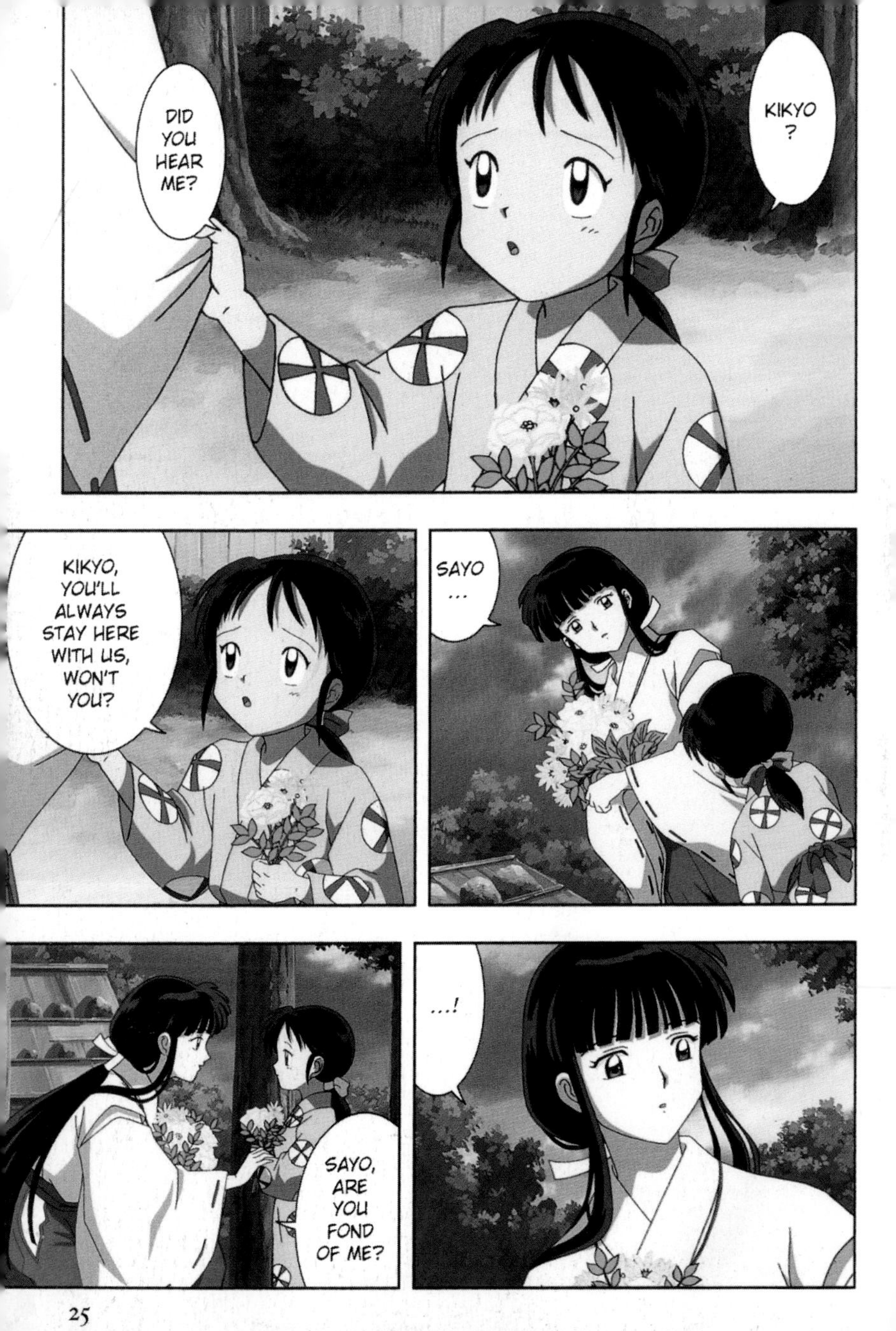
KIKYO ?
DID YOU HEAR ME?
SAYO ...
KIKYO, YOU'LL ALWAYS STAY HERE WITH US, WON'T YOU?
...!
SAYO, ARE YOU FOND OF ME?

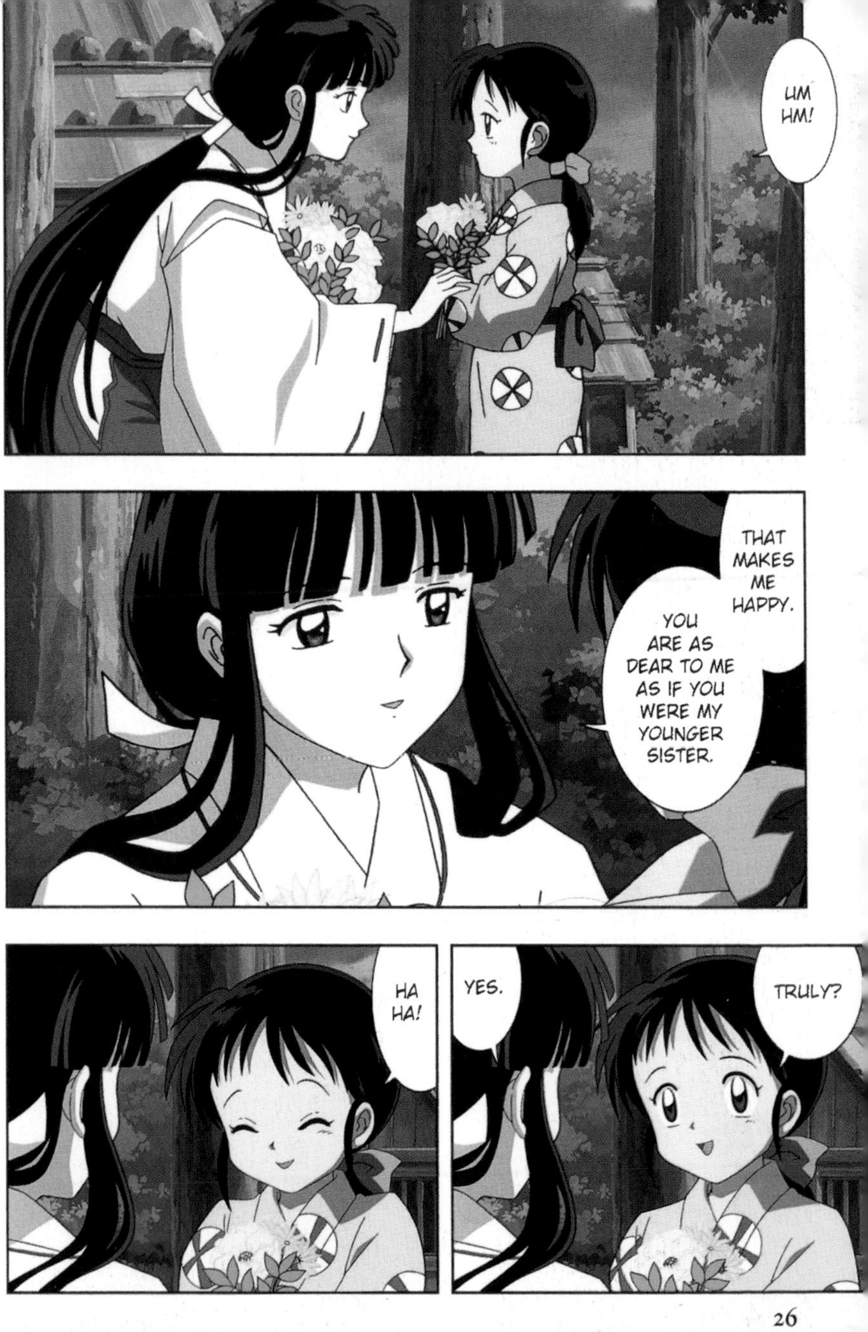
UM HM!
THAT MAKES ME HAPPY.
YOU ARE AS DEAR TO ME AS IF YOU WERE MY YOUNGER SISTER.
TRULY?
YES.
HA HA!

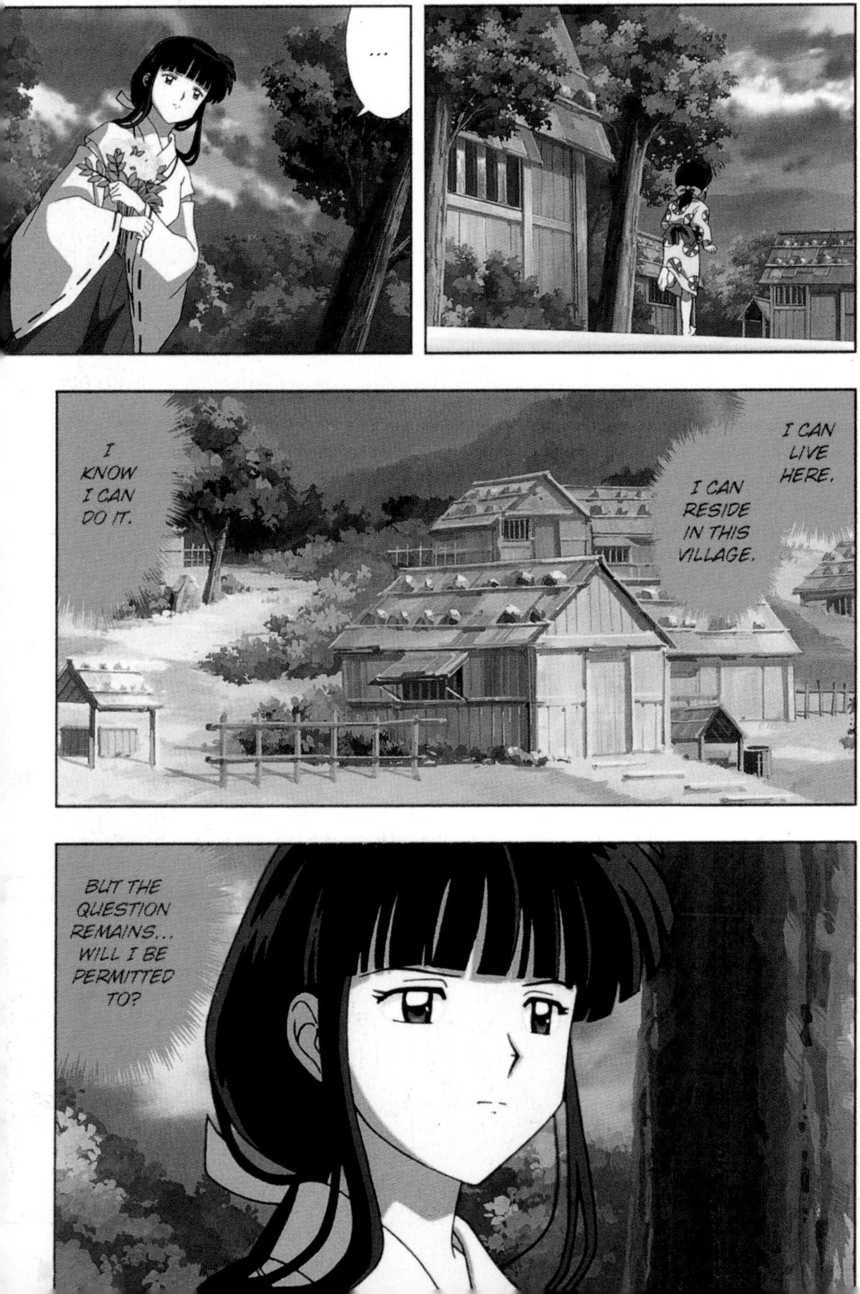
...
I CAN LIVE HERE.
I CAN RESIDE IN THIS VILLAGE.
I KNOW I CAN DO IT.
BUT THE QUESTION REMAINS... WILL I BE PERMITTED TO?

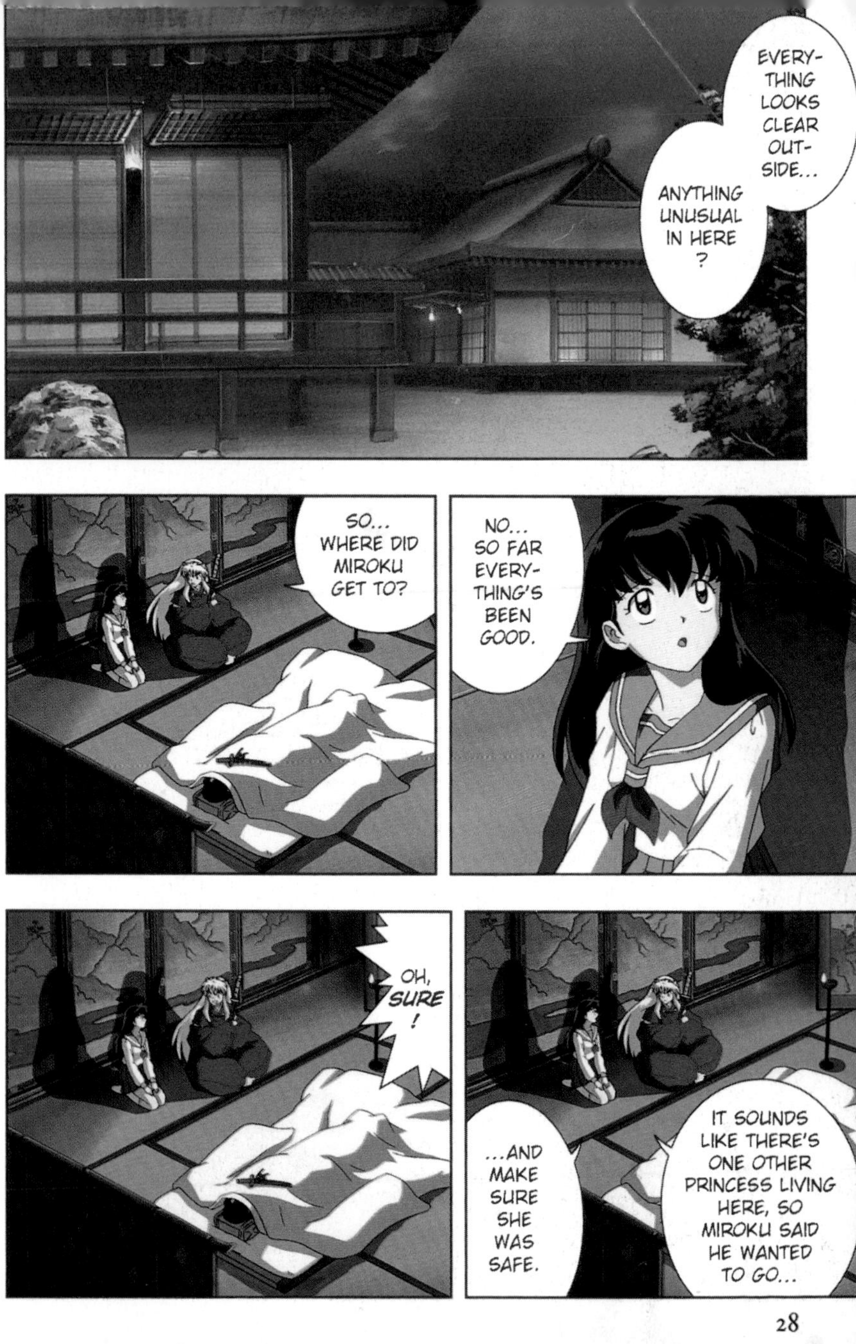
EVERY-THING LOOKS CLEAR OUT-SIDE...
ANYTHING UNUSUAL IN HERE ?
NO... SO FAR EVERY-THING'S BEEN GOOD.
SO... WHERE DID MIROKU GET TO?
IT SOUNDS LIKE THERE'S ONE OTHER PRINCESS LIVING HERE, SO MIROKU SAID HE WANTED TO GO...
...AND MAKE SURE SHE WAS SAFE.
OH, **SURE** !

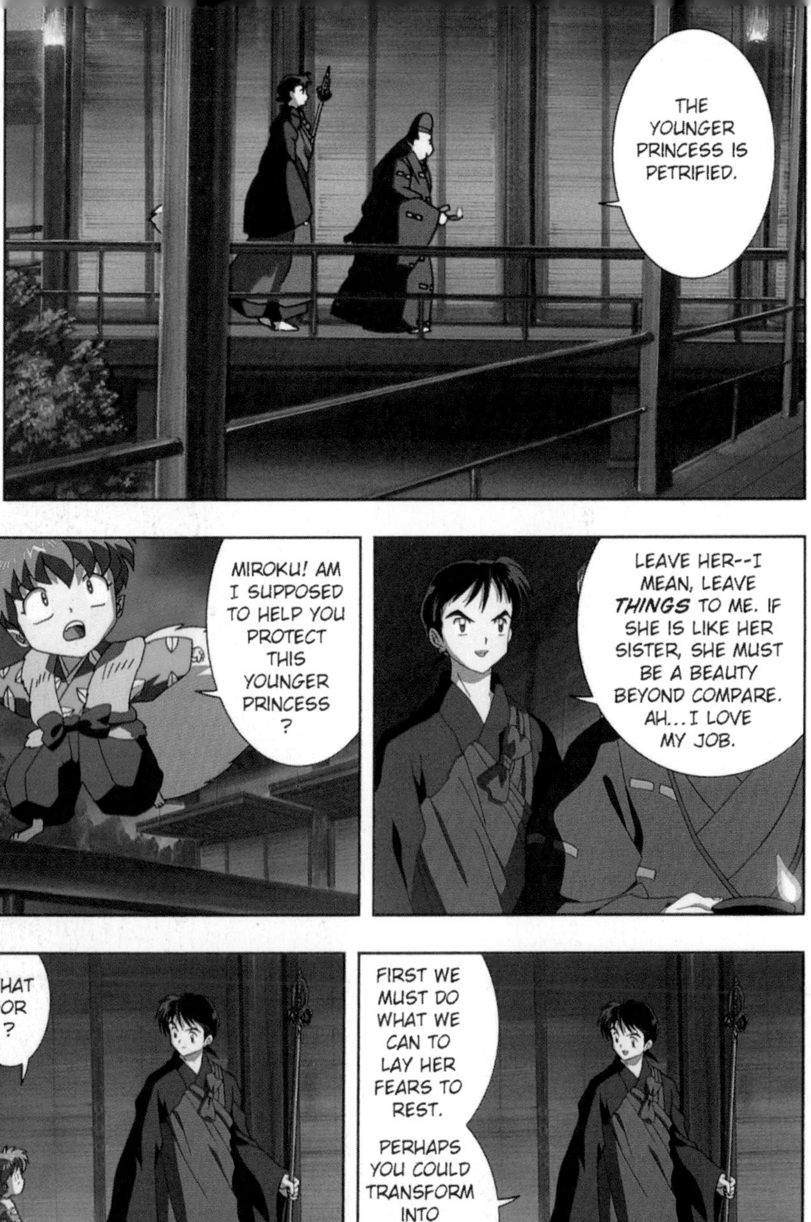
THE YOUNGER PRINCESS IS PETRIFIED.
MIROKU! AM I SUPPOSED TO HELP YOU PROTECT THIS YOUNGER PRINCESS?
LEAVE HER--I MEAN, LEAVE *THINGS* TO ME. IF SHE IS LIKE HER SISTER, SHE MUST BE A BEAUTY BEYOND COMPARE. AH...I LOVE MY JOB.
WHAT FOR?
FIRST WE MUST DO WHAT WE CAN TO LAY HER FEARS TO REST.
PERHAPS YOU COULD TRANSFORM INTO SOMETHING CUTE AND FUZZY?

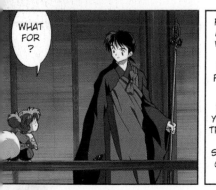

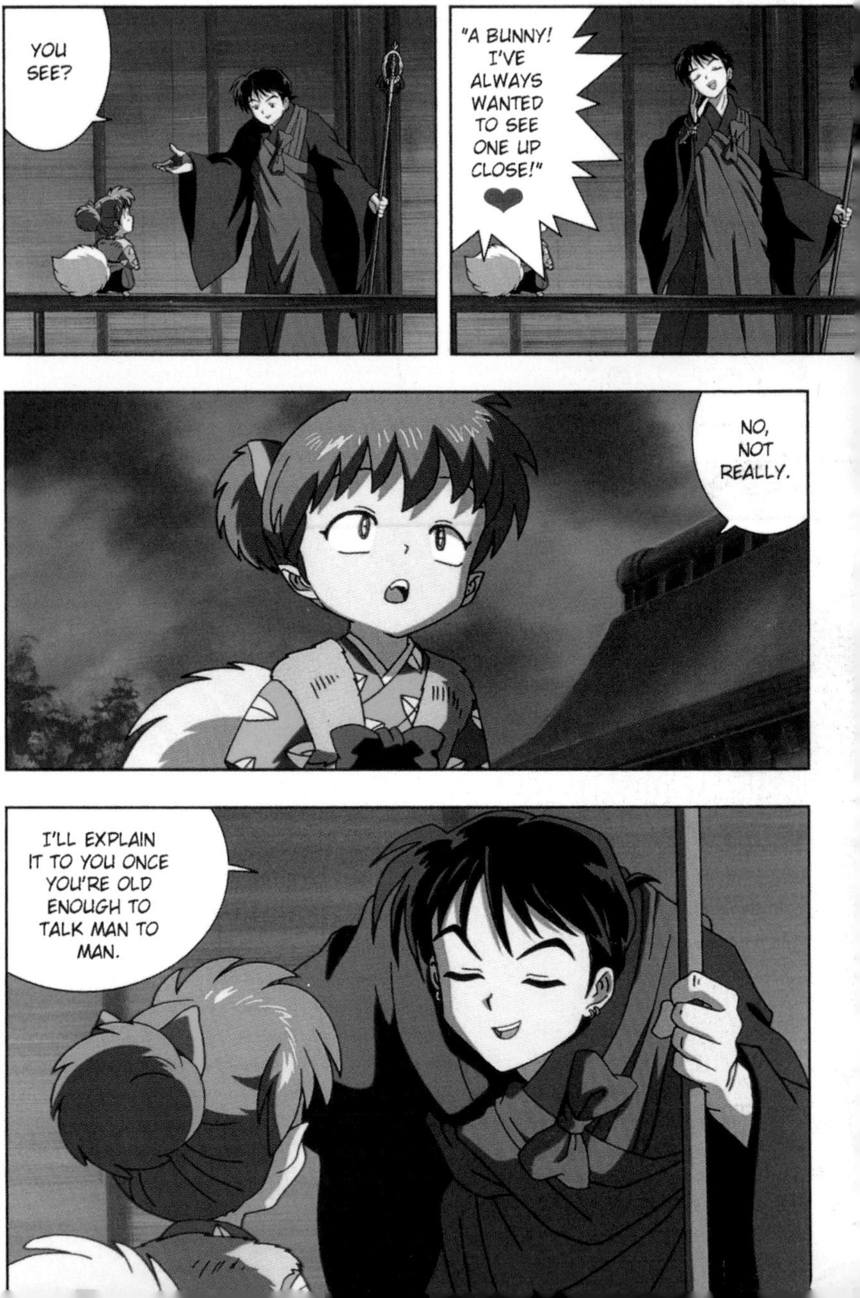
"A BUNNY! I'VE ALWAYS WANTED TO SEE ONE UP CLOSE!" ♥
YOU SEE?
NO, NOT REALLY.
I'LL EXPLAIN IT TO YOU ONCE YOU'RE OLD ENOUGH TO TALK MAN TO MAN.

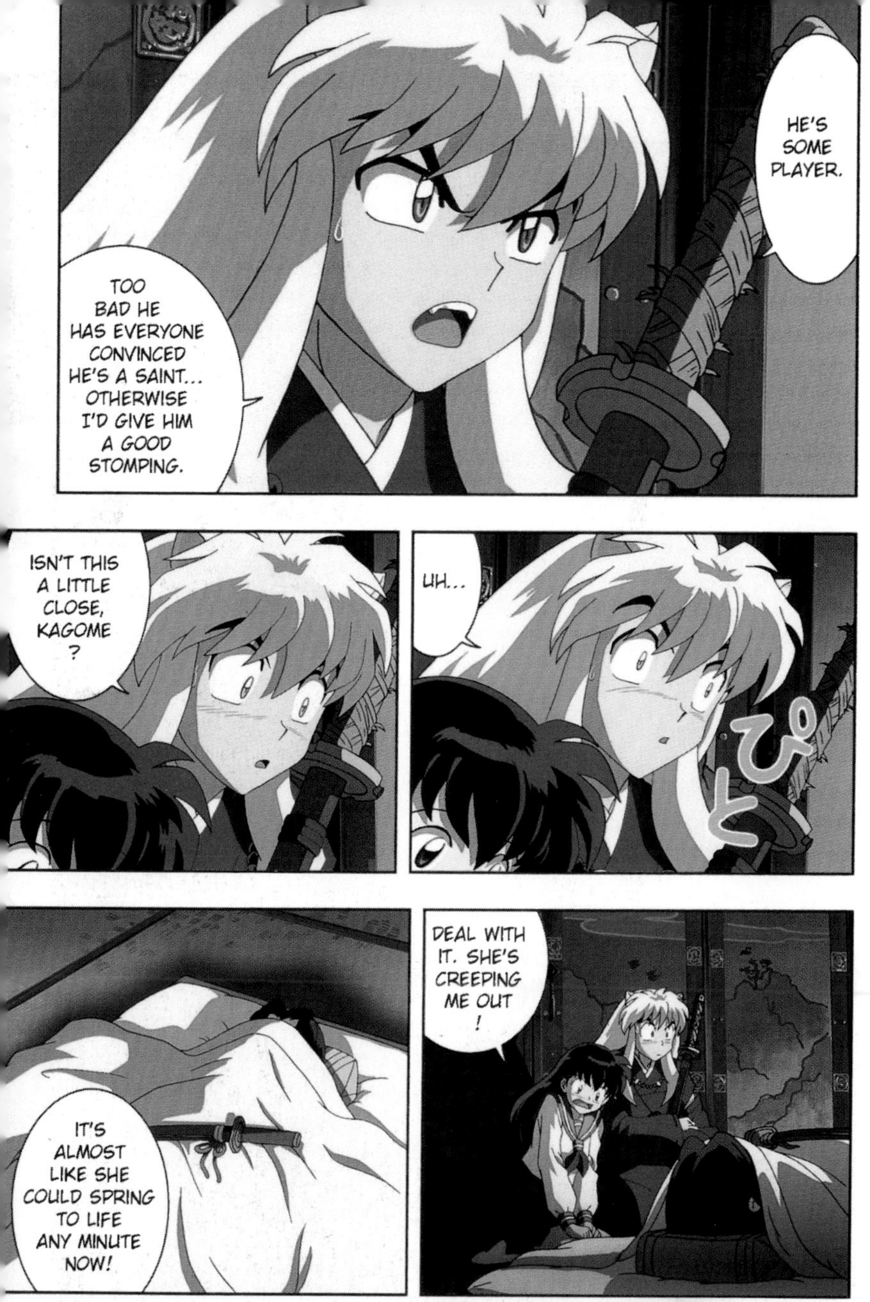
HE'S SOME PLAYER.
TOO BAD HE HAS EVERYONE CONVINCED HE'S A SAINT... OTHERWISE I'D GIVE HIM A GOOD STOMPING.
UH...
ぴと
ISN'T THIS A LITTLE CLOSE, KAGOME?
DEAL WITH IT. SHE'S CREEPING ME OUT!
IT'S ALMOST LIKE SHE COULD SPRING TO LIFE ANY MINUTE NOW!

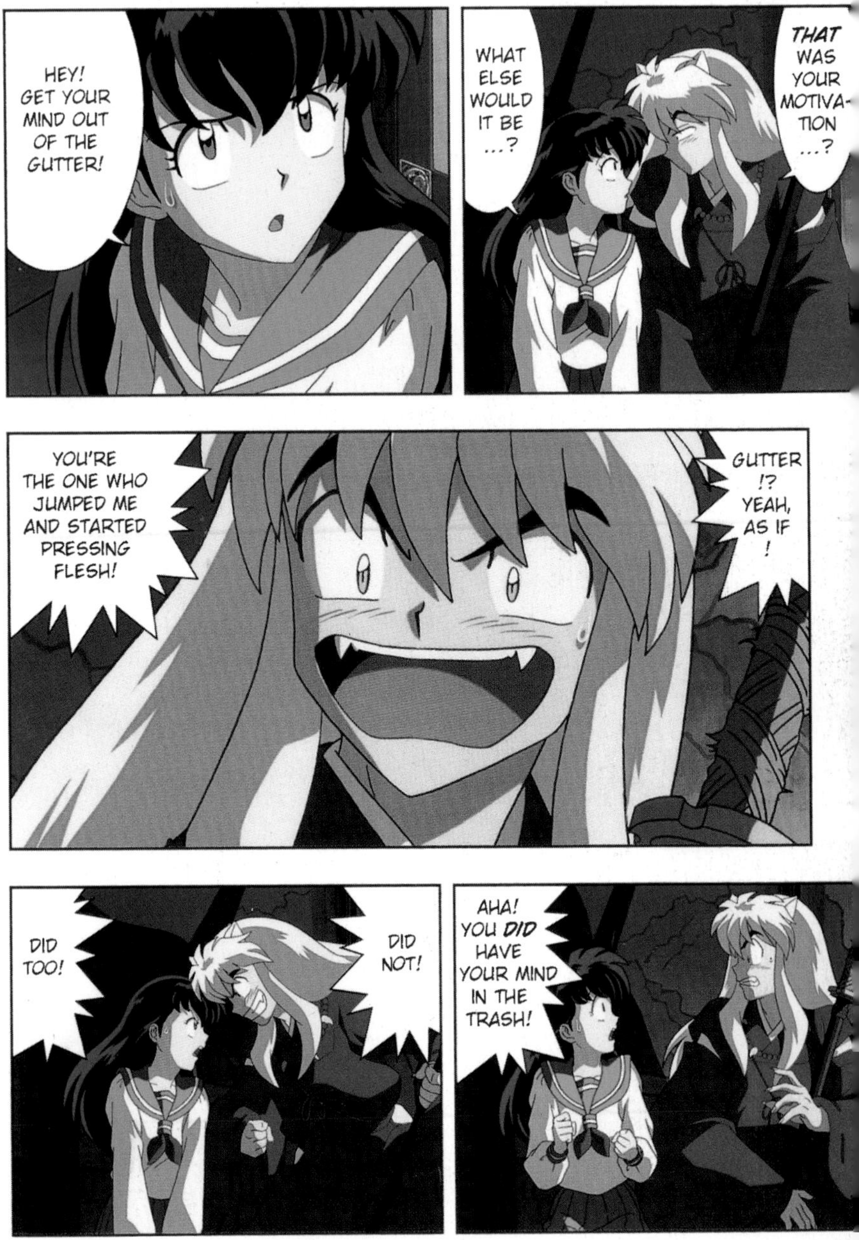
THAT WAS YOUR MOTIVATION ...?
WHAT ELSE WOULD IT BE ...?
HEY! GET YOUR MIND OUT OF THE GUTTER!
GUTTER!? YEAH, AS IF!
YOU'RE THE ONE WHO JUMPED ME AND STARTED PRESSING FLESH!
AHA! YOU DID HAVE YOUR MIND IN THE TRASH!
DID NOT!
DID TOO!

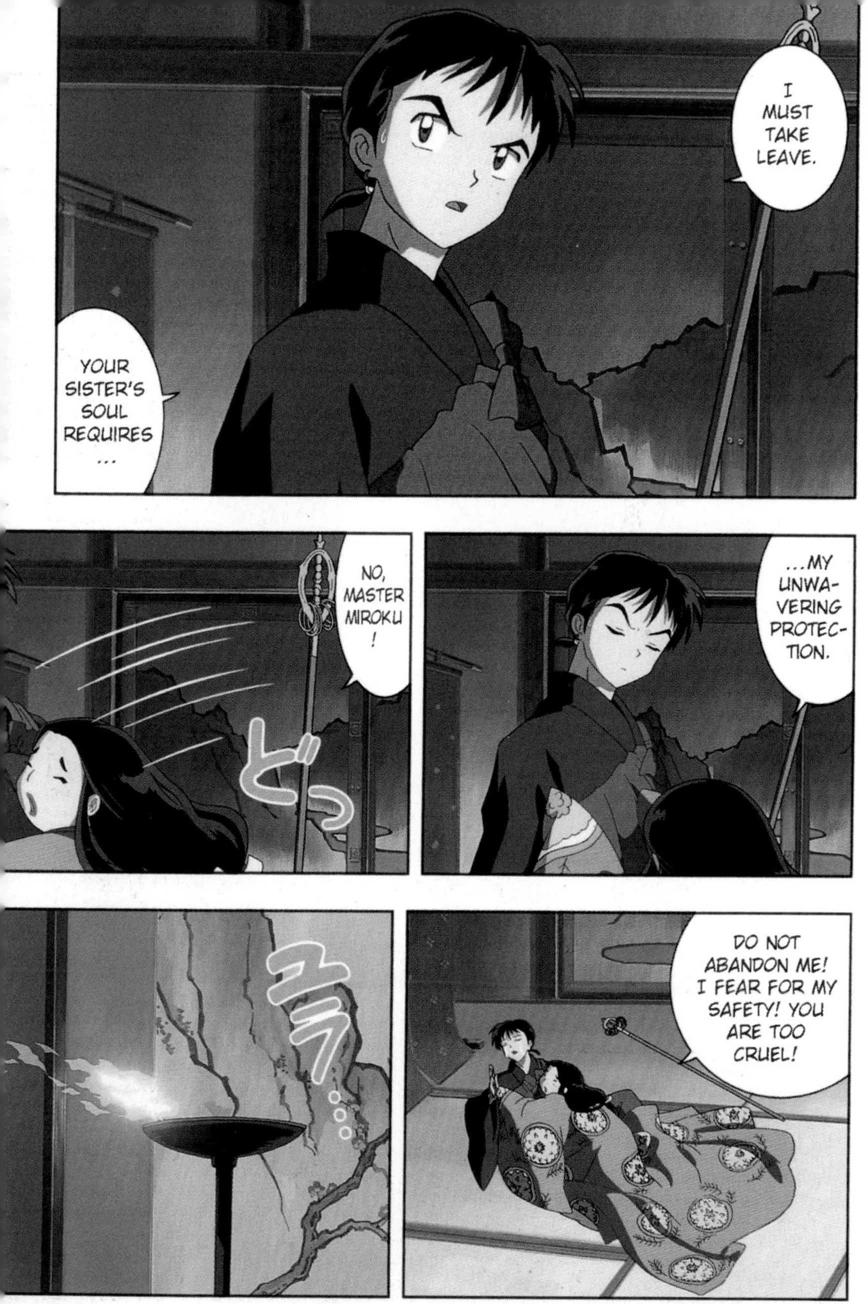
I MUST TAKE LEAVE.
YOUR SISTER'S SOUL REQUIRES ...
...MY UNWAVERING PROTECTION.
NO, MASTER MIROKU!
どっ
DO NOT ABANDON ME! I FEAR FOR MY SAFETY! YOU ARE TOO CRUEL!
ユラ...

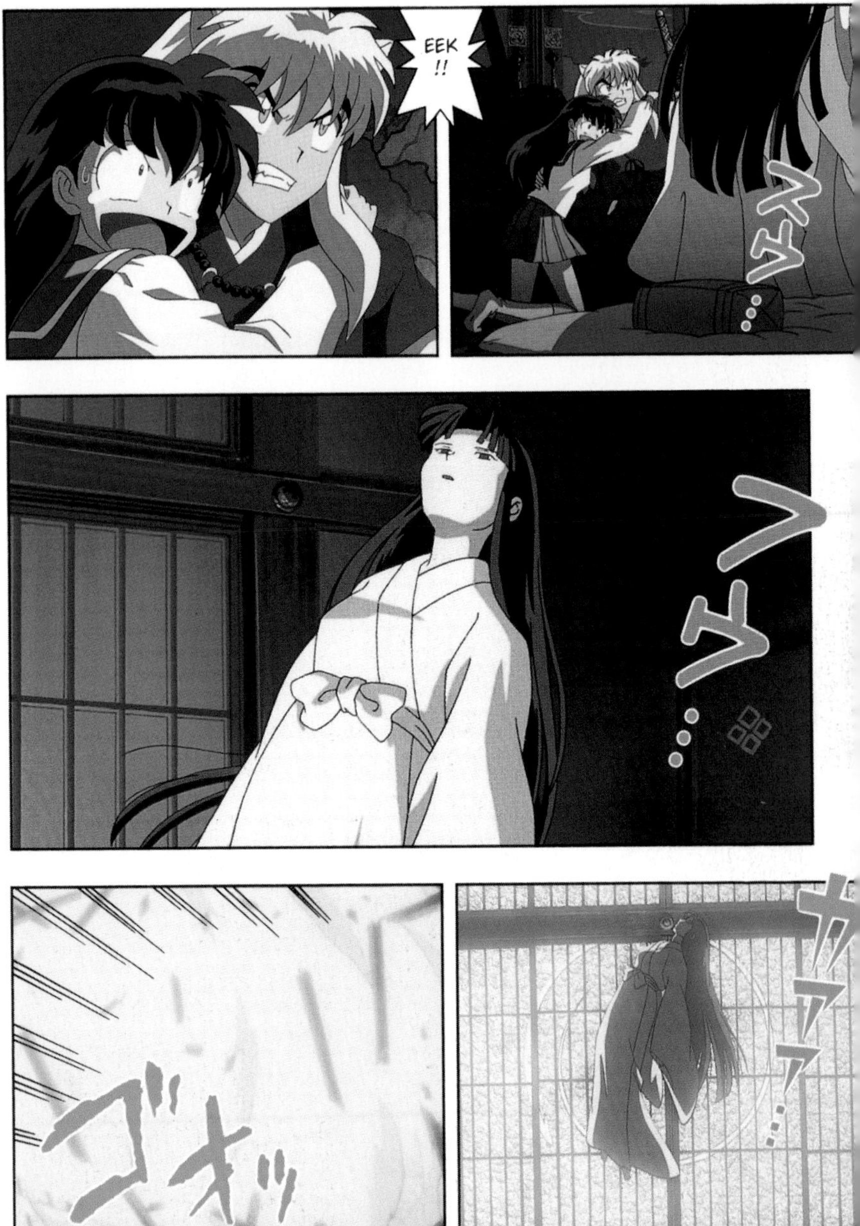
EEK !!
ゴオッ

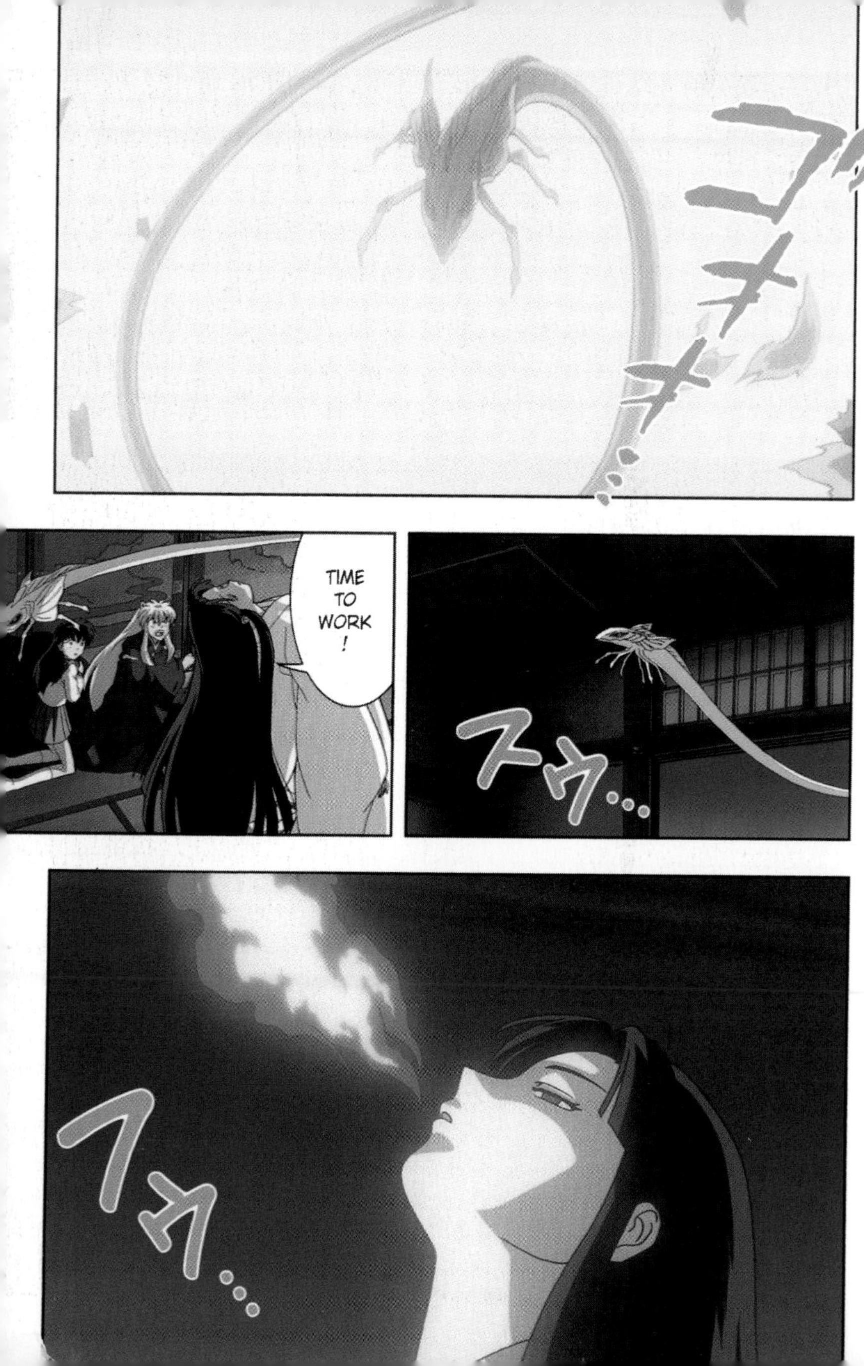
スゥ...
TIME TO WORK !

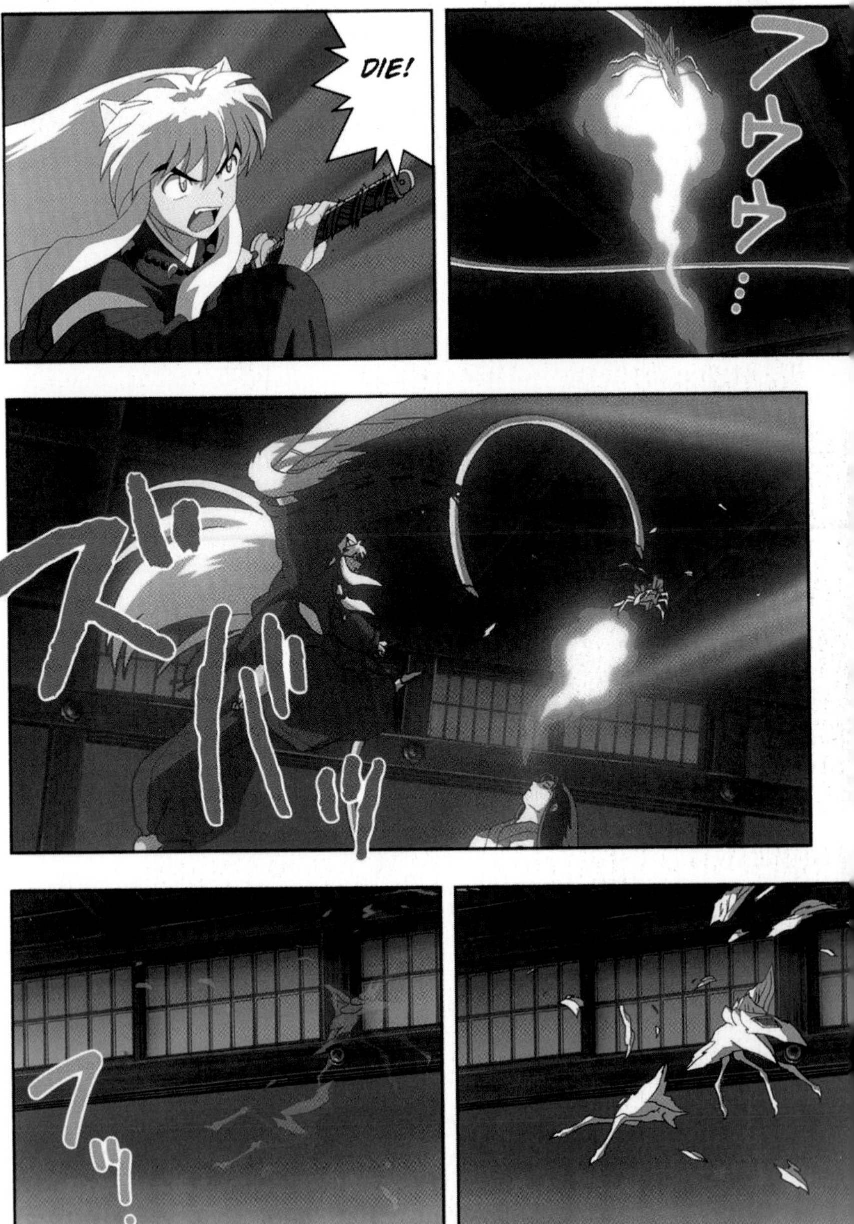
フウウ…
DIE!
ズバッ
フッ…

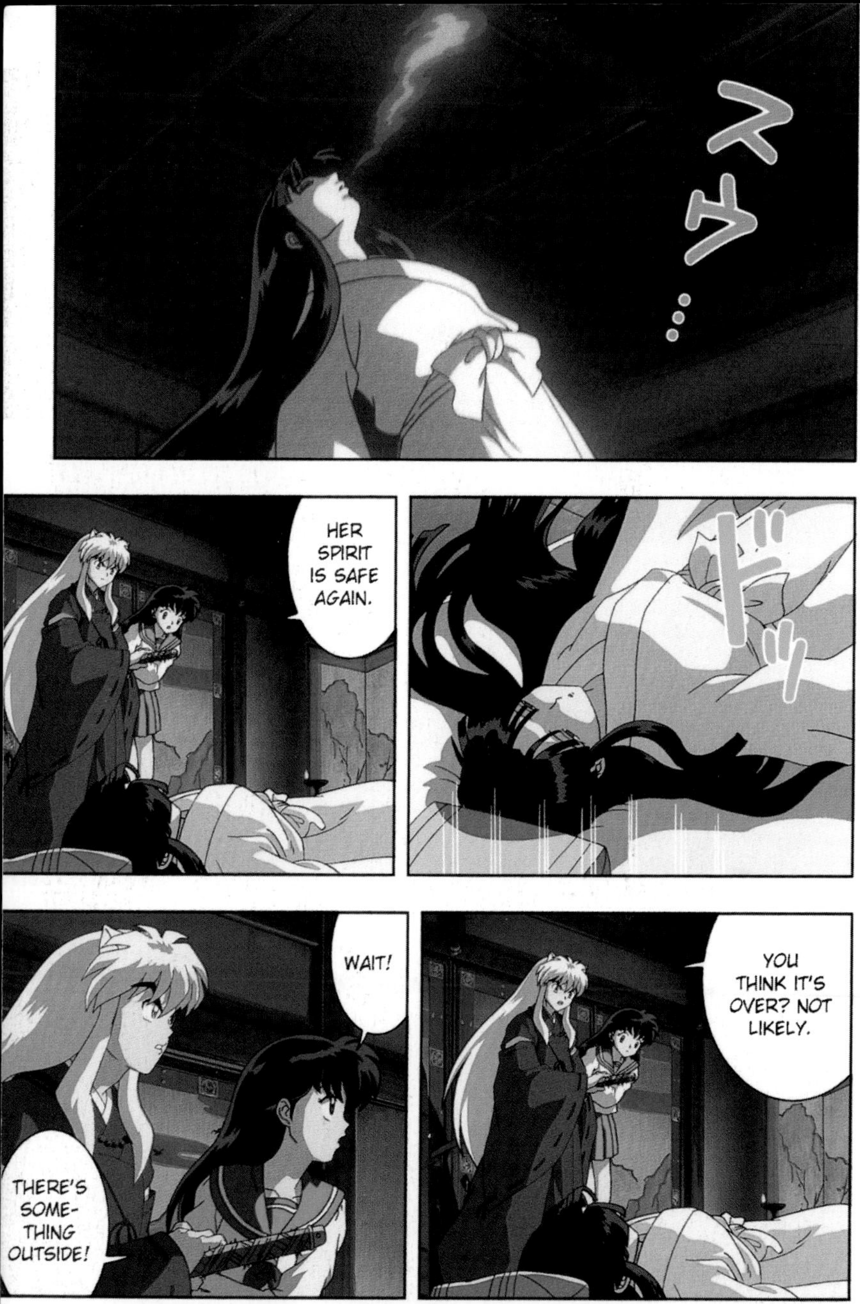
スゥ…
ドッ
HER SPIRIT IS SAFE AGAIN.
YOU THINK IT'S OVER? NOT LIKELY.
WAIT!
THERE'S SOME-THING OUTSIDE!

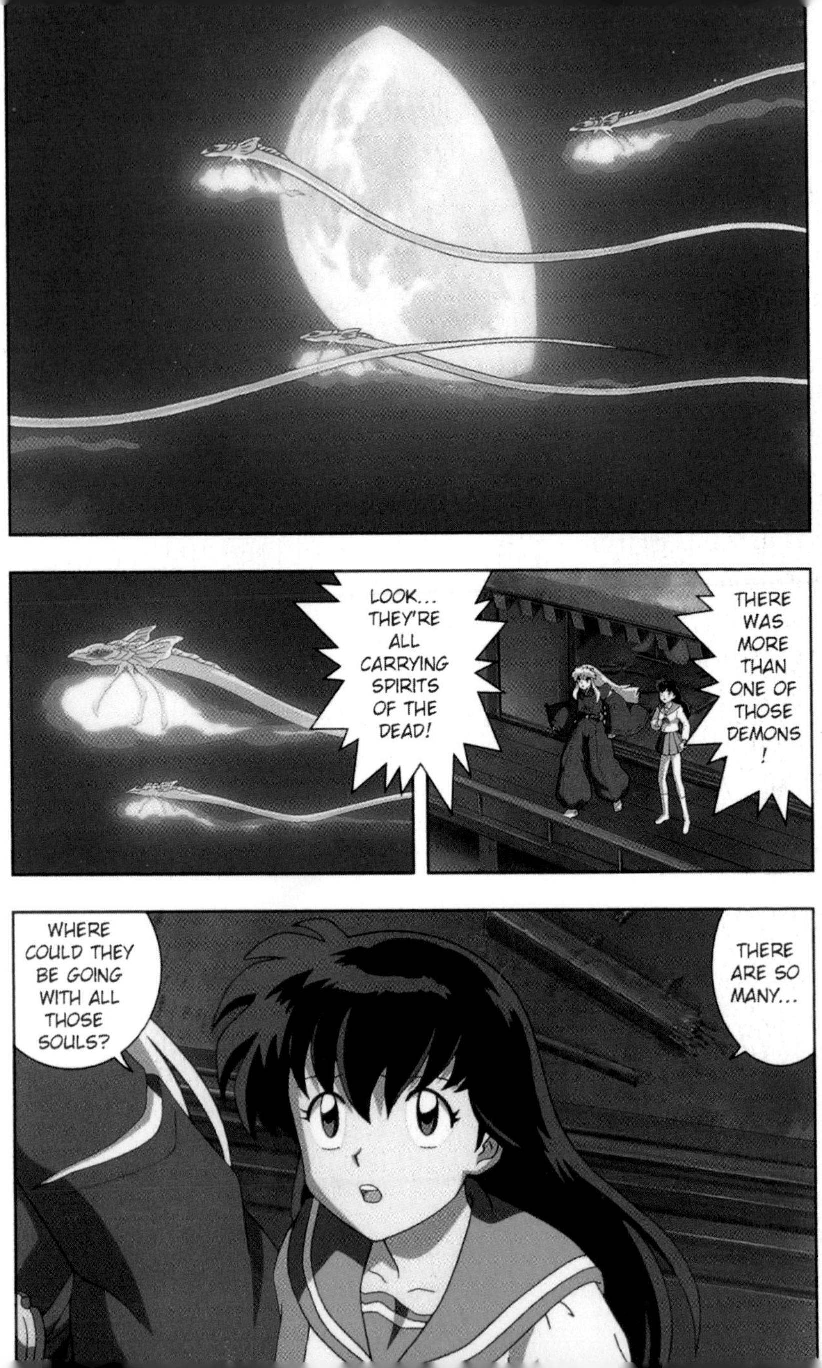
THERE WAS MORE THAN ONE OF THOSE DEMONS!
LOOK... THEY'RE ALL CARRYING SPIRITS OF THE DEAD!
THERE ARE SO MANY...
WHERE COULD THEY BE GOING WITH ALL THOSE SOULS?

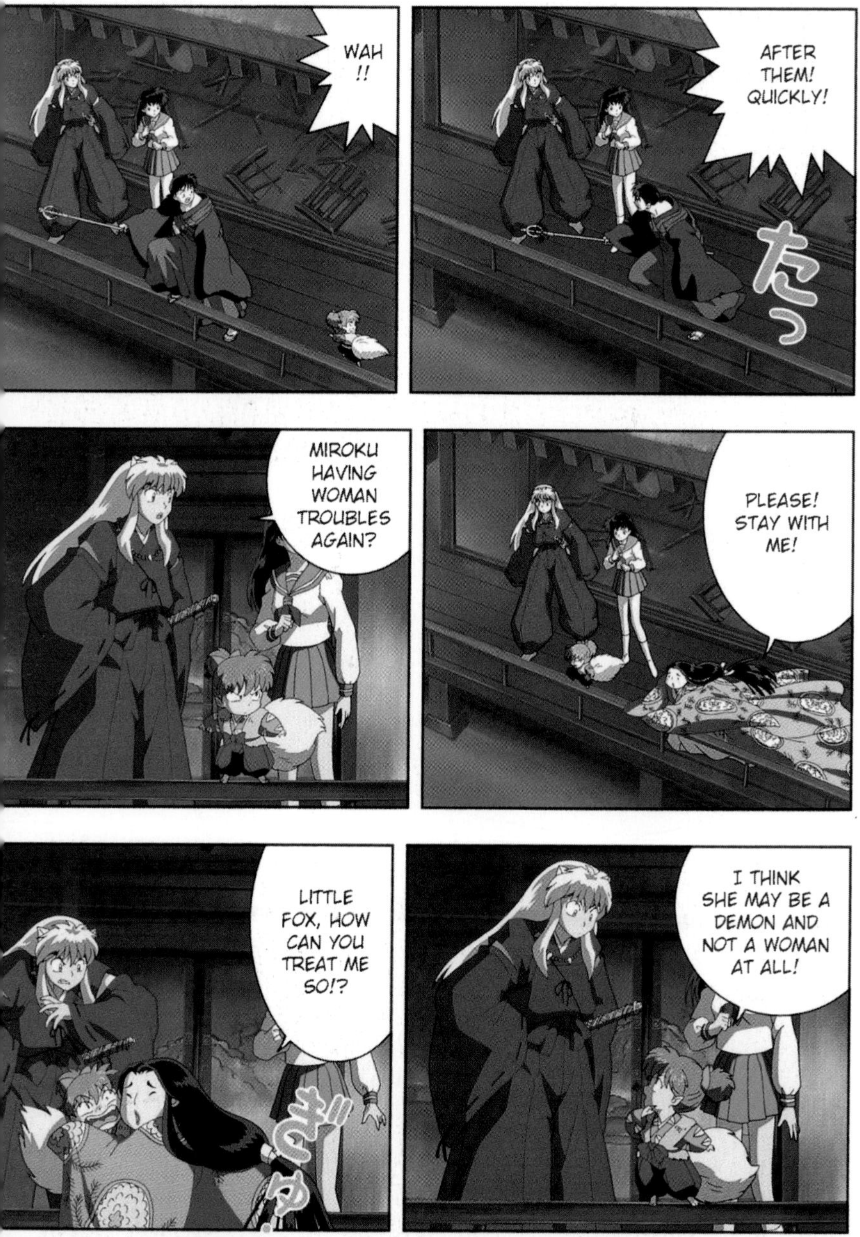
AFTER THEM! QUICKLY!
たっ
WAH !!
PLEASE! STAY WITH ME!
MIROKU HAVING WOMAN TROUBLES AGAIN?
I THINK SHE MAY BE A DEMON AND NOT A WOMAN AT ALL!
LITTLE FOX, HOW CAN YOU TREAT ME SO!?
ぎゅ

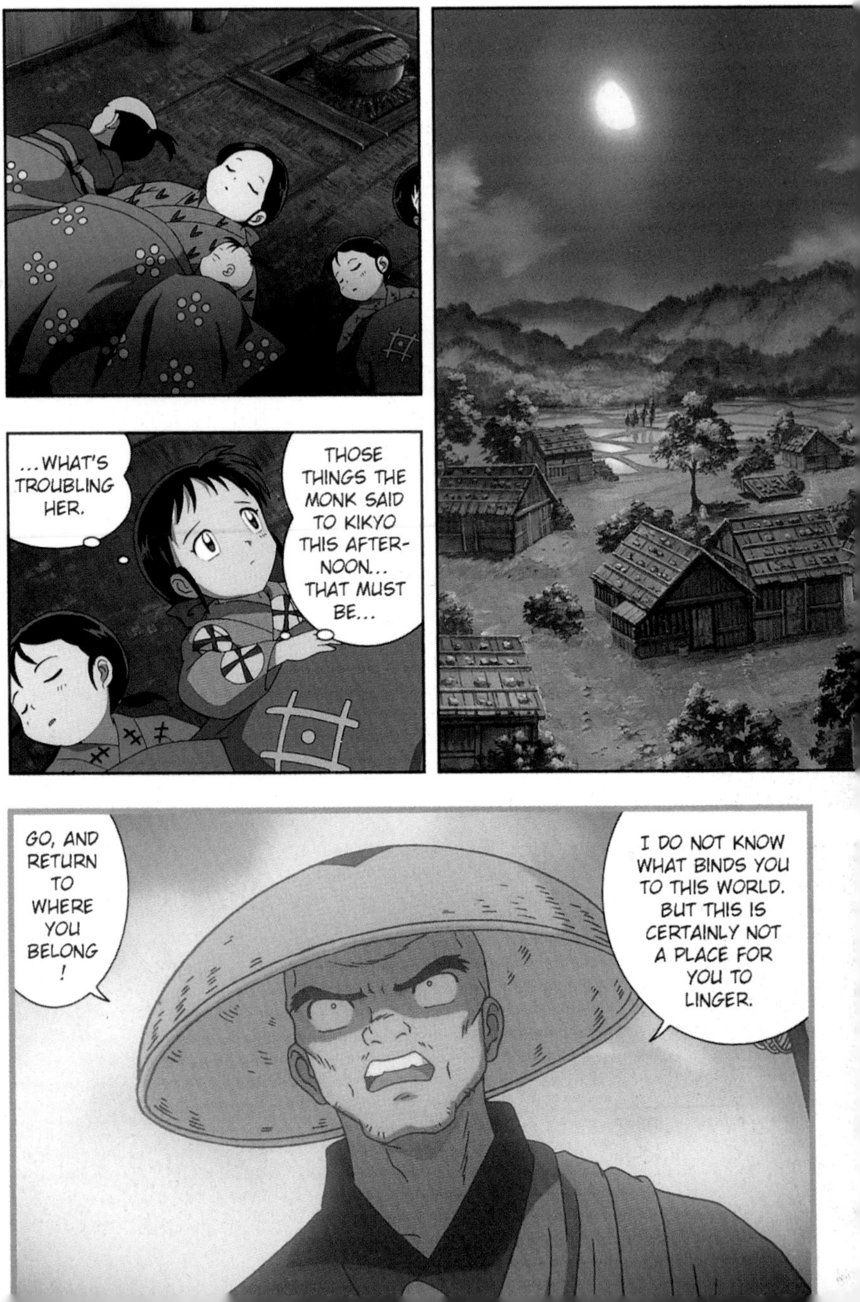
THOSE THINGS THE MONK SAID TO KIKYO THIS AFTERNOON... THAT MUST BE...
...WHAT'S TROUBLING HER.
I DO NOT KNOW WHAT BINDS YOU TO THIS WORLD. BUT THIS IS CERTAINLY NOT A PLACE FOR YOU TO LINGER.
GO, AND RETURN TO WHERE YOU BELONG!

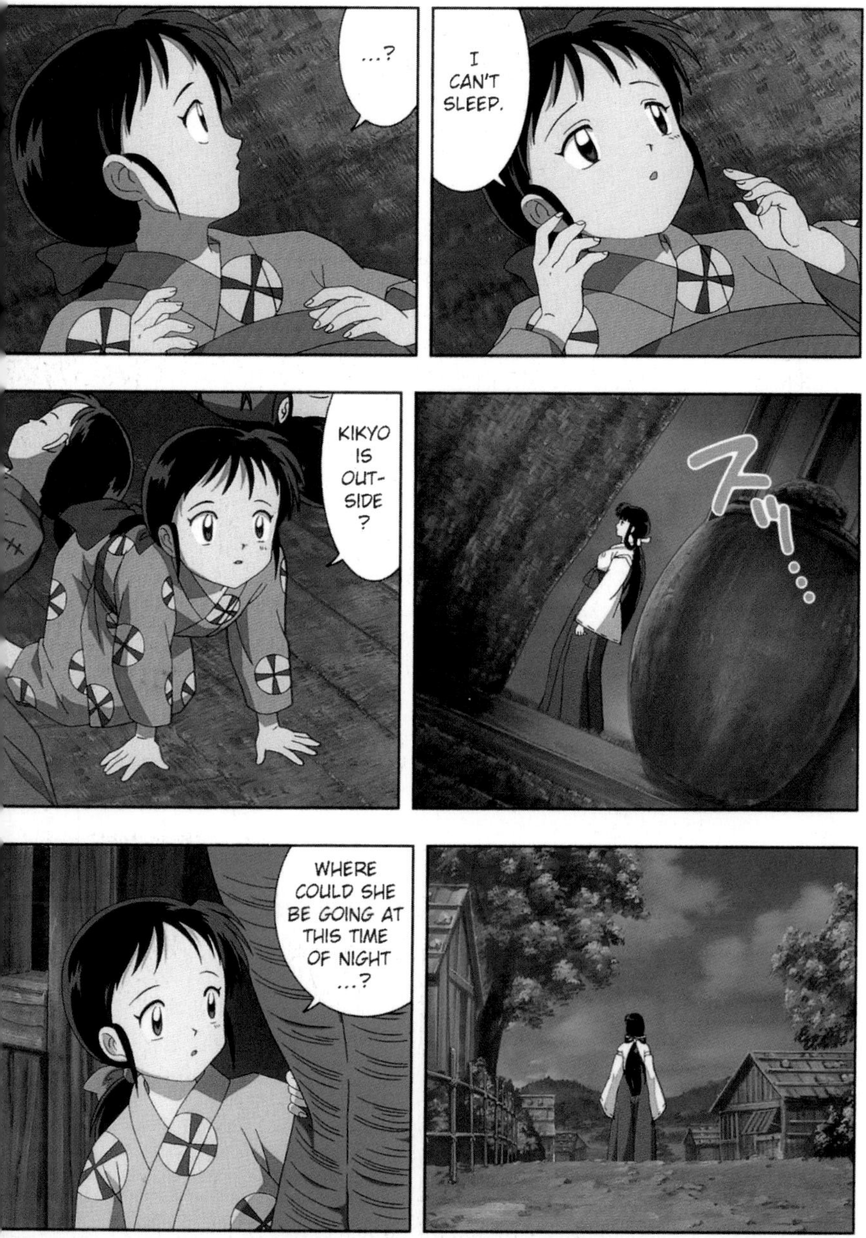
I CAN'T SLEEP.
...?
ズッ...
KIKYO IS OUTSIDE?
WHERE COULD SHE BE GOING AT THIS TIME OF NIGHT...?

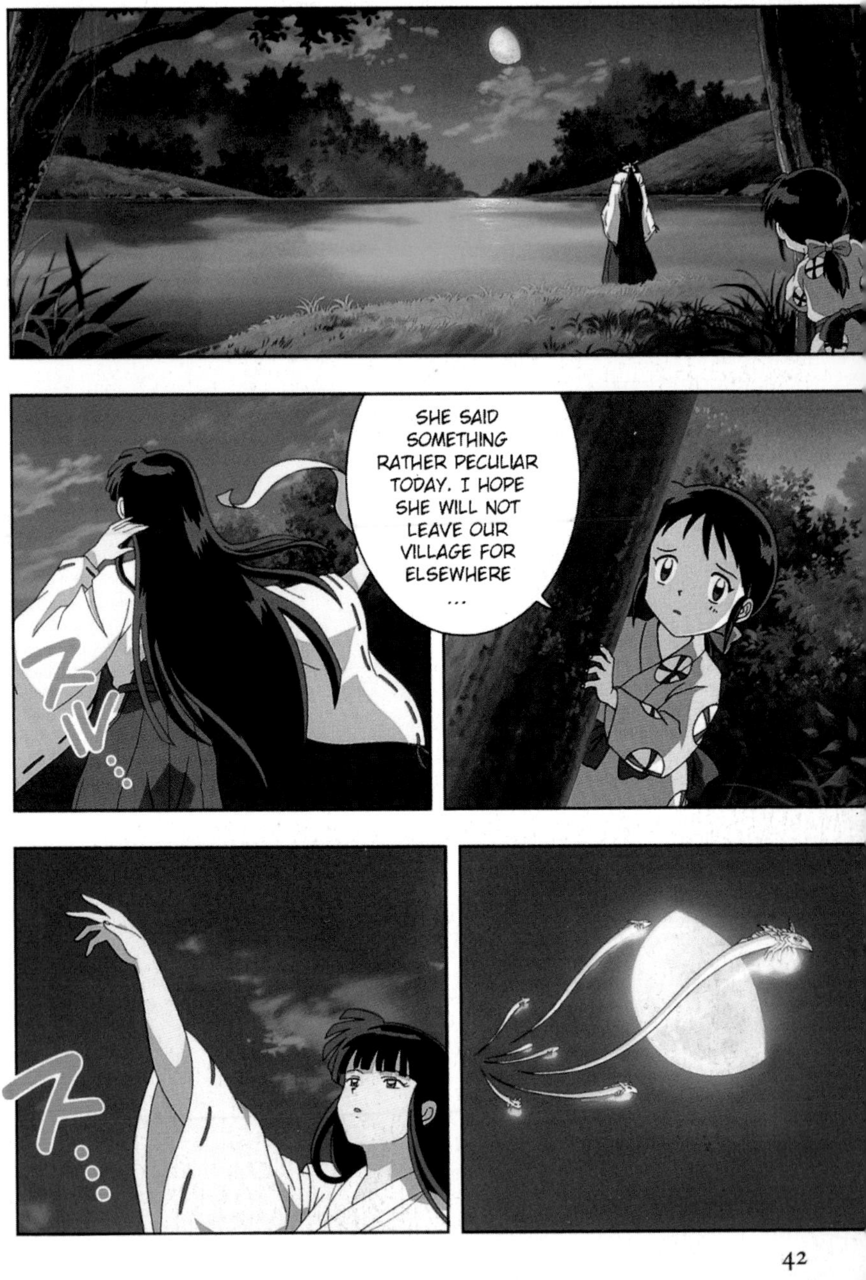
SHE SAID SOMETHING RATHER PECULIAR TODAY. I HOPE SHE WILL NOT LEAVE OUR VILLAGE FOR ELSEWHERE ...

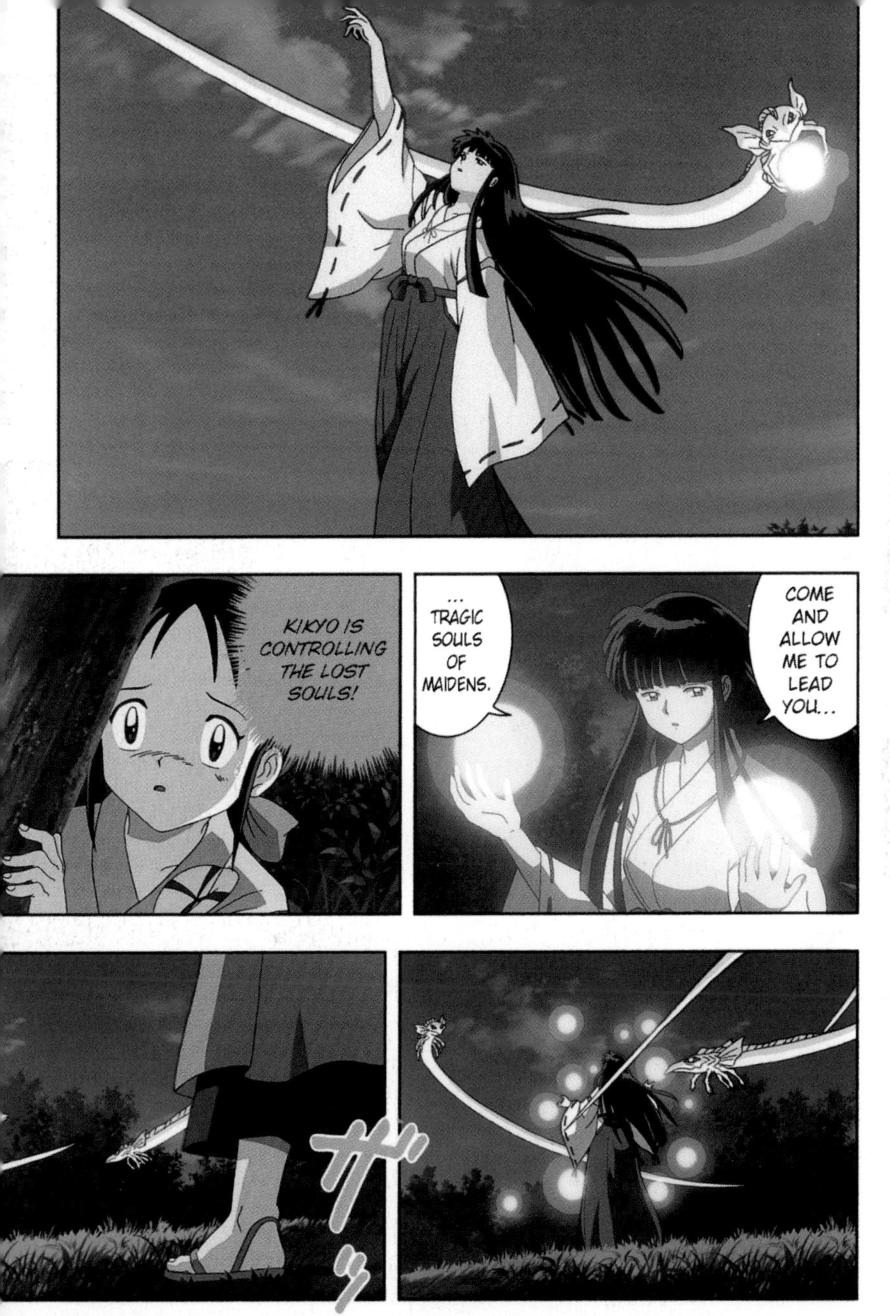
COME AND ALLOW ME TO LEAD YOU...
...TRAGIC SOULS OF MAIDENS.
KIKYO IS CONTROLLING THE LOST SOULS!
ザッ

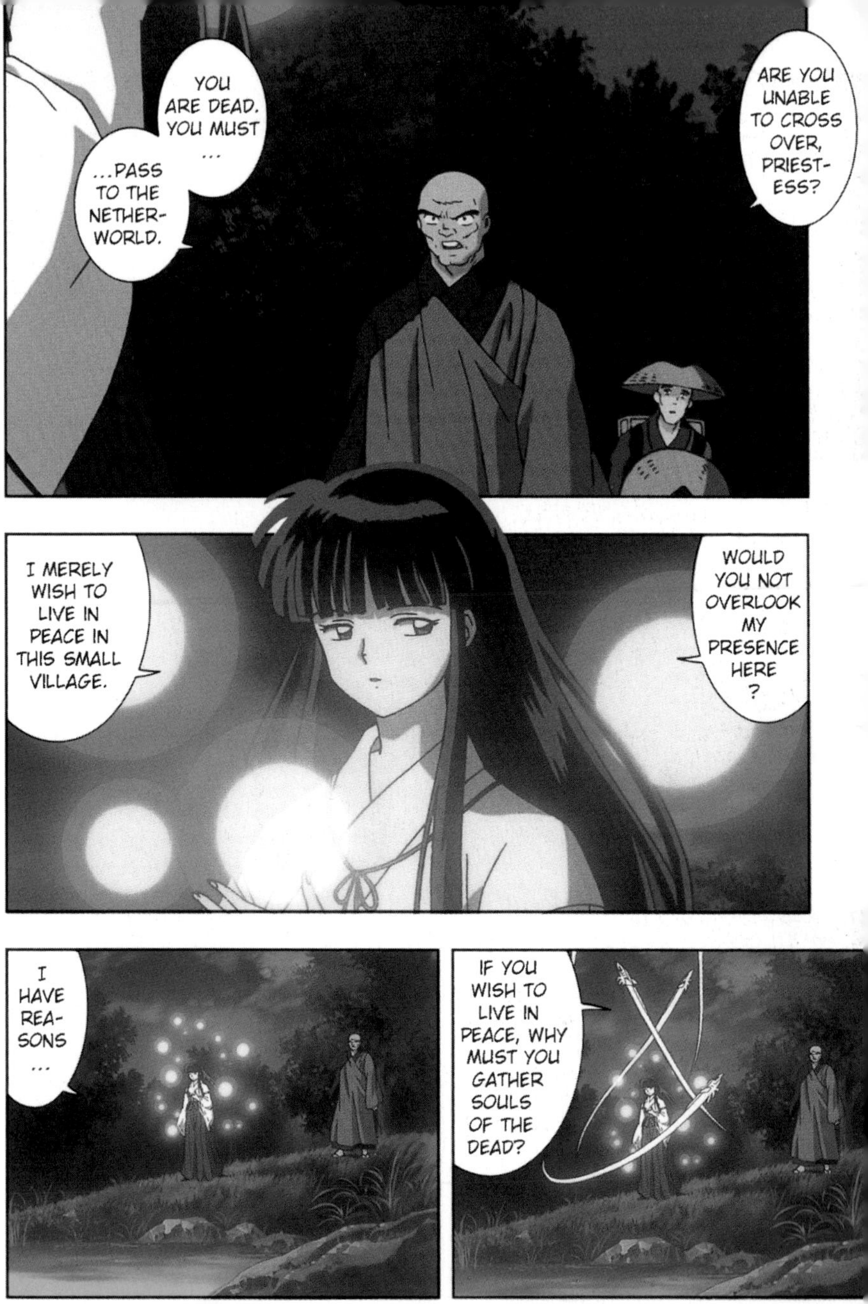
ARE YOU UNABLE TO CROSS OVER, PRIEST-ESS?
YOU ARE DEAD. YOU MUST ...
...PASS TO THE NETHER-WORLD.
WOULD YOU NOT OVERLOOK MY PRESENCE HERE?
I MERELY WISH TO LIVE IN PEACE IN THIS SMALL VILLAGE.
IF YOU WISH TO LIVE IN PEACE, WHY MUST YOU GATHER SOULS OF THE DEAD?
I HAVE REA-SONS ...

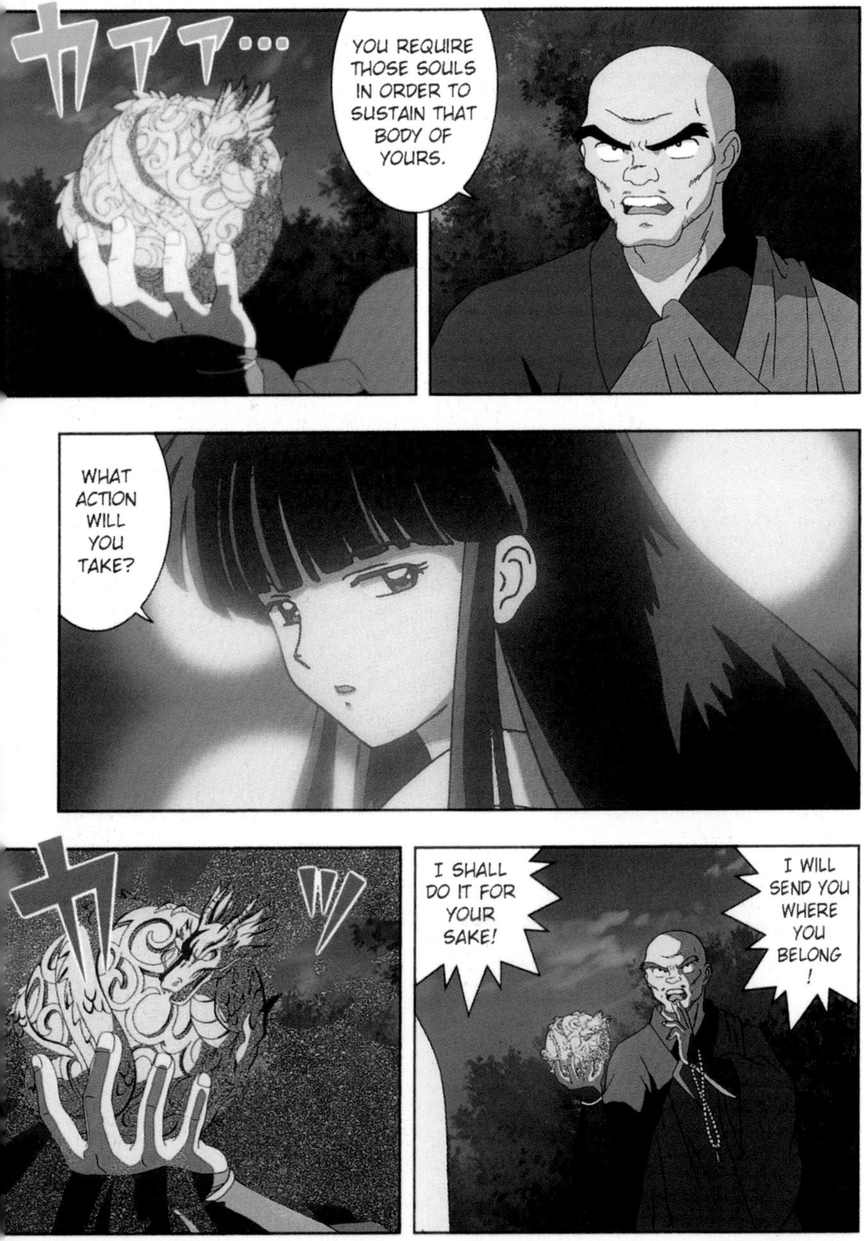
YOU REQUIRE THOSE SOULS IN ORDER TO SUSTAIN THAT BODY OF YOURS.
カァァ...
WHAT ACTION WILL YOU TAKE?
I WILL SEND YOU WHERE YOU BELONG!
I SHALL DO IT FOR YOUR SAKE!
カッ

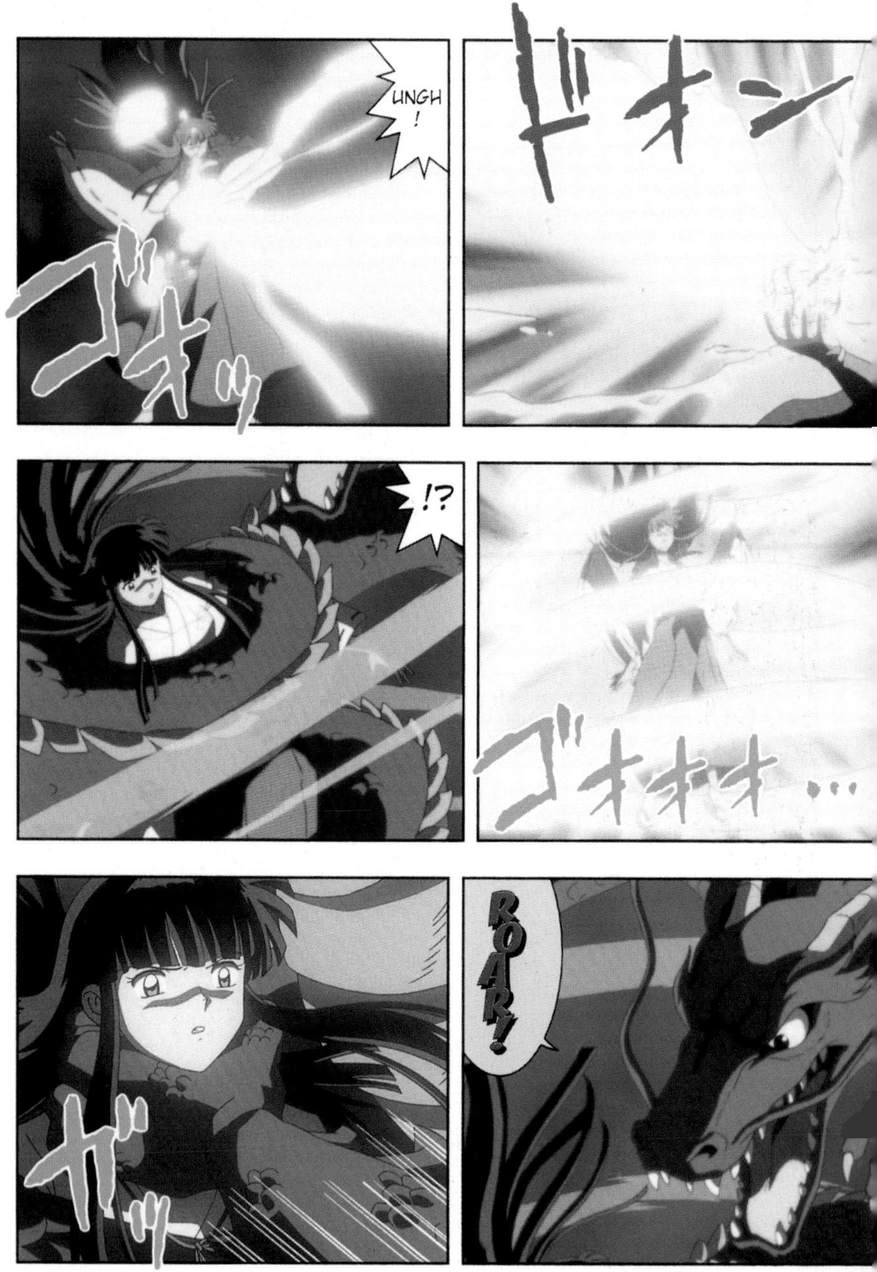
ドオン
UNGH!
ゴオッ
ゴオオオ…
!?
ROAR!
ガッ

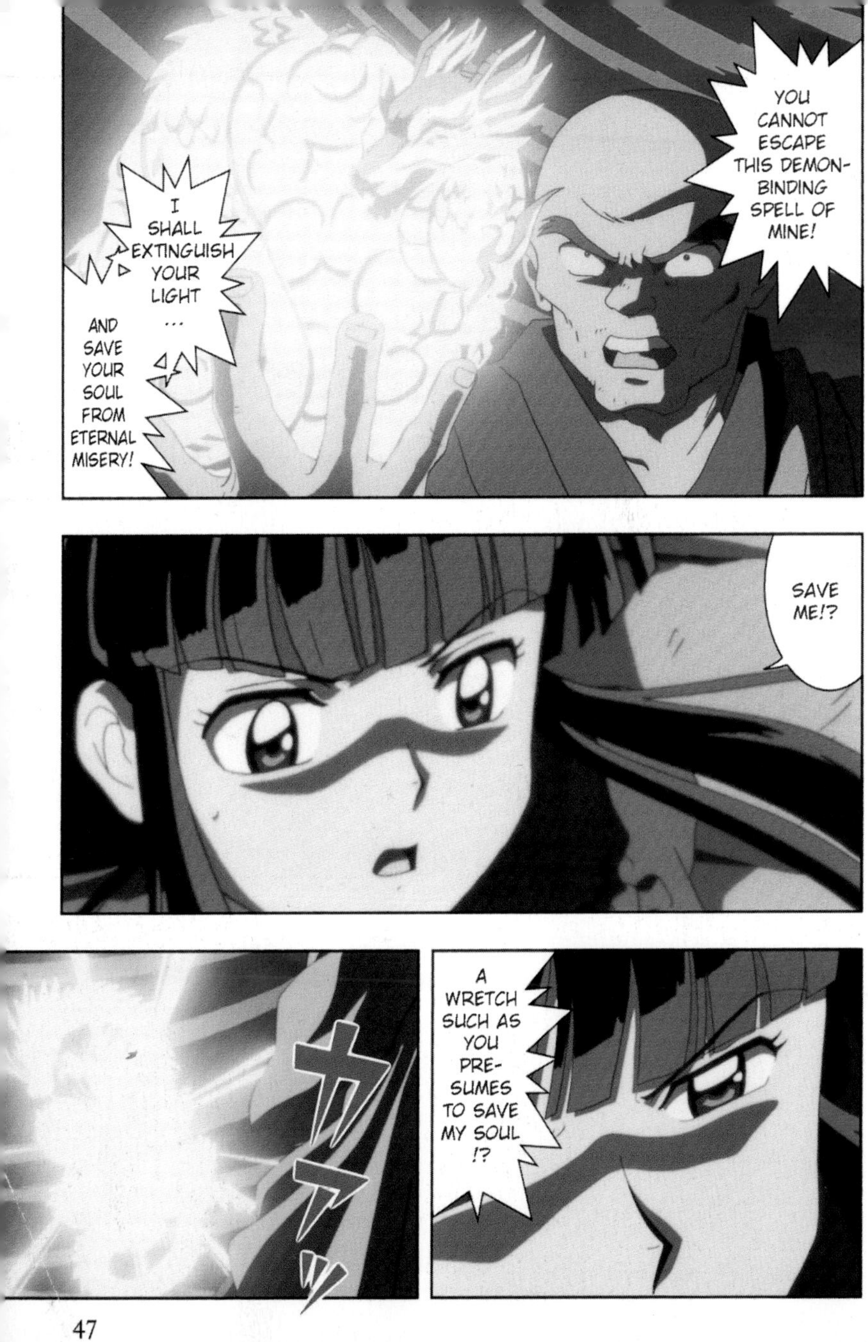
YOU CANNOT ESCAPE THIS DEMON-BINDING SPELL OF MINE!
I SHALL EXTINGUISH YOUR LIGHT ...
AND SAVE YOUR SOUL FROM ETERNAL MISERY!
SAVE ME!?
A WRETCH SUCH AS YOU PRE-SUMES TO SAVE MY SOUL !?
カァッ

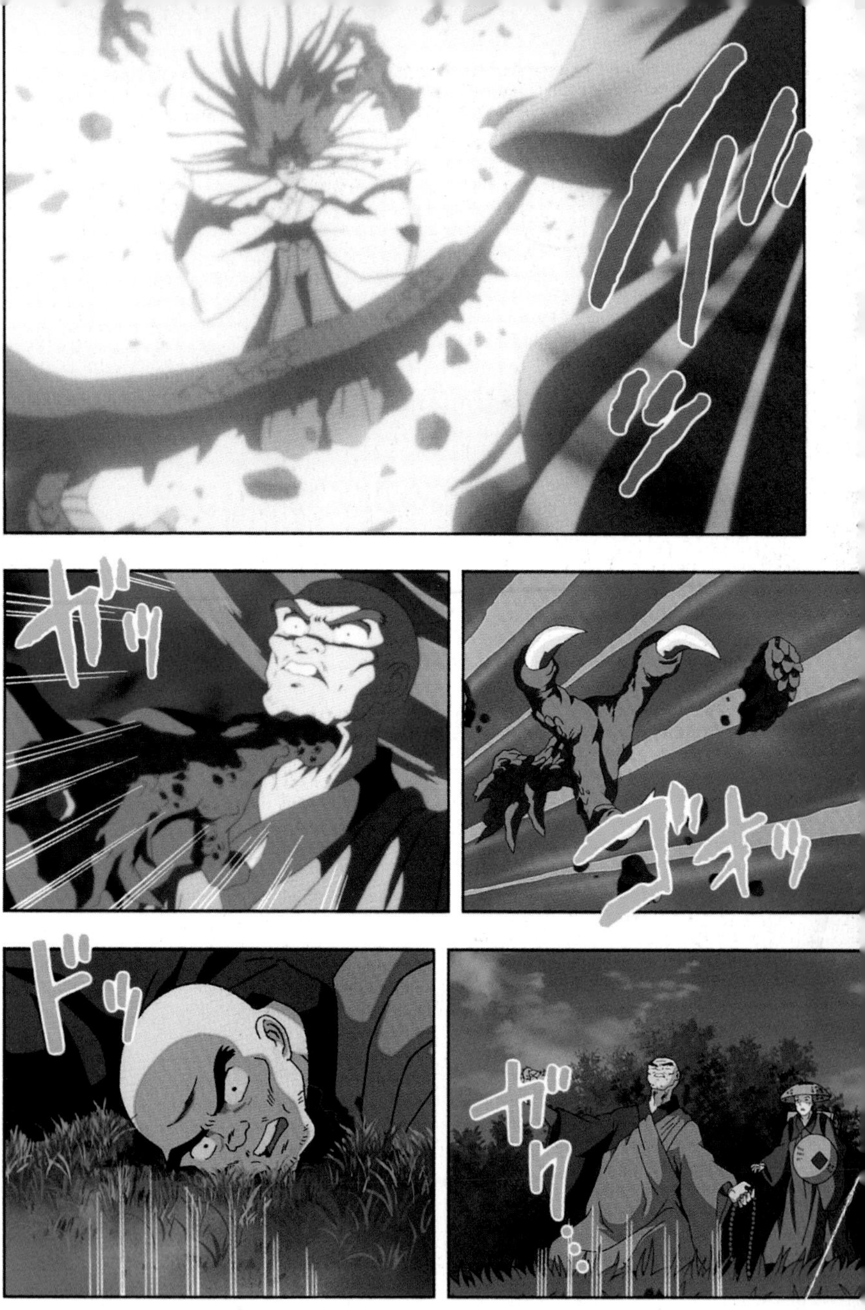
ゴオッ
ガッ
ガク…
ドッ

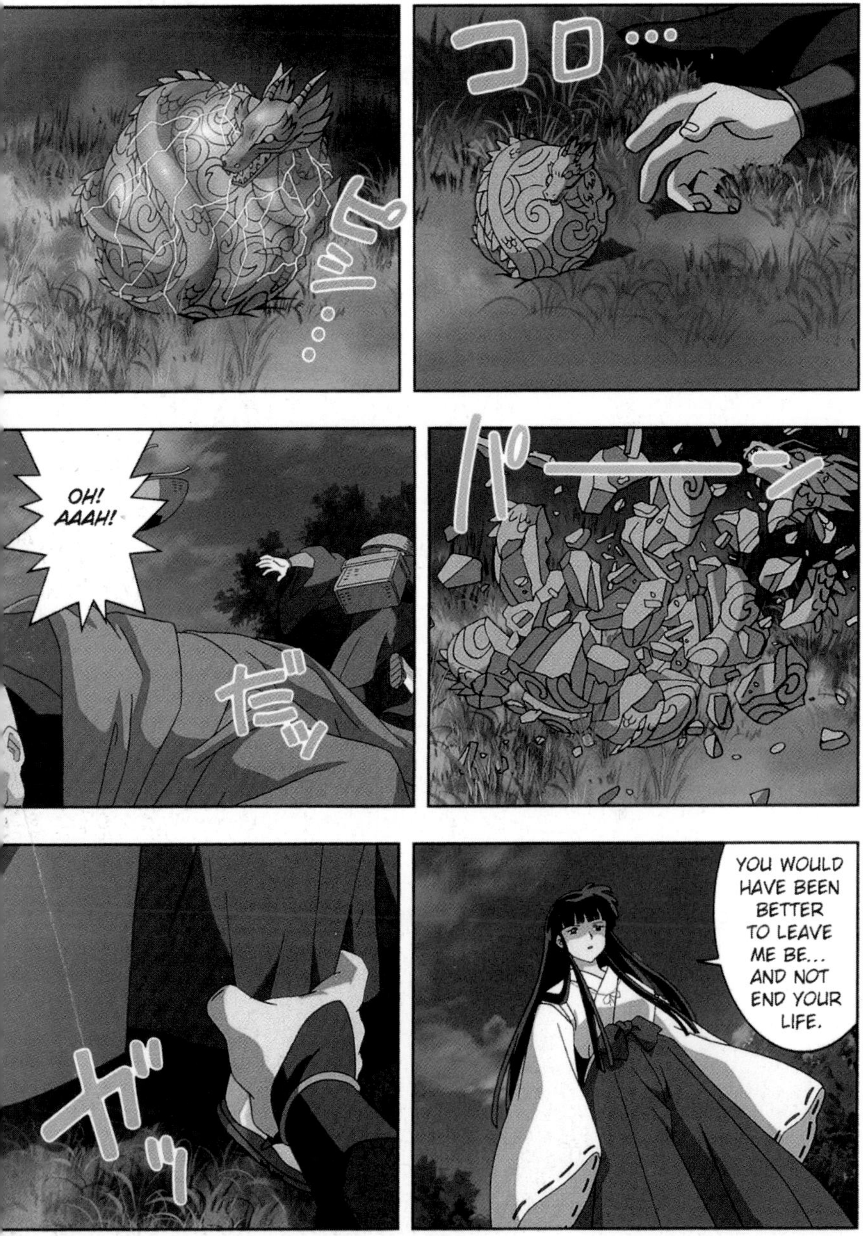
コロ…
ピシッ…
パーーン
OH! AAAH!
だッ
YOU WOULD HAVE BEEN BETTER TO LEAVE ME BE... AND NOT END YOUR LIFE.
ザッ

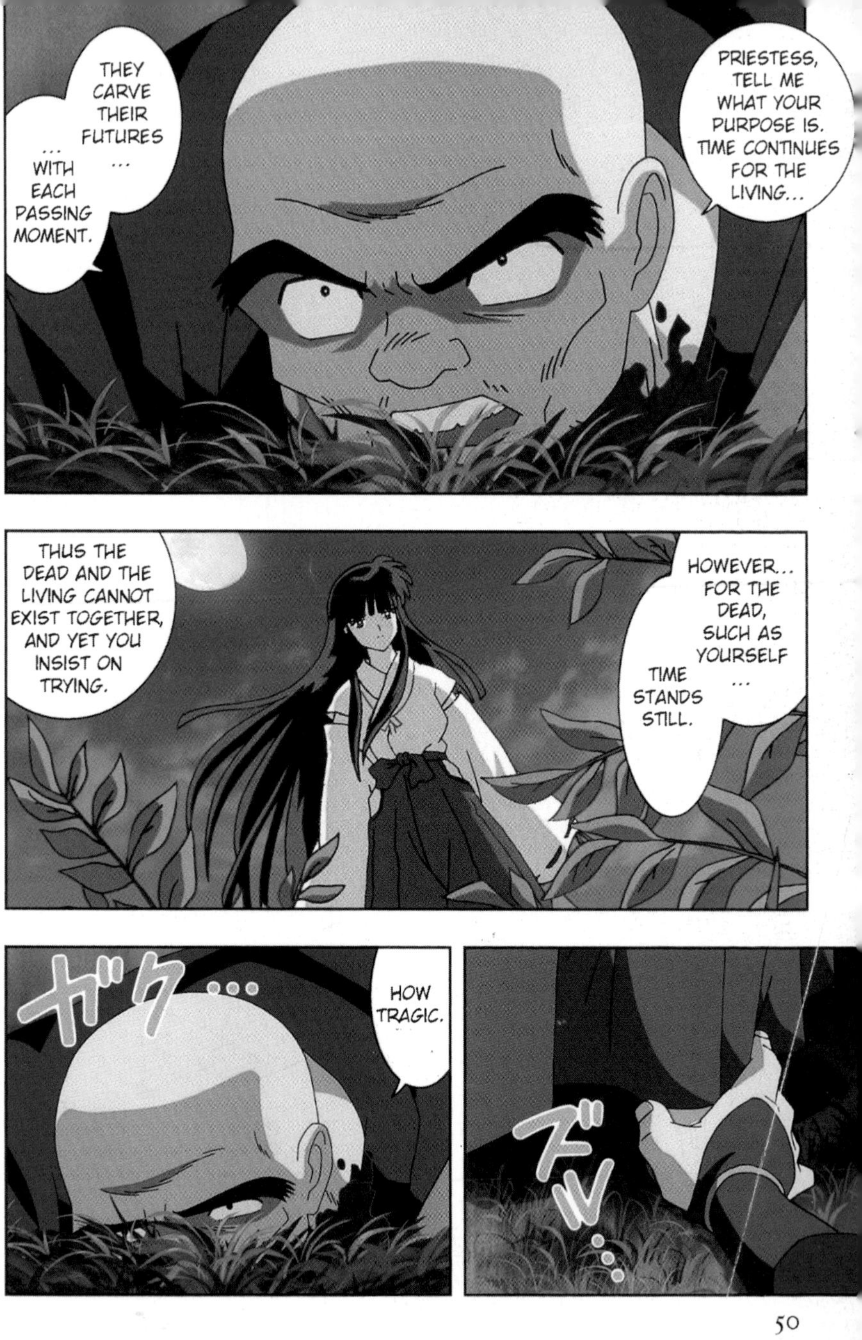
PRIESTESS, TELL ME WHAT YOUR PURPOSE IS. TIME CONTINUES FOR THE LIVING...
THEY CARVE THEIR FUTURES...
...WITH EACH PASSING MOMENT.
HOWEVER... FOR THE DEAD, SUCH AS YOURSELF...
TIME STANDS STILL.
THUS THE DEAD AND THE LIVING CANNOT EXIST TOGETHER, AND YET YOU INSIST ON TRYING.
ズ...
ガク...
HOW TRAGIC.

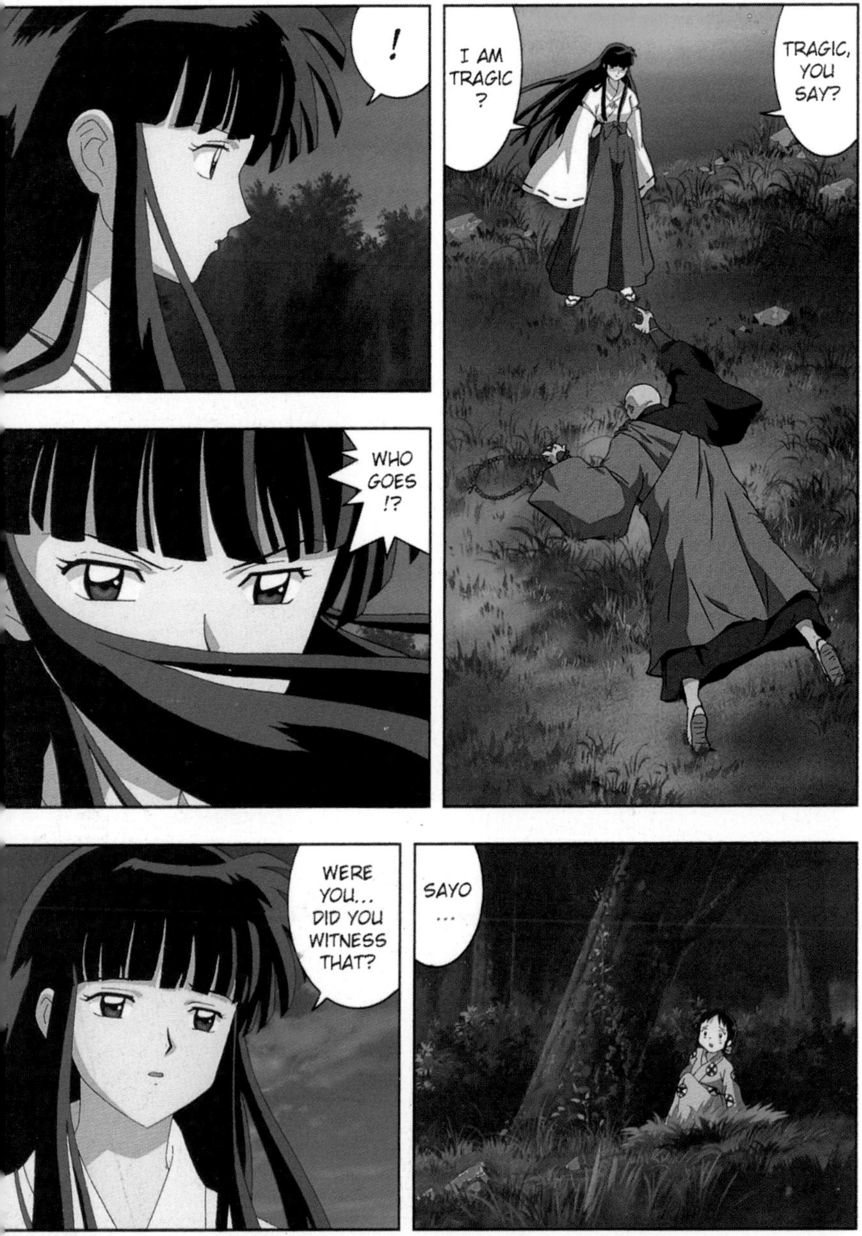
TRAGIC, YOU SAY?
I AM TRAGIC ?
!
WHO GOES !?
SAYO ...
WERE YOU... DID YOU WITNESS THAT?

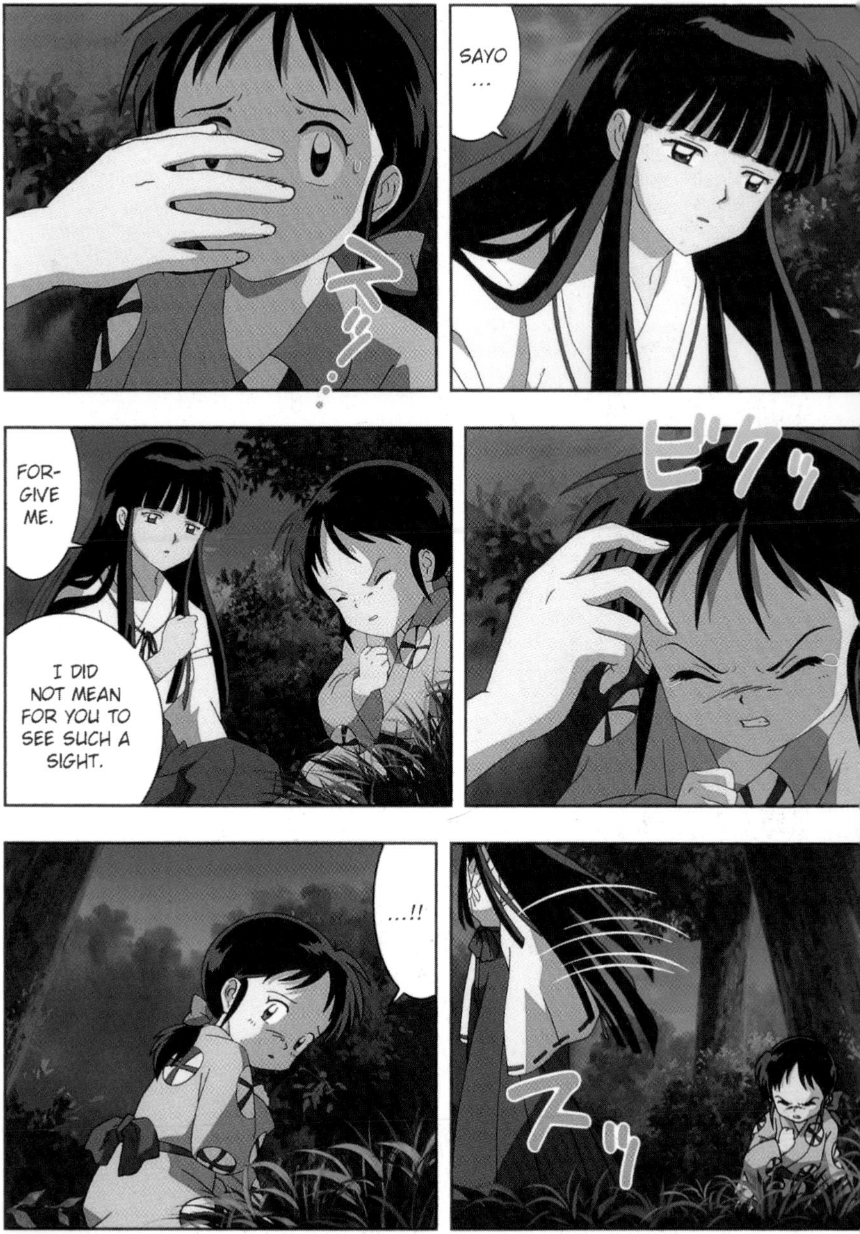
SAYO ...
スッ...
ビクッ
FOR-GIVE ME.
I DID NOT MEAN FOR YOU TO SEE SUCH A SIGHT.
スッ
...!!

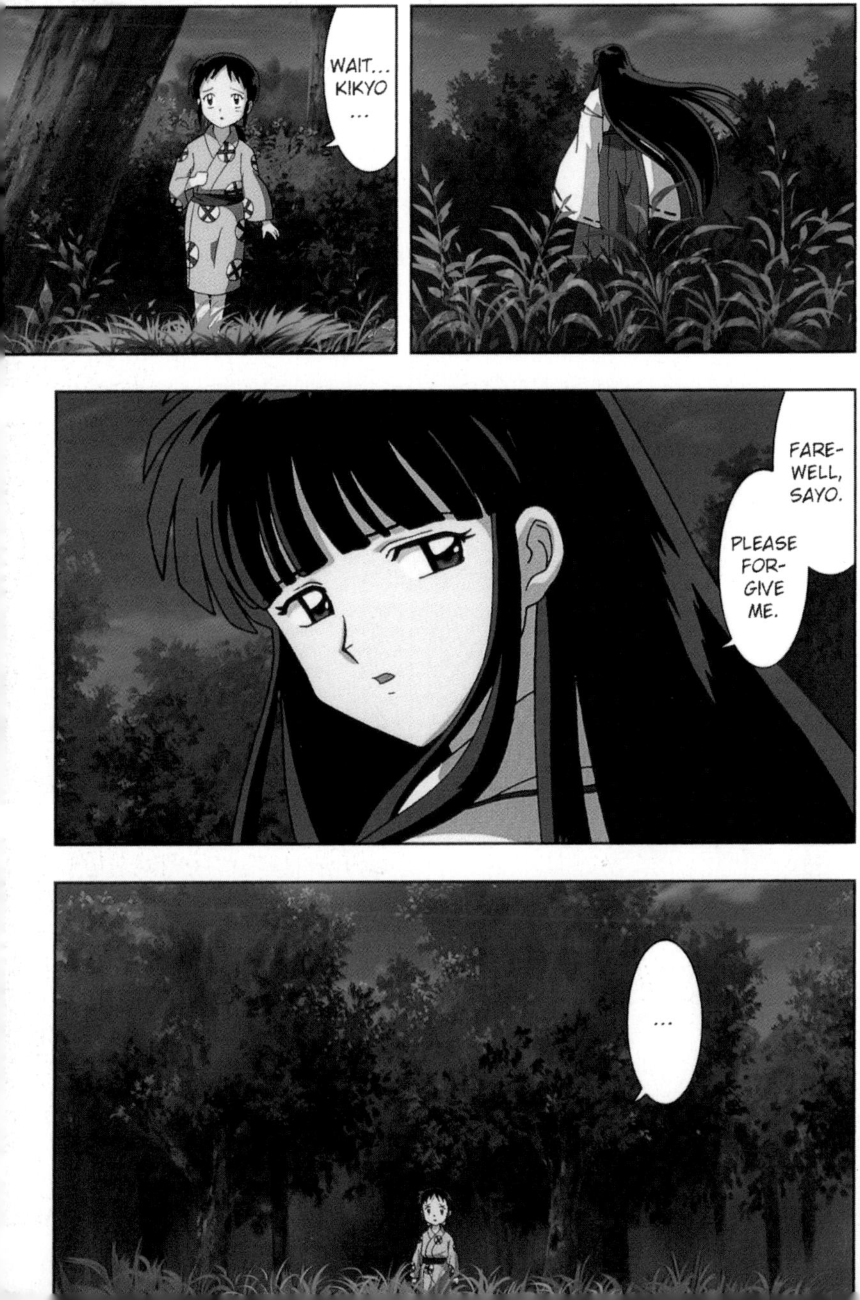
WAIT… KIKYO …
FAREWELL, SAYO.
PLEASE FORGIVE ME.
…

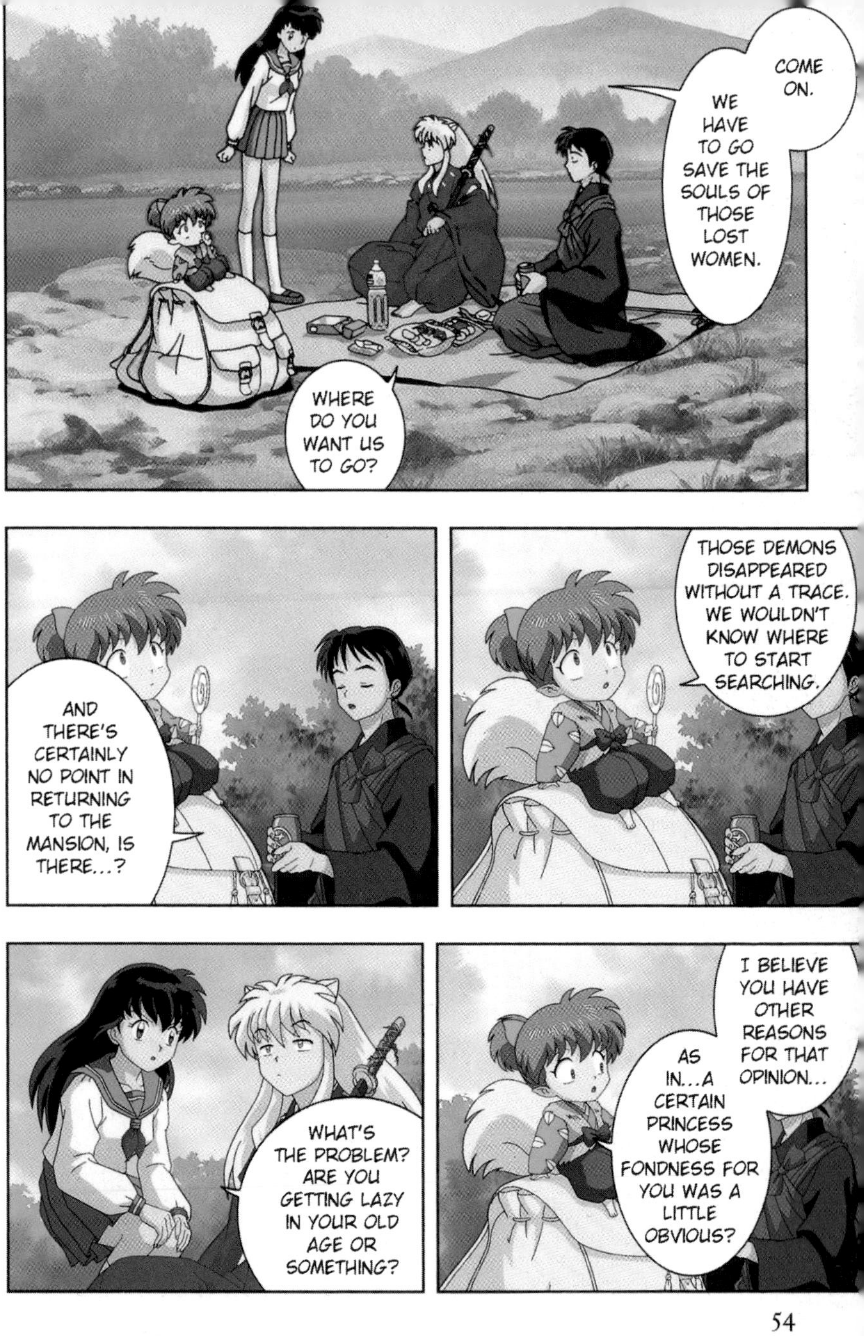
COME ON.
WE HAVE TO GO SAVE THE SOULS OF THOSE LOST WOMEN.
WHERE DO YOU WANT US TO GO?
THOSE DEMONS DISAPPEARED WITHOUT A TRACE. WE WOULDN'T KNOW WHERE TO START SEARCHING.
AND THERE'S CERTAINLY NO POINT IN RETURNING TO THE MANSION, IS THERE...?
I BELIEVE YOU HAVE OTHER REASONS FOR THAT OPINION...
AS IN...A CERTAIN PRINCESS WHOSE FONDNESS FOR YOU WAS A LITTLE OBVIOUS?
WHAT'S THE PROBLEM? ARE YOU GETTING LAZY IN YOUR OLD AGE OR SOMETHING?

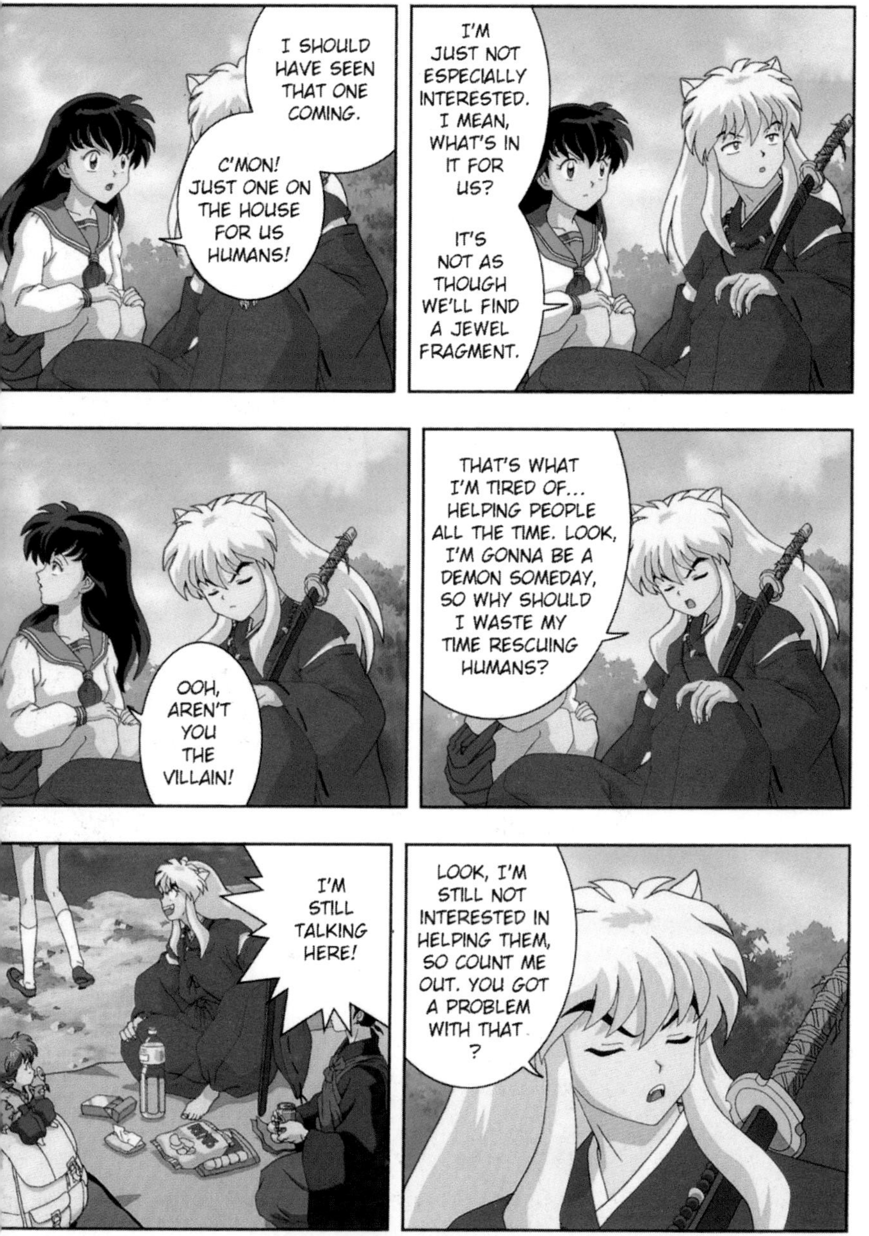
I'M JUST NOT ESPECIALLY INTERESTED. I MEAN, WHAT'S IN IT FOR US?
IT'S NOT AS THOUGH WE'LL FIND A JEWEL FRAGMENT.
I SHOULD HAVE SEEN THAT ONE COMING.
C'MON! JUST ONE ON THE HOUSE FOR US HUMANS!
THAT'S WHAT I'M TIRED OF... HELPING PEOPLE ALL THE TIME. LOOK, I'M GONNA BE A DEMON SOMEDAY, SO WHY SHOULD I WASTE MY TIME RESCUING HUMANS?
OOH, AREN'T YOU THE VILLAIN!
LOOK, I'M STILL NOT INTERESTED IN HELPING THEM, SO COUNT ME OUT. YOU GOT A PROBLEM WITH THAT ?
I'M STILL TALKING HERE!

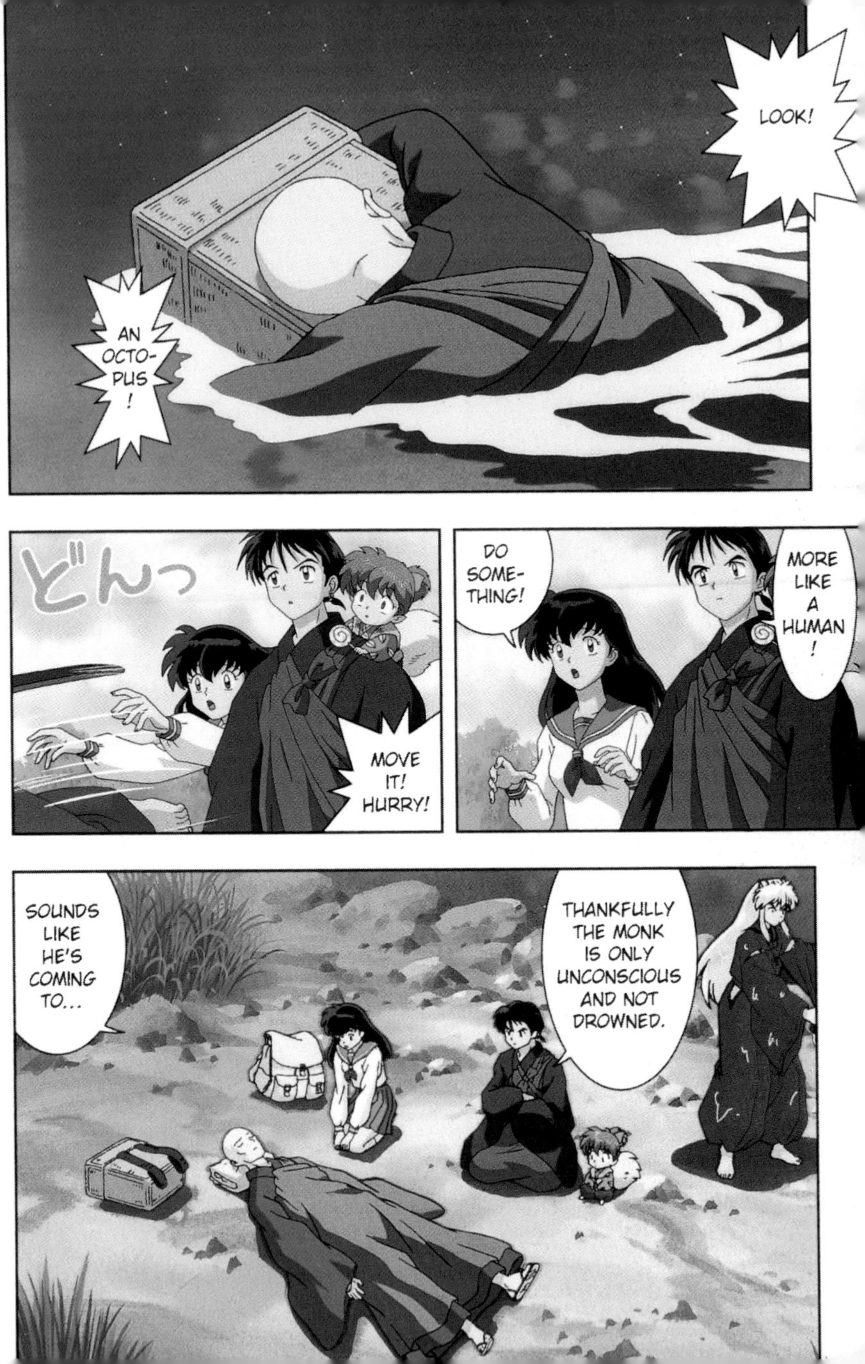
LOOK!
AN OCTOPUS!
MORE LIKE A HUMAN!
DO SOMETHING!
どんっ
MOVE IT! HURRY!
THANKFULLY THE MONK IS ONLY UNCONSCIOUS AND NOT DROWNED.
SOUNDS LIKE HE'S COMING TO...

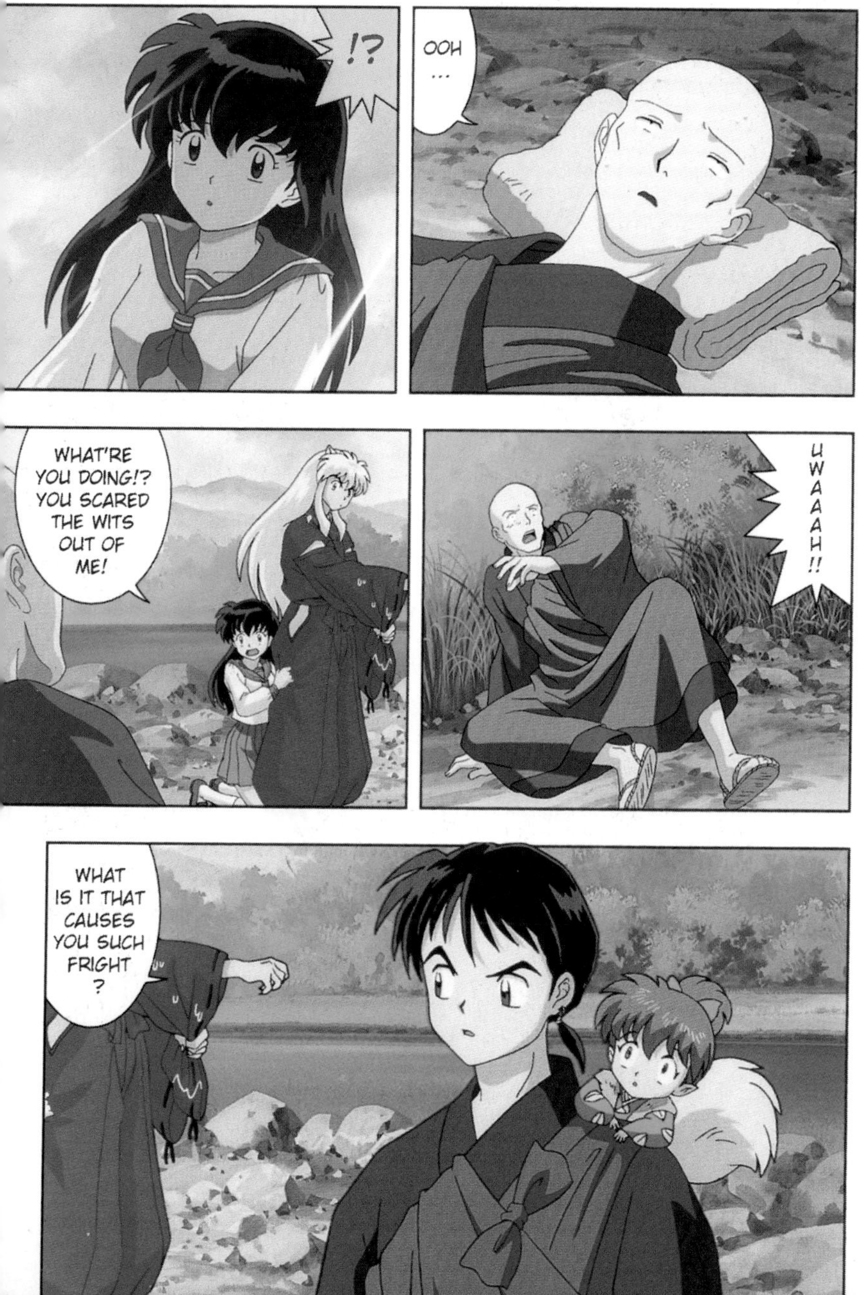
OOH ...
!?
UWAAAH!!
WHAT'RE YOU DOING!? YOU SCARED THE WITS OUT OF ME!
WHAT IS IT THAT CAUSES YOU SUCH FRIGHT ?

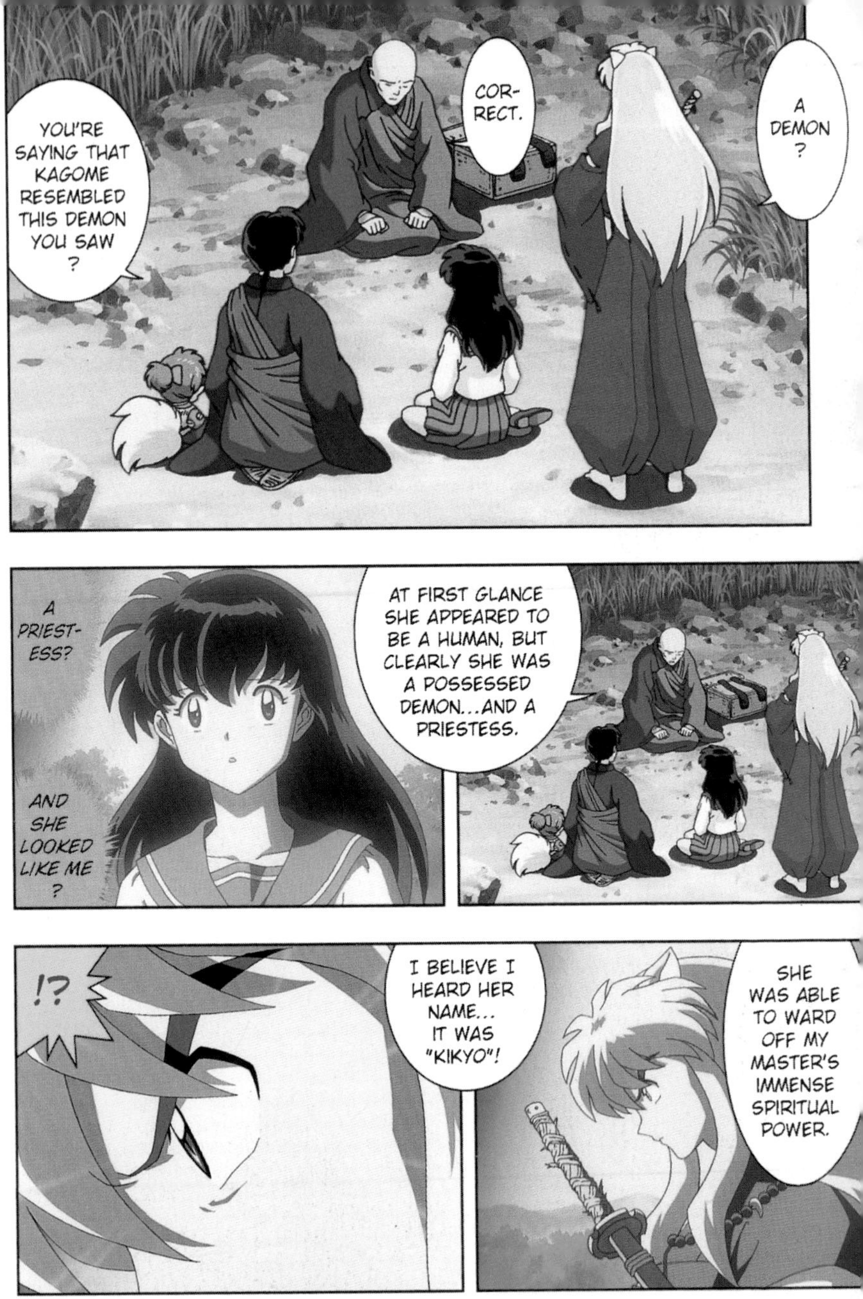
A DEMON?
COR-RECT.
YOU'RE SAYING THAT KAGOME RESEMBLED THIS DEMON YOU SAW?
AT FIRST GLANCE SHE APPEARED TO BE A HUMAN, BUT CLEARLY SHE WAS A POSSESSED DEMON...AND A PRIESTESS.
A PRIEST-ESS?
AND SHE LOOKED LIKE ME?
SHE WAS ABLE TO WARD OFF MY MASTER'S IMMENSE SPIRITUAL POWER.
I BELIEVE I HEARD HER NAME... IT WAS "KIKYO"!
!?

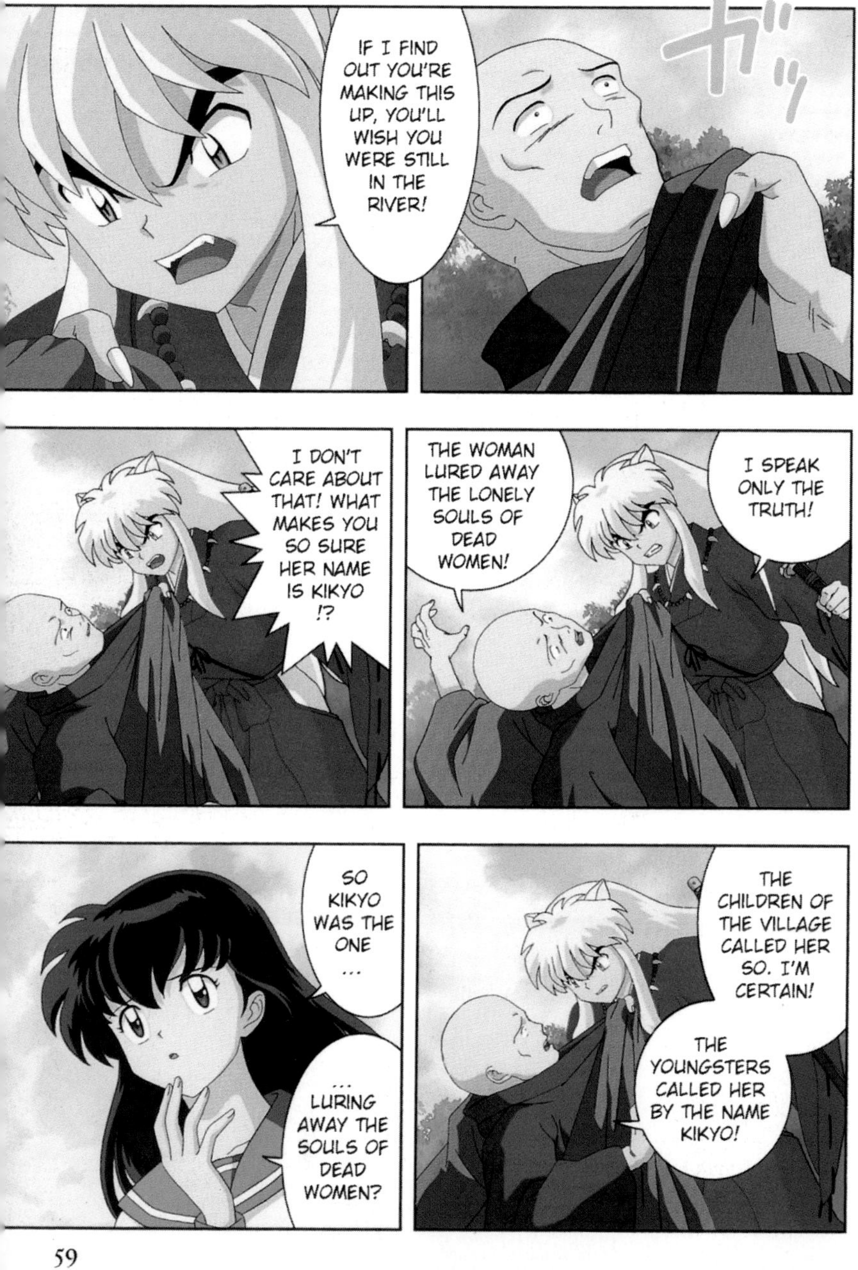
ガッ
IF I FIND OUT YOU'RE MAKING THIS UP, YOU'LL WISH YOU WERE STILL IN THE RIVER!
I SPEAK ONLY THE TRUTH!
THE WOMAN LURED AWAY THE LONELY SOULS OF DEAD WOMEN!
I DON'T CARE ABOUT THAT! WHAT MAKES YOU SO SURE HER NAME IS KIKYO !?
THE CHILDREN OF THE VILLAGE CALLED HER SO. I'M CERTAIN!
THE YOUNGSTERS CALLED HER BY THE NAME KIKYO!
SO KIKYO WAS THE ONE ...
... LURING AWAY THE SOULS OF DEAD WOMEN?

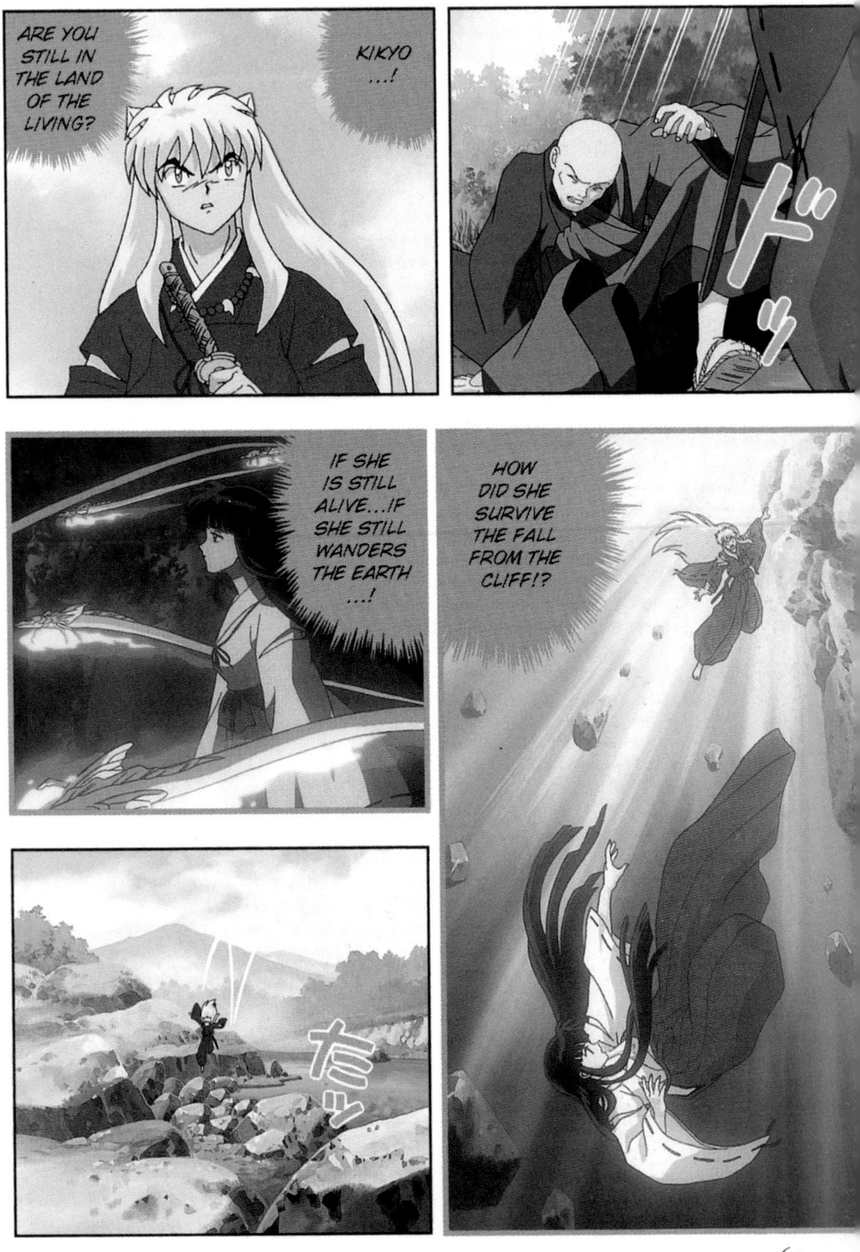
ドッ
KIKYO ...!
ARE YOU STILL IN THE LAND OF THE LIVING?
HOW DID SHE SURVIVE THE FALL FROM THE CLIFF!?
IF SHE IS STILL ALIVE...IF SHE STILL WANDERS THE EARTH ...!
タッ

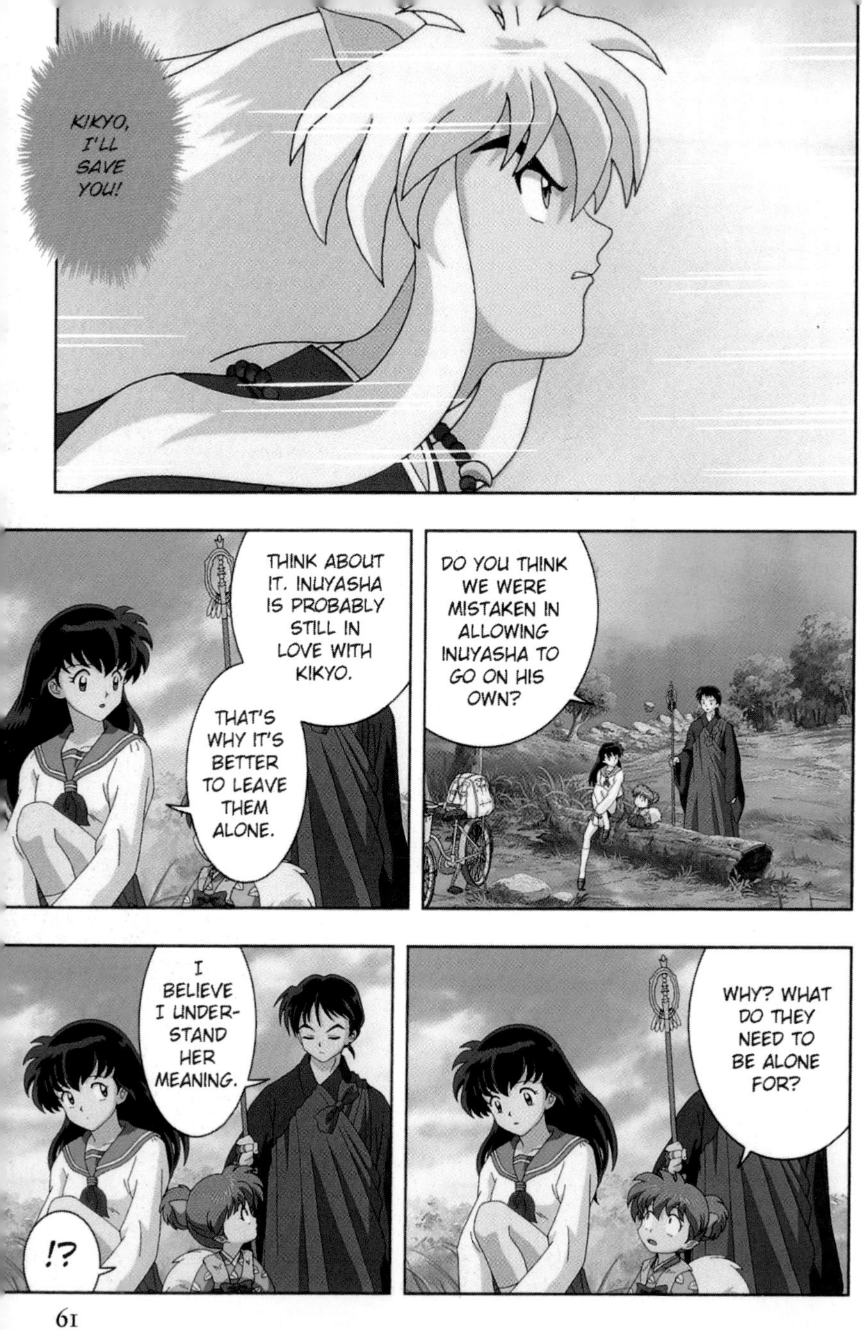
KIKYO, I'LL SAVE YOU!
DO YOU THINK WE WERE MISTAKEN IN ALLOWING INUYASHA TO GO ON HIS OWN?
THINK ABOUT IT. INUYASHA IS PROBABLY STILL IN LOVE WITH KIKYO.
THAT'S WHY IT'S BETTER TO LEAVE THEM ALONE.
WHY? WHAT DO THEY NEED TO BE ALONE FOR?
I BELIEVE I UNDER-STAND HER MEANING.
!?

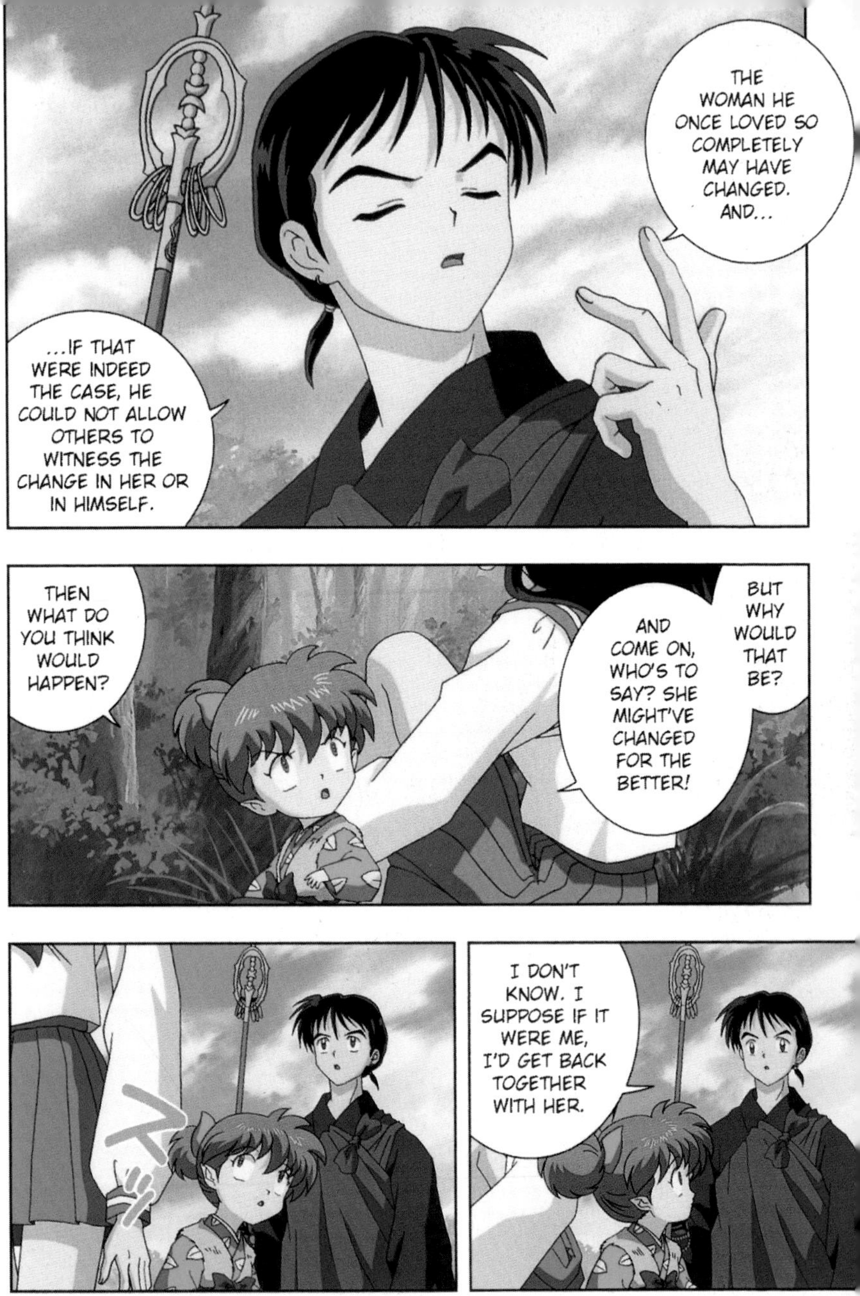
THE WOMAN HE ONCE LOVED SO COMPLETELY MAY HAVE CHANGED. AND...
...IF THAT WERE INDEED THE CASE, HE COULD NOT ALLOW OTHERS TO WITNESS THE CHANGE IN HER OR IN HIMSELF.
BUT WHY WOULD THAT BE?
AND COME ON, WHO'S TO SAY? SHE MIGHT'VE CHANGED FOR THE BETTER!
THEN WHAT DO YOU THINK WOULD HAPPEN?
I DON'T KNOW. I SUPPOSE IF IT WERE ME, I'D GET BACK TOGETHER WITH HER.

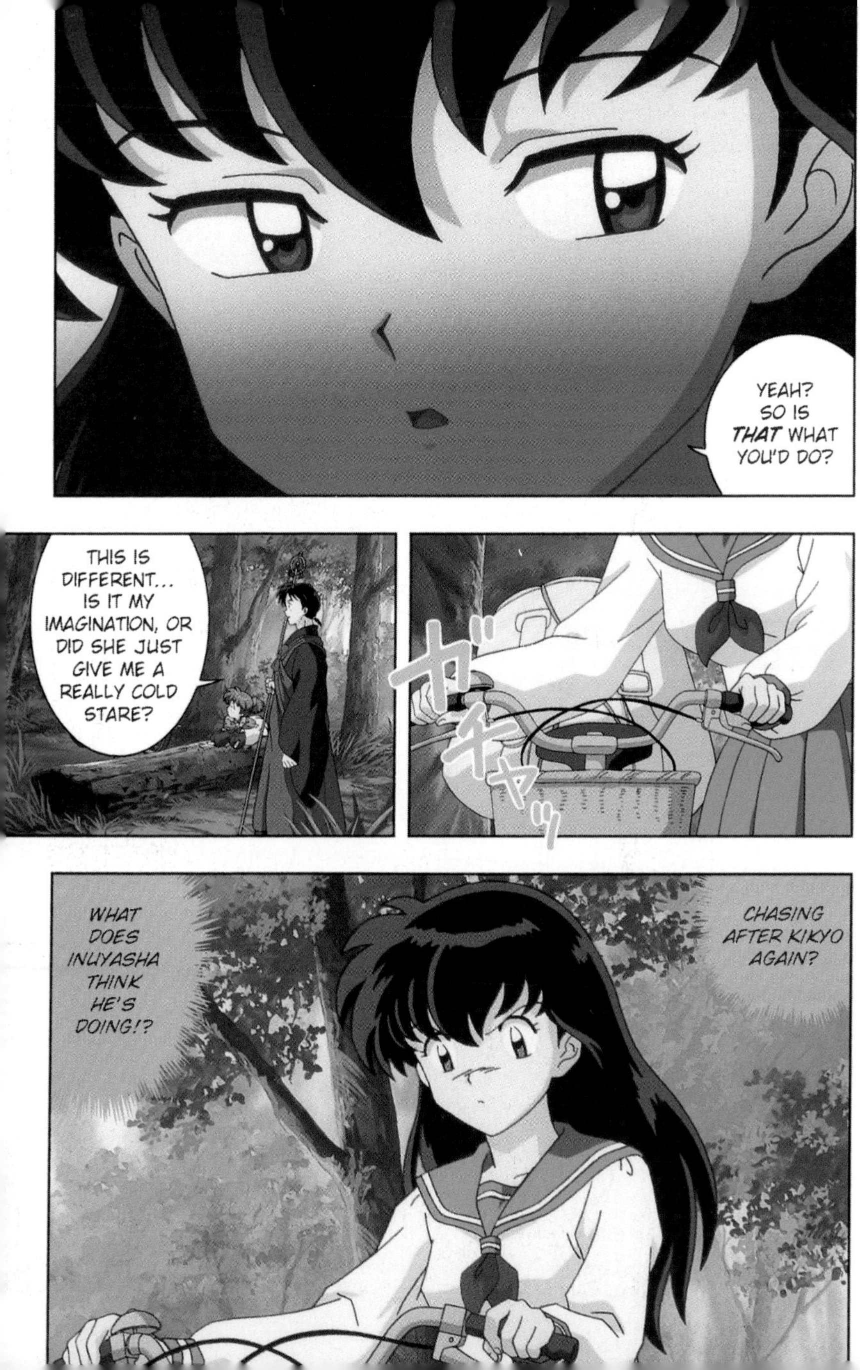
YEAH? SO IS *THAT* WHAT YOU'D DO?
ガチャッ
THIS IS DIFFERENT... IS IT MY IMAGINATION, OR DID SHE JUST GIVE ME A REALLY COLD STARE?
CHASING AFTER KIKYO AGAIN?
WHAT DOES INUYASHA THINK HE'S DOING!?

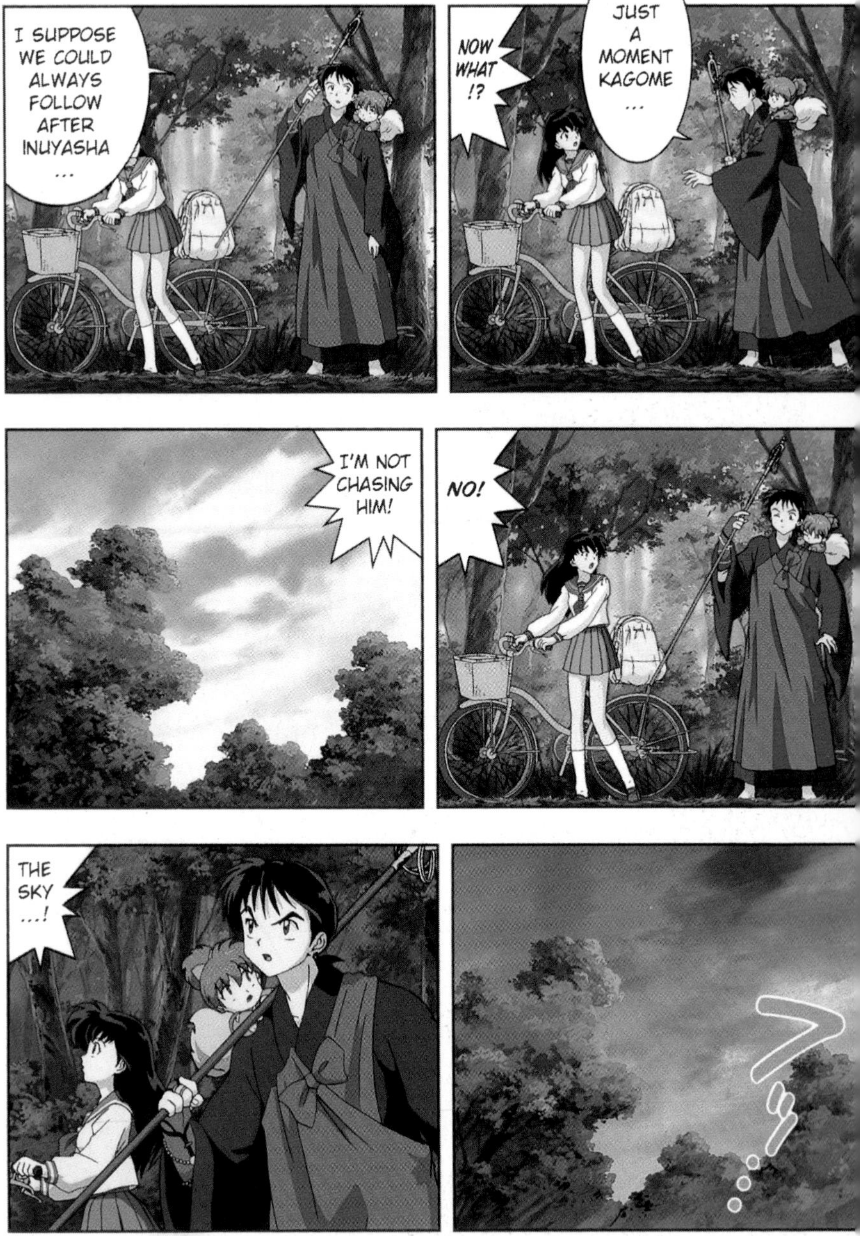
JUST A MOMENT KAGOME ...
NOW WHAT !?
I SUPPOSE WE COULD ALWAYS FOLLOW AFTER INUYASHA ...
NO!
I'M NOT CHASING HIM!
THE SKY ...!

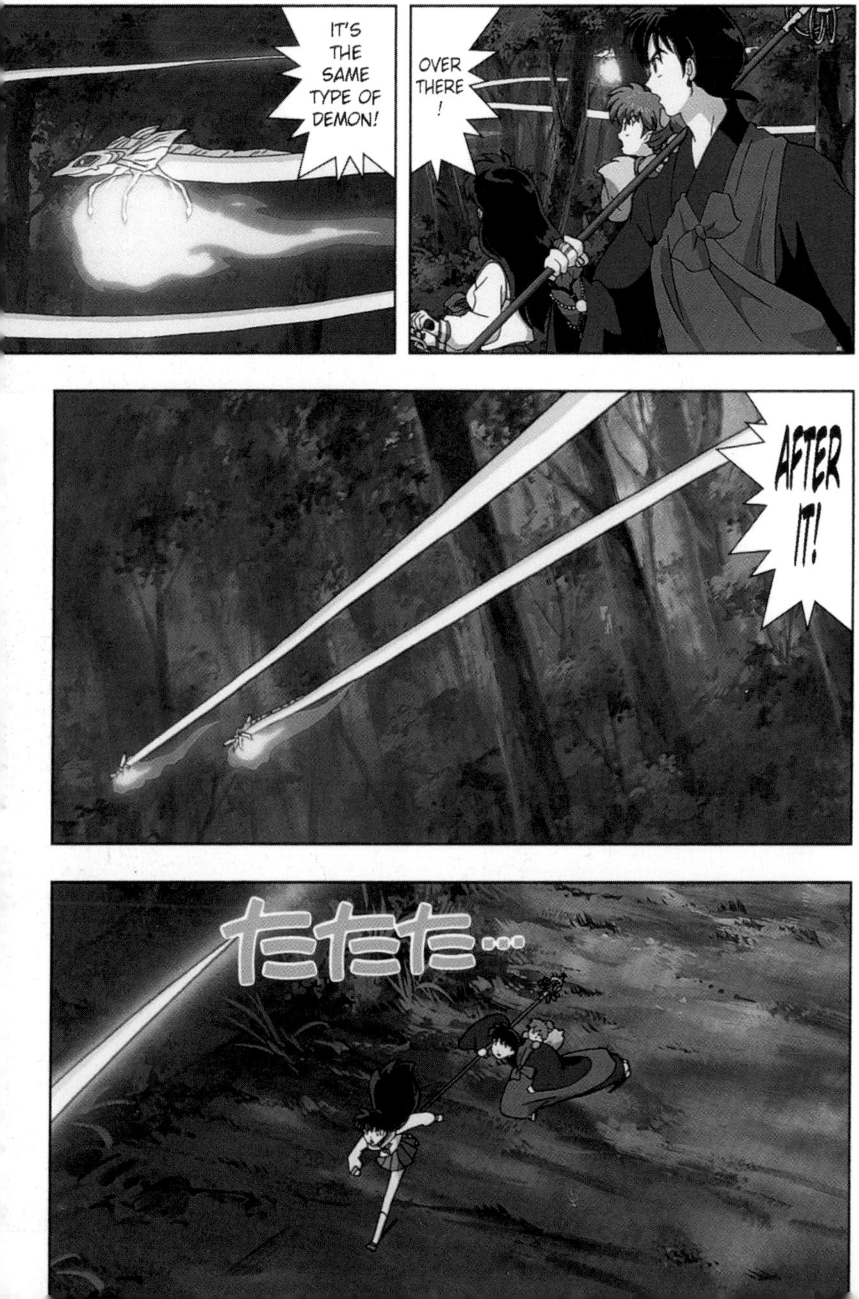
OVER THERE!
IT'S THE SAME TYPE OF DEMON!
AFTER IT!
たたたた…

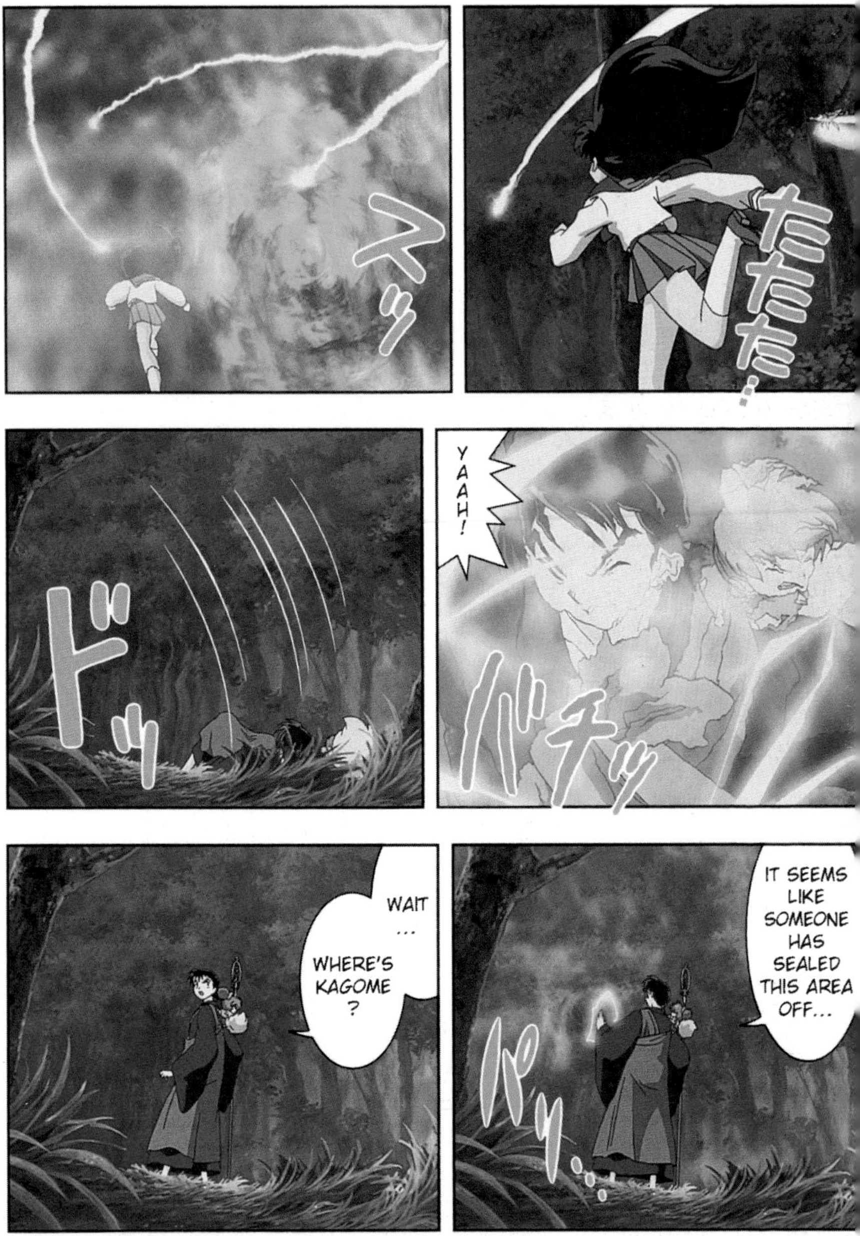

たたた…
スッ
YAAH!
バチッ
ドッ
IT SEEMS LIKE SOMEONE HAS SEALED THIS AREA OFF…
パッ…
WAIT … WHERE'S KAGOME ?

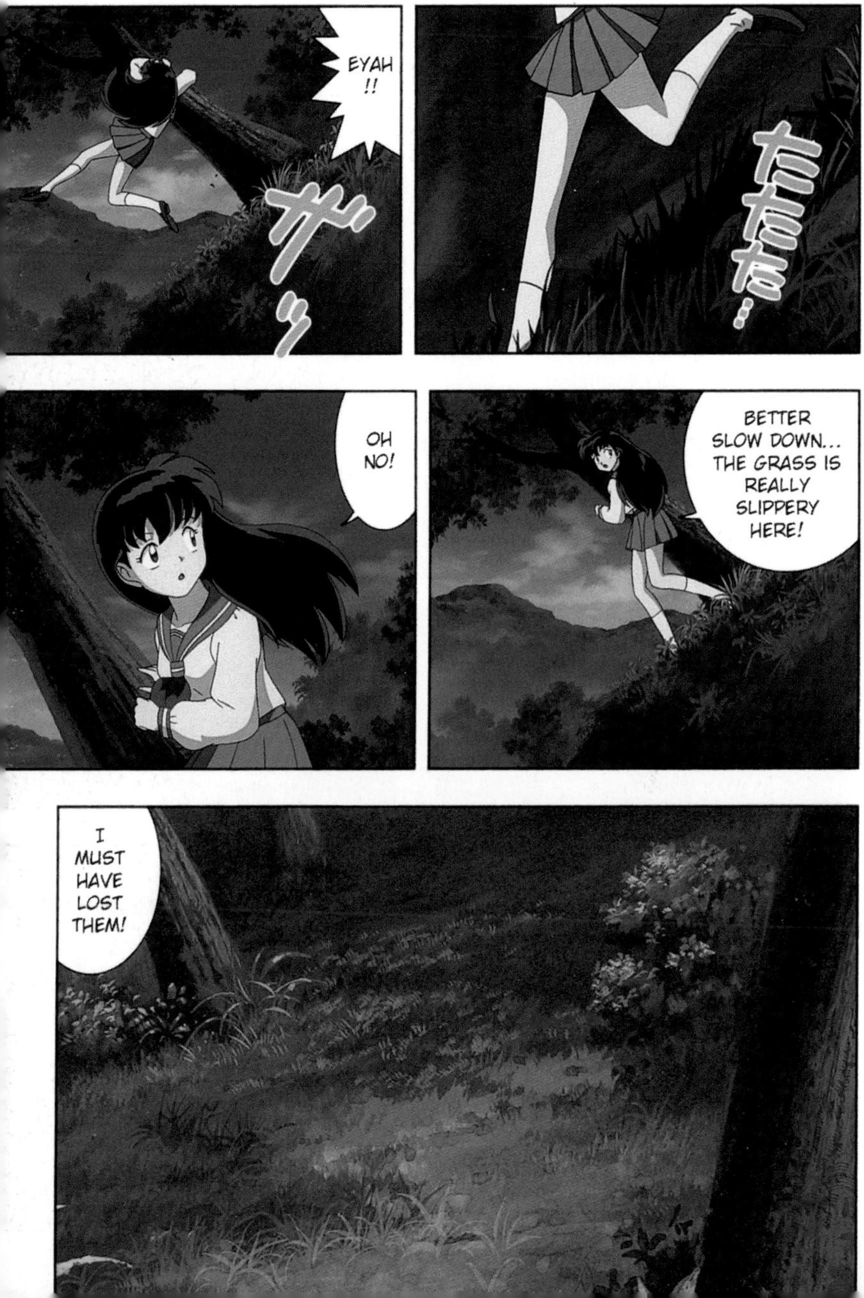
たたた…
EYAH !!
ザッ
BETTER SLOW DOWN... THE GRASS IS REALLY SLIPPERY HERE!
OH NO!
I MUST HAVE LOST THEM!

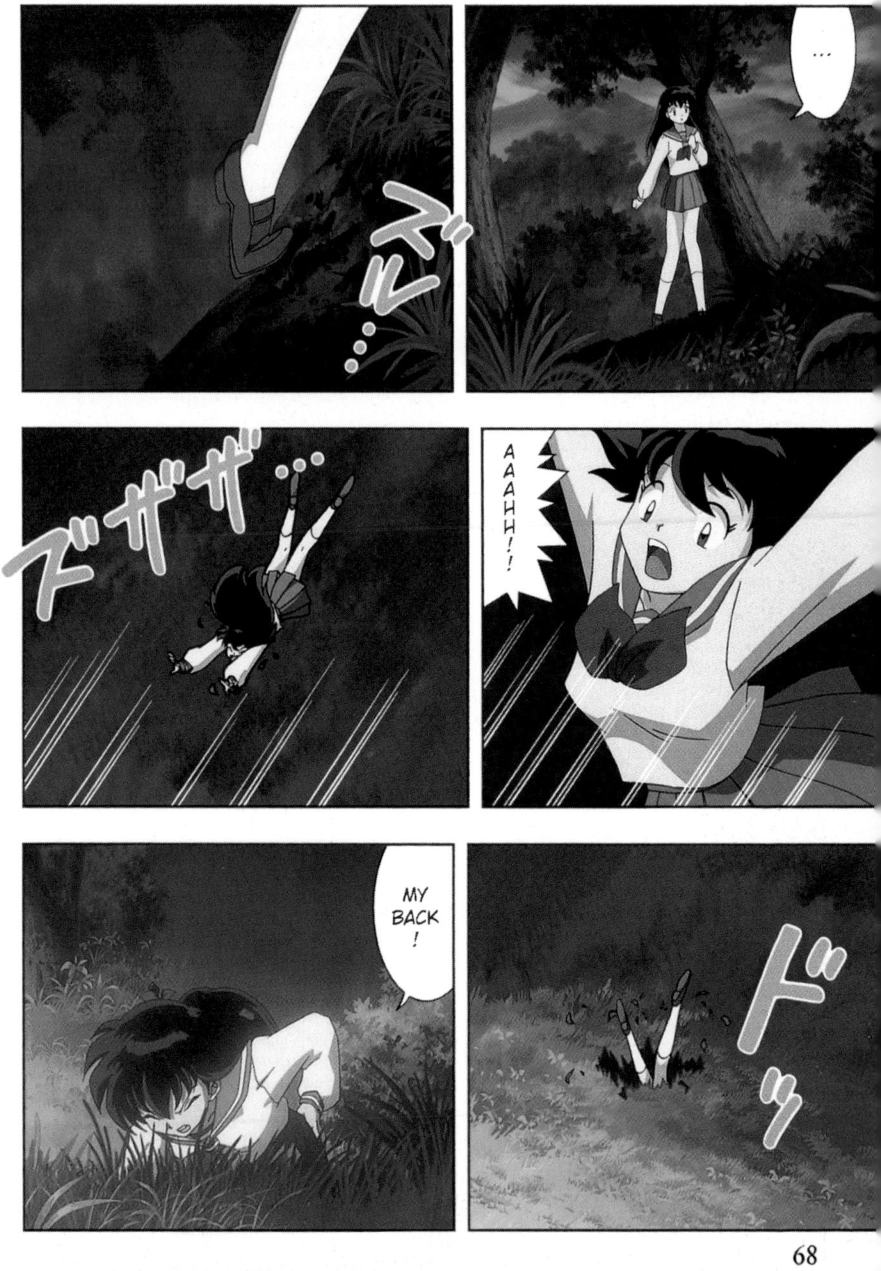
...
ズル…
AAAHH!!
ズザザ…
ドッ
MY BACK!

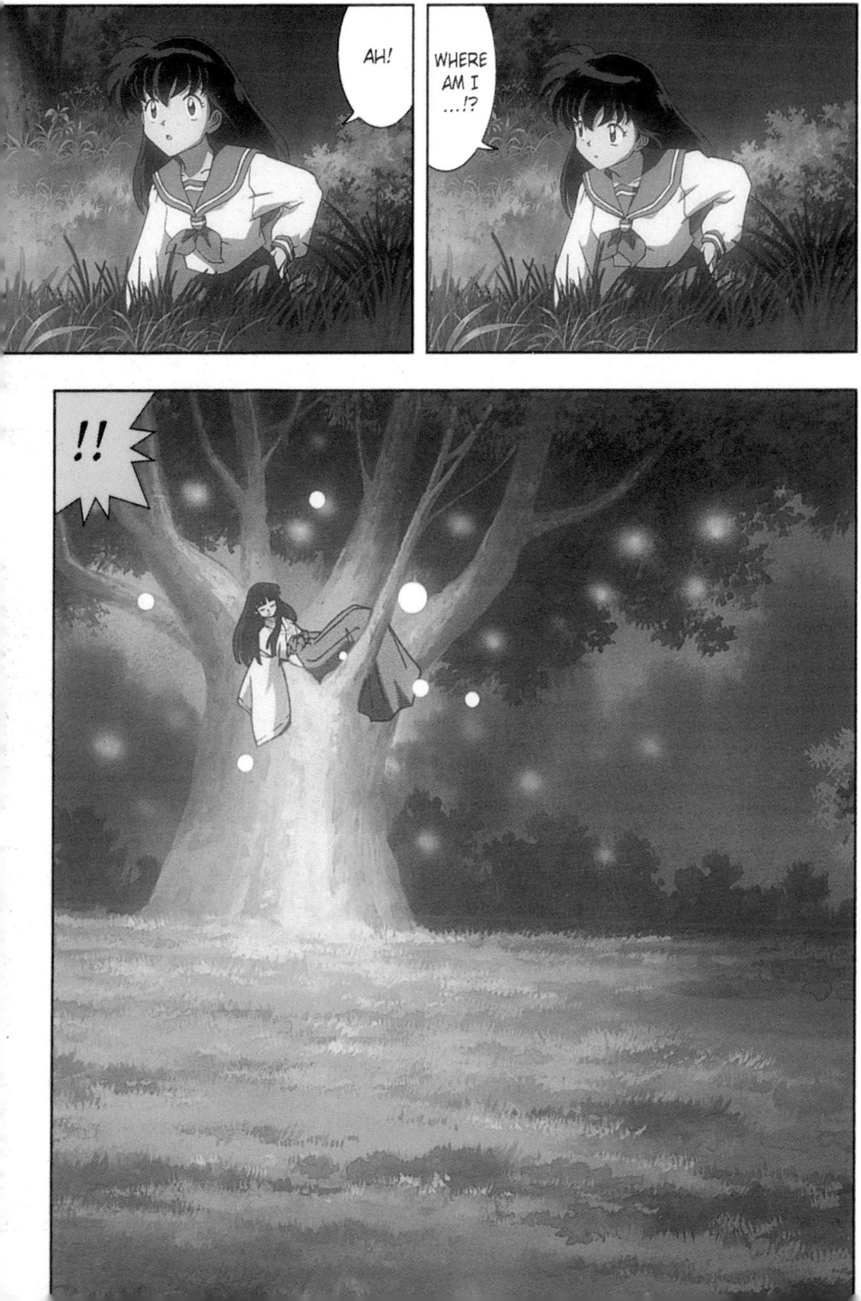
WHERE AM I ...!?
AH!
!!

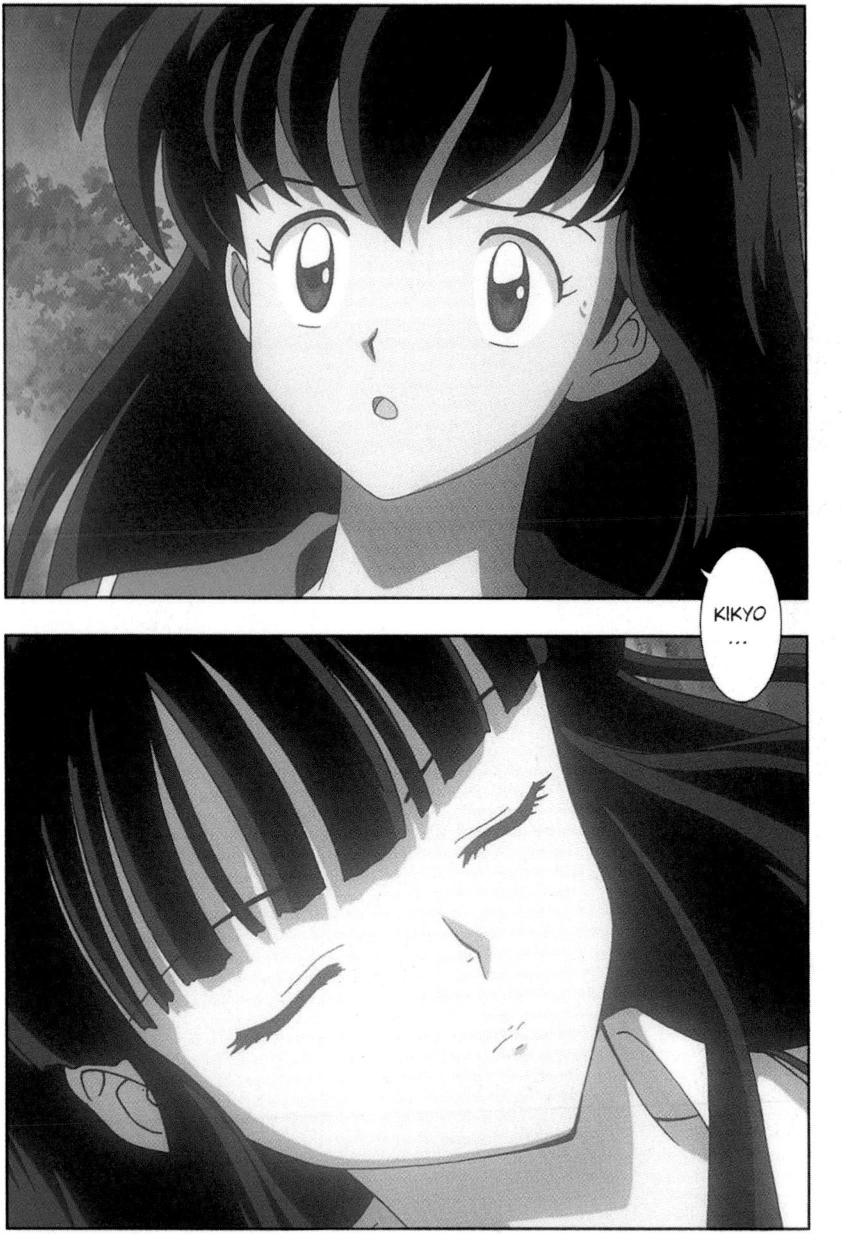
KIKYO ...

23
Kagome's Voice and Kikyo's Kiss

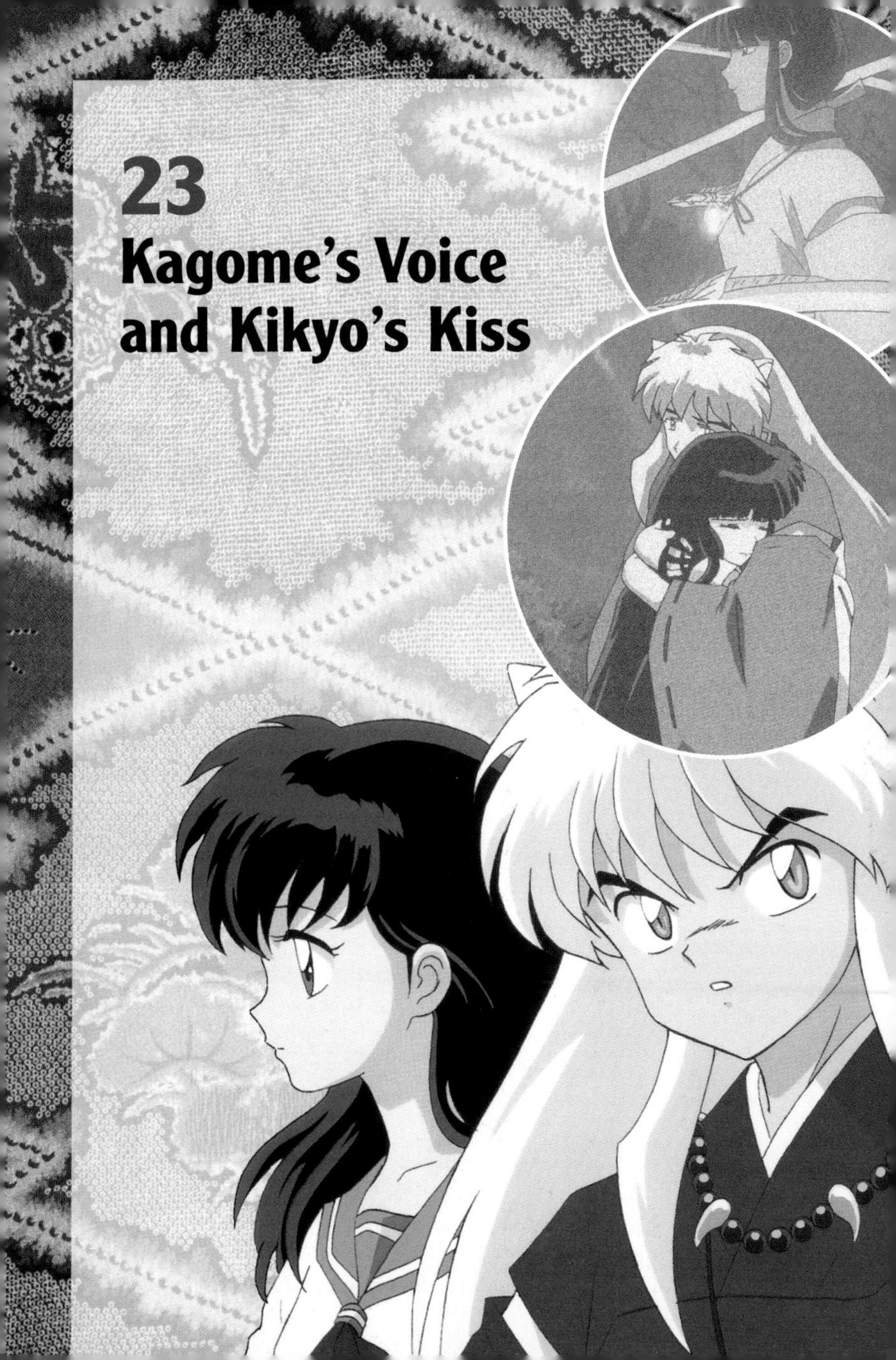

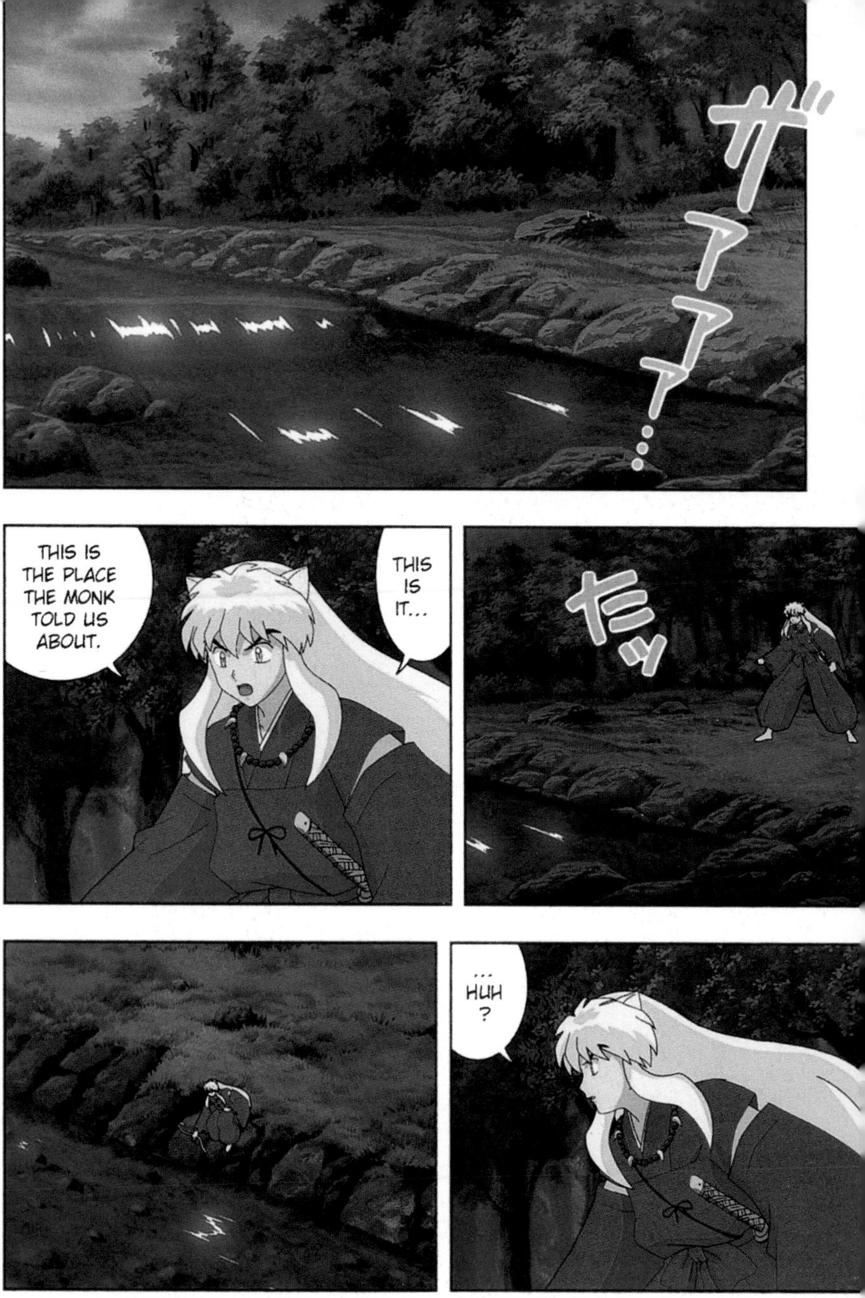
ザァァァ…
たッ
THIS IS IT...
THIS IS THE PLACE THE MONK TOLD US ABOUT.
...HUH?

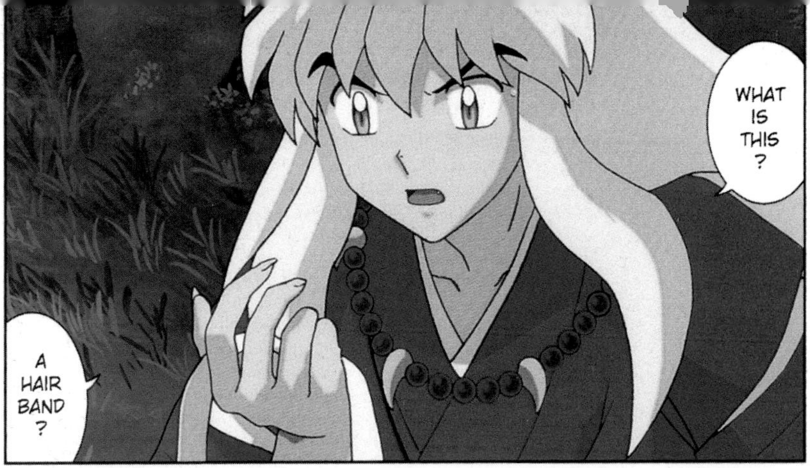
WHAT IS THIS?
A HAIR BAND?

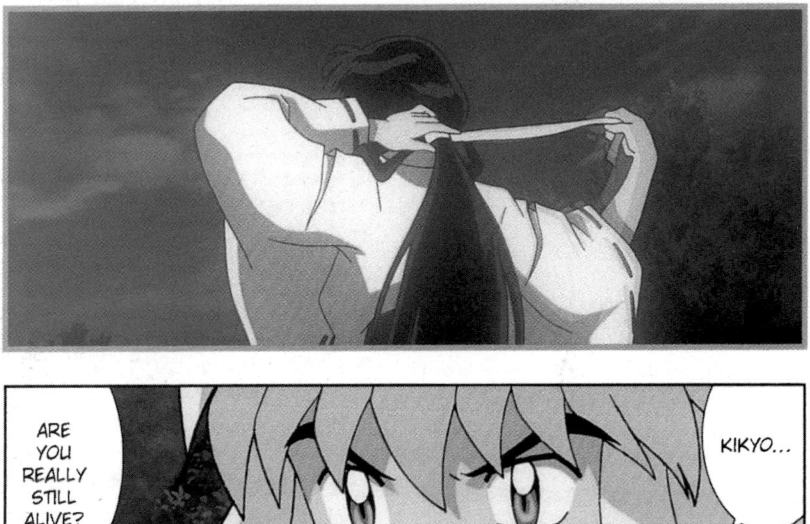

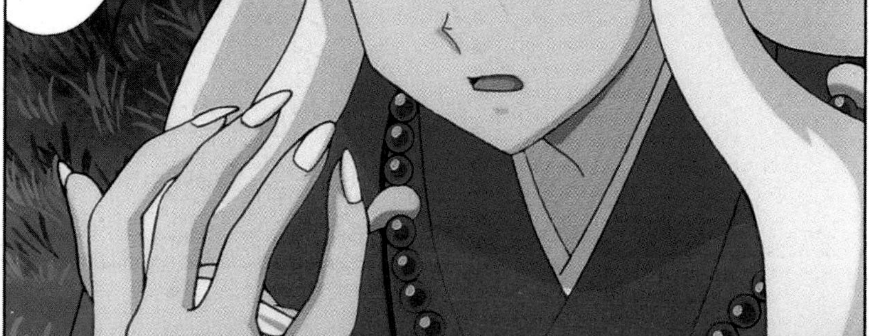
KIKYO...
ARE YOU REALLY STILL ALIVE?

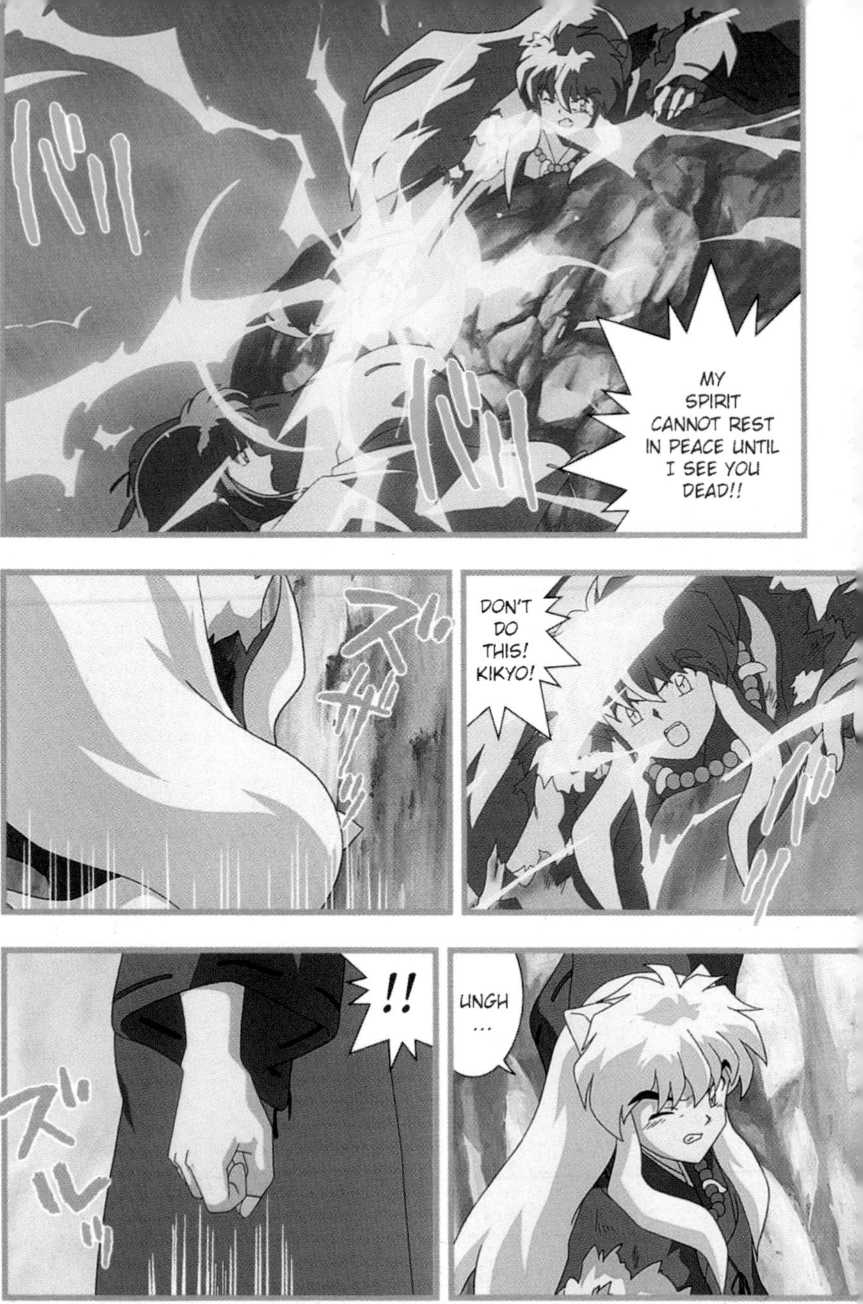
MY SPIRIT CANNOT REST IN PEACE UNTIL I SEE YOU DEAD!!
DON'T DO THIS! KIKYO!
UNGH ...
!!

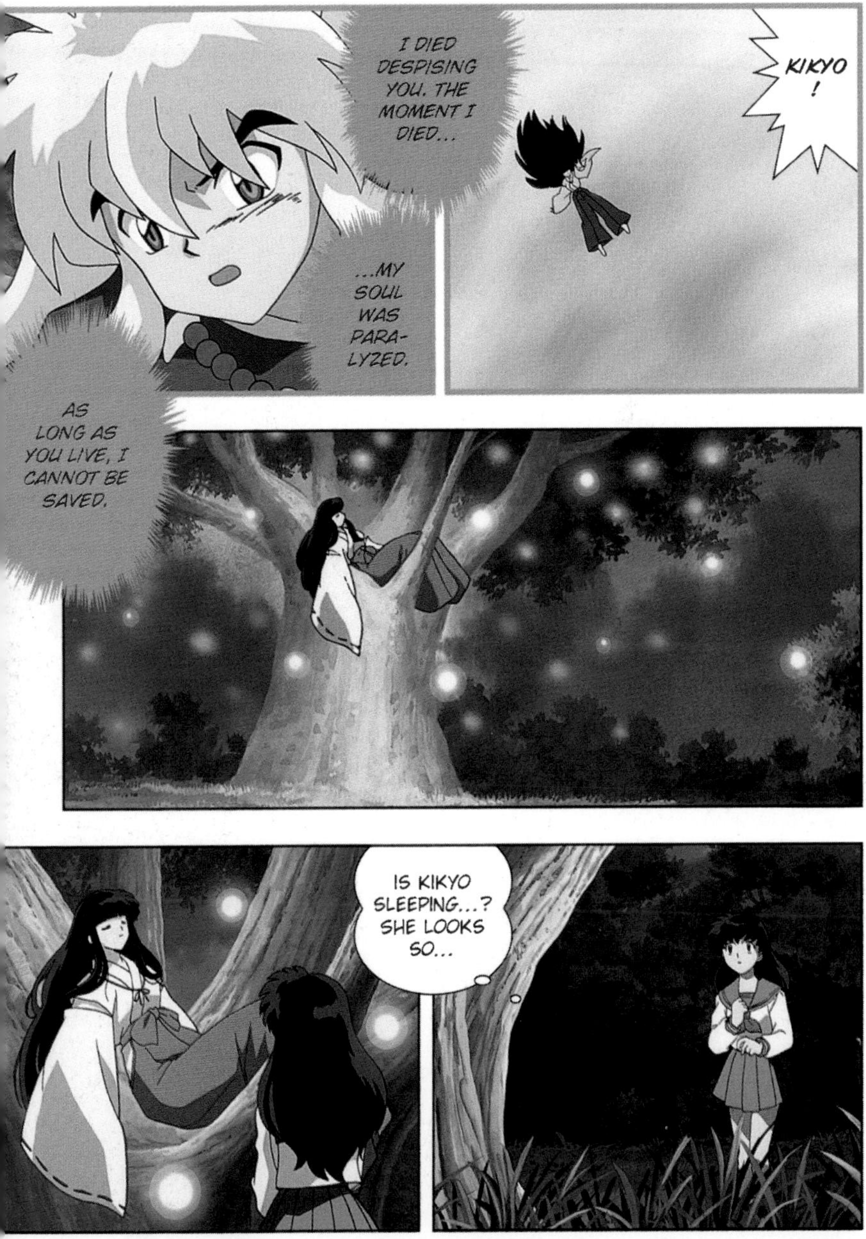
KIKYO!
I DIED DESPISING YOU. THE MOMENT I DIED...
...MY SOUL WAS PARALYZED.
AS LONG AS YOU LIVE, I CANNOT BE SAVED.
IS KIKYO SLEEPING...? SHE LOOKS SO...

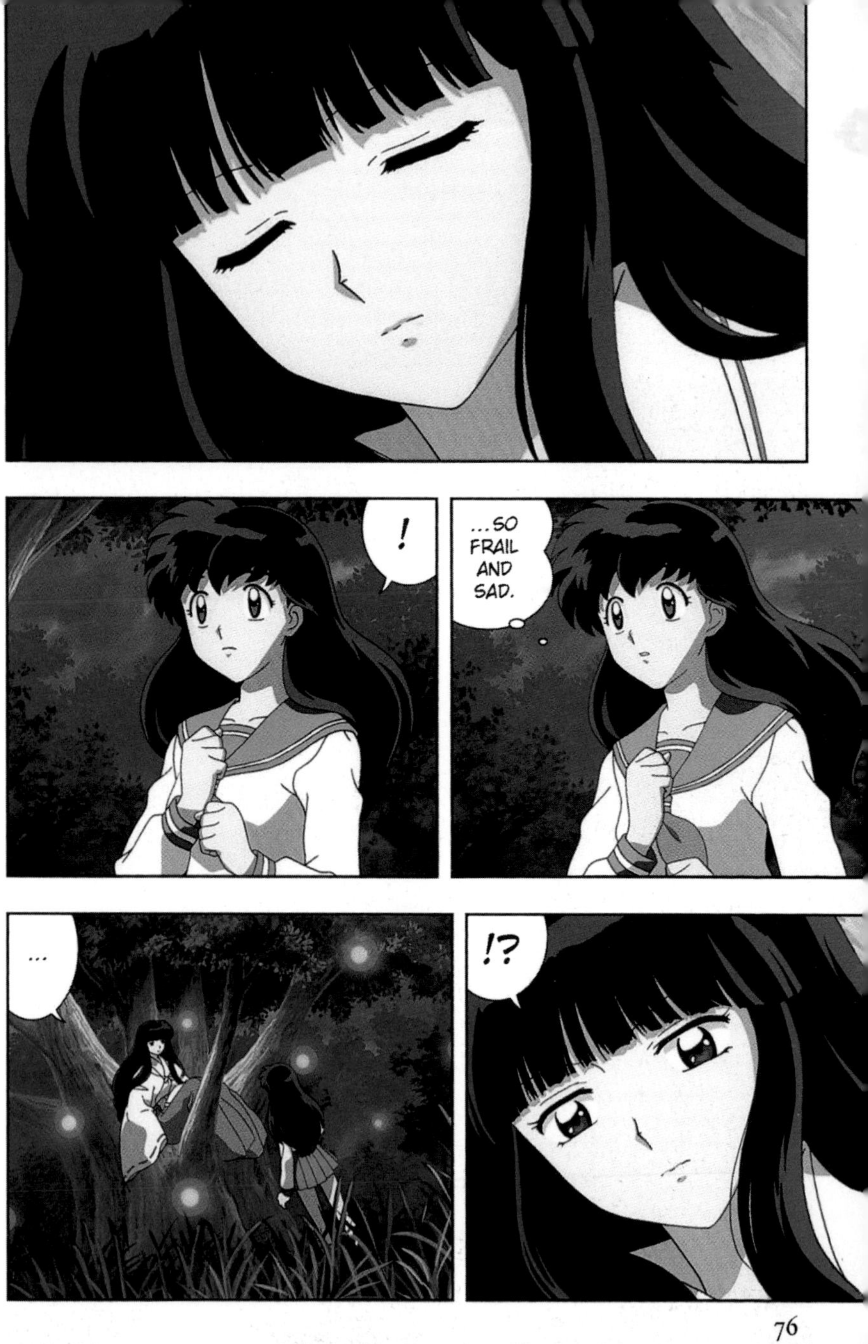
...SO FRAIL AND SAD.
!
!?
...

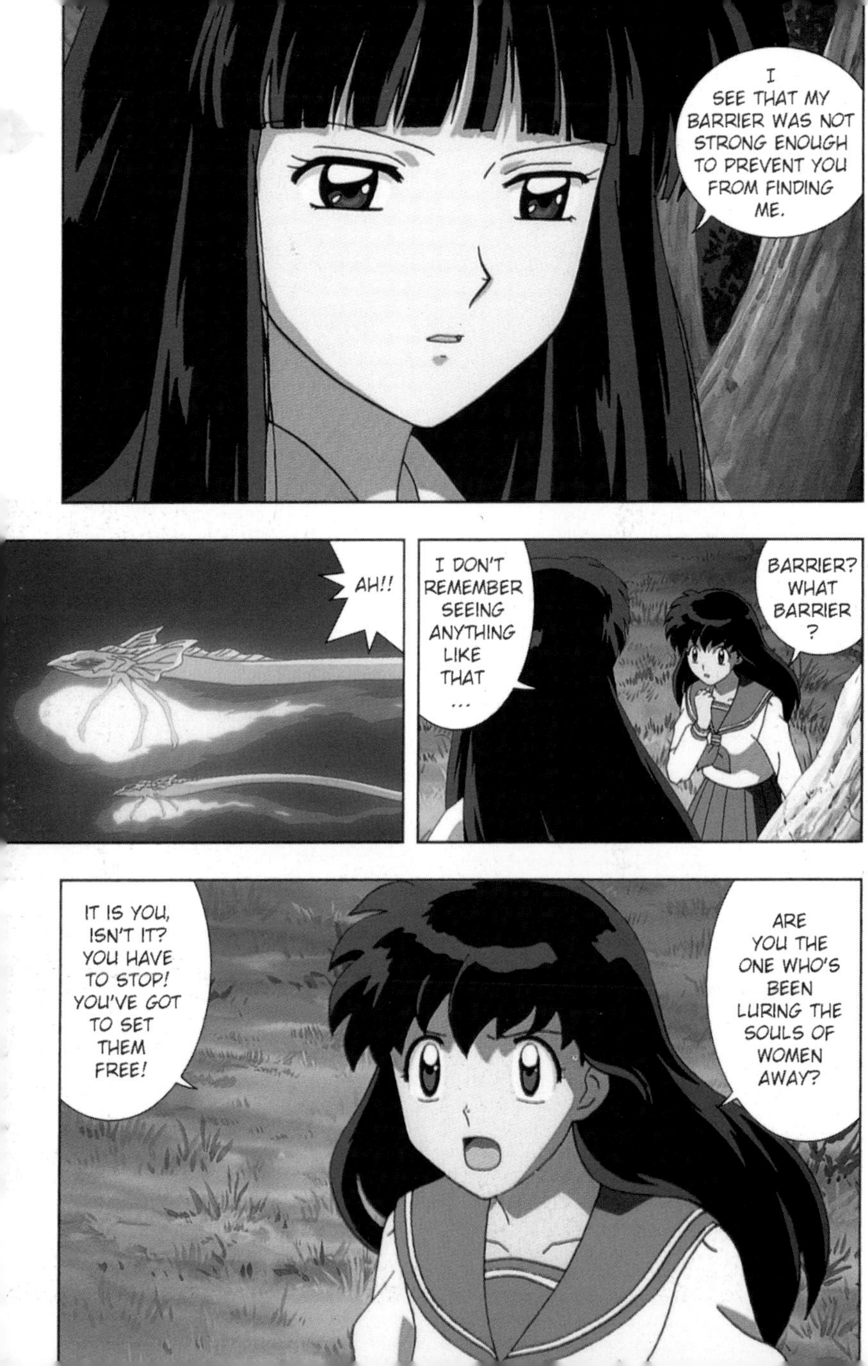
I SEE THAT MY BARRIER WAS NOT STRONG ENOUGH TO PREVENT YOU FROM FINDING ME.
BARRIER? WHAT BARRIER ?
I DON'T REMEMBER SEEING ANYTHING LIKE THAT ...
AH!!
ARE YOU THE ONE WHO'S BEEN LURING THE SOULS OF WOMEN AWAY?
IT IS YOU, ISN'T IT? YOU HAVE TO STOP! YOU'VE GOT TO SET THEM FREE!

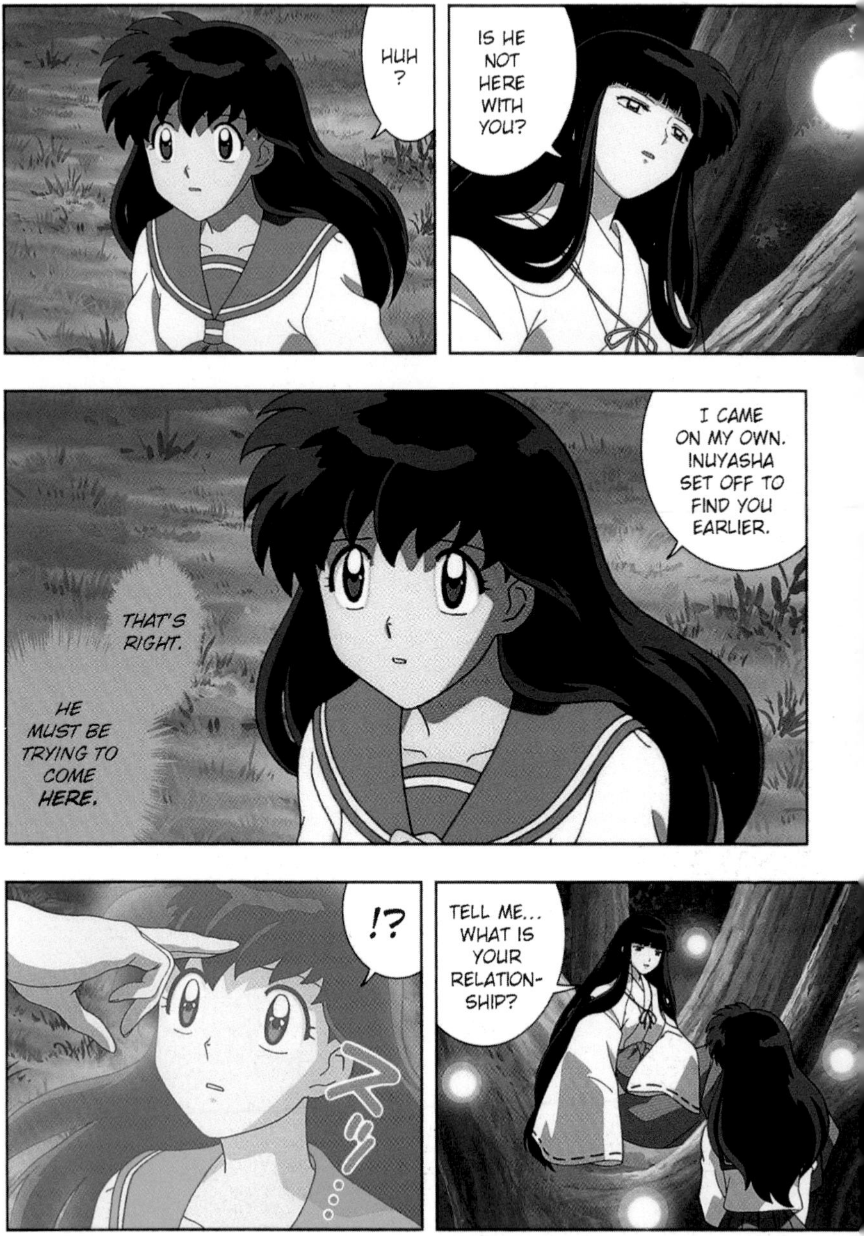
IS HE NOT HERE WITH YOU?
HUH?
I CAME ON MY OWN. INUYASHA SET OFF TO FIND YOU EARLIER.
THAT'S RIGHT.
HE MUST BE TRYING TO COME HERE.
TELL ME... WHAT IS YOUR RELATIONSHIP?
!?

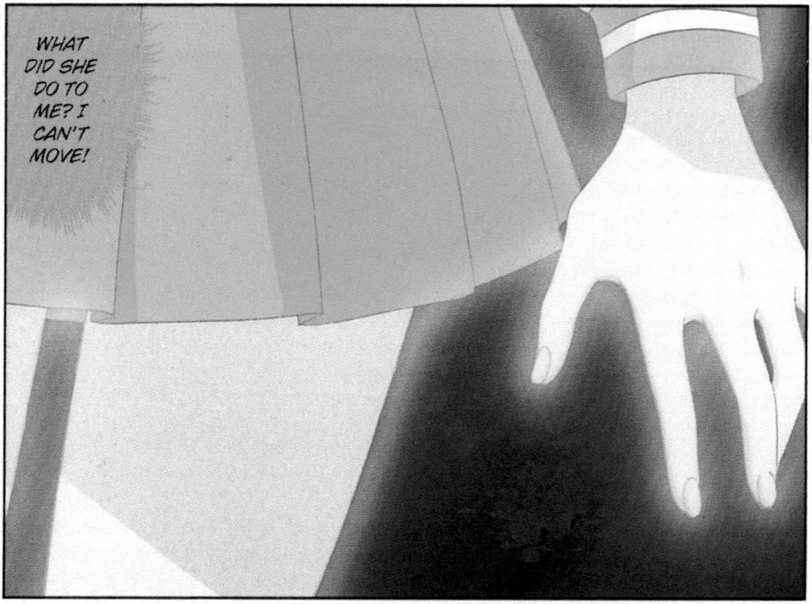
WHAT DID SHE DO TO ME? I CAN'T MOVE!

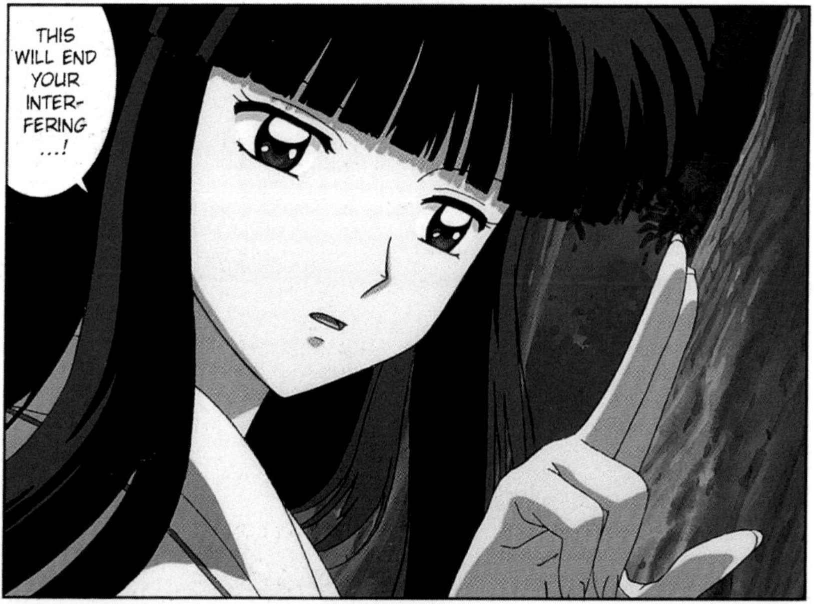
THIS WILL END YOUR INTER-FERING ...!

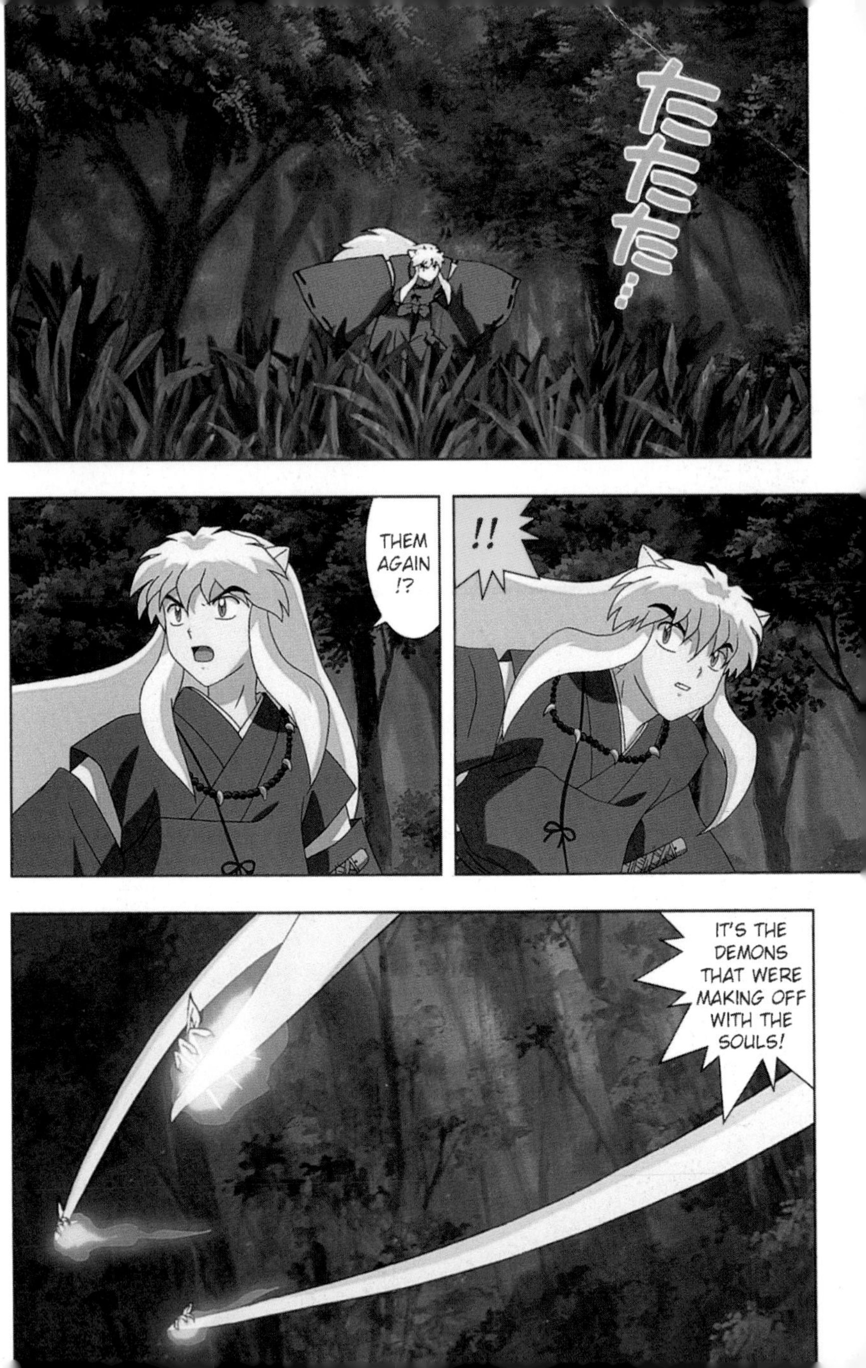
たたた…
!!
THEM AGAIN!?
IT'S THE DEMONS THAT WERE MAKING OFF WITH THE SOULS!

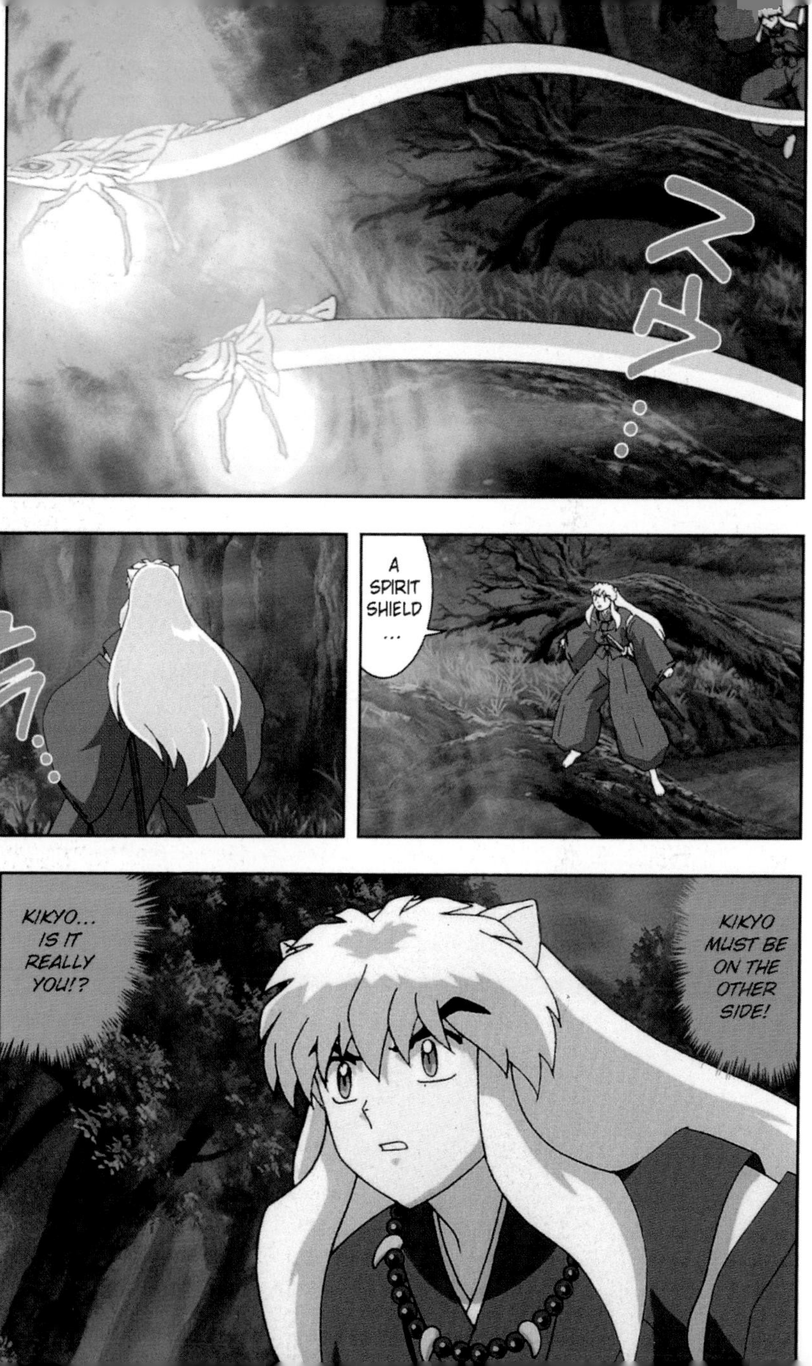
A SPIRIT SHIELD ...
KIKYO MUST BE ON THE OTHER SIDE!
KIKYO... IS IT REALLY YOU!?

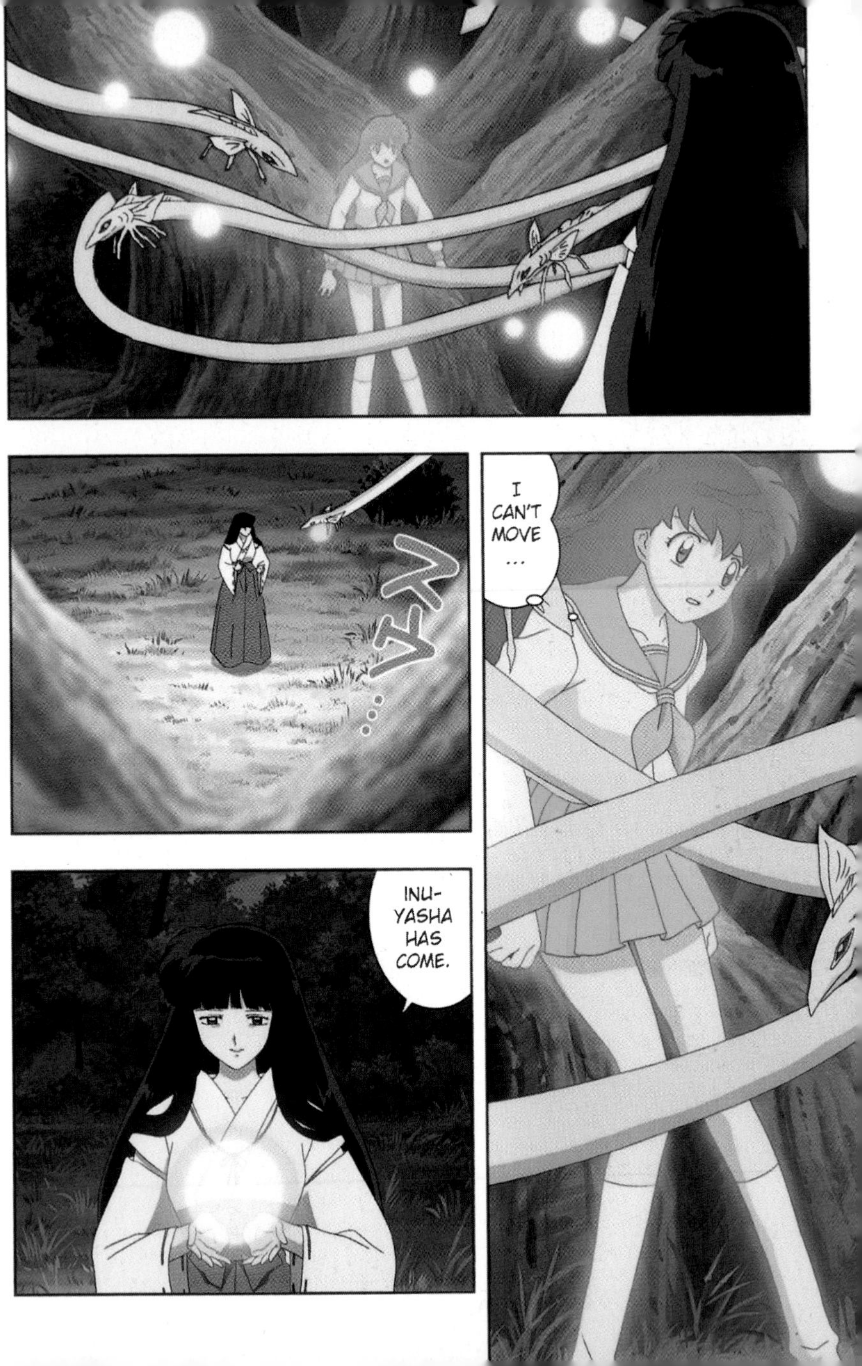
I CAN'T MOVE ...
スッ…
INU-YASHA HAS COME.

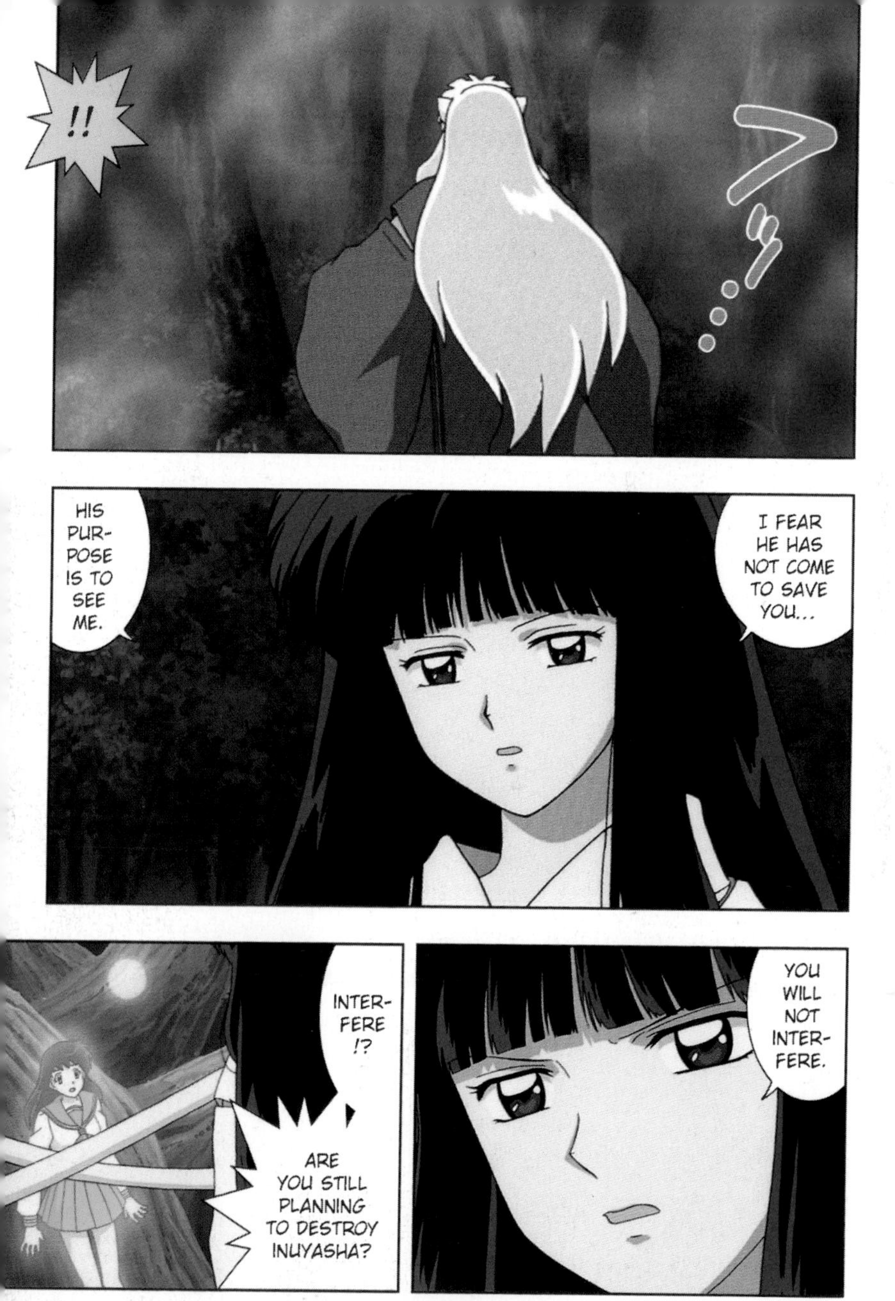
!!
I FEAR HE HAS NOT COME TO SAVE YOU...
HIS PURPOSE IS TO SEE ME.
YOU WILL NOT INTERFERE.
INTERFERE!?
ARE YOU STILL PLANNING TO DESTROY INUYASHA?

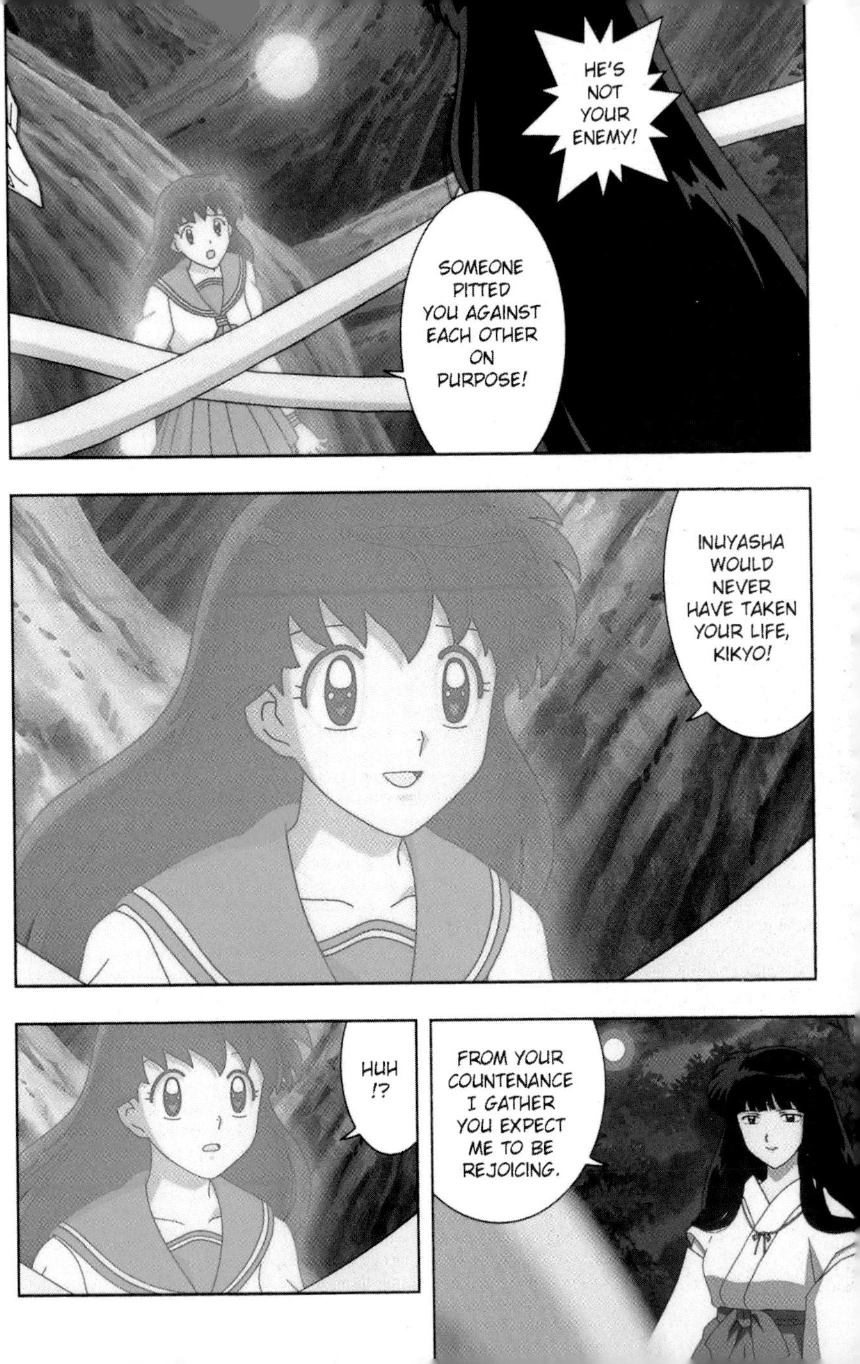
HE'S NOT YOUR ENEMY!
SOMEONE PITTED YOU AGAINST EACH OTHER ON PURPOSE!
INUYASHA WOULD NEVER HAVE TAKEN YOUR LIFE, KIKYO!
FROM YOUR COUNTENANCE I GATHER YOU EXPECT ME TO BE REJOICING.
HUH !?

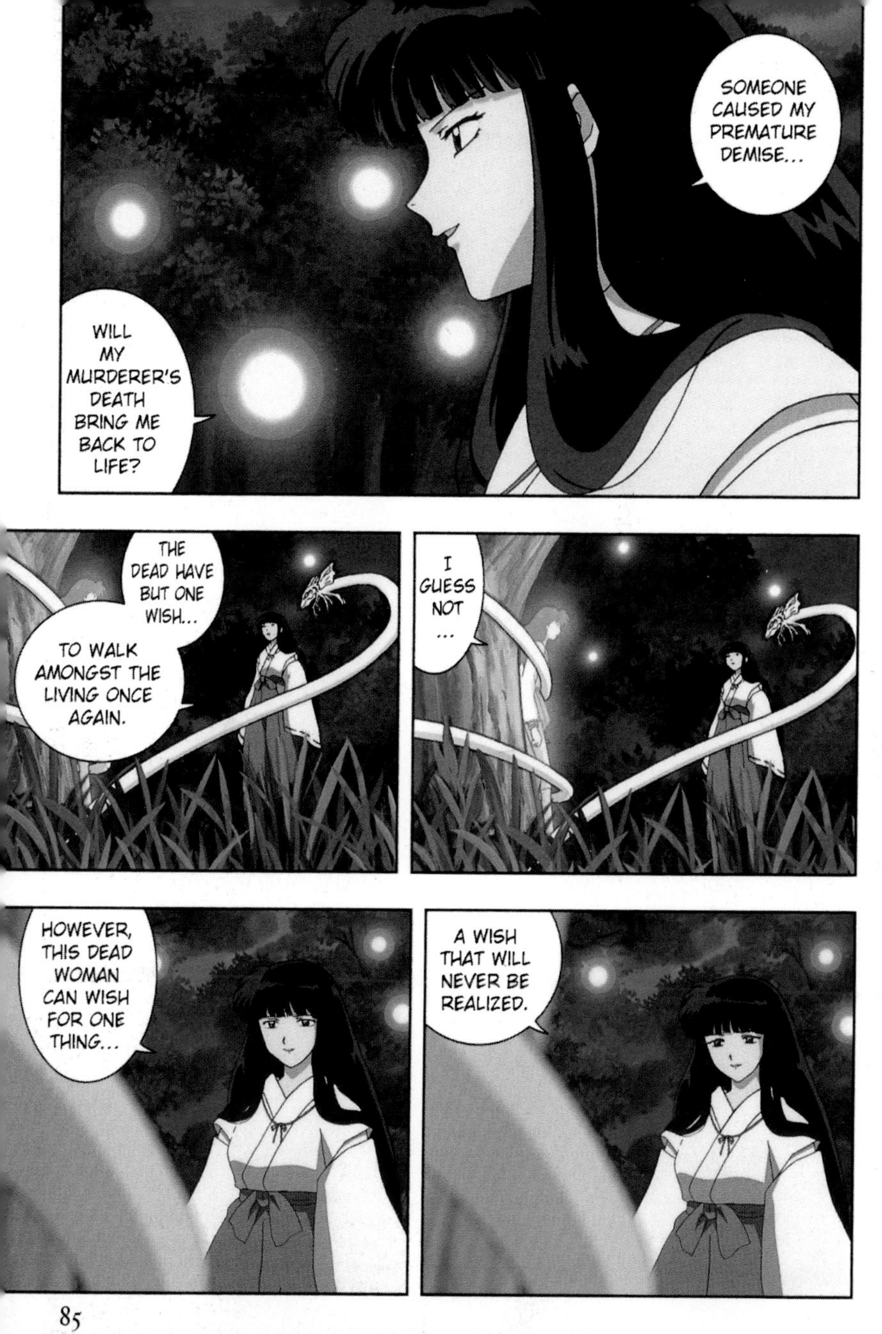
SOMEONE CAUSED MY PREMATURE DEMISE...
WILL MY MURDERER'S DEATH BRING ME BACK TO LIFE?
I GUESS NOT ...
THE DEAD HAVE BUT ONE WISH...
TO WALK AMONGST THE LIVING ONCE AGAIN.
A WISH THAT WILL NEVER BE REALIZED.
HOWEVER, THIS DEAD WOMAN CAN WISH FOR ONE THING...

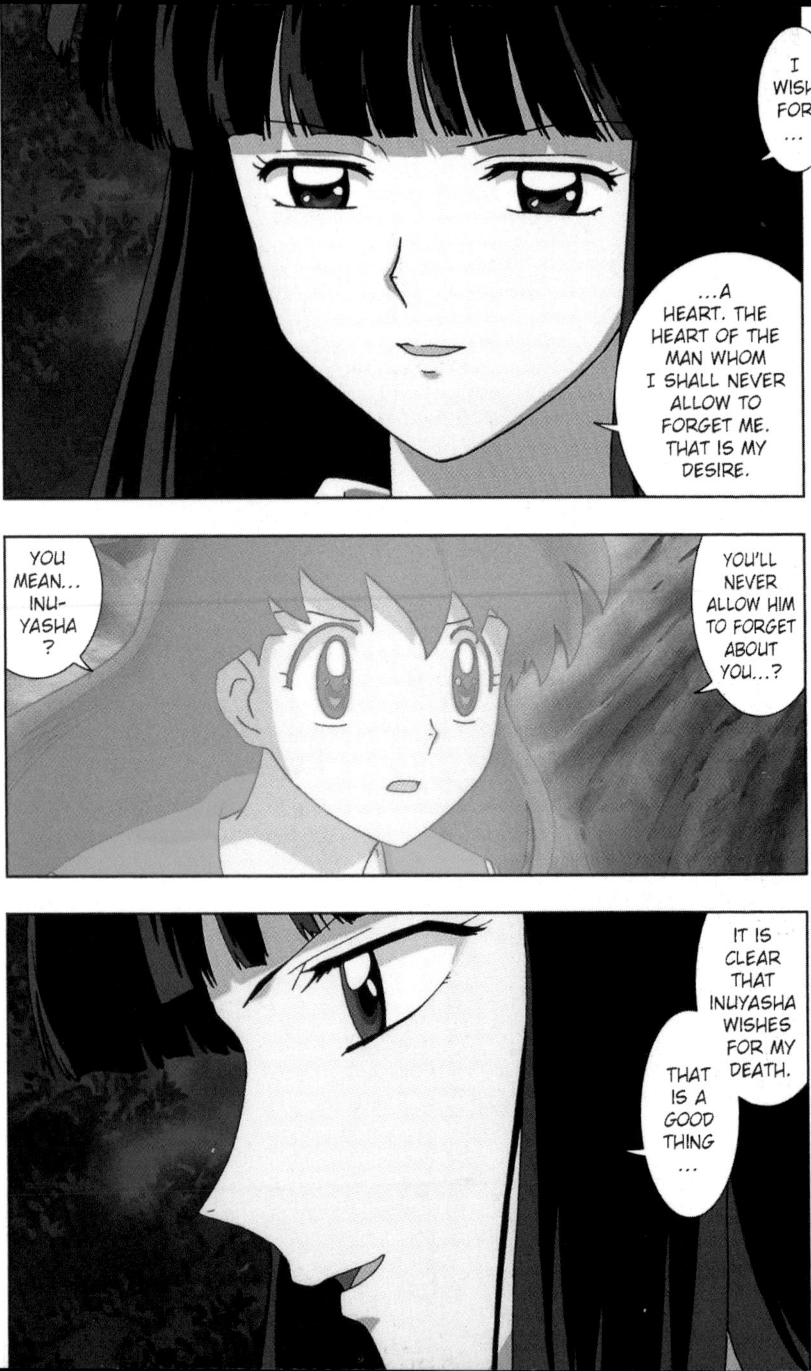
I WISH FOR...
...A HEART. THE HEART OF THE MAN WHOM I SHALL NEVER ALLOW TO FORGET ME. THAT IS MY DESIRE.
YOU'LL NEVER ALLOW HIM TO FORGET ABOUT YOU...?
YOU MEAN... INU-YASHA?
IT IS CLEAR THAT INUYASHA WISHES FOR MY DEATH.
THAT IS A GOOD THING...

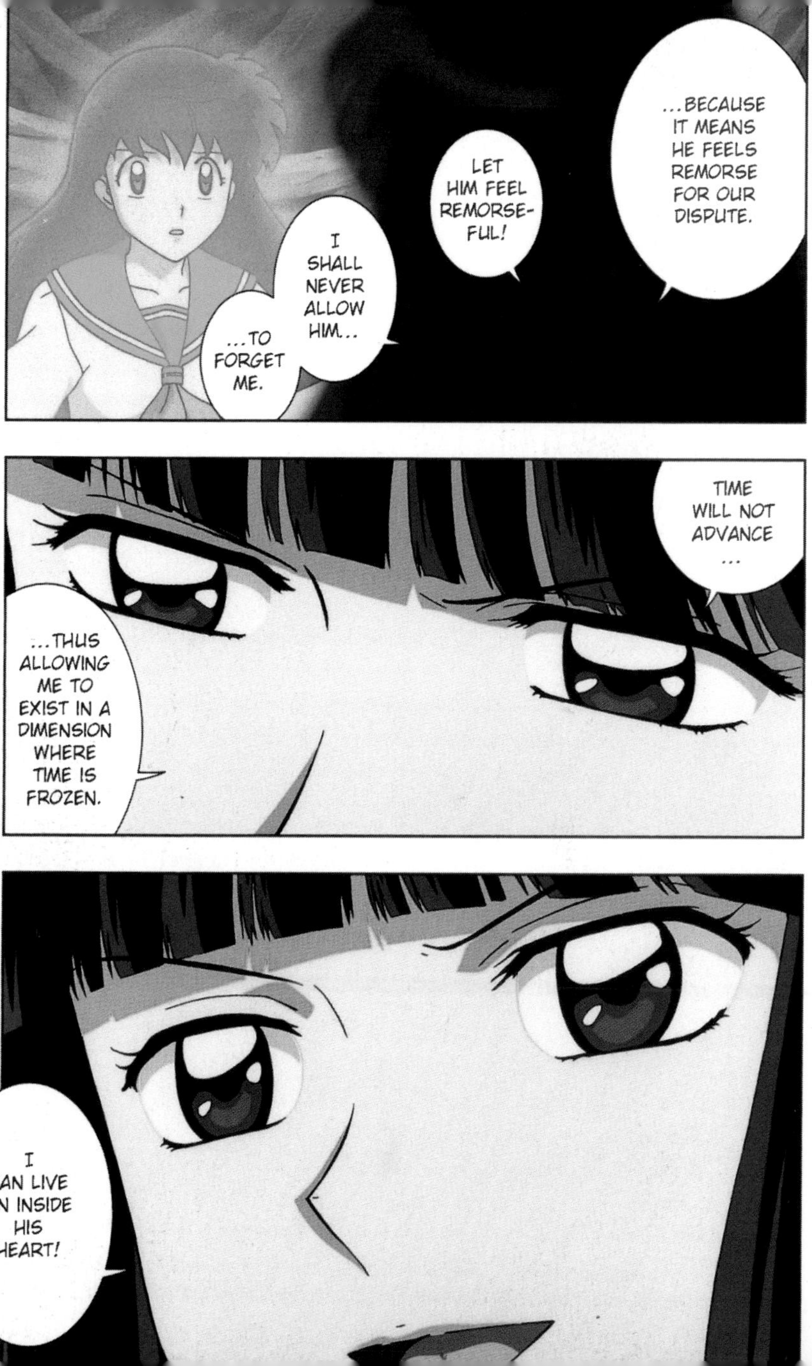
...BECAUSE IT MEANS HE FEELS REMORSE FOR OUR DISPUTE.
LET HIM FEEL REMORSE-FUL!
I SHALL NEVER ALLOW HIM...
...TO FORGET ME.
TIME WILL NOT ADVANCE ...
...THUS ALLOWING ME TO EXIST IN A DIMENSION WHERE TIME IS FROZEN.
I CAN LIVE ON INSIDE HIS HEART!

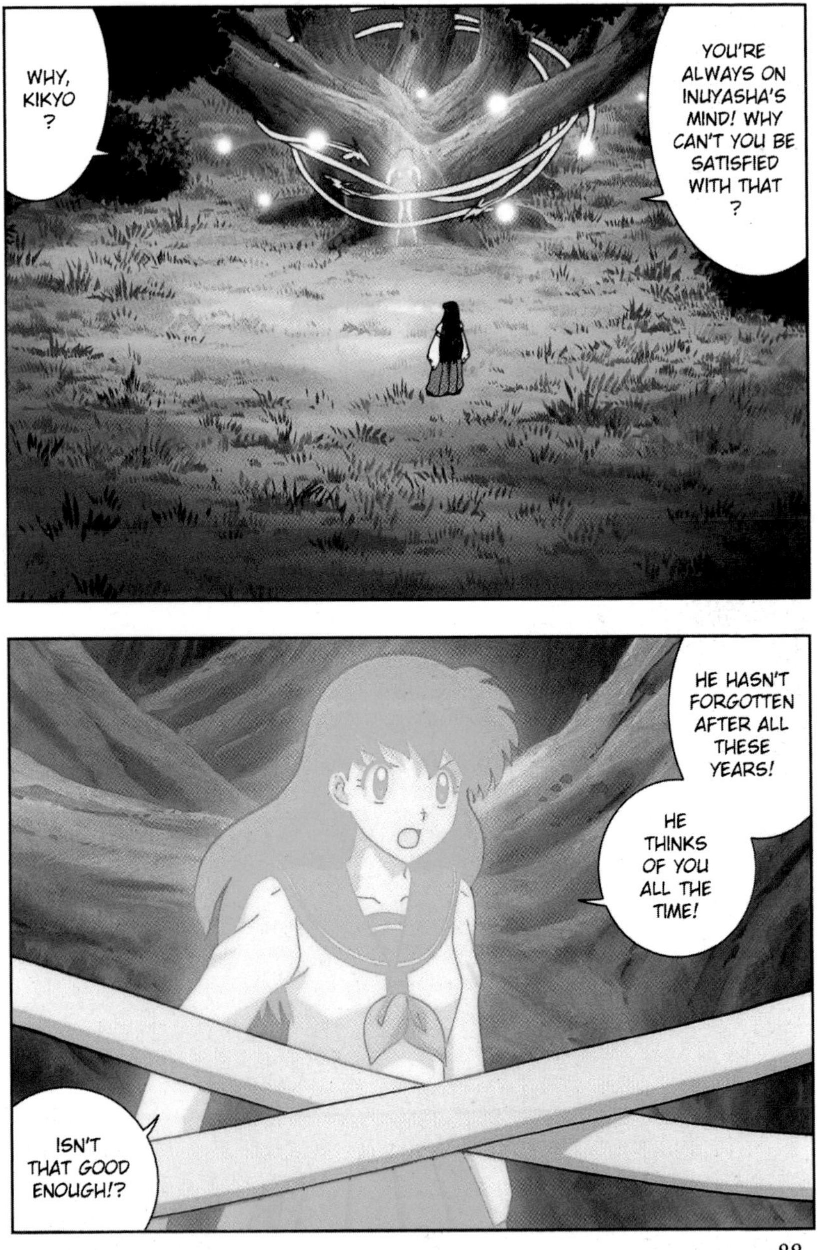
YOU'RE ALWAYS ON INUYASHA'S MIND! WHY CAN'T YOU BE SATISFIED WITH THAT ?
WHY, KIKYO ?
HE HASN'T FORGOTTEN AFTER ALL THESE YEARS!
HE THINKS OF YOU ALL THE TIME!
ISN'T THAT GOOD ENOUGH!?

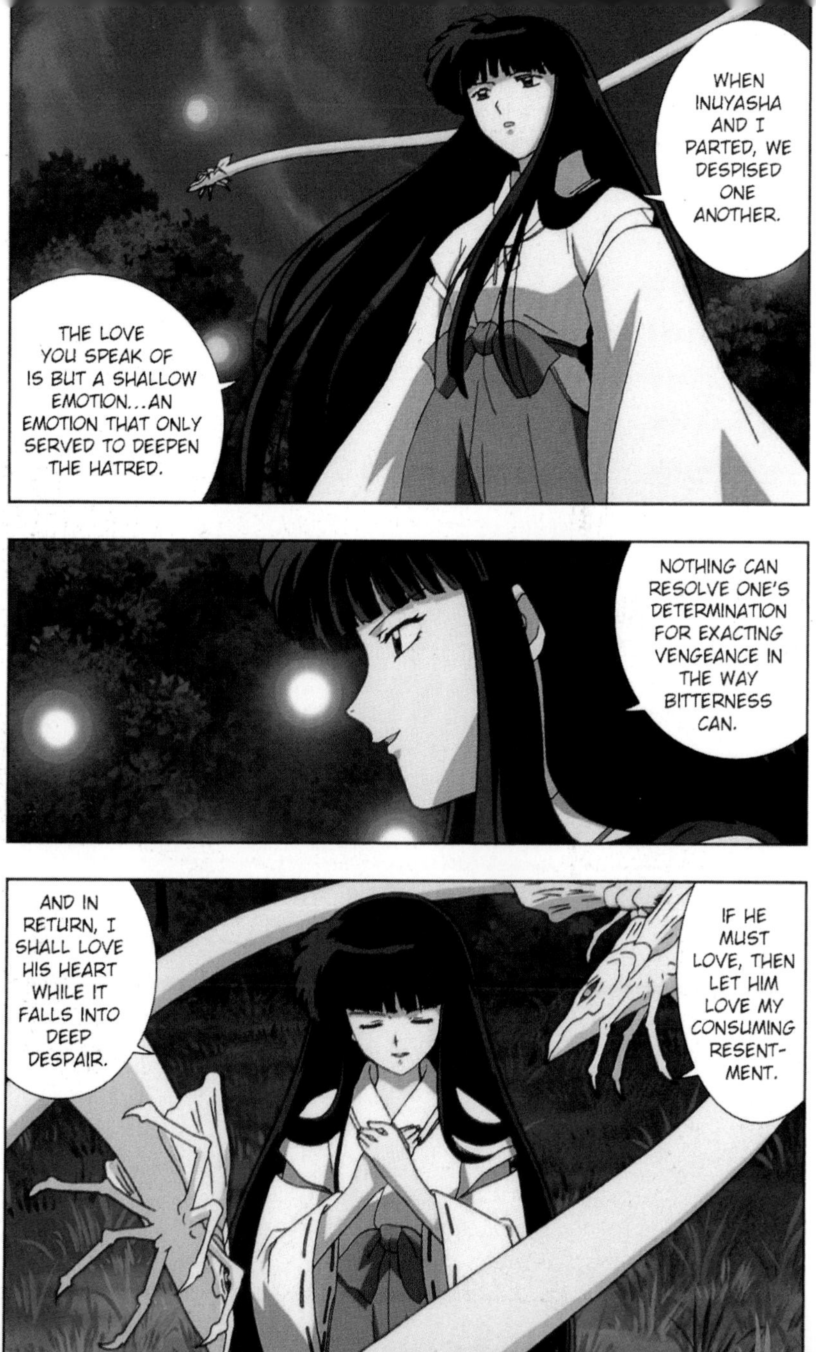
WHEN INUYASHA AND I PARTED, WE DESPISED ONE ANOTHER.
THE LOVE YOU SPEAK OF IS BUT A SHALLOW EMOTION...AN EMOTION THAT ONLY SERVED TO DEEPEN THE HATRED.
NOTHING CAN RESOLVE ONE'S DETERMINATION FOR EXACTING VENGEANCE IN THE WAY BITTERNESS CAN.
IF HE MUST LOVE, THEN LET HIM LOVE MY CONSUMING RESENT-MENT.
AND IN RETURN, I SHALL LOVE HIS HEART WHILE IT FALLS INTO DEEP DESPAIR.

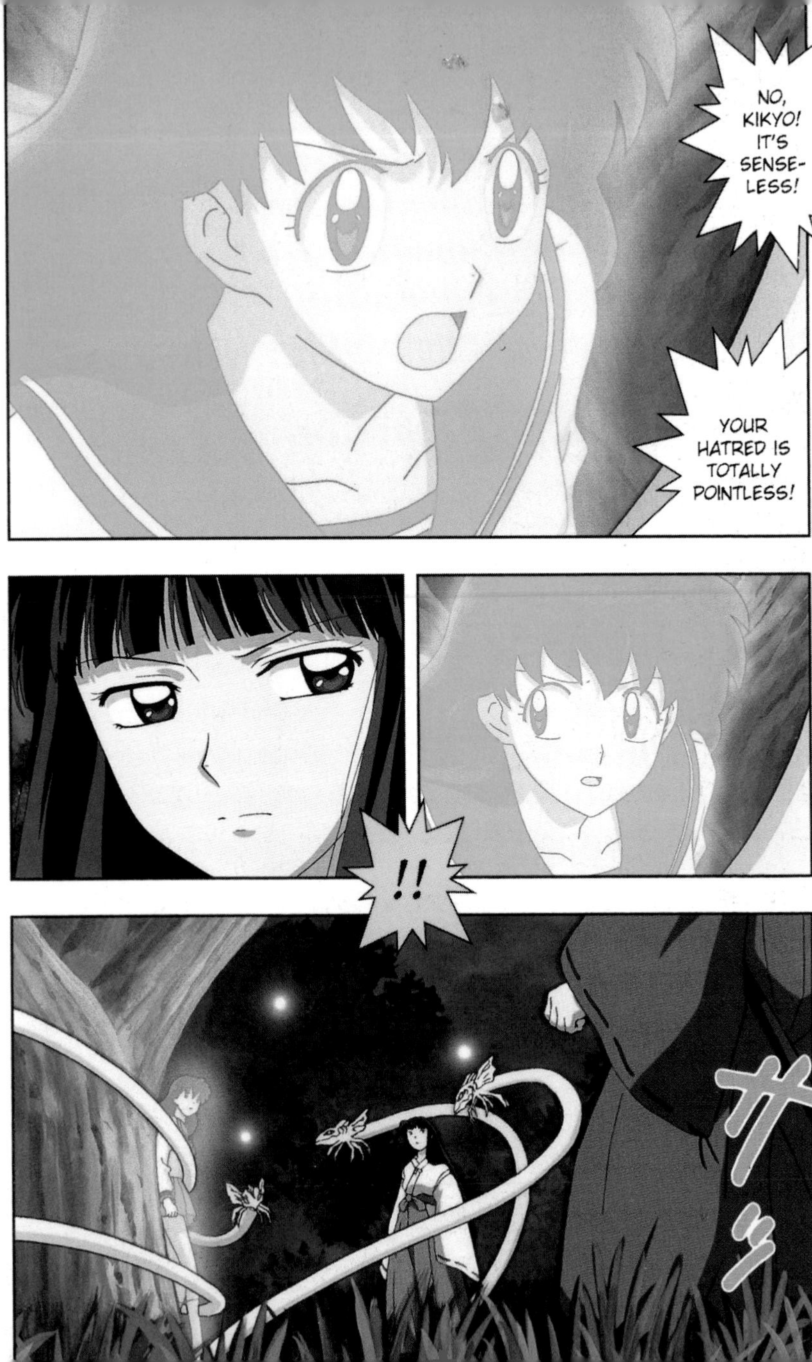
NO, KIKYO! IT'S SENSE-LESS!
YOUR HATRED IS TOTALLY POINTLESS!
!!
ザッ

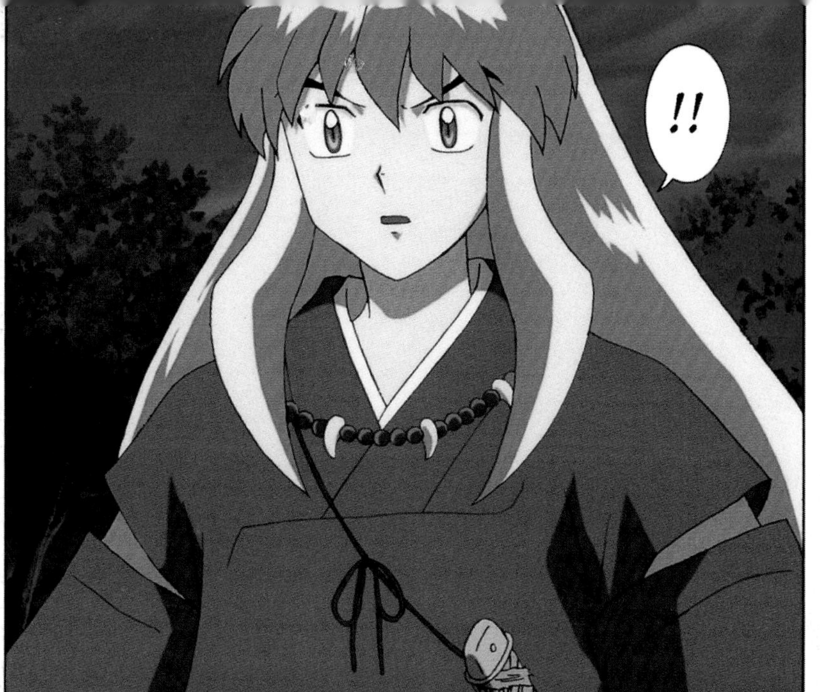
!!

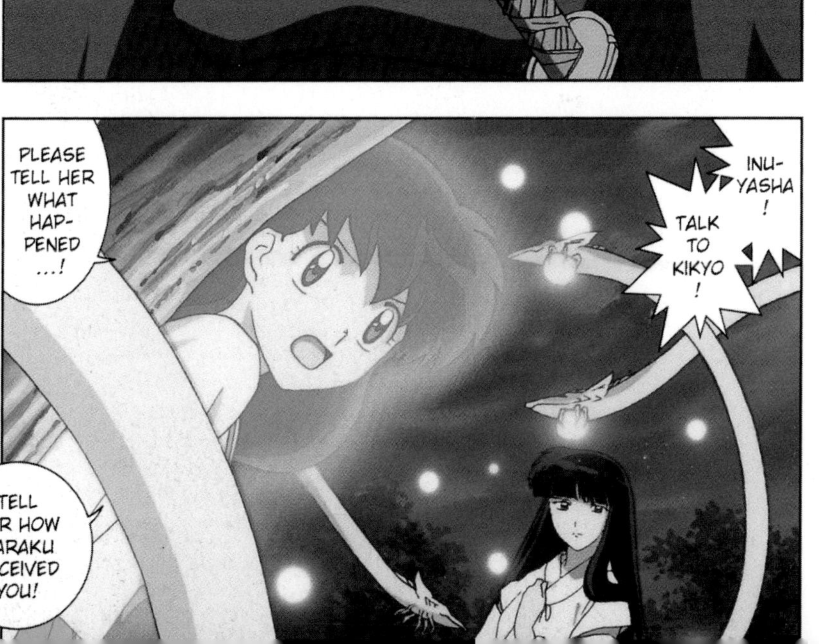
INU-YASHA!
TALK TO KIKYO!
PLEASE TELL HER WHAT HAP-PENED ...!
TELL HER HOW NARAKU DECEIVED YOU!

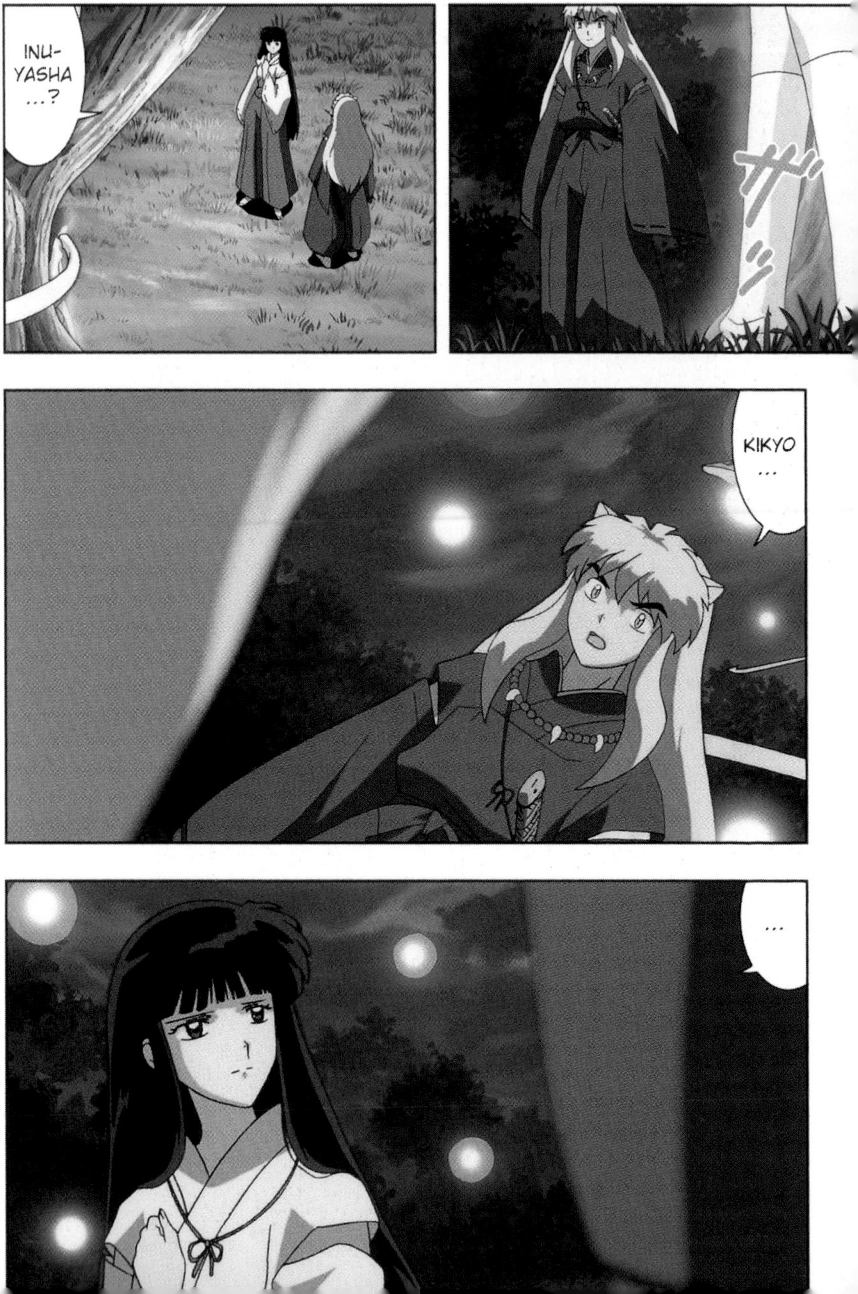
ザッ
INU-YASHA ...?
KIKYO ...
...

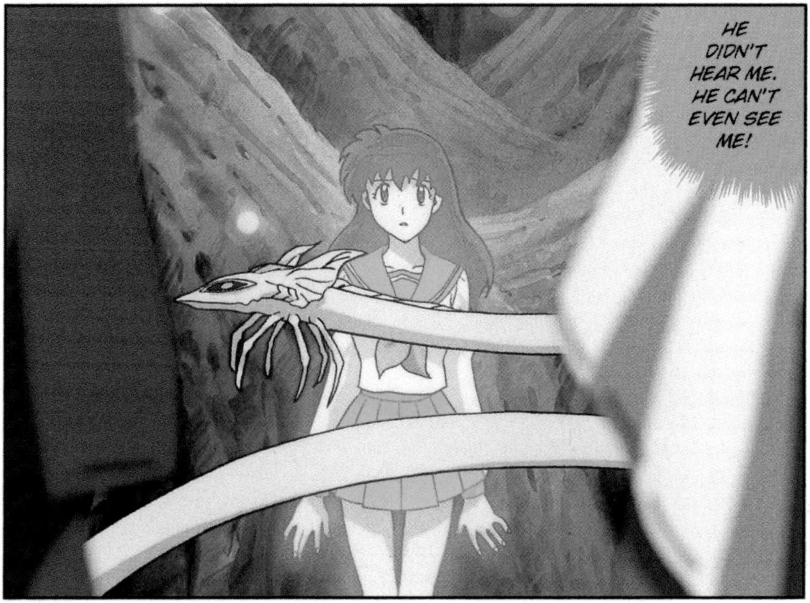
HE DIDN'T HEAR ME. HE CAN'T EVEN SEE ME!

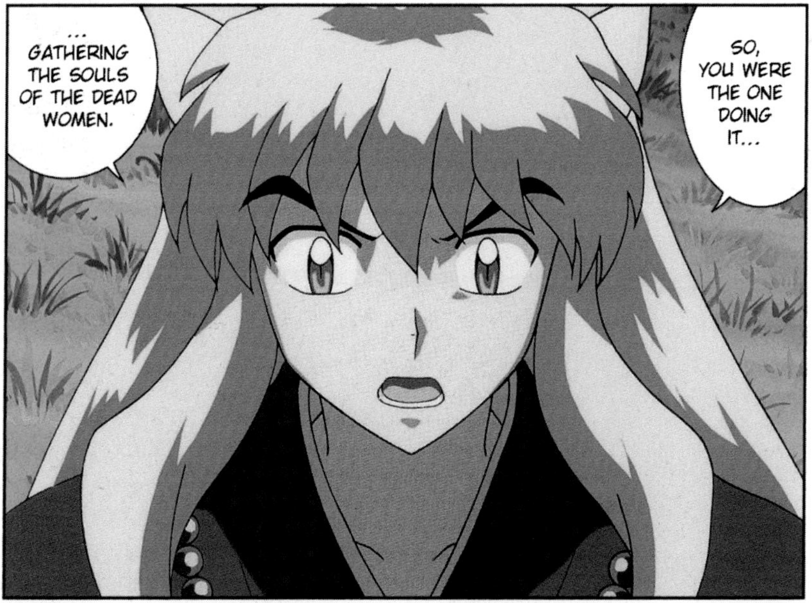
SO, YOU WERE THE ONE DOING IT...
...GATHERING THE SOULS OF THE DEAD WOMEN.

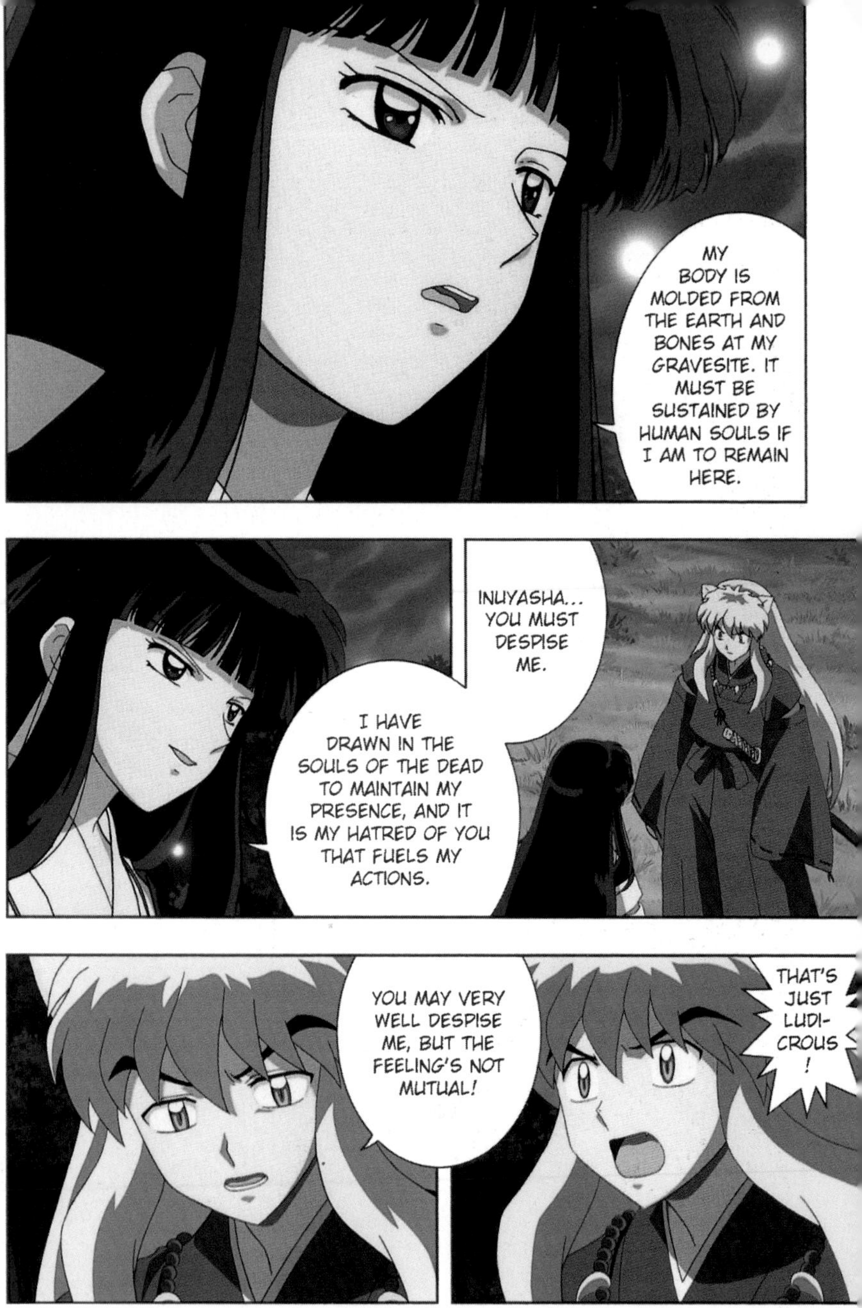
MY BODY IS MOLDED FROM THE EARTH AND BONES AT MY GRAVESITE. IT MUST BE SUSTAINED BY HUMAN SOULS IF I AM TO REMAIN HERE.
INUYASHA... YOU MUST DESPISE ME.
I HAVE DRAWN IN THE SOULS OF THE DEAD TO MAINTAIN MY PRESENCE, AND IT IS MY HATRED OF YOU THAT FUELS MY ACTIONS.
THAT'S JUST LUDICROUS!
YOU MAY VERY WELL DESPISE ME, BUT THE FEELING'S NOT MUTUAL!

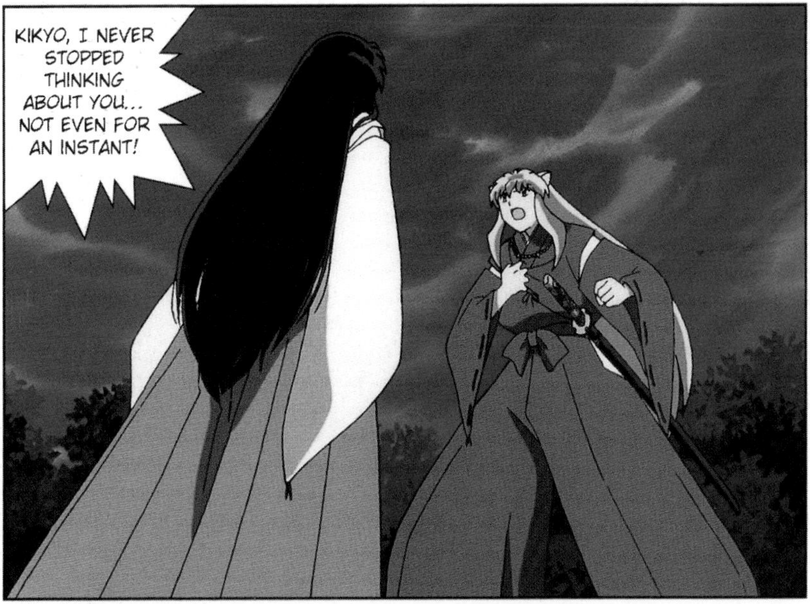
KIKYO, I NEVER STOPPED THINKING ABOUT YOU... NOT EVEN FOR AN INSTANT!

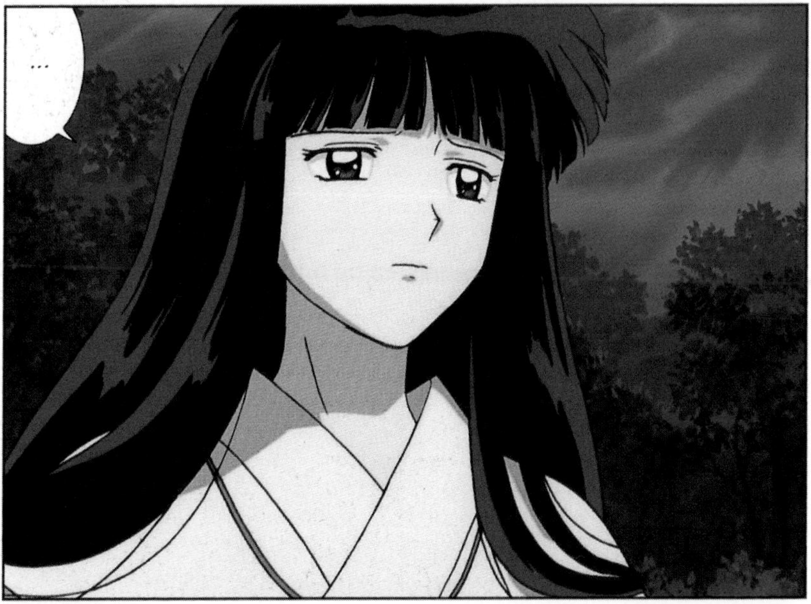
...

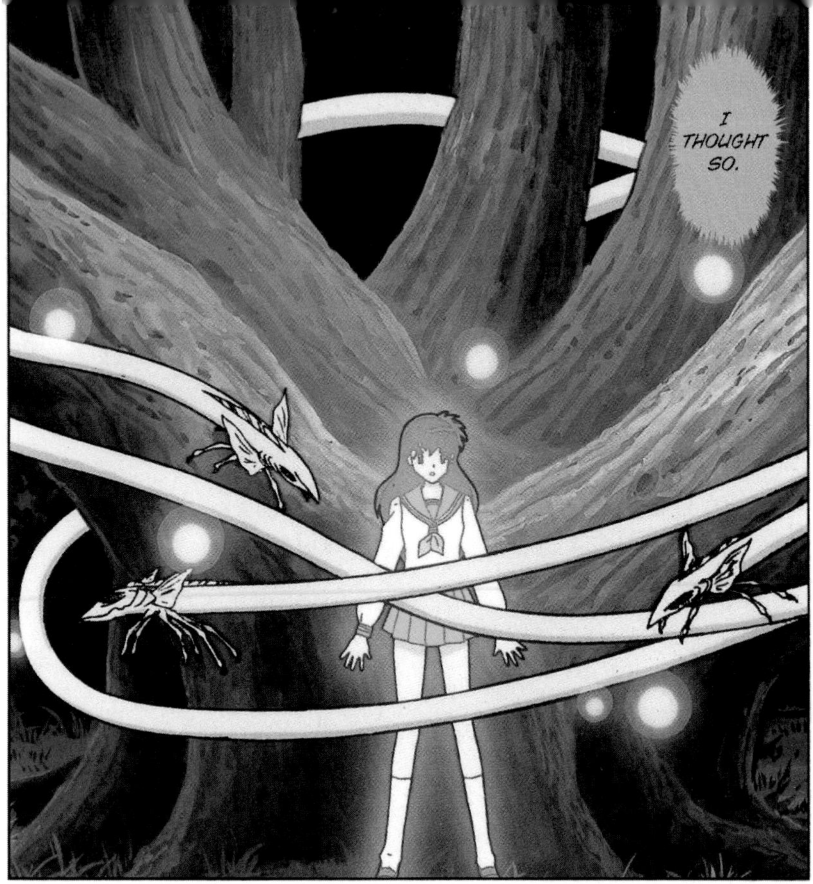
I THOUGHT SO.
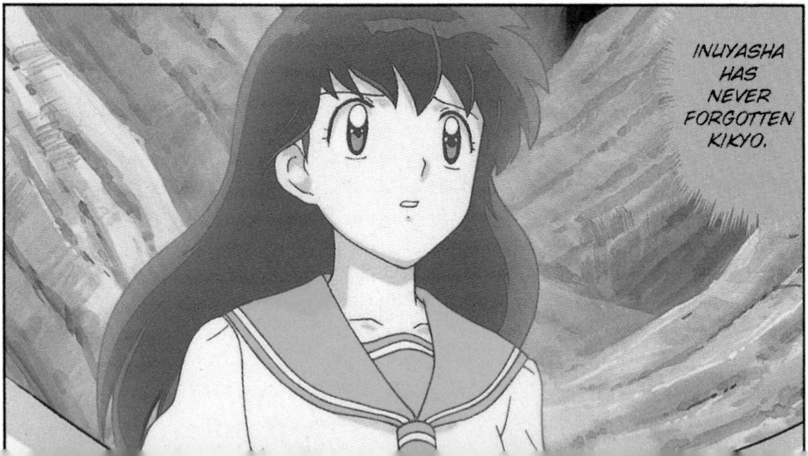
INUYASHA HAS NEVER FORGOTTEN KIKYO.

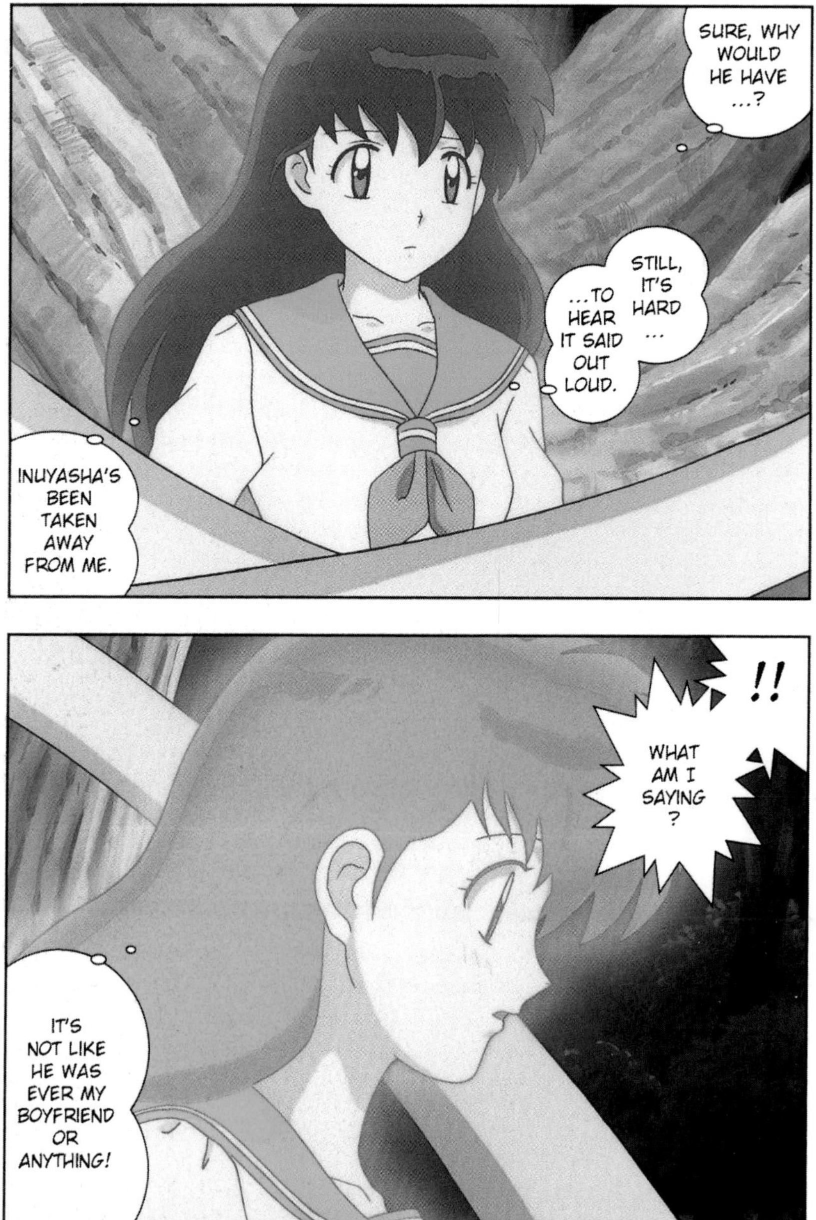
SURE, WHY WOULD HE HAVE ...?
STILL, IT'S HARD ...
...TO HEAR IT SAID OUT LOUD.
INUYASHA'S BEEN TAKEN AWAY FROM ME.
!!
WHAT AM I SAYING?
IT'S NOT LIKE HE WAS EVER MY BOYFRIEND OR ANYTHING!

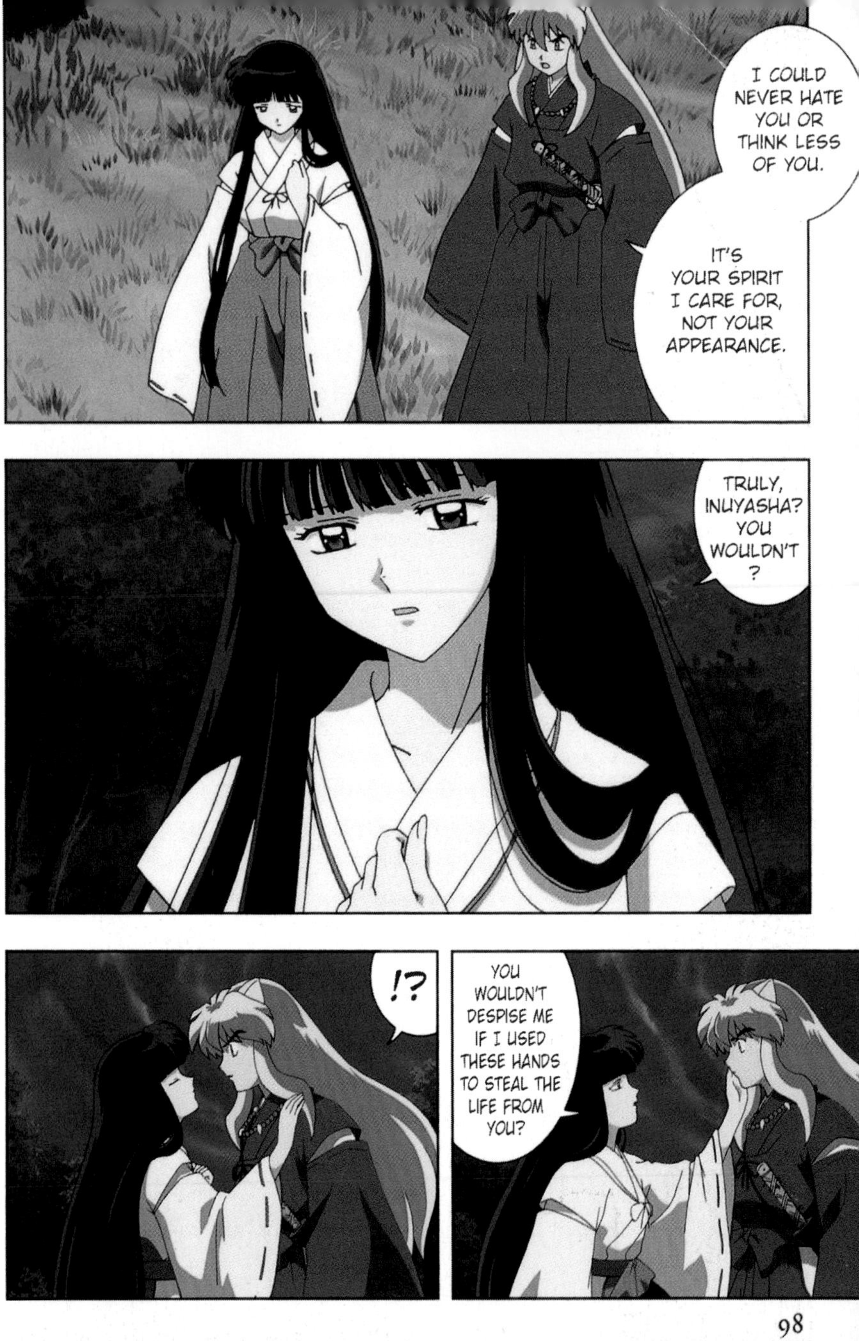
I COULD NEVER HATE YOU OR THINK LESS OF YOU.
IT'S YOUR SPIRIT I CARE FOR, NOT YOUR APPEARANCE.
TRULY, INUYASHA? YOU WOULDN'T ?
YOU WOULDN'T DESPISE ME IF I USED THESE HANDS TO STEAL THE LIFE FROM YOU?
!?

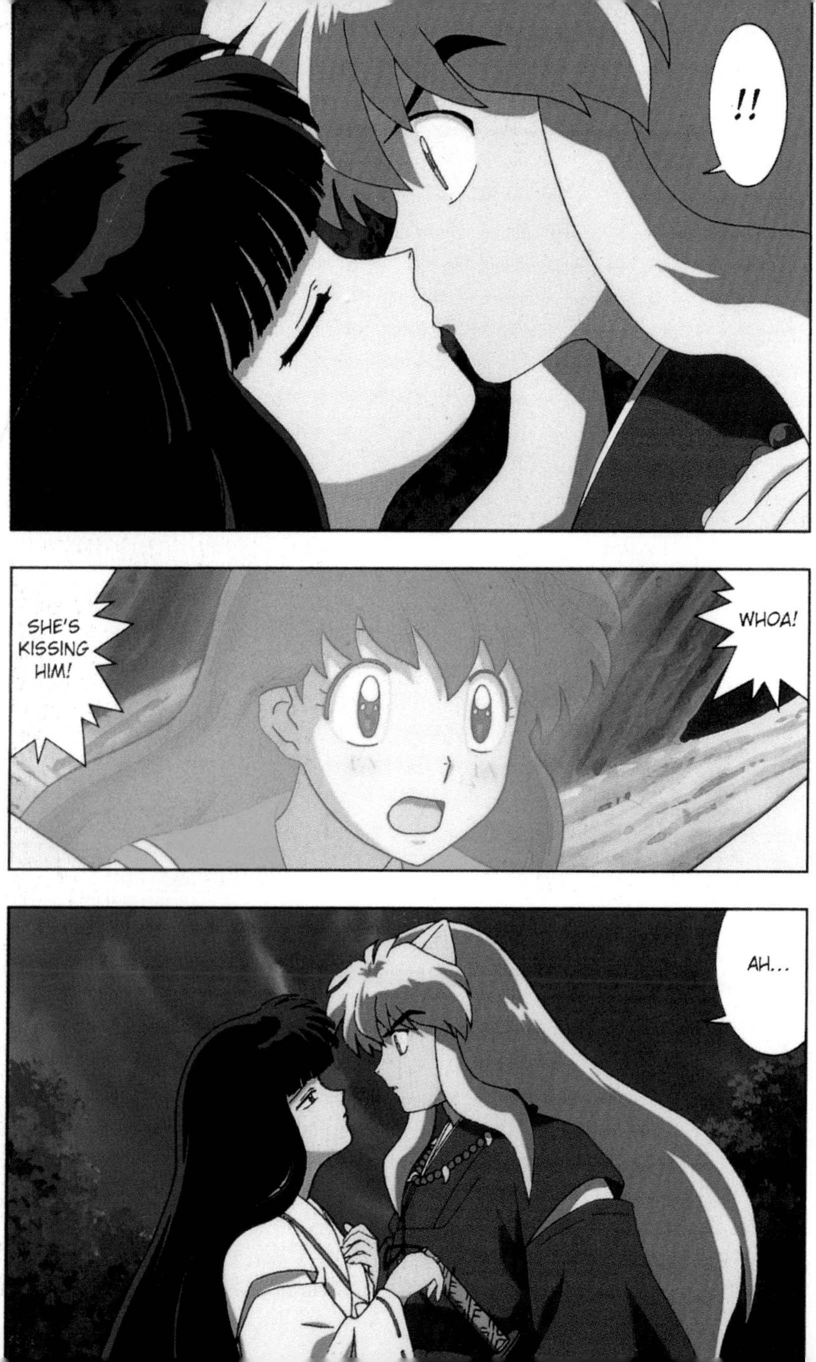
!!
WHOA!
SHE'S KISSING HIM!
AH...

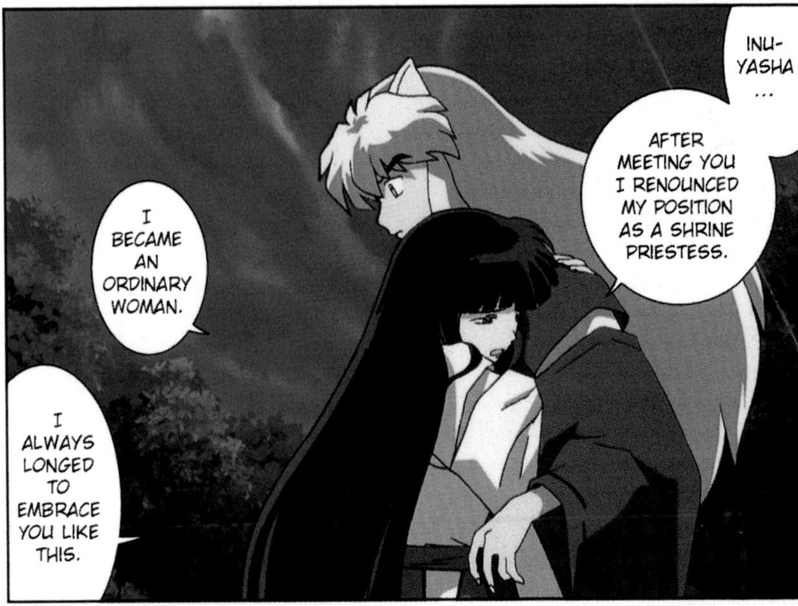
INU-YASHA ...
AFTER MEETING YOU I RENOUNCED MY POSITION AS A SHRINE PRIESTESS.
I BECAME AN ORDINARY WOMAN.
I ALWAYS LONGED TO EMBRACE YOU LIKE THIS.

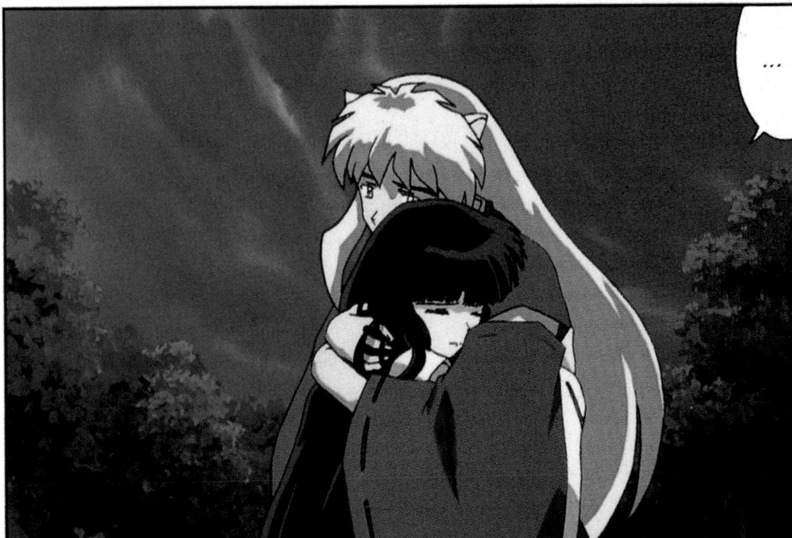
...

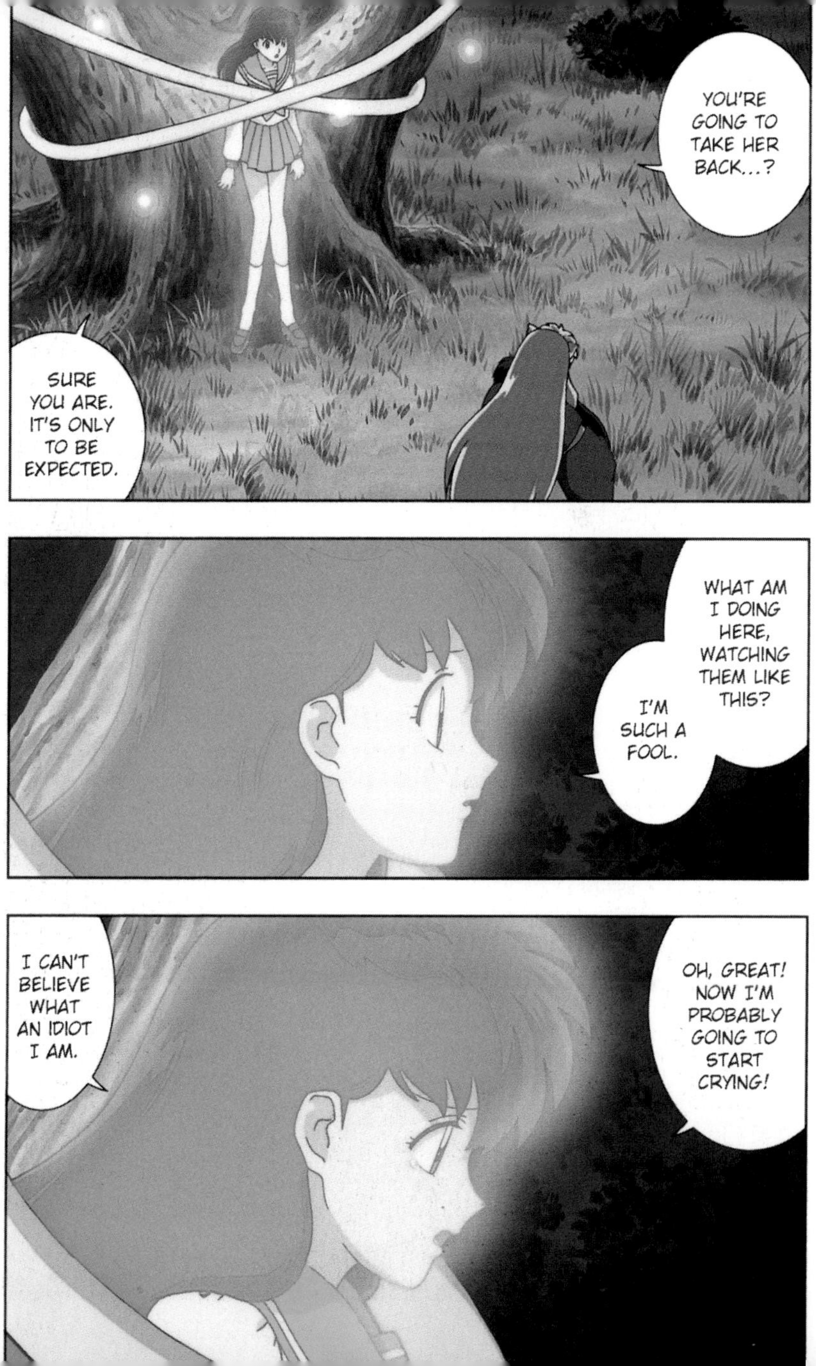
YOU'RE GOING TO TAKE HER BACK...?
SURE YOU ARE. IT'S ONLY TO BE EXPECTED.
WHAT AM I DOING HERE, WATCHING THEM LIKE THIS?
I'M SUCH A FOOL.
OH, GREAT! NOW I'M PROBABLY GOING TO START CRYING!
I CAN'T BELIEVE WHAT AN IDIOT I AM.

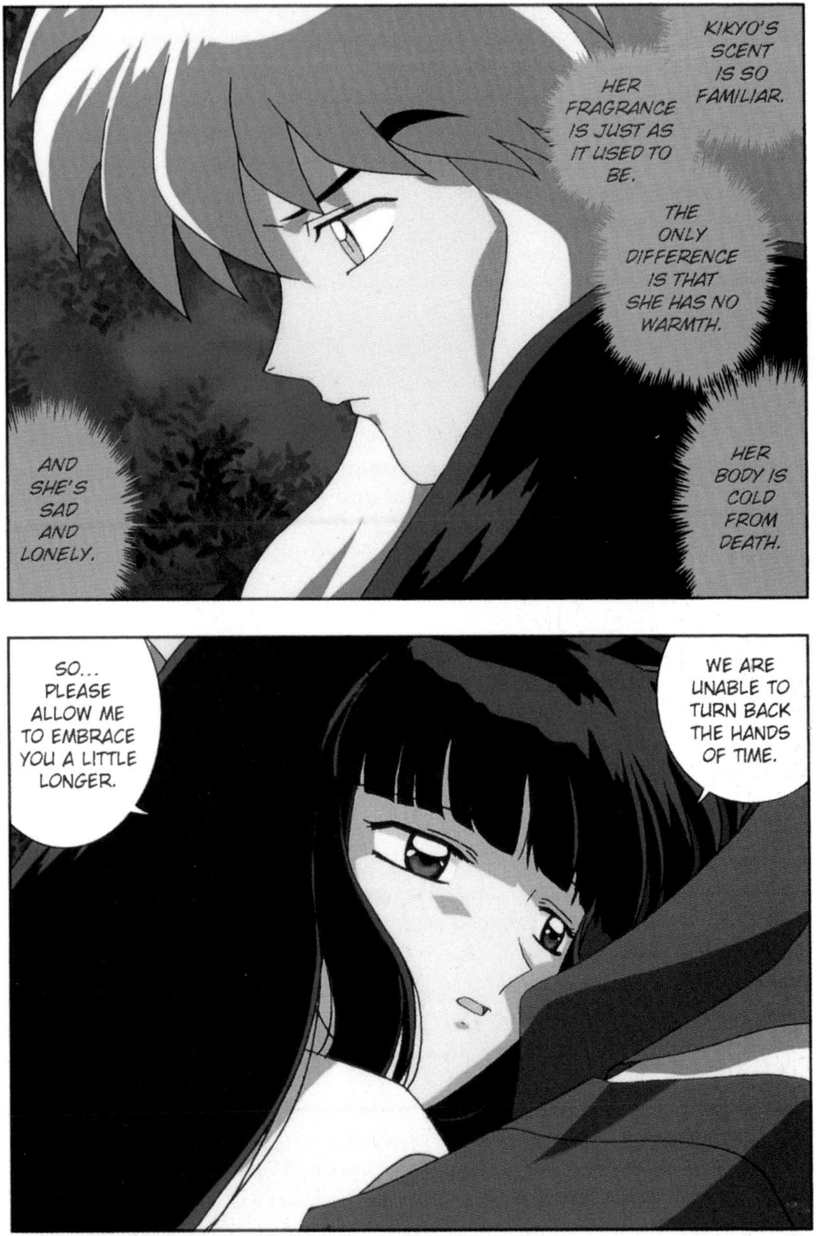
KIKYO'S SCENT IS SO FAMILIAR.
HER FRAGRANCE IS JUST AS IT USED TO BE.
THE ONLY DIFFERENCE IS THAT SHE HAS NO WARMTH.
HER BODY IS COLD FROM DEATH.
AND SHE'S SAD AND LONELY.
WE ARE UNABLE TO TURN BACK THE HANDS OF TIME.
SO... PLEASE ALLOW ME TO EMBRACE YOU A LITTLE LONGER.

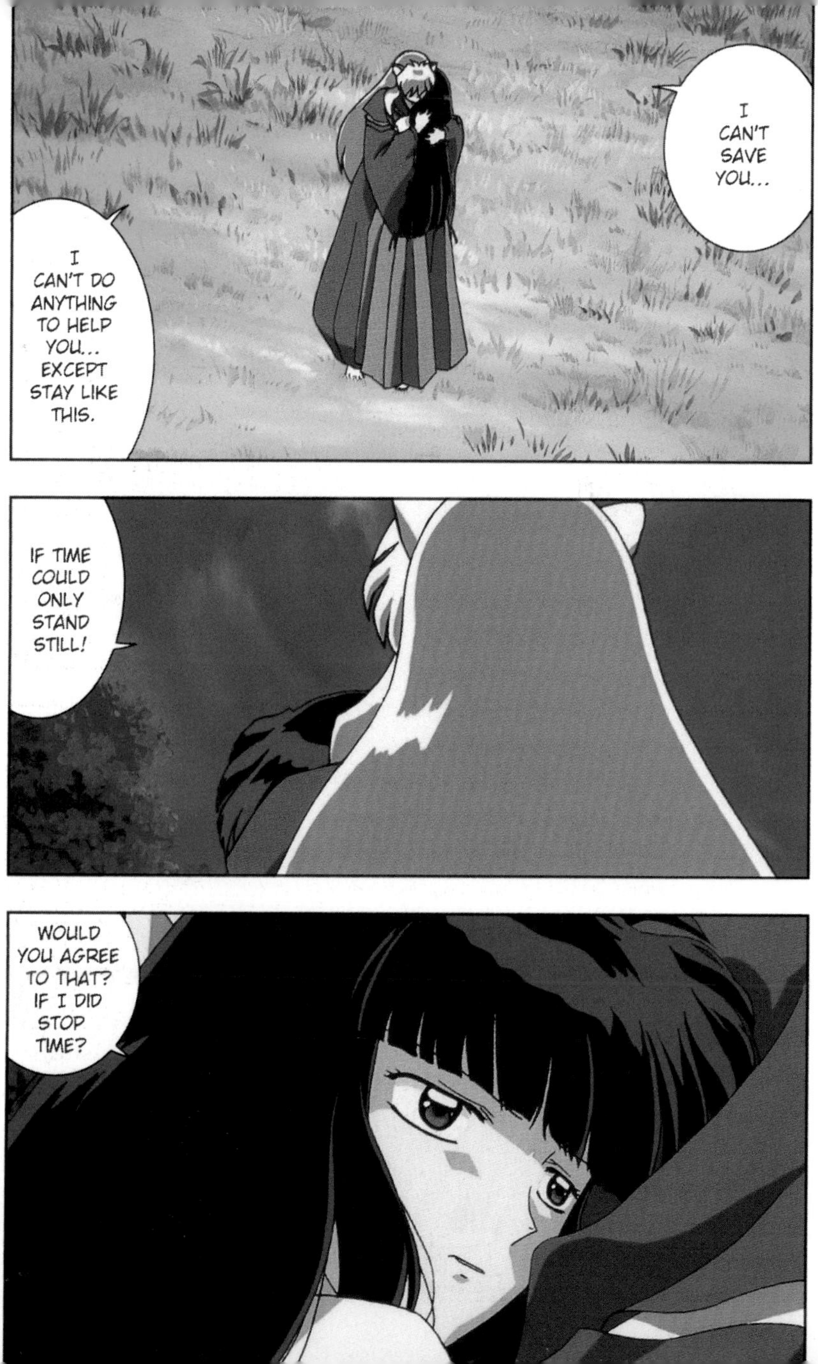
I CAN'T SAVE YOU...
I CAN'T DO ANYTHING TO HELP YOU... EXCEPT STAY LIKE THIS.
IF TIME COULD ONLY STAND STILL!
WOULD YOU AGREE TO THAT? IF I DID STOP TIME?

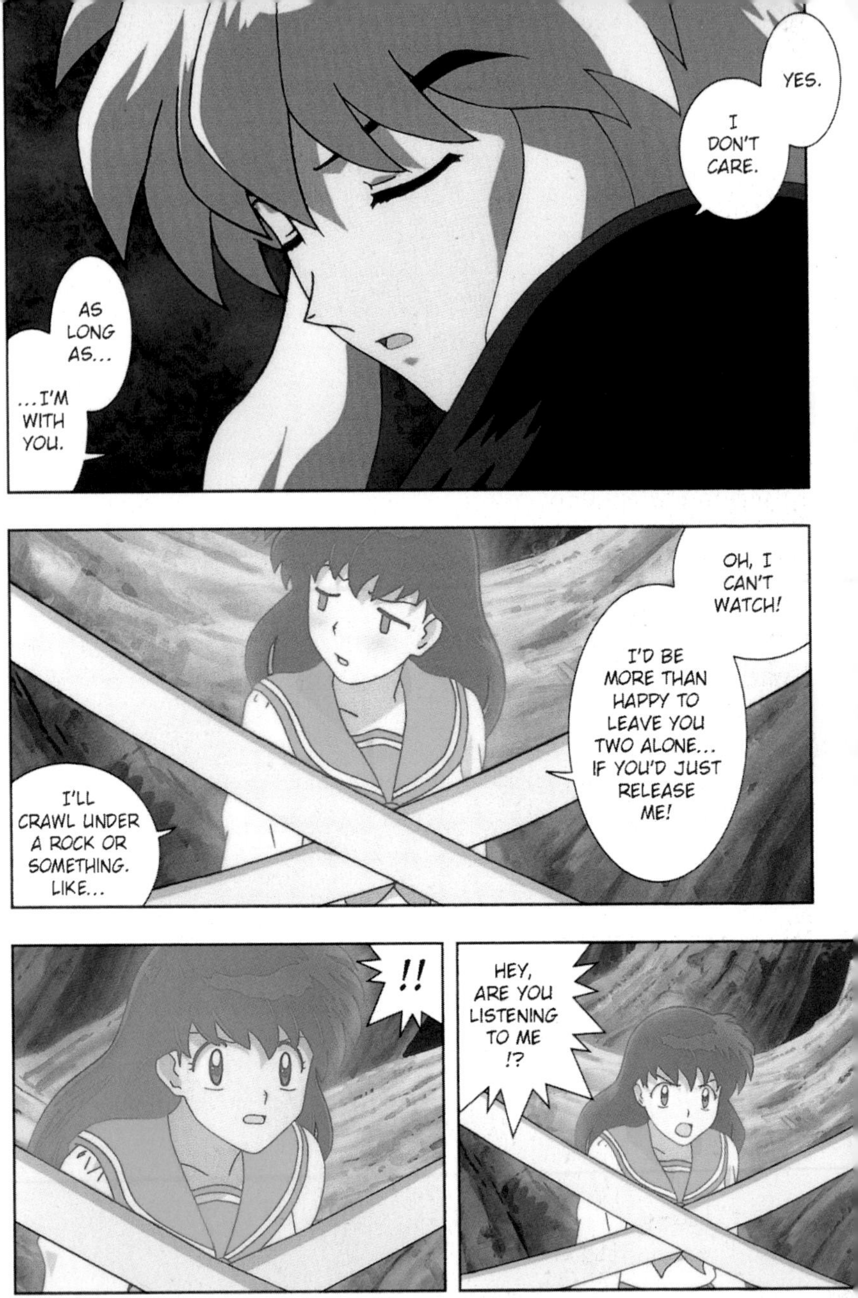
YES.
I DON'T CARE.
AS LONG AS...
...I'M WITH YOU.
OH, I CAN'T WATCH!
I'D BE MORE THAN HAPPY TO LEAVE YOU TWO ALONE... IF YOU'D JUST RELEASE ME!
I'LL CRAWL UNDER A ROCK OR SOMETHING. LIKE...
HEY, ARE YOU LISTENING TO ME !?
!!

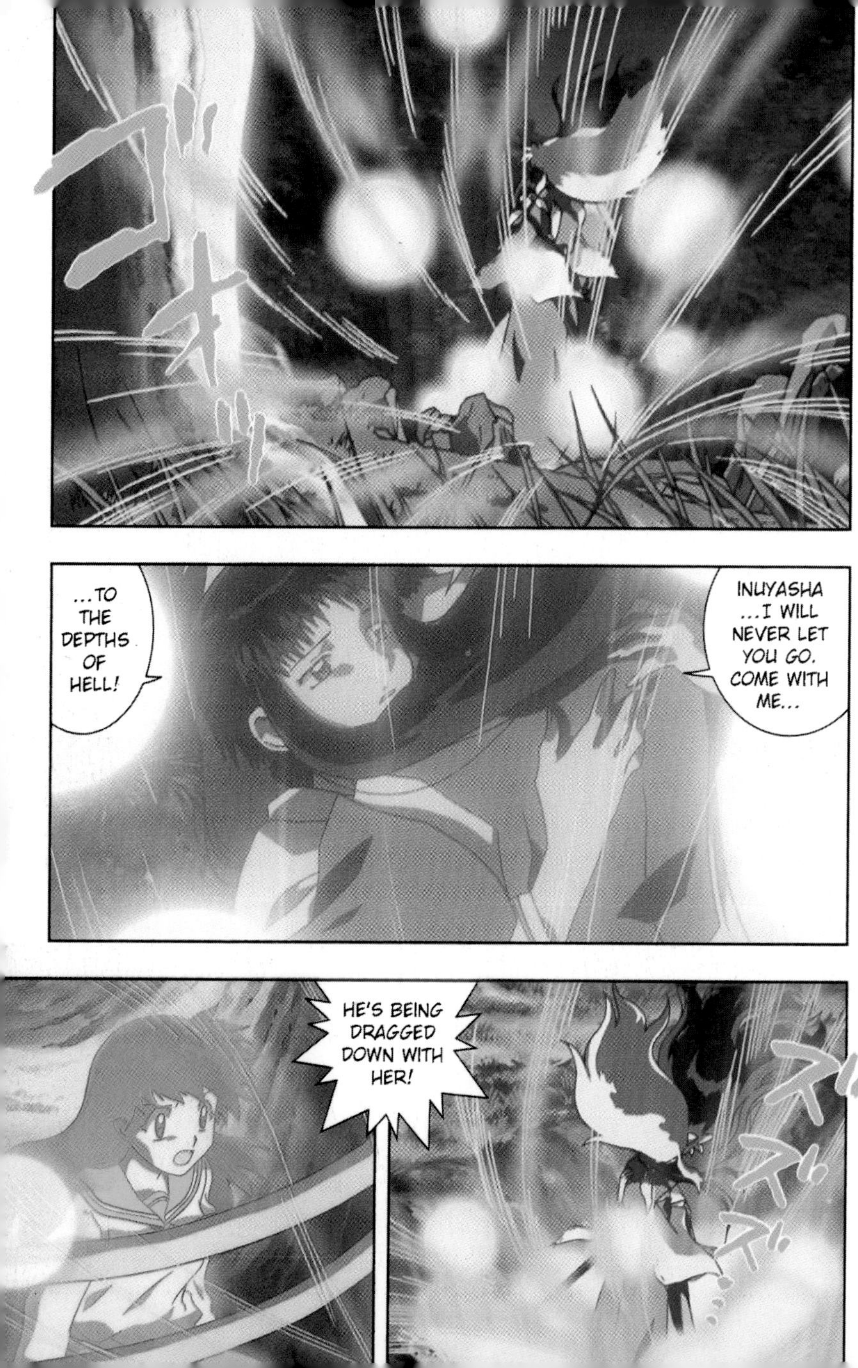
INUYASHA ...I WILL NEVER LET YOU GO. COME WITH ME...
...TO THE DEPTHS OF HELL!
HE'S BEING DRAGGED DOWN WITH HER!

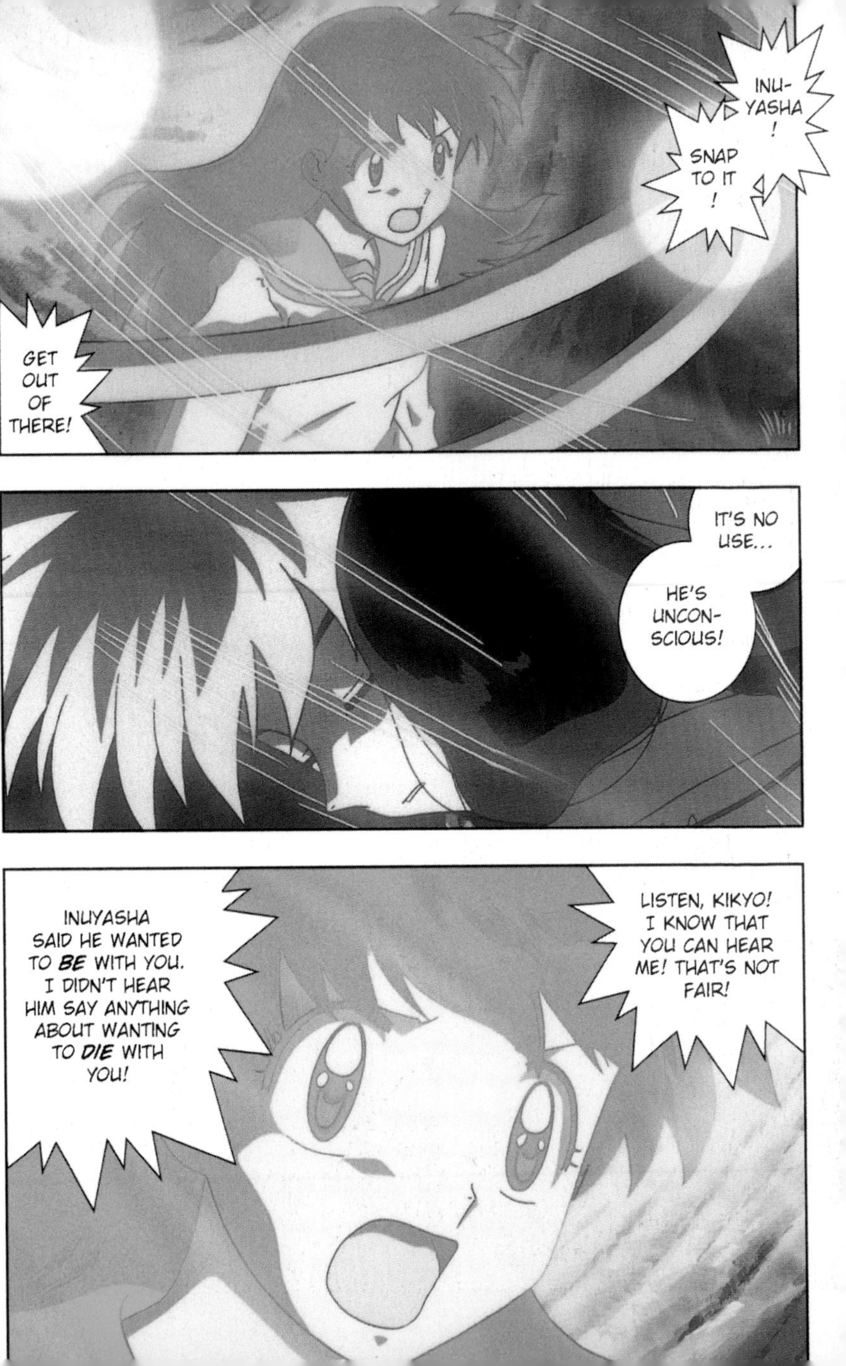
INU-YASHA!
SNAP TO IT!
GET OUT OF THERE!
IT'S NO USE...
HE'S UNCONSCIOUS!
LISTEN, KIKYO! I KNOW THAT YOU CAN HEAR ME! THAT'S NOT FAIR!
INUYASHA SAID HE WANTED TO **BE** WITH YOU. I DIDN'T HEAR HIM SAY ANYTHING ABOUT WANTING TO **DIE** WITH YOU!

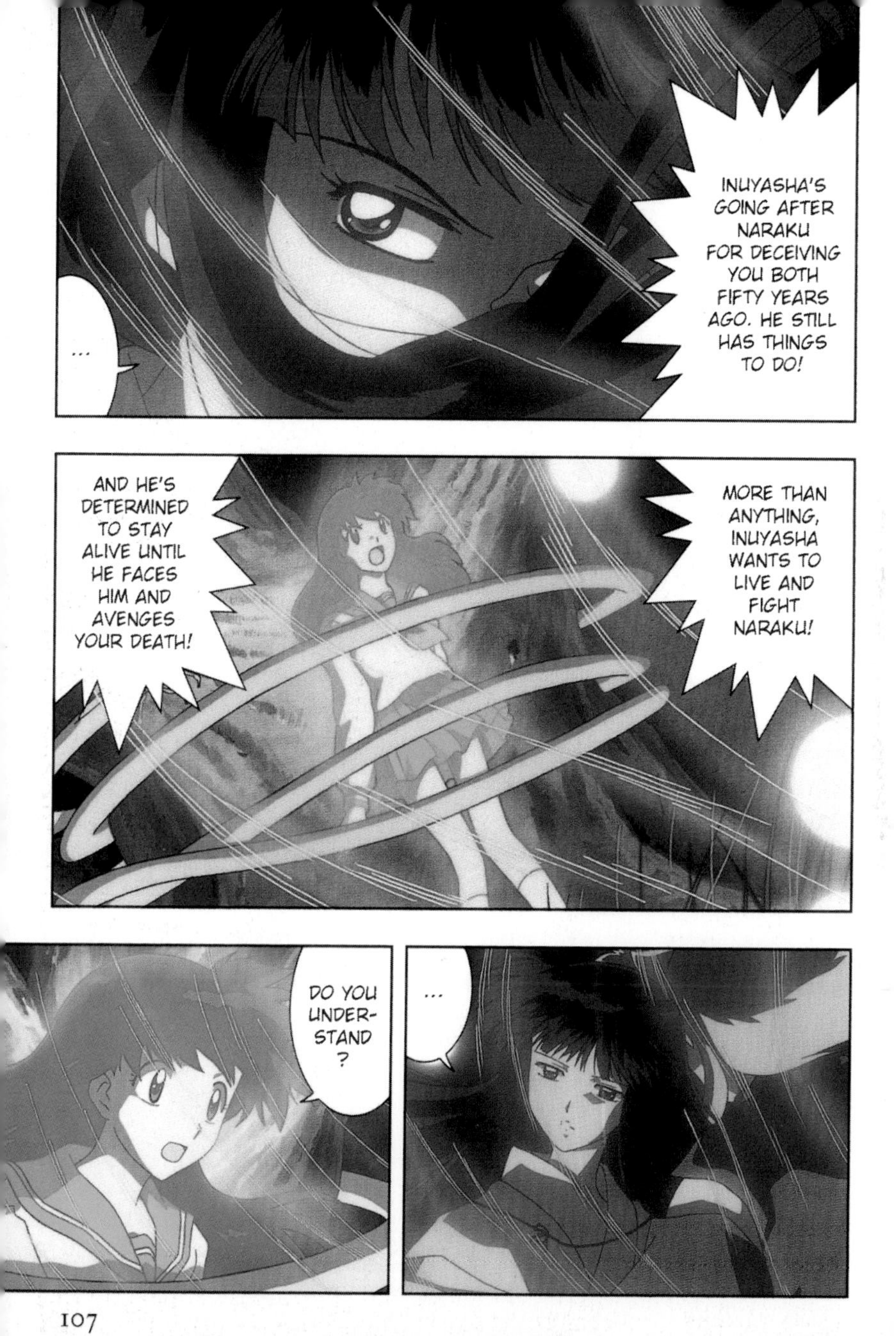
INUYASHA'S GOING AFTER NARAKU FOR DECEIVING YOU BOTH FIFTY YEARS AGO. HE STILL HAS THINGS TO DO!
...
MORE THAN ANYTHING, INUYASHA WANTS TO LIVE AND FIGHT NARAKU!
AND HE'S DETERMINED TO STAY ALIVE UNTIL HE FACES HIM AND AVENGES YOUR DEATH!
...
DO YOU UNDER-STAND?

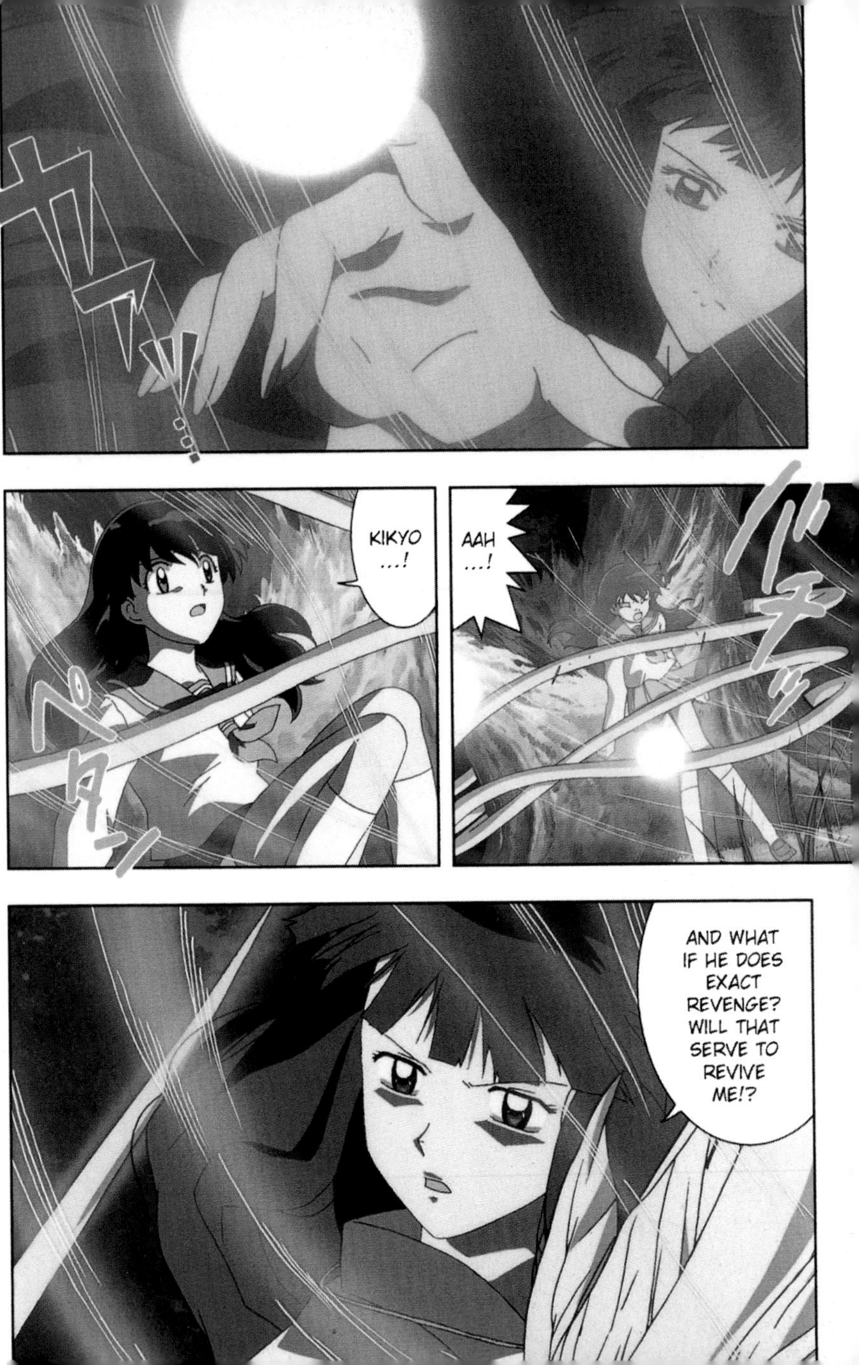
AAH ...!
KIKYO ...!
AND WHAT IF HE DOES EXACT REVENGE? WILL THAT SERVE TO REVIVE ME!?

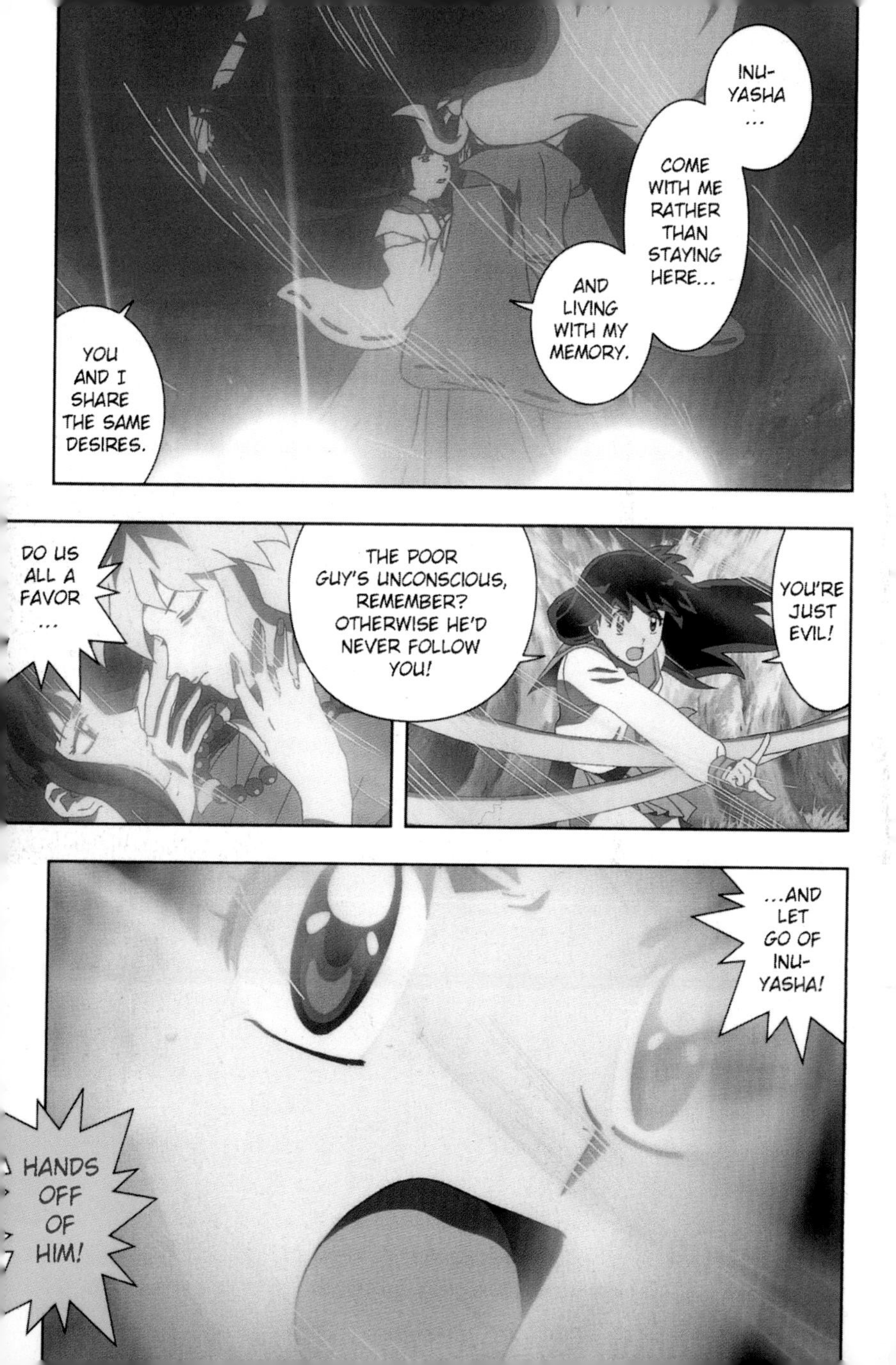

INU-YASHA...
COME WITH ME RATHER THAN STAYING HERE...
AND LIVING WITH MY MEMORY.
YOU AND I SHARE THE SAME DESIRES.
YOU'RE JUST EVIL!
THE POOR GUY'S UNCONSCIOUS, REMEMBER? OTHERWISE HE'D NEVER FOLLOW YOU!
DO US ALL A FAVOR...
...AND LET GO OF INU-YASHA!
HANDS OFF OF HIM!

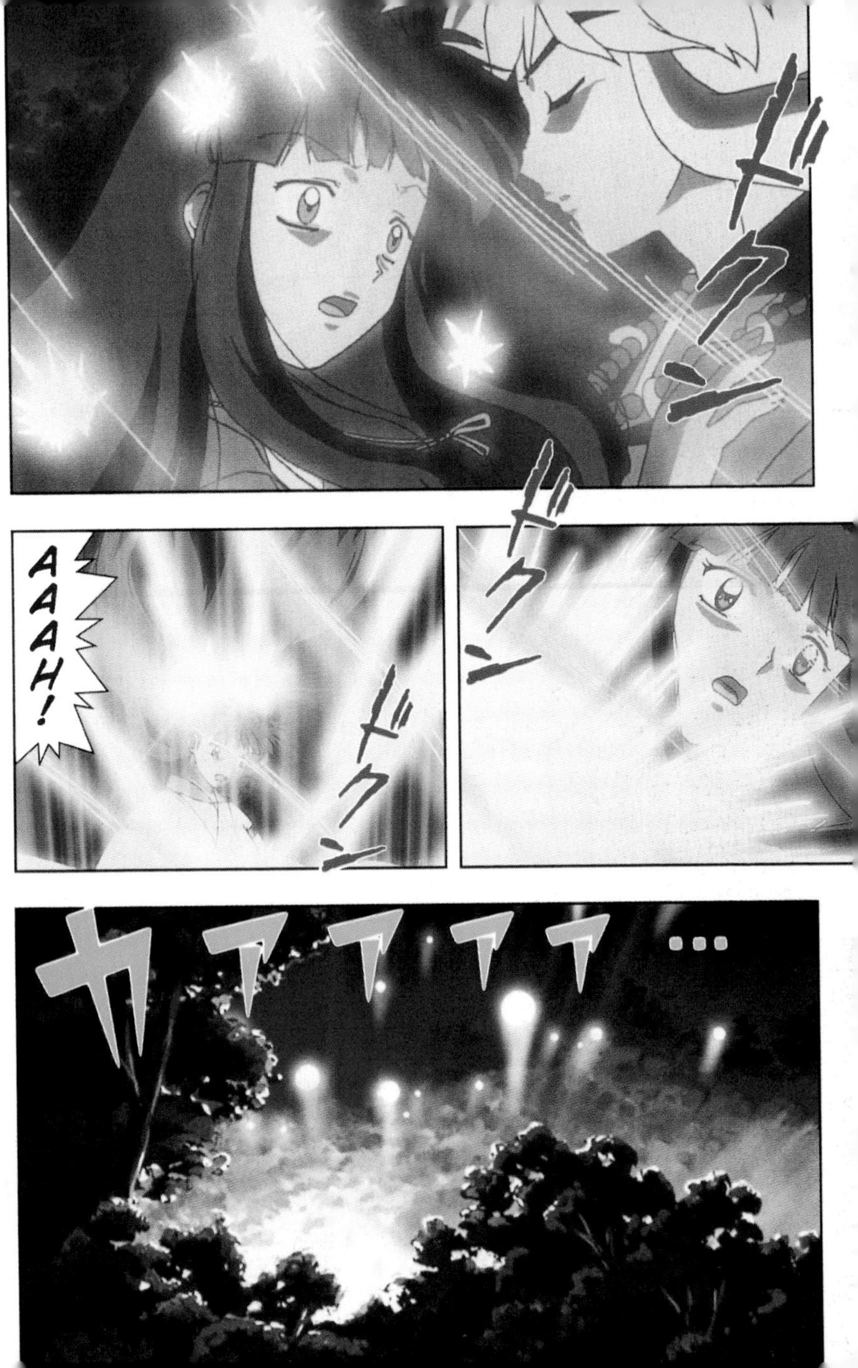
ドクン
ドクン
AAAAH!
ドクン
ヤァァァァ…

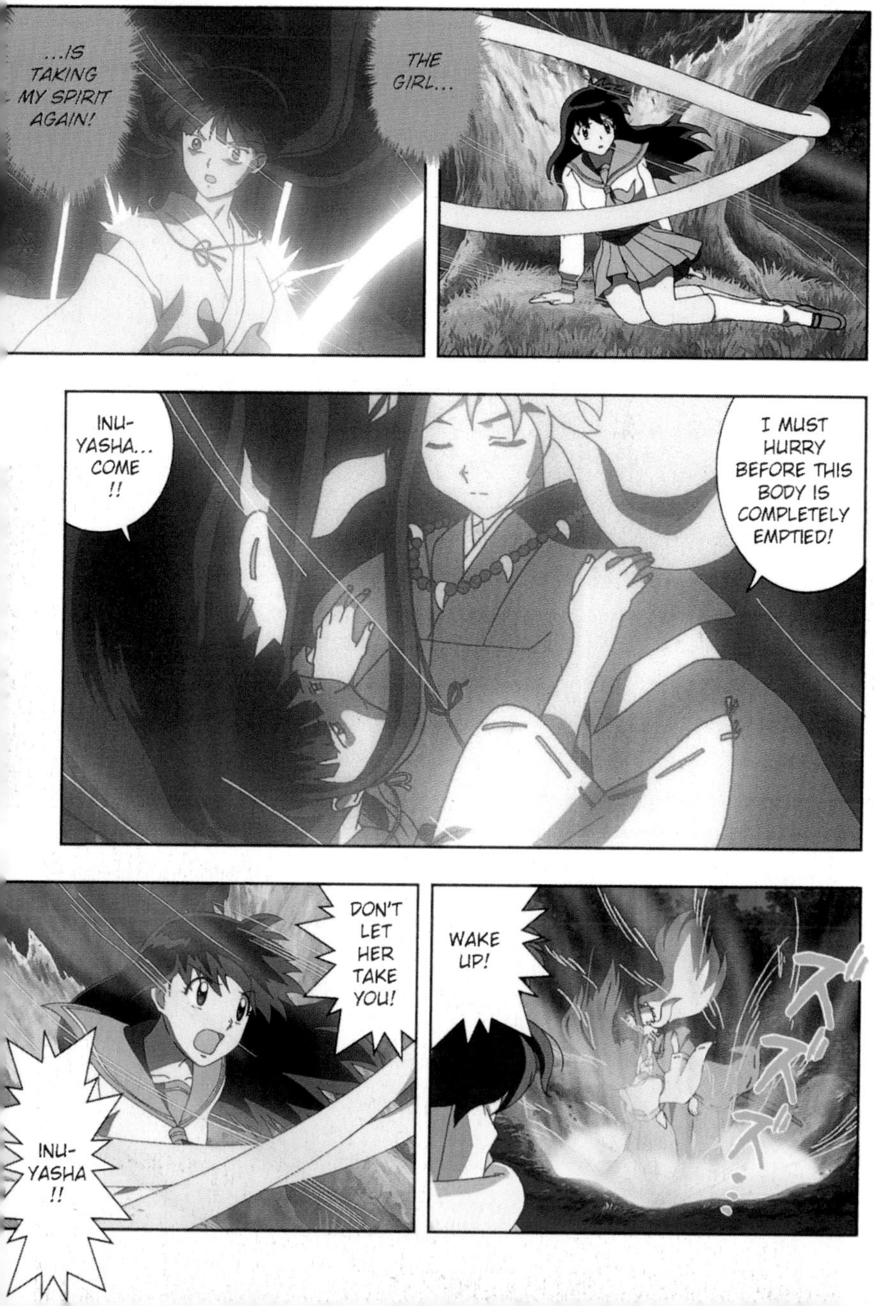
THE GIRL...
...IS TAKING MY SPIRIT AGAIN!
I MUST HURRY BEFORE THIS BODY IS COMPLETELY EMPTIED!
INU-YASHA... COME !!
WAKE UP!
DON'T LET HER TAKE YOU!
INU-YASHA !!

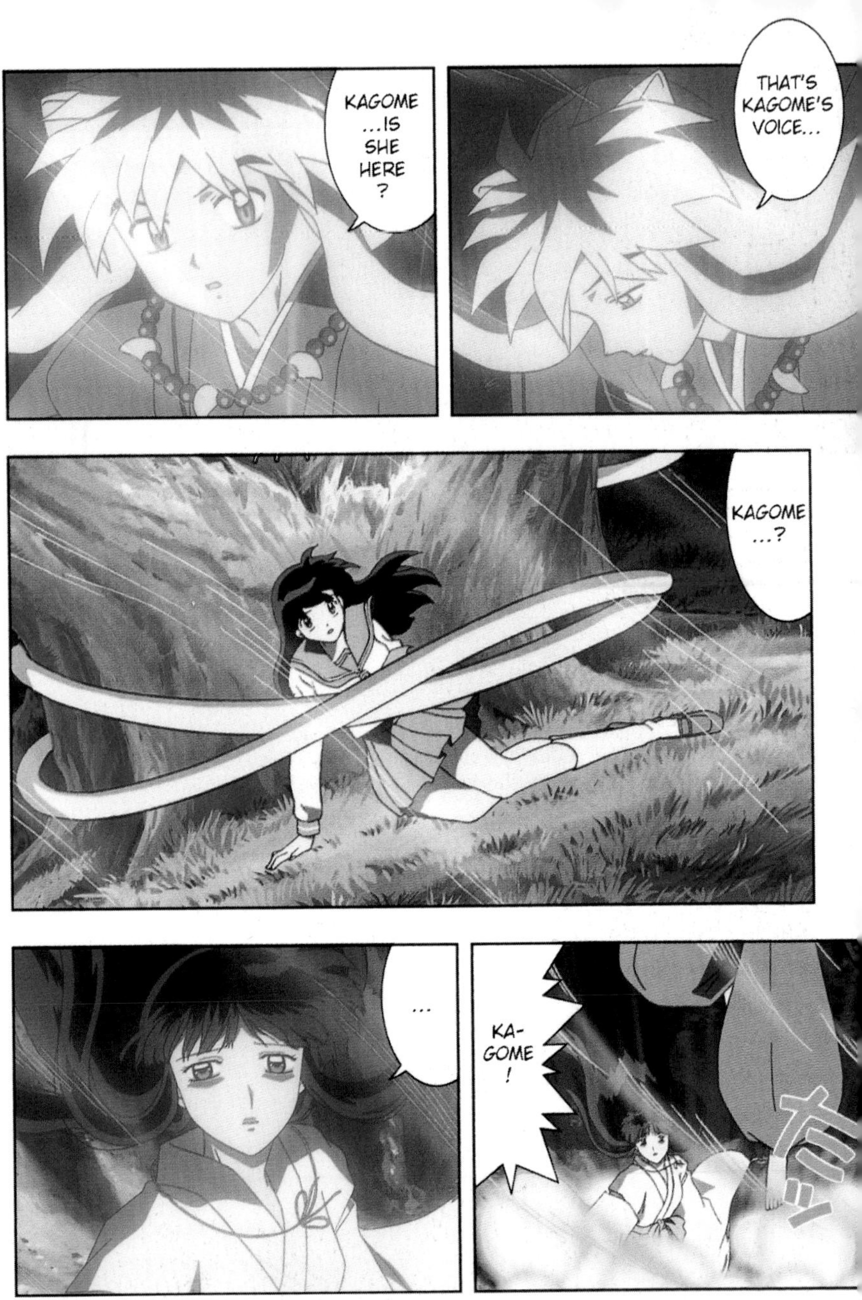
THAT'S KAGOME'S VOICE...
KAGOME ...IS SHE HERE ?
KAGOME ...?
KA- GOME !
...

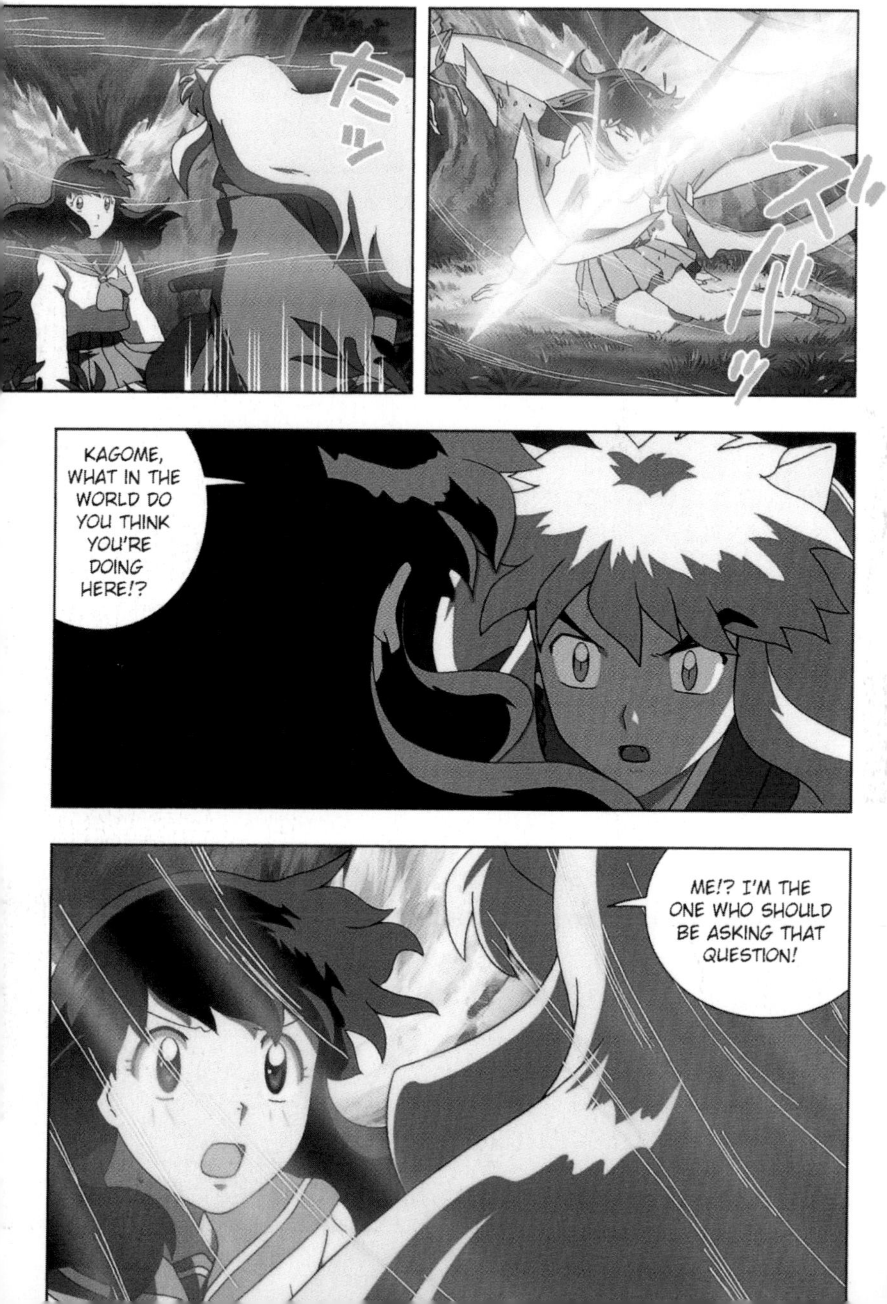
タッ
KAGOME, WHAT IN THE WORLD DO YOU THINK YOU'RE DOING HERE!?
ME!? I'M THE ONE WHO SHOULD BE ASKING THAT QUESTION!

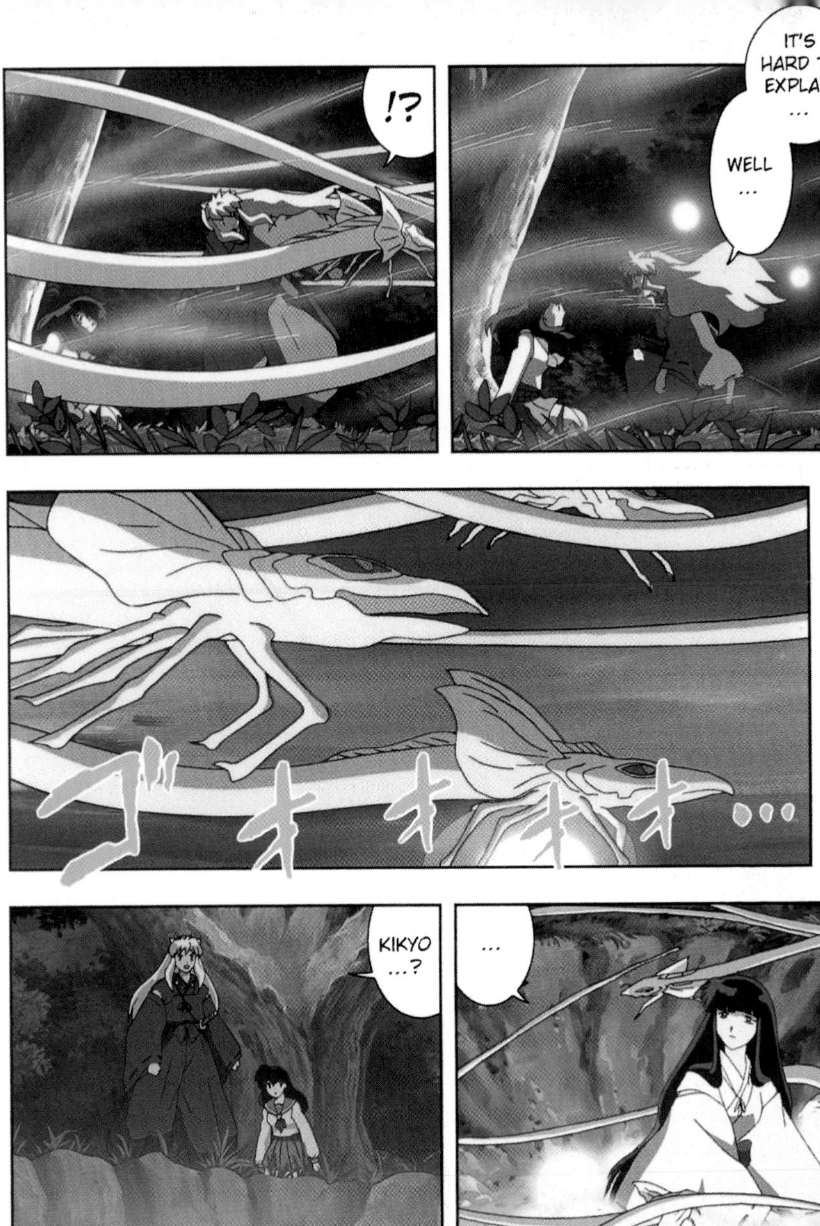
IT'S HARD TO EXPLAIN ...
WELL ...
!?
ゴオオオ…
...
KIKYO ...?

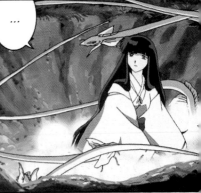

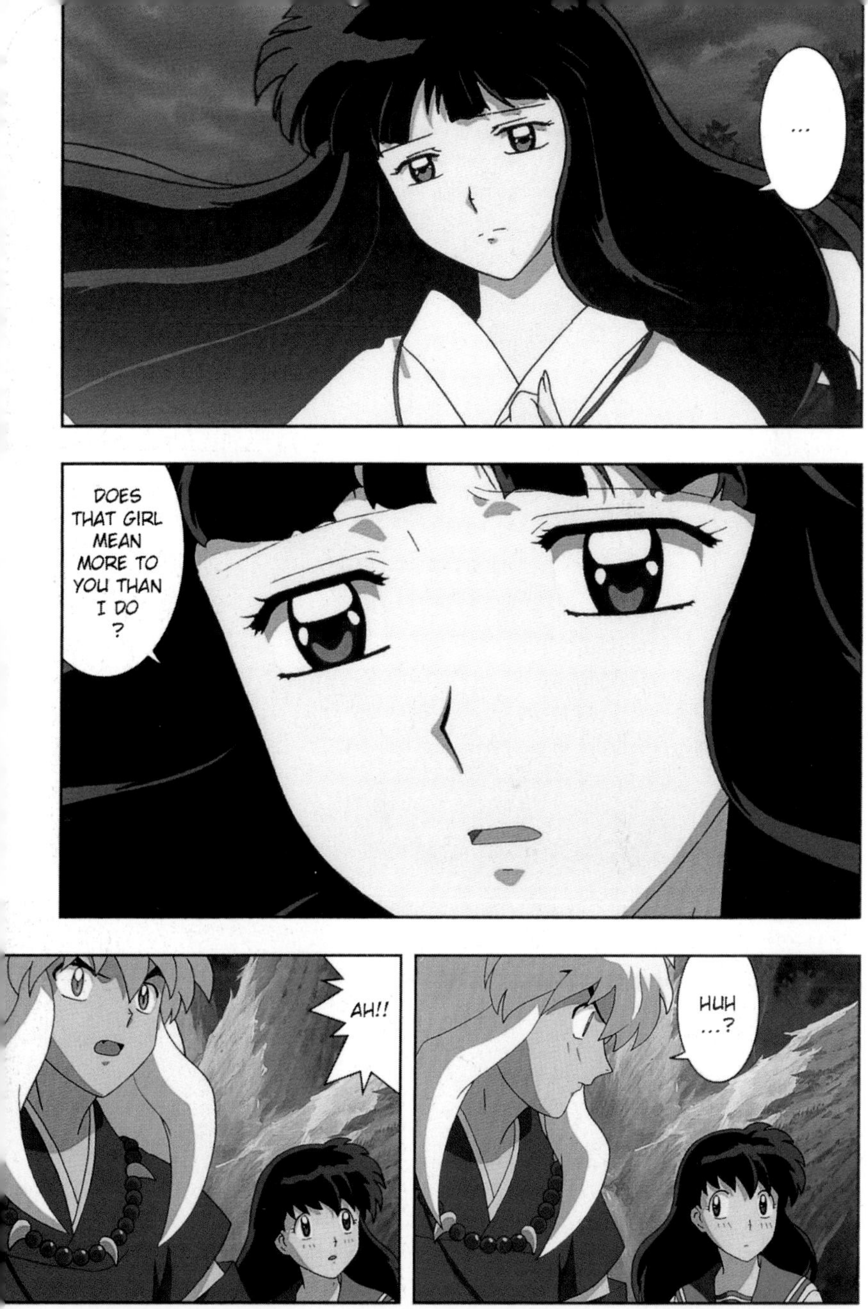
...
DOES THAT GIRL MEAN MORE TO YOU THAN I DO ?
HUH ...?
AH!!

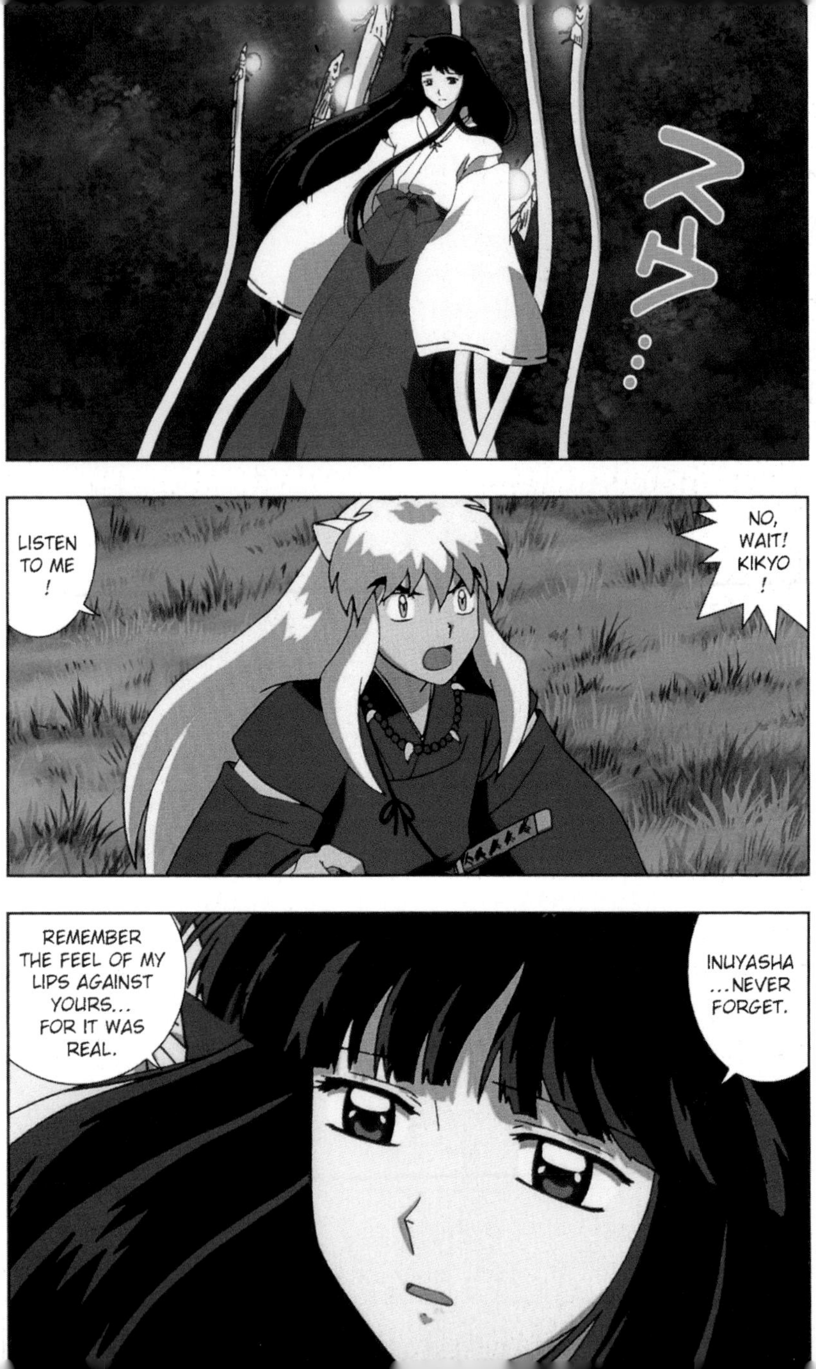
スッ…
NO, WAIT! KIKYO!
LISTEN TO ME!
INUYASHA ...NEVER FORGET.
REMEMBER THE FEEL OF MY LIPS AGAINST YOURS... FOR IT WAS REAL.

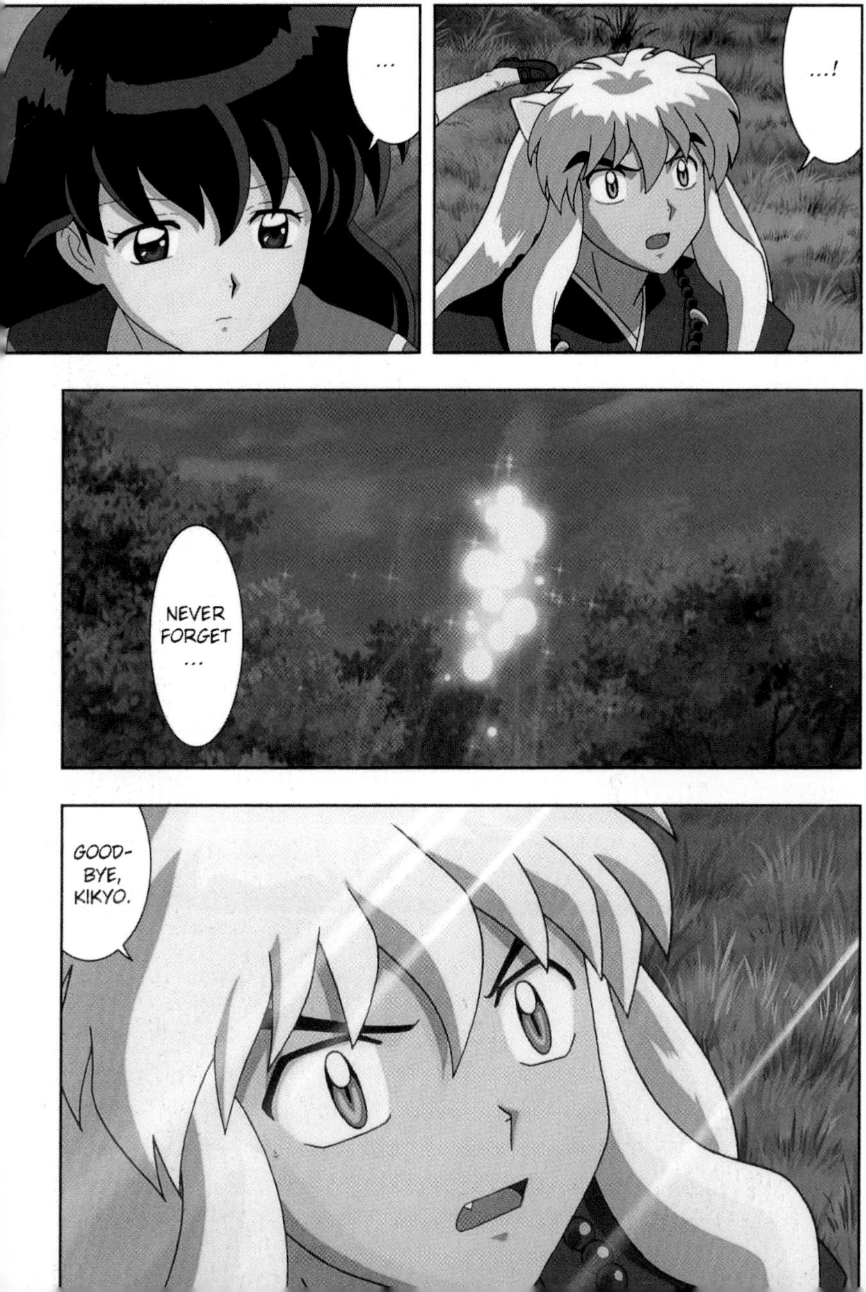
...!
...
NEVER FORGET ...
GOOD-BYE, KIKYO.

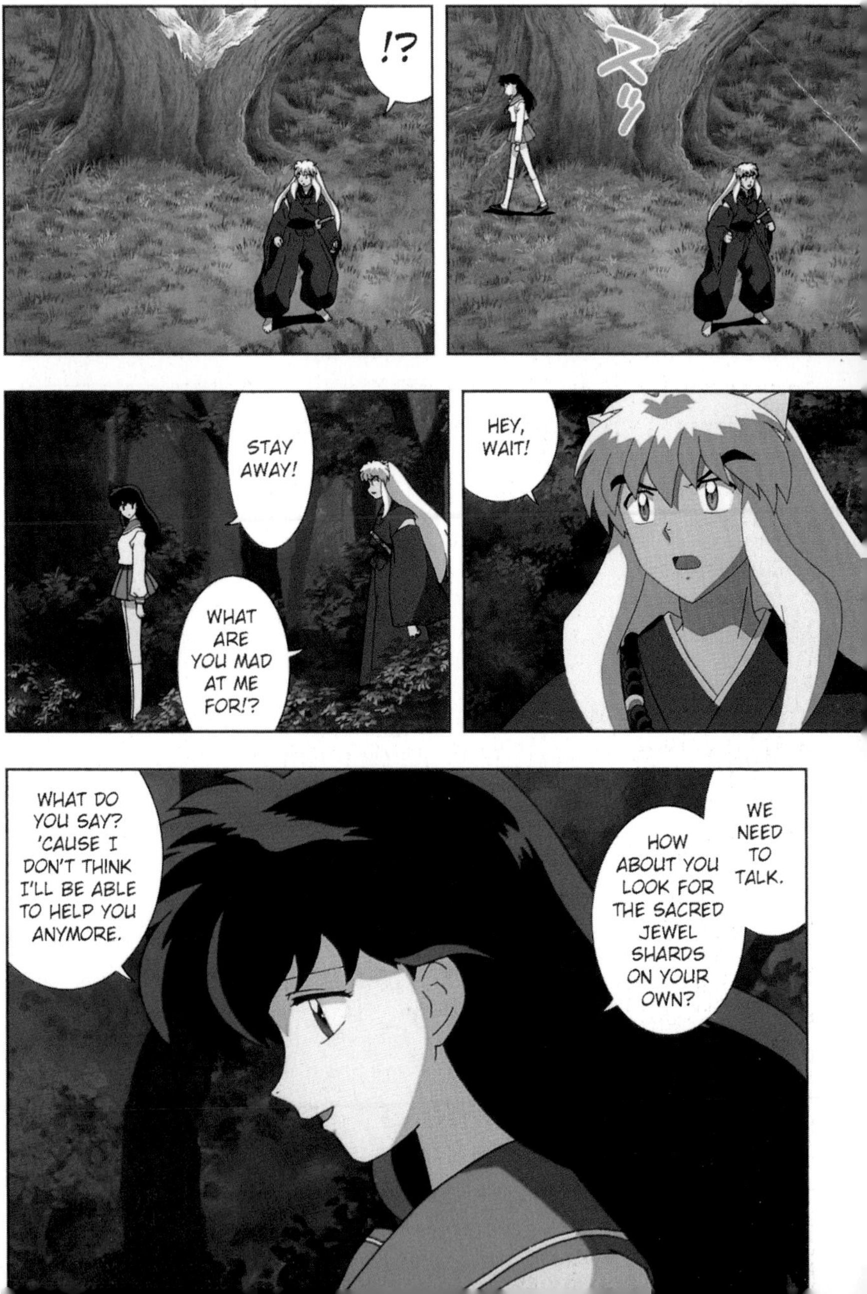
スッ
!?
HEY, WAIT!
STAY AWAY!
WHAT ARE YOU MAD AT ME FOR!?
WE NEED TO TALK.
HOW ABOUT YOU LOOK FOR THE SACRED JEWEL SHARDS ON YOUR OWN?
WHAT DO YOU SAY? 'CAUSE I DON'T THINK I'LL BE ABLE TO HELP YOU ANYMORE.

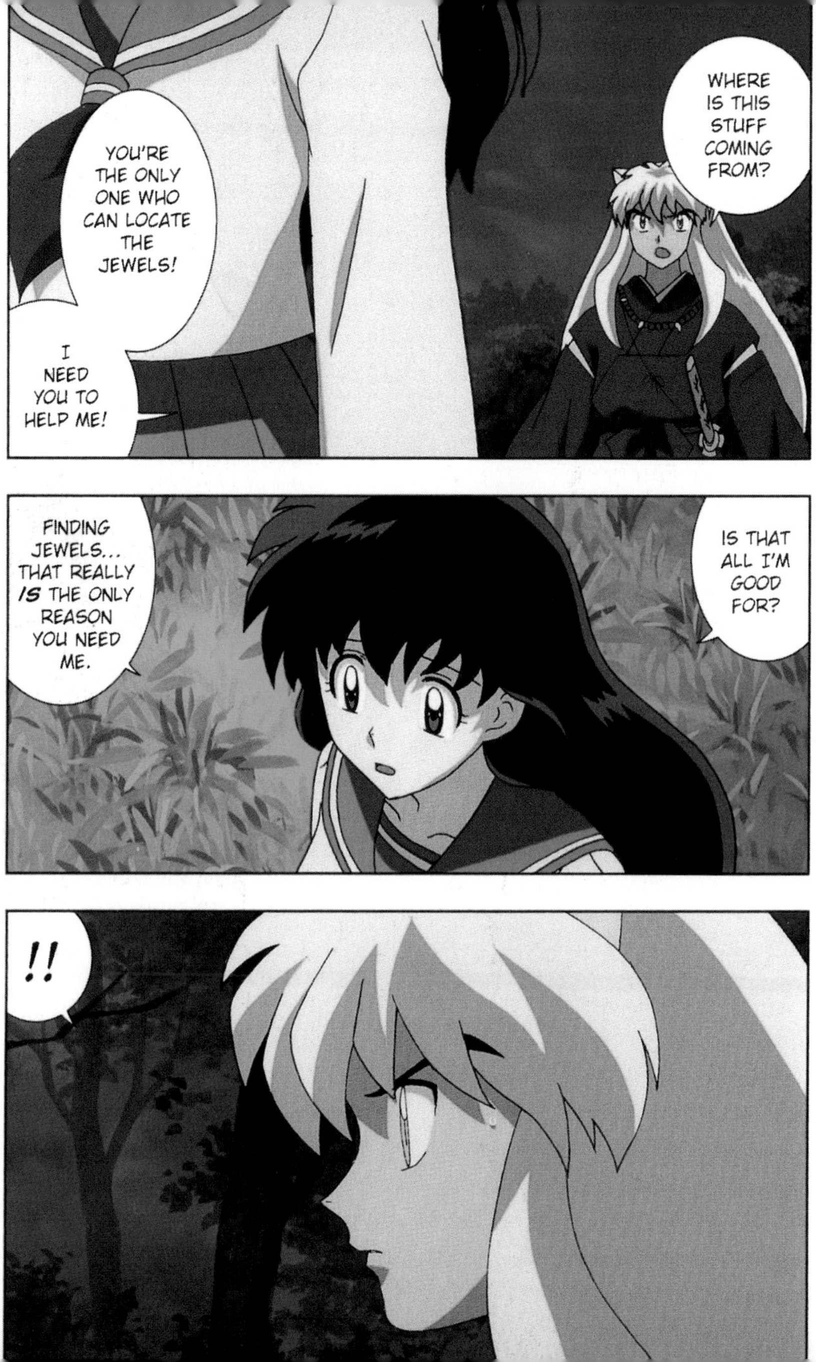
WHERE IS THIS STUFF COMING FROM?
YOU'RE THE ONLY ONE WHO CAN LOCATE THE JEWELS!
I NEED YOU TO HELP ME!
IS THAT ALL I'M GOOD FOR?
FINDING JEWELS... THAT REALLY *IS* THE ONLY REASON YOU NEED ME.
!!

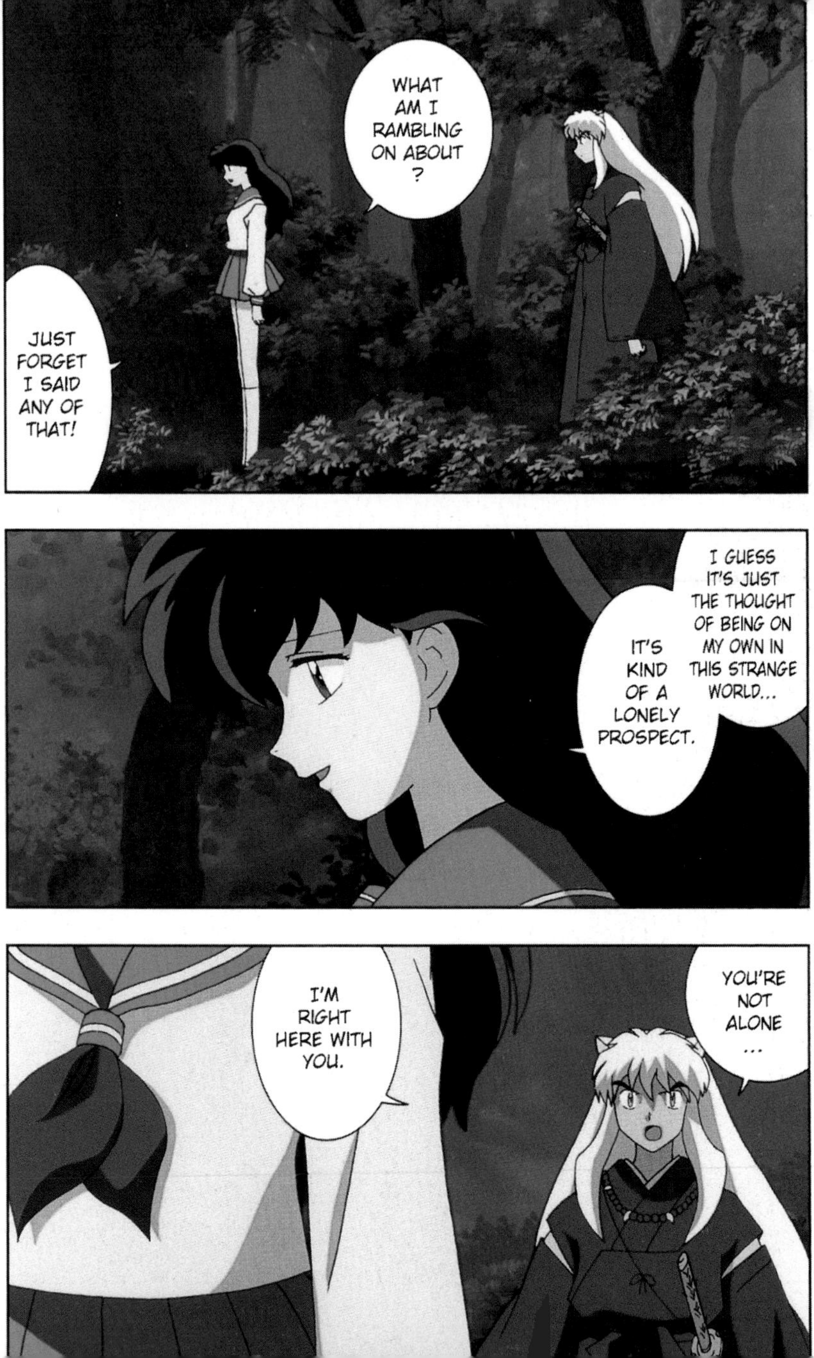
WHAT AM I RAMBLING ON ABOUT?
JUST FORGET I SAID ANY OF THAT!
I GUESS IT'S JUST THE THOUGHT OF BEING ON MY OWN IN THIS STRANGE WORLD...
IT'S KIND OF A LONELY PROSPECT.
YOU'RE NOT ALONE...
I'M RIGHT HERE WITH YOU.

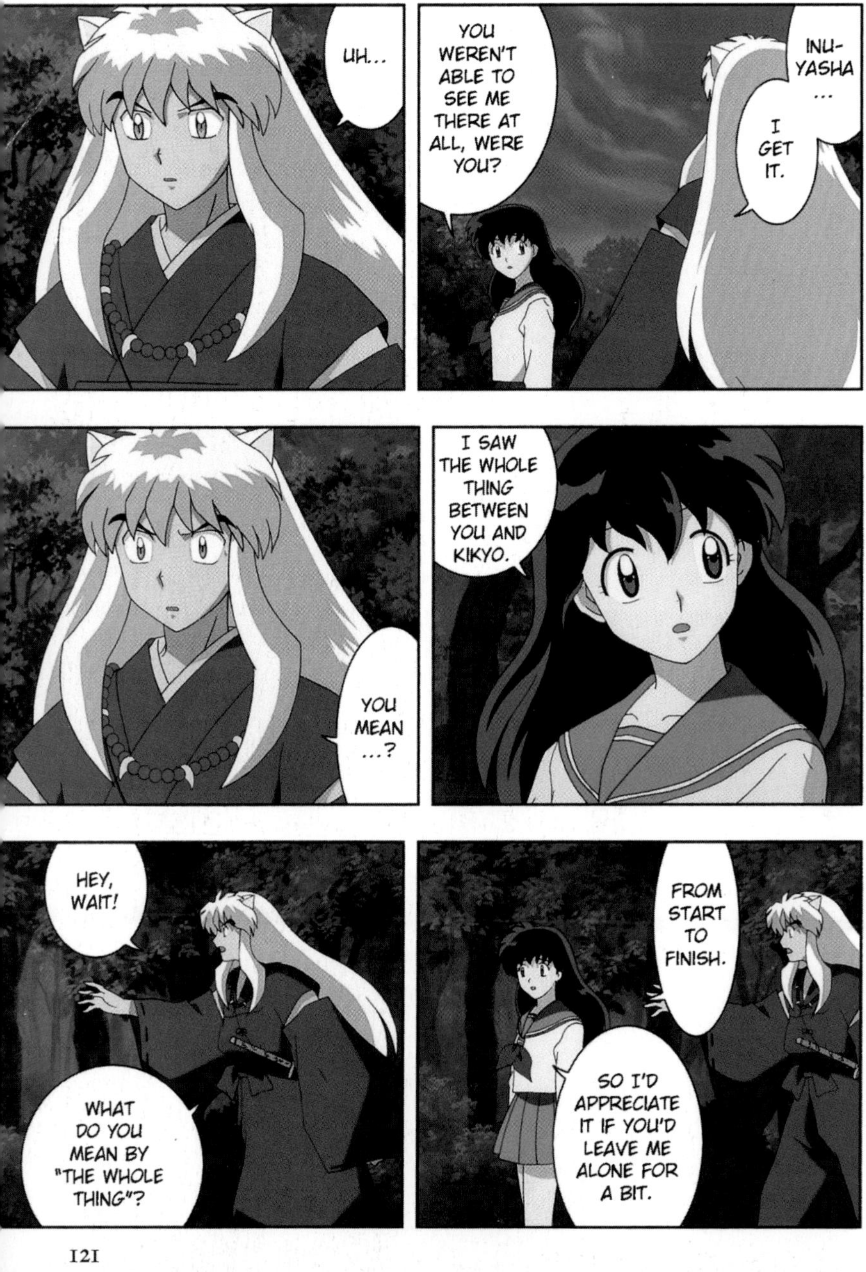
INU-YASHA... I GET IT.
YOU WEREN'T ABLE TO SEE ME THERE AT ALL, WERE YOU?
UH...
I SAW THE WHOLE THING BETWEEN YOU AND KIKYO.
YOU MEAN ...?
FROM START TO FINISH.
SO I'D APPRECIATE IT IF YOU'D LEAVE ME ALONE FOR A BIT.
HEY, WAIT!
WHAT DO YOU MEAN BY "THE WHOLE THING"?

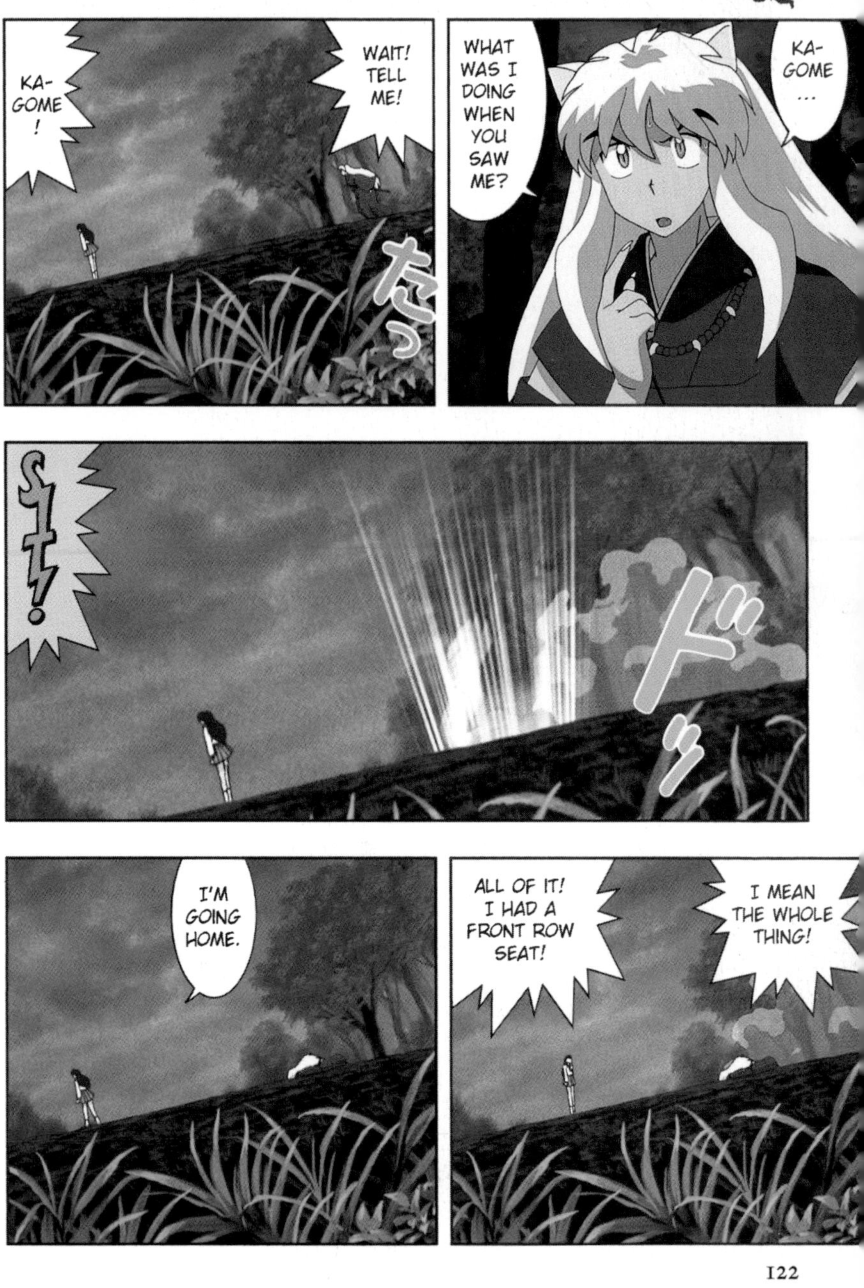
KA-GOME ...
WHAT WAS I DOING WHEN YOU SAW ME?
WAIT! TELL ME!
KA-GOME!
たっ
ドッ
I MEAN THE WHOLE THING!
ALL OF IT! I HAD A FRONT ROW SEAT!
I'M GOING HOME.

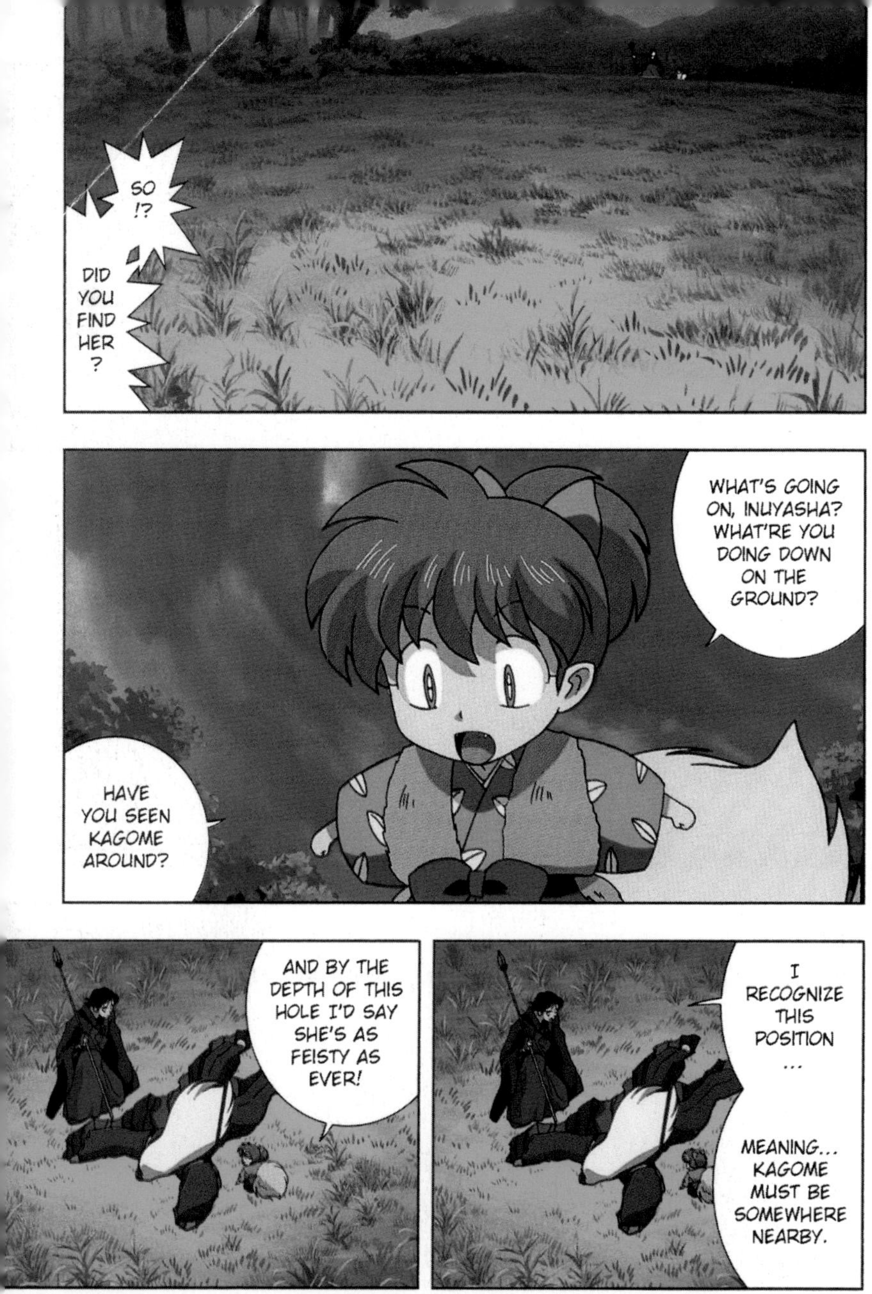
SO !?
DID YOU FIND HER ?
WHAT'S GOING ON, INUYASHA? WHAT'RE YOU DOING DOWN ON THE GROUND?
HAVE YOU SEEN KAGOME AROUND?
I RECOGNIZE THIS POSITION …
MEANING… KAGOME MUST BE SOMEWHERE NEARBY.
AND BY THE DEPTH OF THIS HOLE I'D SAY SHE'S AS FEISTY AS EVER!

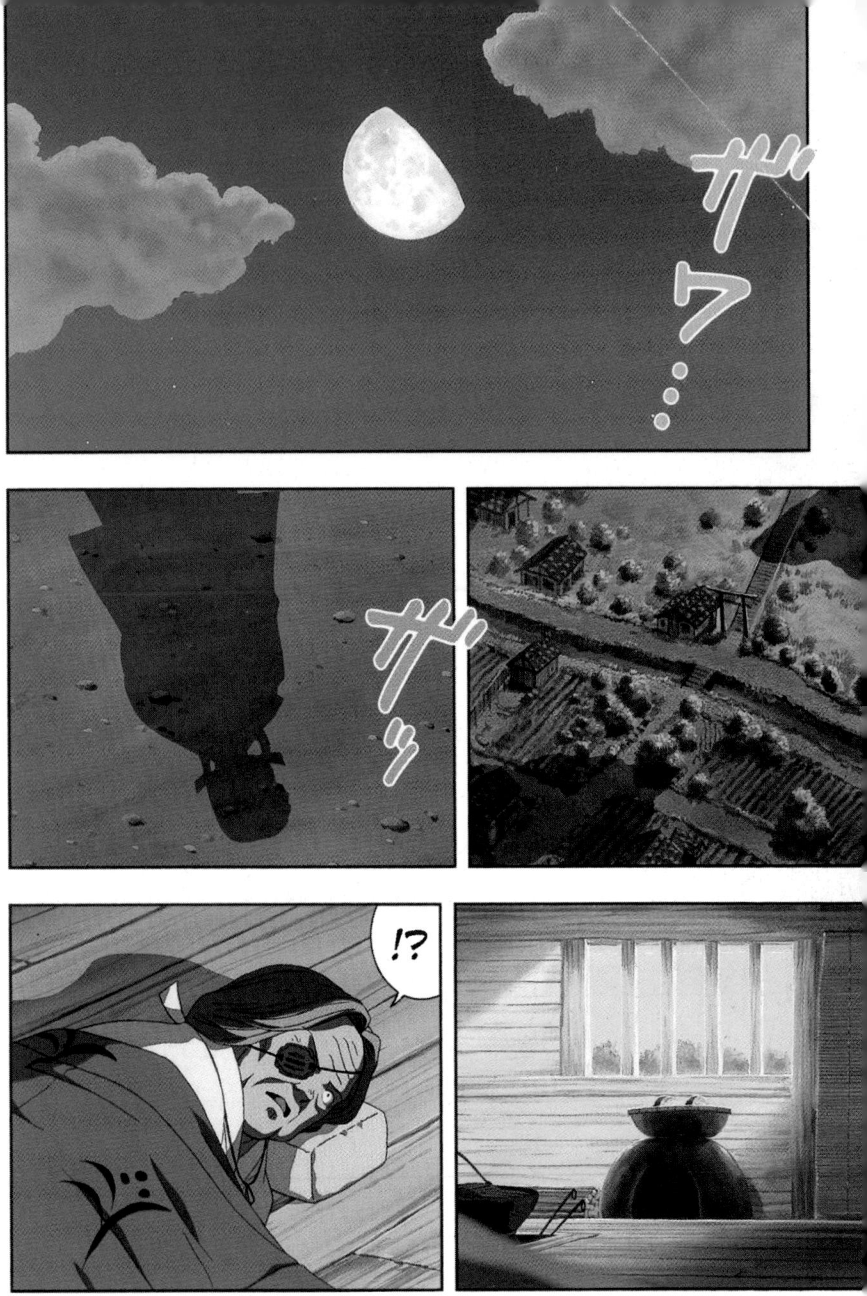
ザワ…
ザッ
!?

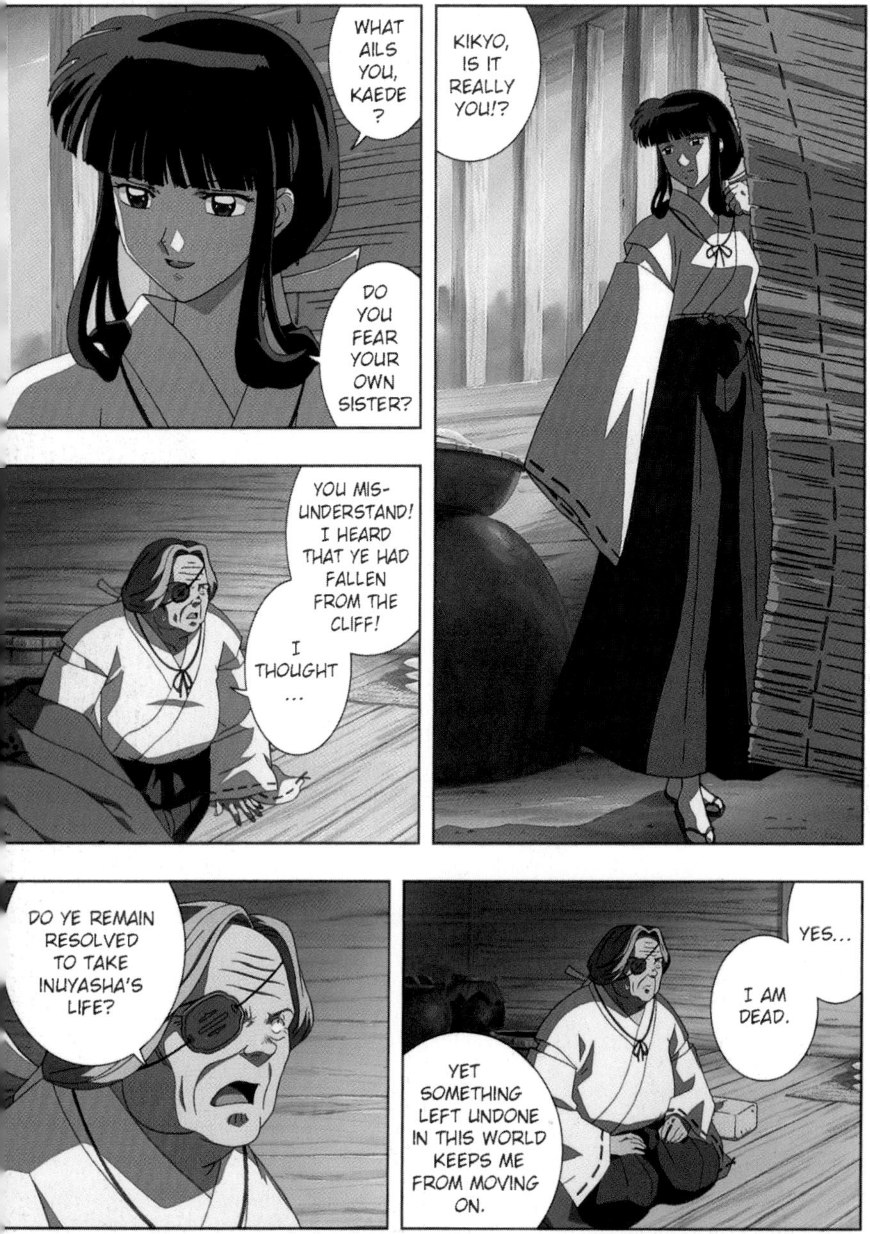
KIKYO, IS IT REALLY YOU!?
WHAT AILS YOU, KAEDE?
DO YOU FEAR YOUR OWN SISTER?
YOU MIS-UNDERSTAND! I HEARD THAT YE HAD FALLEN FROM THE CLIFF!
I THOUGHT...
YES...
I AM DEAD.
YET SOMETHING LEFT UNDONE IN THIS WORLD KEEPS ME FROM MOVING ON.
DO YE REMAIN RESOLVED TO TAKE INUYASHA'S LIFE?

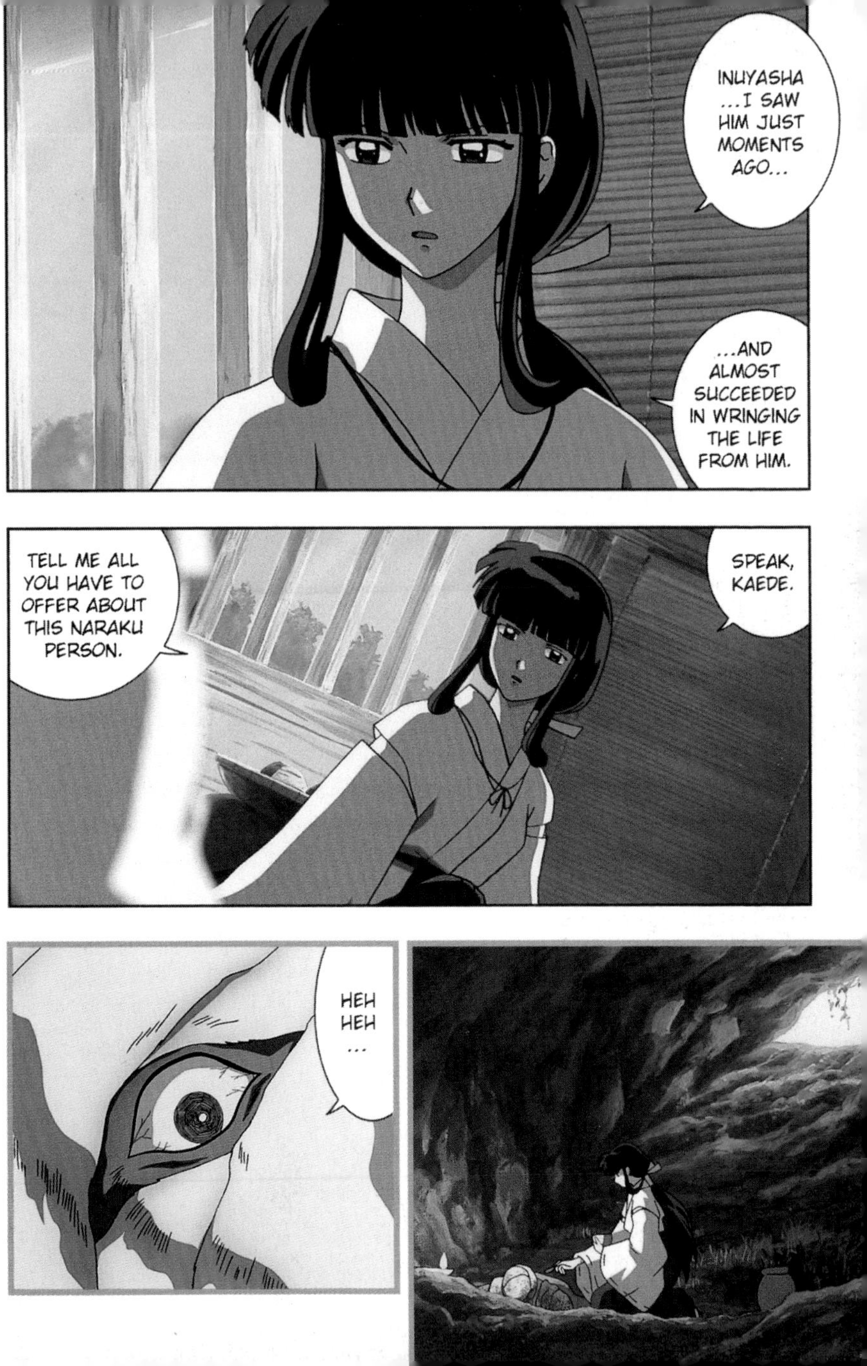
INUYASHA ...I SAW HIM JUST MOMENTS AGO...
...AND ALMOST SUCCEEDED IN WRINGING THE LIFE FROM HIM.
SPEAK, KAEDE.
TELL ME ALL YOU HAVE TO OFFER ABOUT THIS NARAKU PERSON.
HEH HEH ...

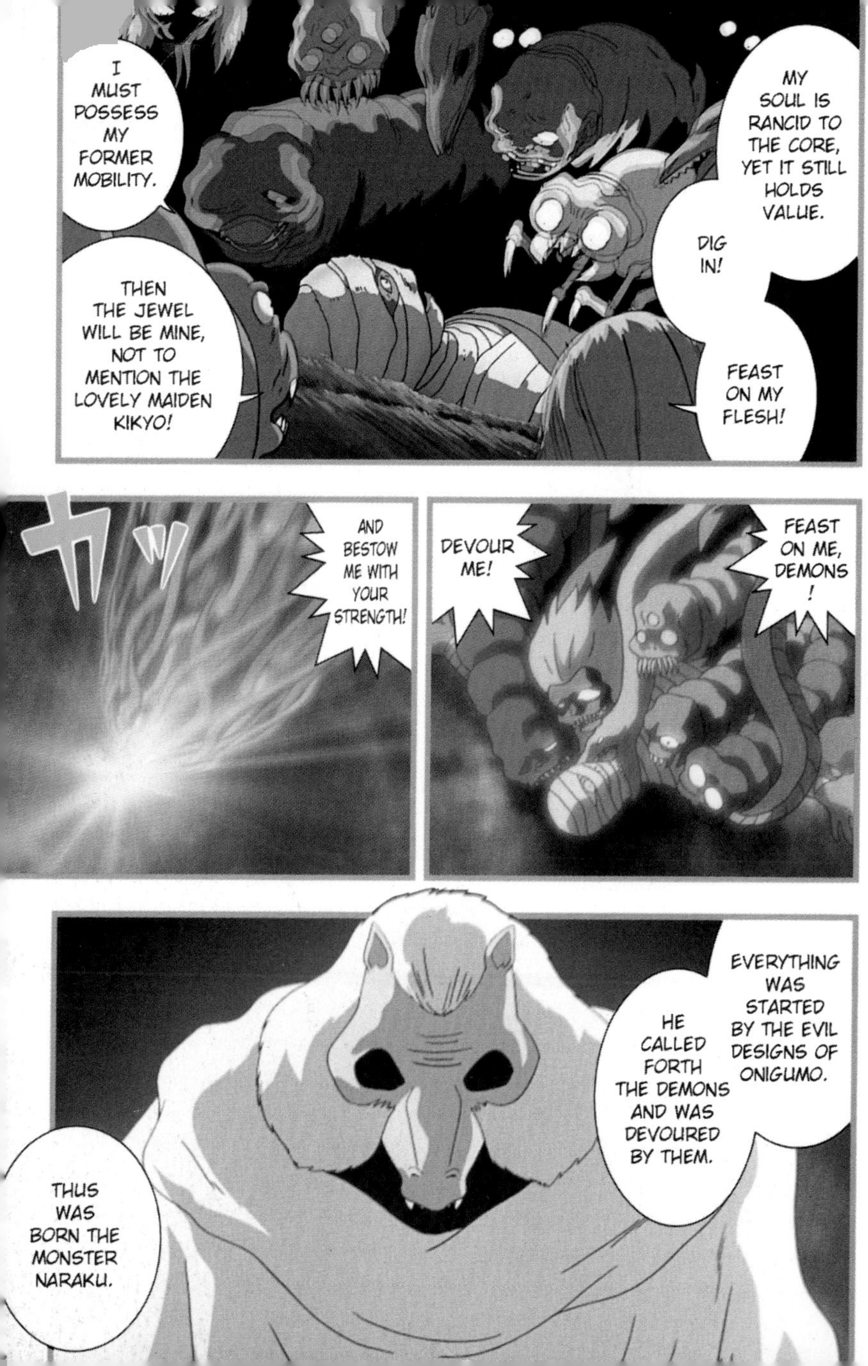
MY SOUL IS RANCID TO THE CORE, YET IT STILL HOLDS VALUE.
DIG IN!
FEAST ON MY FLESH!
I MUST POSSESS MY FORMER MOBILITY.
THEN THE JEWEL WILL BE MINE, NOT TO MENTION THE LOVELY MAIDEN KIKYO!
FEAST ON ME, DEMONS!
DEVOUR ME!
AND BESTOW ME WITH YOUR STRENGTH!
カッ
EVERYTHING WAS STARTED BY THE EVIL DESIGNS OF ONIGUMO.
HE CALLED FORTH THE DEMONS AND WAS DEVOURED BY THEM.
THUS WAS BORN THE MONSTER NARAKU.

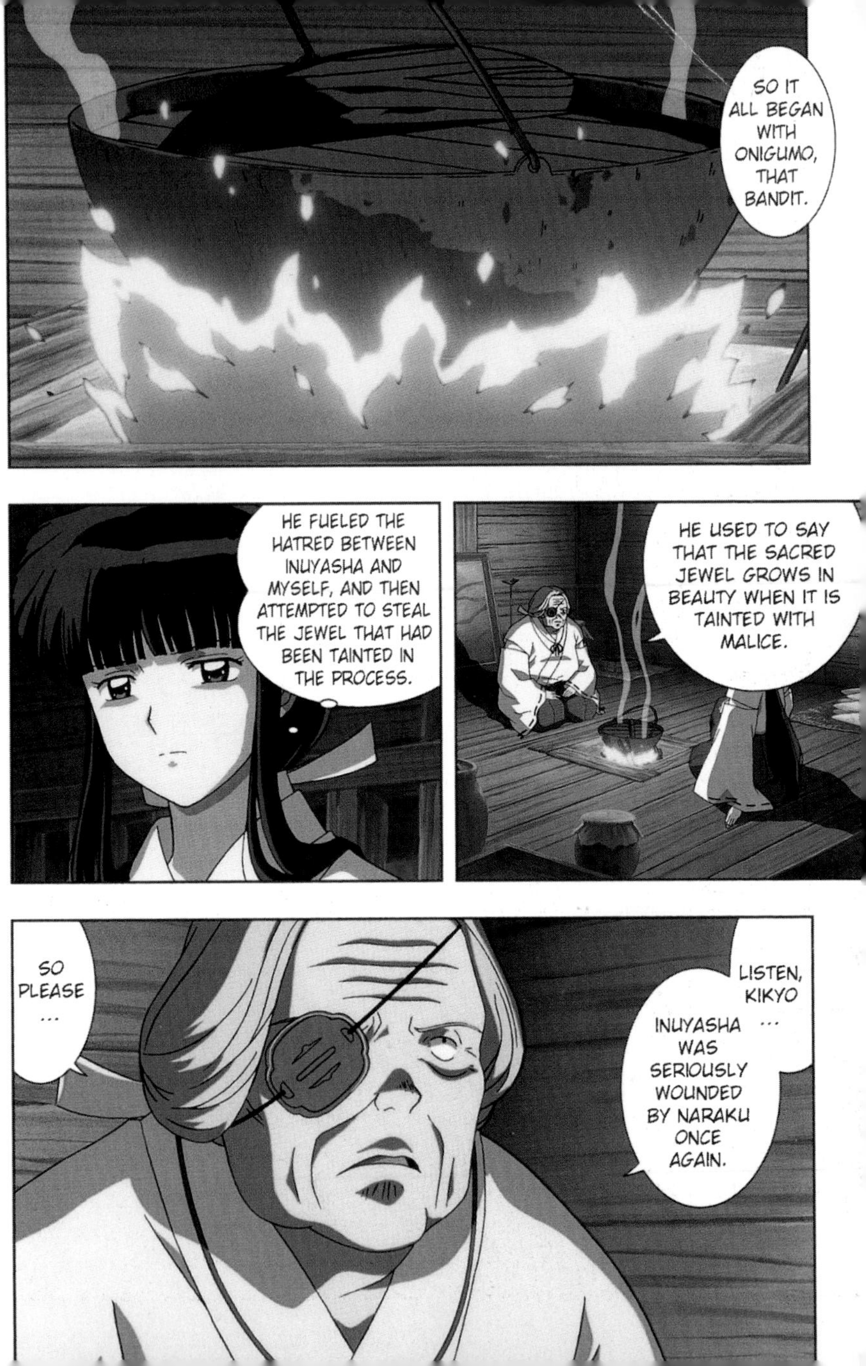
SO IT ALL BEGAN WITH ONIGUMO, THAT BANDIT.
HE USED TO SAY THAT THE SACRED JEWEL GROWS IN BEAUTY WHEN IT IS TAINTED WITH MALICE.
HE FUELED THE HATRED BETWEEN INUYASHA AND MYSELF, AND THEN ATTEMPTED TO STEAL THE JEWEL THAT HAD BEEN TAINTED IN THE PROCESS.
LISTEN, KIKYO ... INUYASHA WAS SERIOUSLY WOUNDED BY NARAKU ONCE AGAIN.
SO PLEASE ...

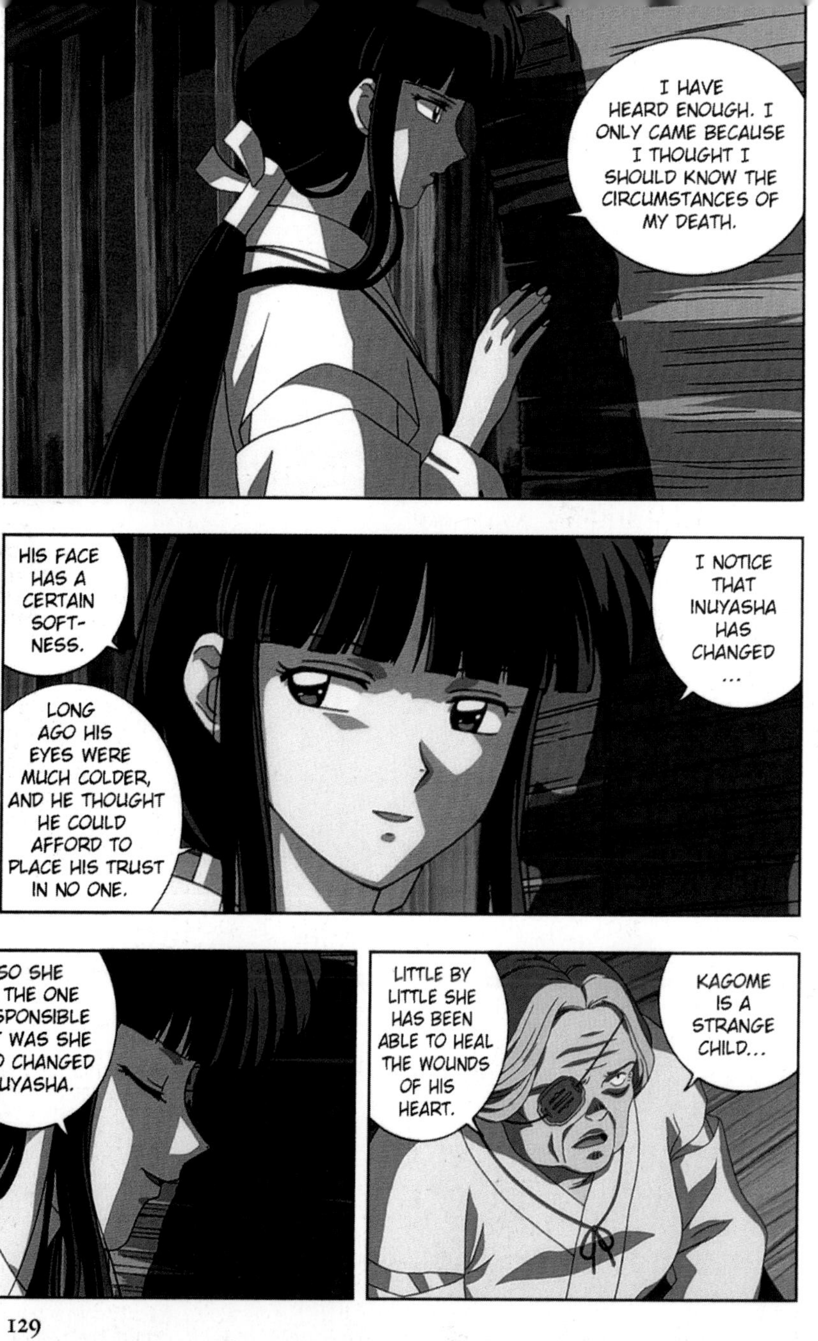
I HAVE HEARD ENOUGH. I ONLY CAME BECAUSE I THOUGHT I SHOULD KNOW THE CIRCUMSTANCES OF MY DEATH.
I NOTICE THAT INUYASHA HAS CHANGED ...
HIS FACE HAS A CERTAIN SOFT-NESS.
LONG AGO HIS EYES WERE MUCH COLDER, AND HE THOUGHT HE COULD AFFORD TO PLACE HIS TRUST IN NO ONE.
KAGOME IS A STRANGE CHILD...
LITTLE BY LITTLE SHE HAS BEEN ABLE TO HEAL THE WOUNDS OF HIS HEART.
SO SHE IS THE ONE RESPONSIBLE ...IT WAS SHE WHO CHANGED INUYASHA.

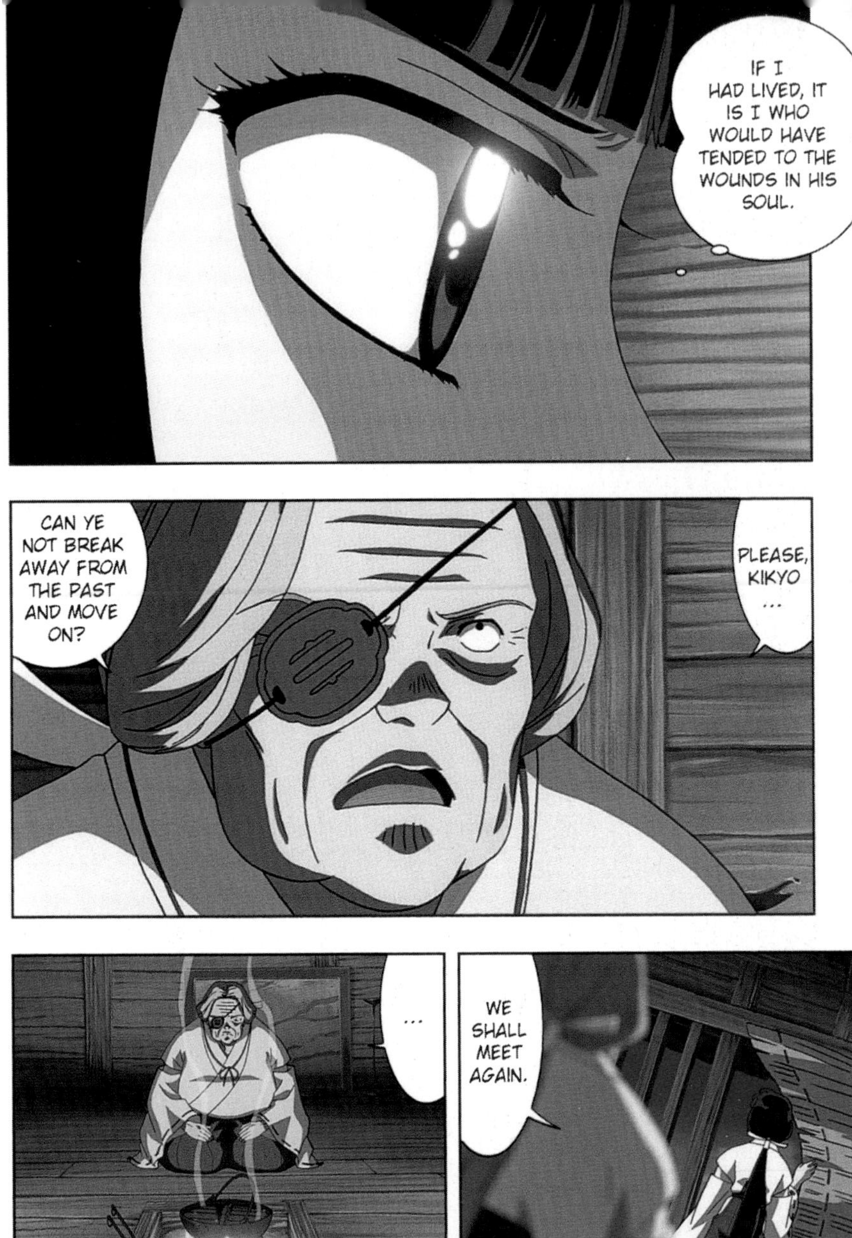
IF I HAD LIVED, IT IS I WHO WOULD HAVE TENDED TO THE WOUNDS IN HIS SOUL.
PLEASE, KIKYO ...
CAN YE NOT BREAK AWAY FROM THE PAST AND MOVE ON?
WE SHALL MEET AGAIN.
...

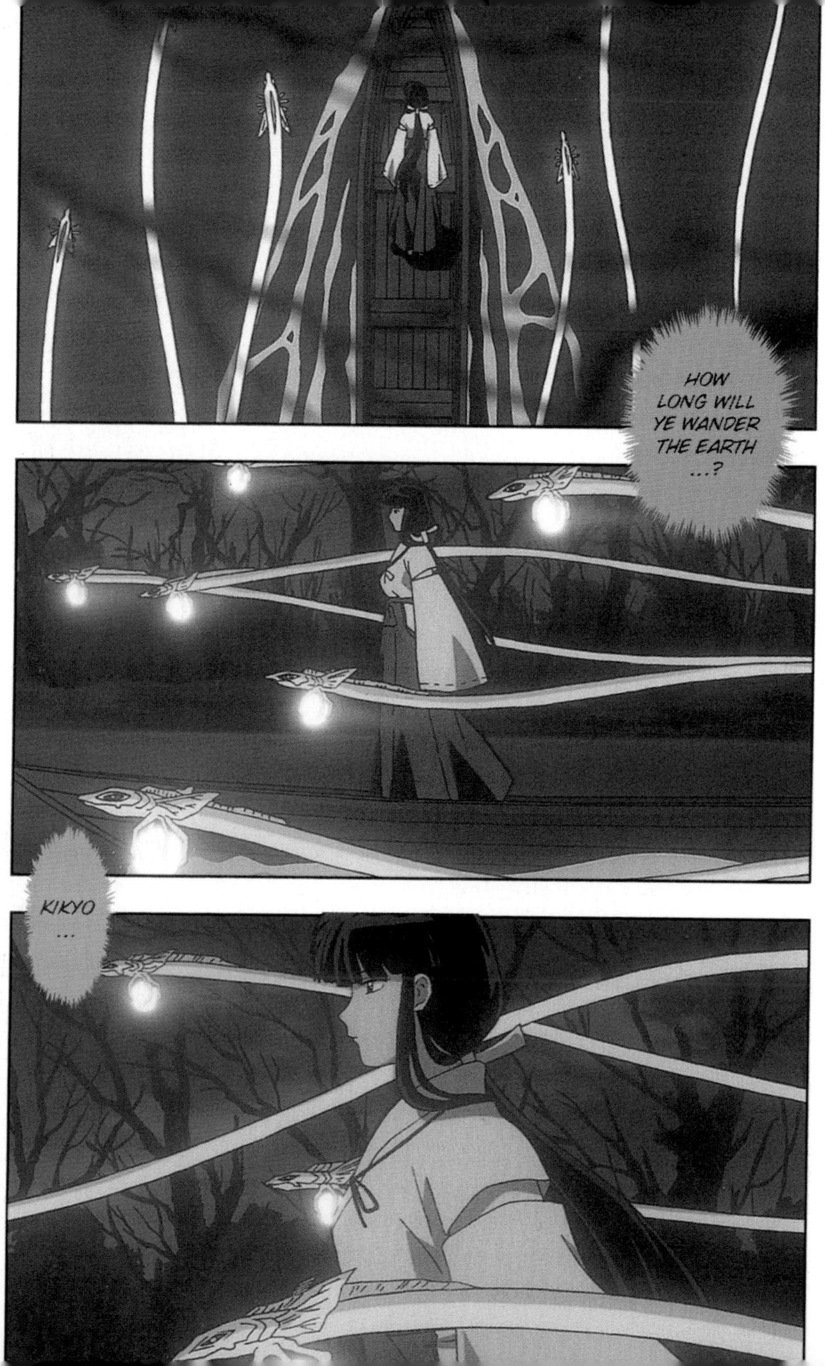
HOW LONG WILL YE WANDER THE EARTH ...?
KIKYO ...

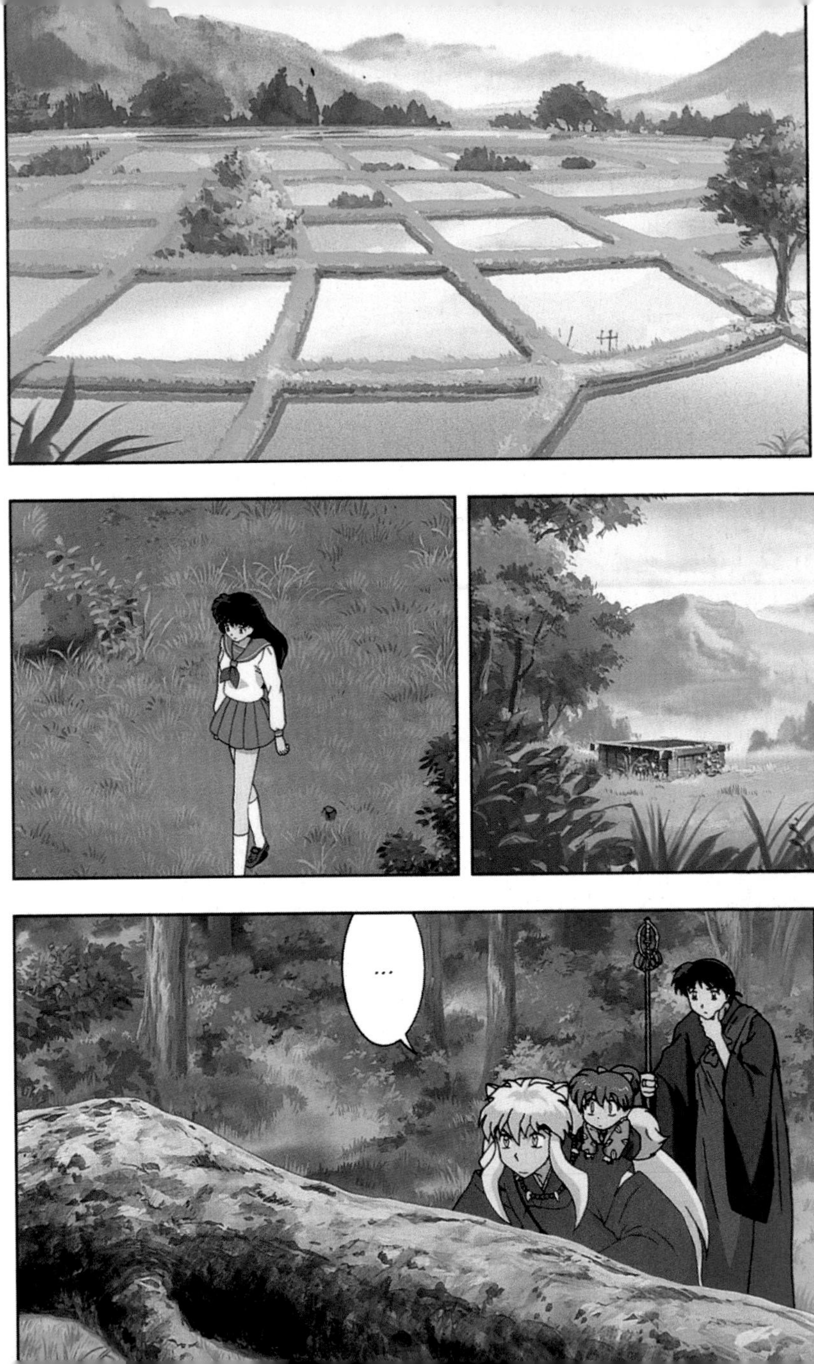
...

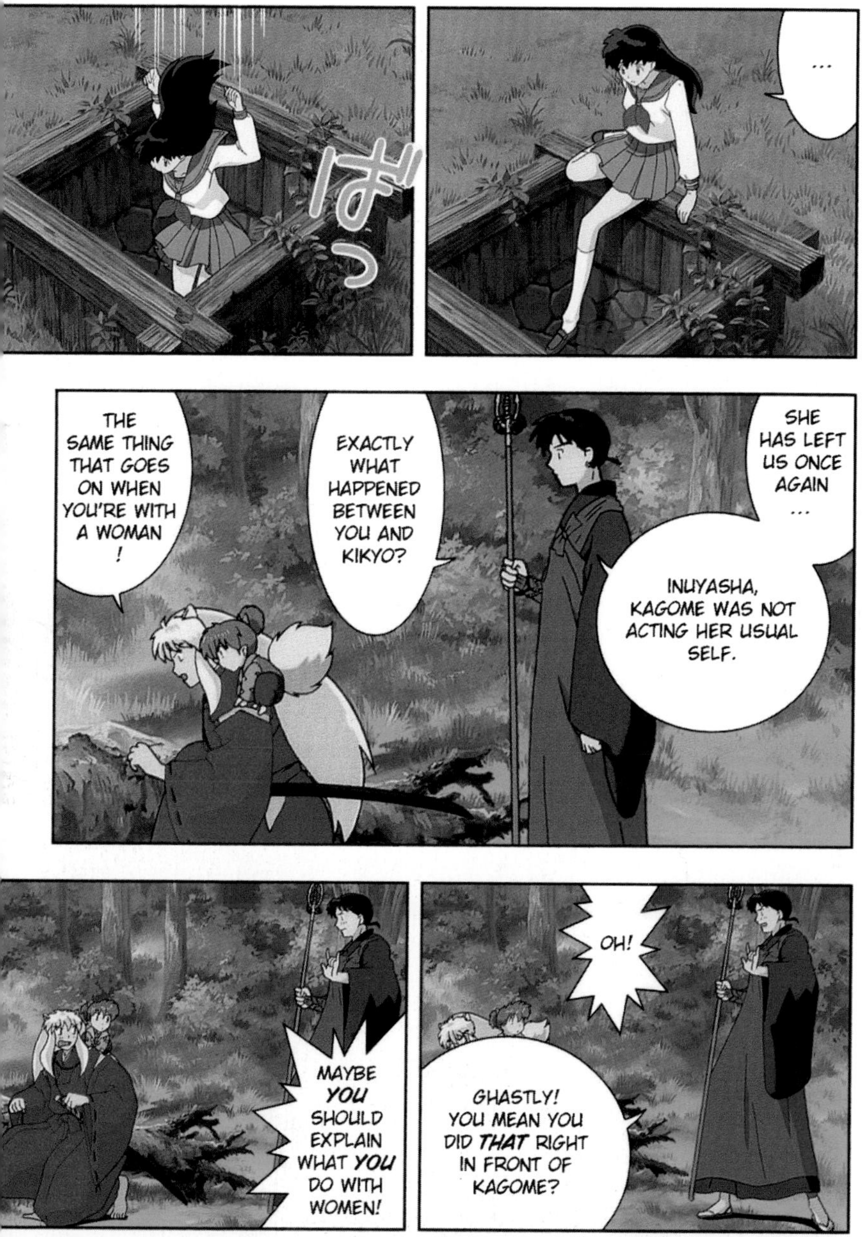
ぱっ
...
SHE HAS LEFT US ONCE AGAIN ...
INUYASHA, KAGOME WAS NOT ACTING HER USUAL SELF.
EXACTLY WHAT HAPPENED BETWEEN YOU AND KIKYO?
THE SAME THING THAT GOES ON WHEN YOU'RE WITH A WOMAN!
MAYBE *YOU* SHOULD EXPLAIN WHAT *YOU* DO WITH WOMEN!
OH!
GHASTLY! YOU MEAN YOU DID *THAT* RIGHT IN FRONT OF KAGOME?

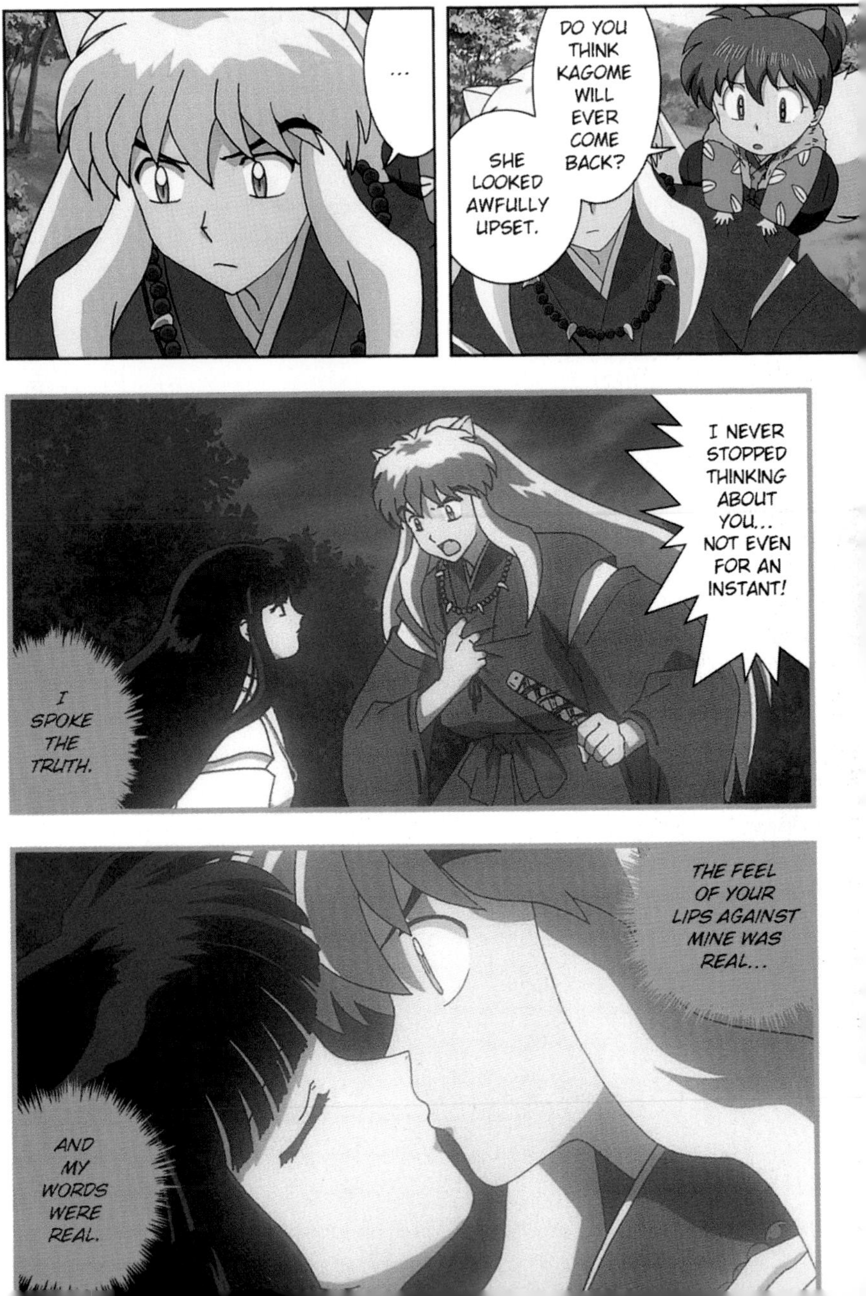
DO YOU THINK KAGOME WILL EVER COME BACK?
SHE LOOKED AWFULLY UPSET.
...
I NEVER STOPPED THINKING ABOUT YOU... NOT EVEN FOR AN INSTANT!
I SPOKE THE TRUTH.
THE FEEL OF YOUR LIPS AGAINST MINE WAS REAL...
AND MY WORDS WERE REAL.

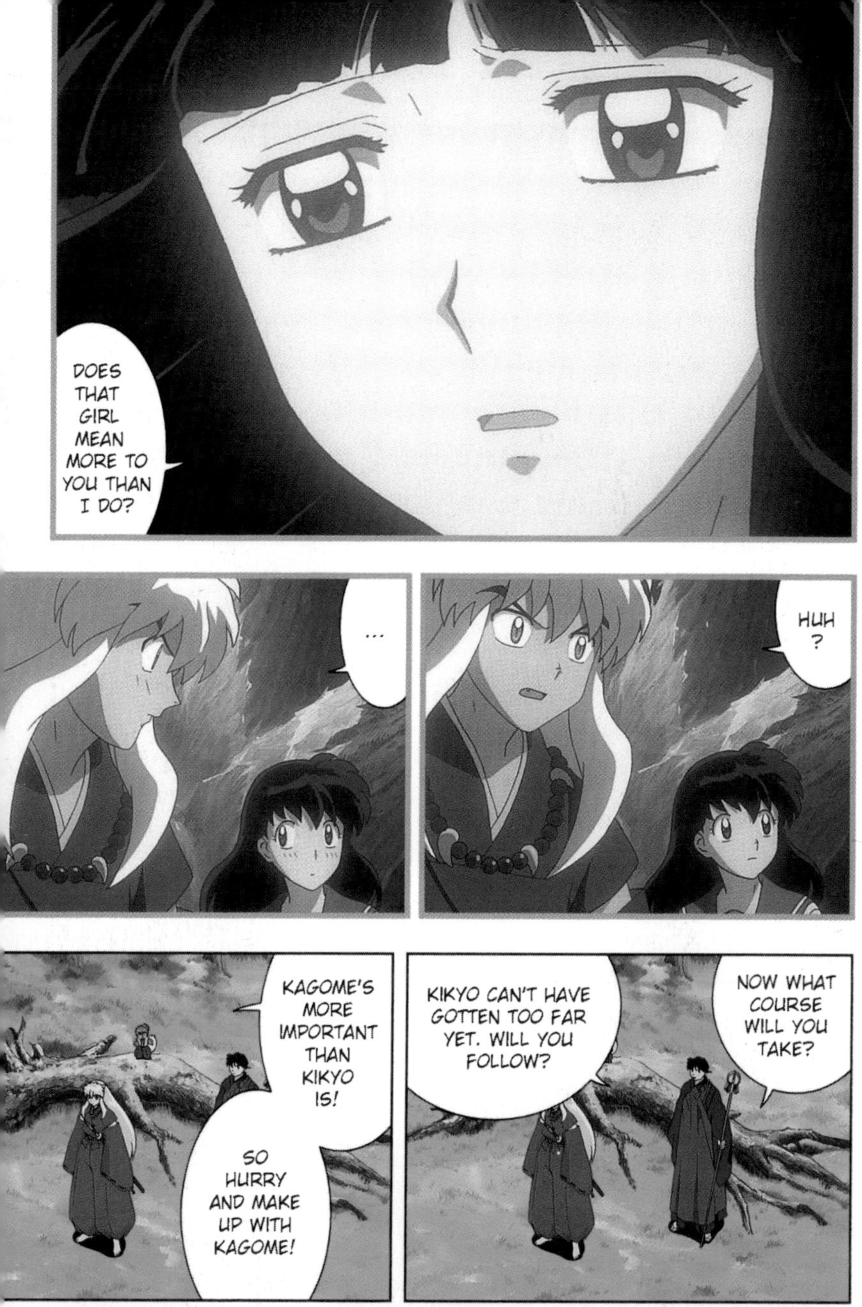
DOES THAT GIRL MEAN MORE TO YOU THAN I DO?
HUH?
...
NOW WHAT COURSE WILL YOU TAKE?
KIKYO CAN'T HAVE GOTTEN TOO FAR YET. WILL YOU FOLLOW?
KAGOME'S MORE IMPORTANT THAN KIKYO IS!
SO HURRY AND MAKE UP WITH KAGOME!

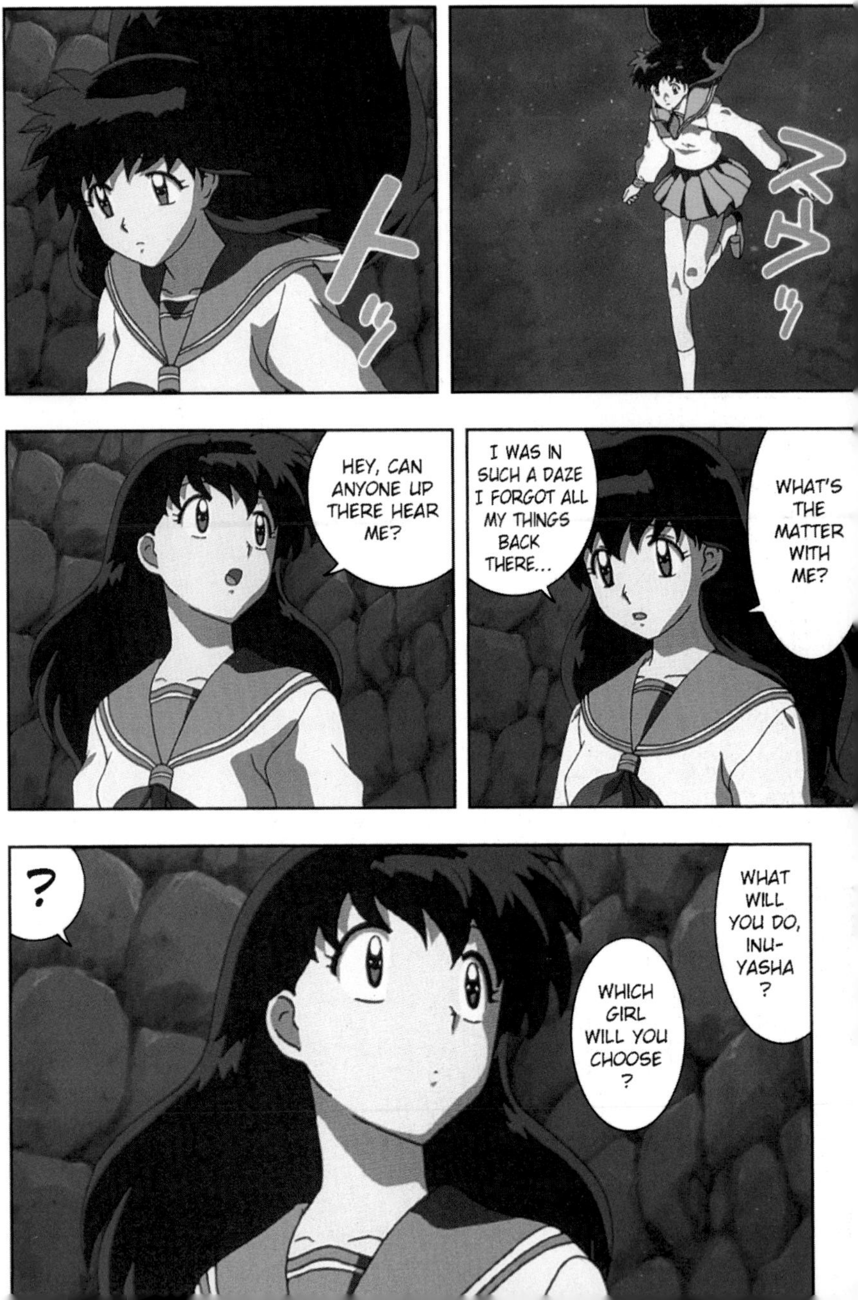

スウッ
トッ
WHAT'S THE MATTER WITH ME?
I WAS IN SUCH A DAZE I FORGOT ALL MY THINGS BACK THERE...
HEY, CAN ANYONE UP THERE HEAR ME?
WHAT WILL YOU DO, INU-YASHA?
WHICH GIRL WILL YOU CHOOSE?
?

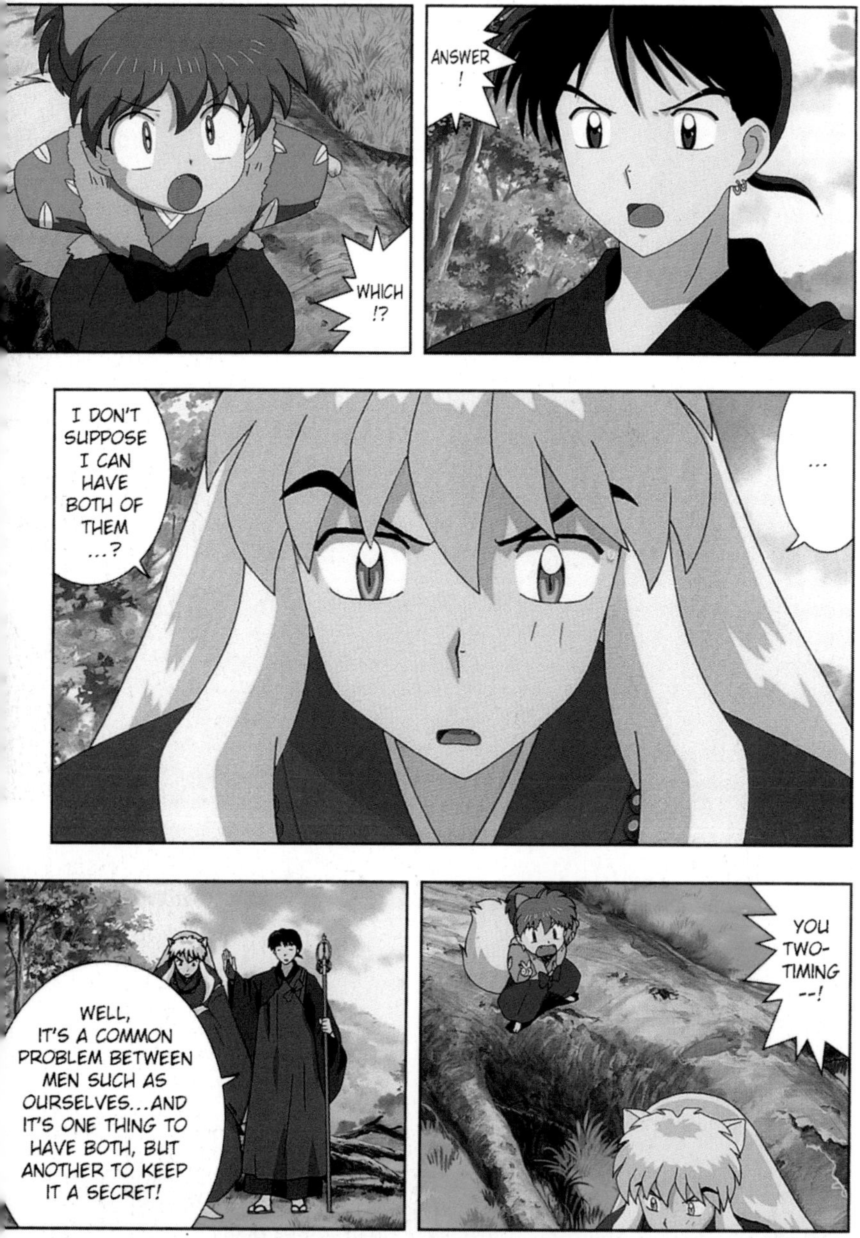

ANSWER!
WHICH!?
...
I DON'T SUPPOSE I CAN HAVE BOTH OF THEM...?
YOU TWO-TIMING--!
WELL, IT'S A COMMON PROBLEM BETWEEN MEN SUCH AS OURSELVES...AND IT'S ONE THING TO HAVE BOTH, BUT ANOTHER TO KEEP IT A SECRET!

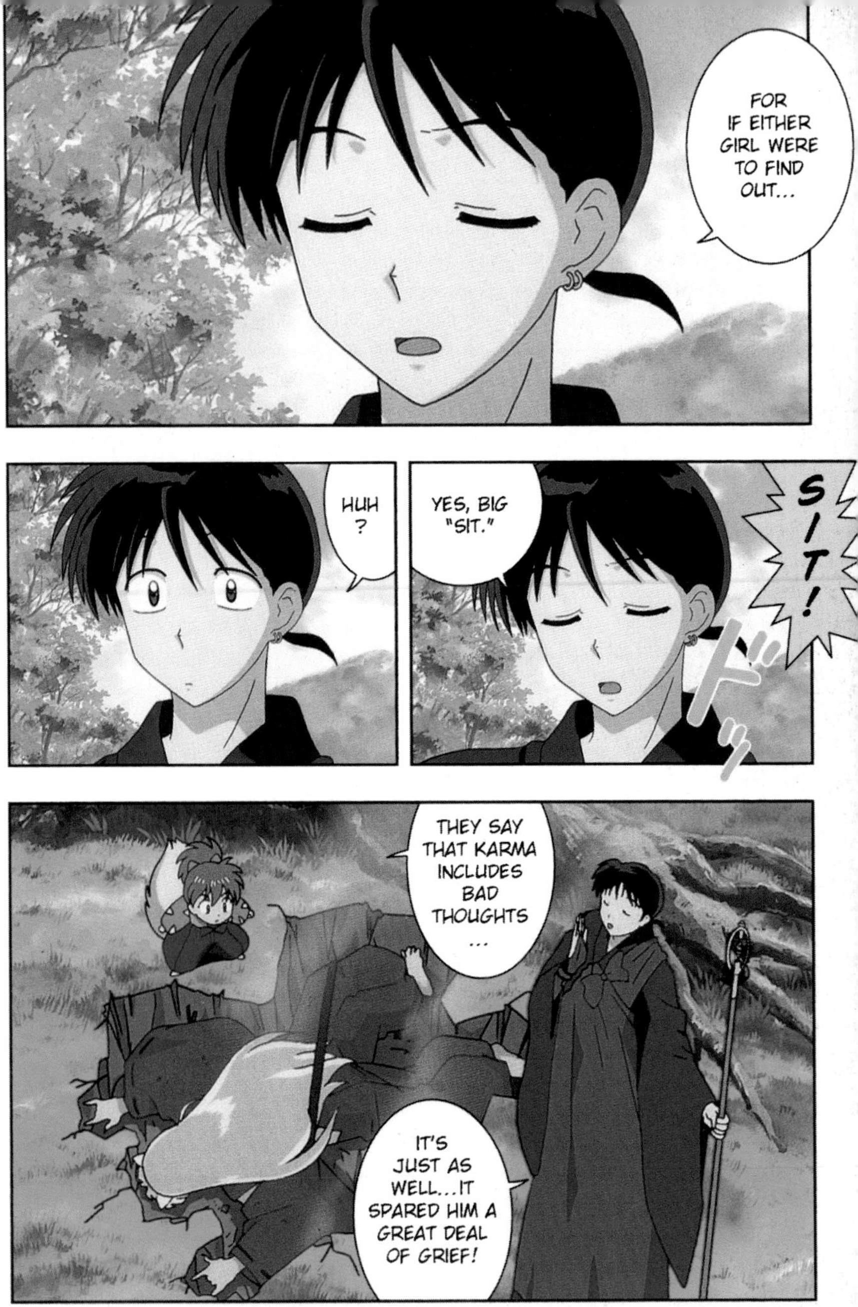
FOR IF EITHER GIRL WERE TO FIND OUT...
YES, BIG "SIT."
SIT!
HUH ?
THEY SAY THAT KARMA INCLUDES BAD THOUGHTS ...
IT'S JUST AS WELL...IT SPARED HIM A GREAT DEAL OF GRIEF!

24
Enter Sango, the Demon Slayer

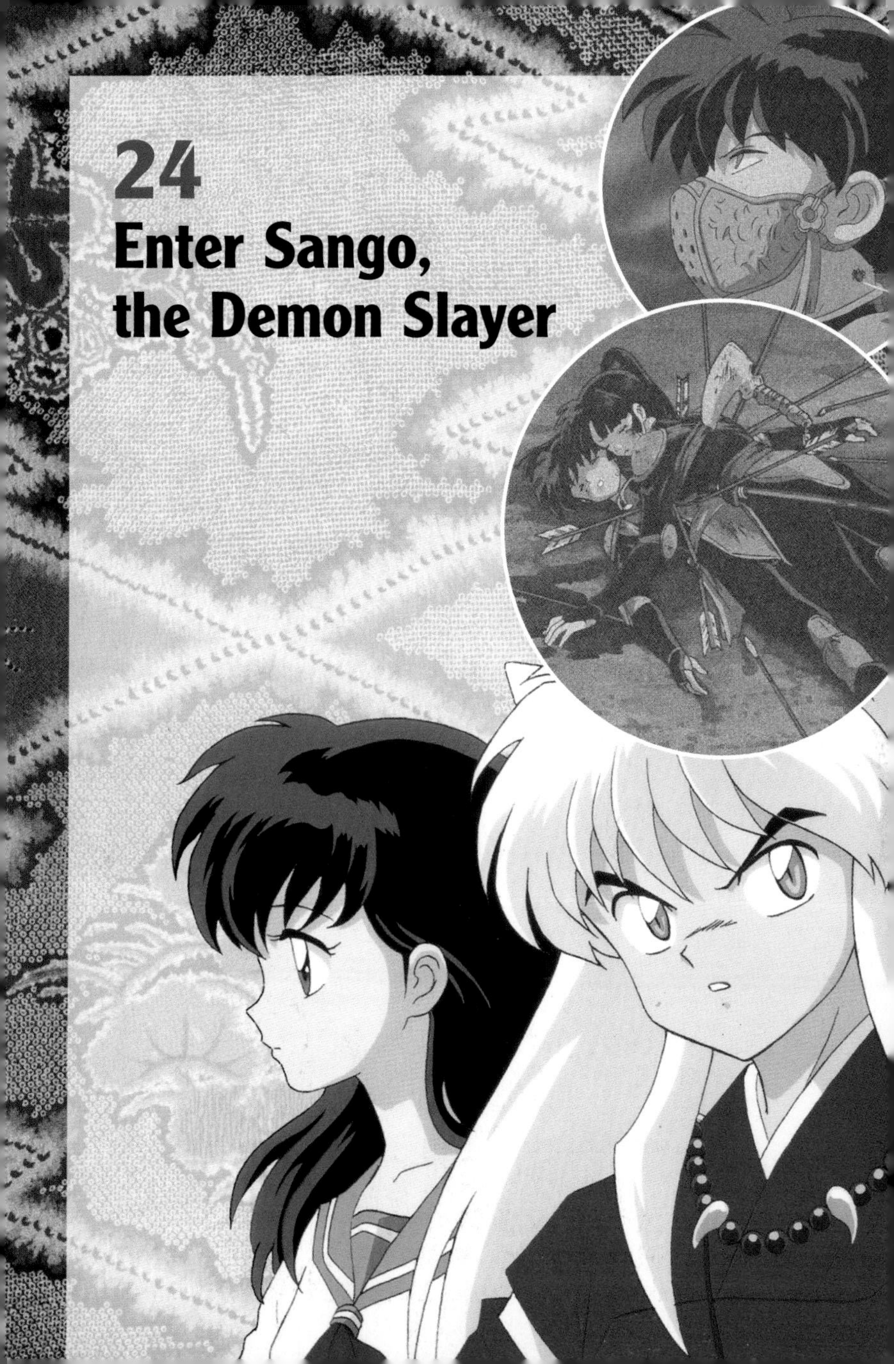

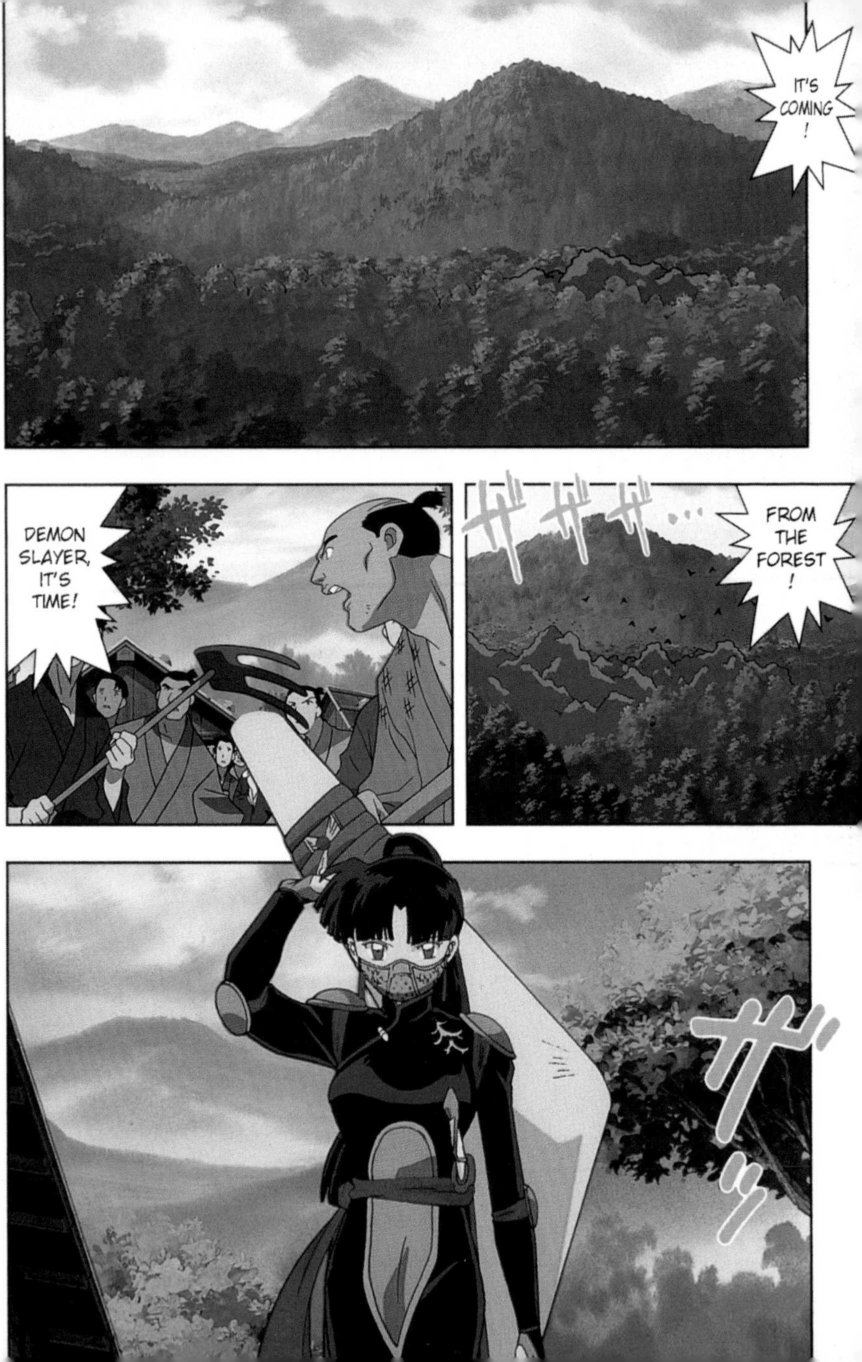
IT'S COMING!
FROM THE FOREST!
ザザザ…
DEMON SLAYER, IT'S TIME!
ザッ

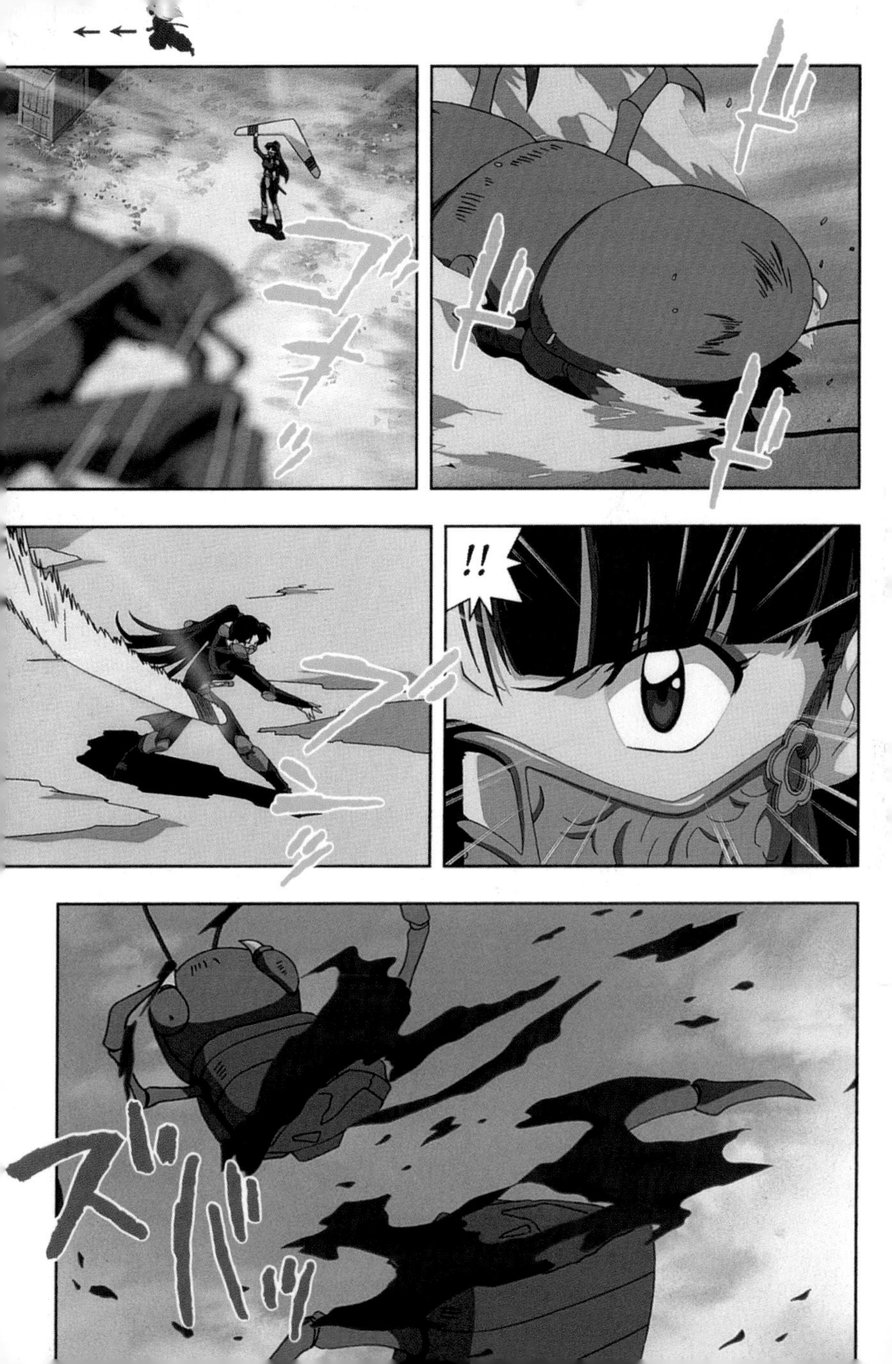
!!
ズバッ

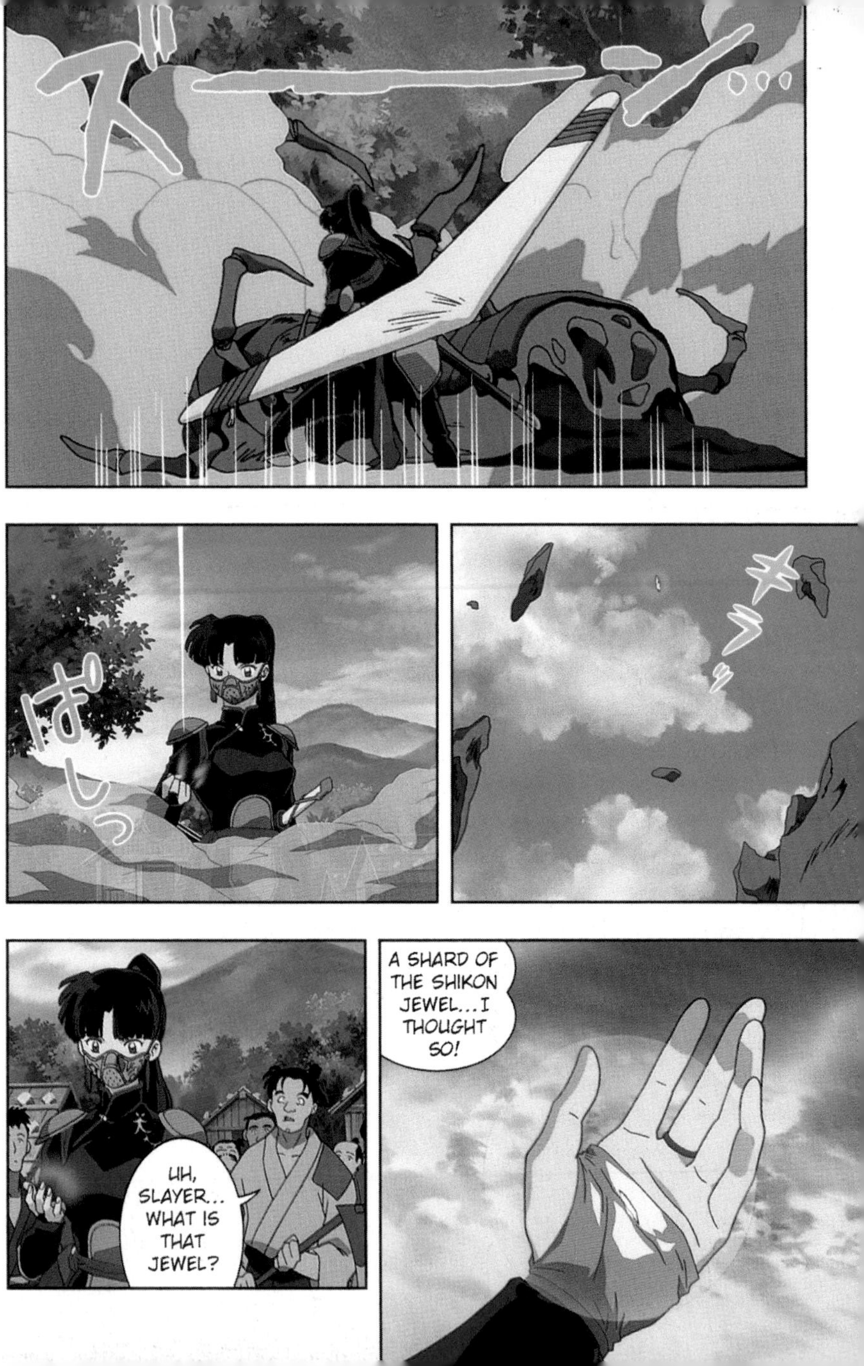
ズーーン…
キラッ
ぱしっ
A SHARD OF THE SHIKON JEWEL...I THOUGHT SO!
UH, SLAYER... WHAT IS THAT JEWEL?

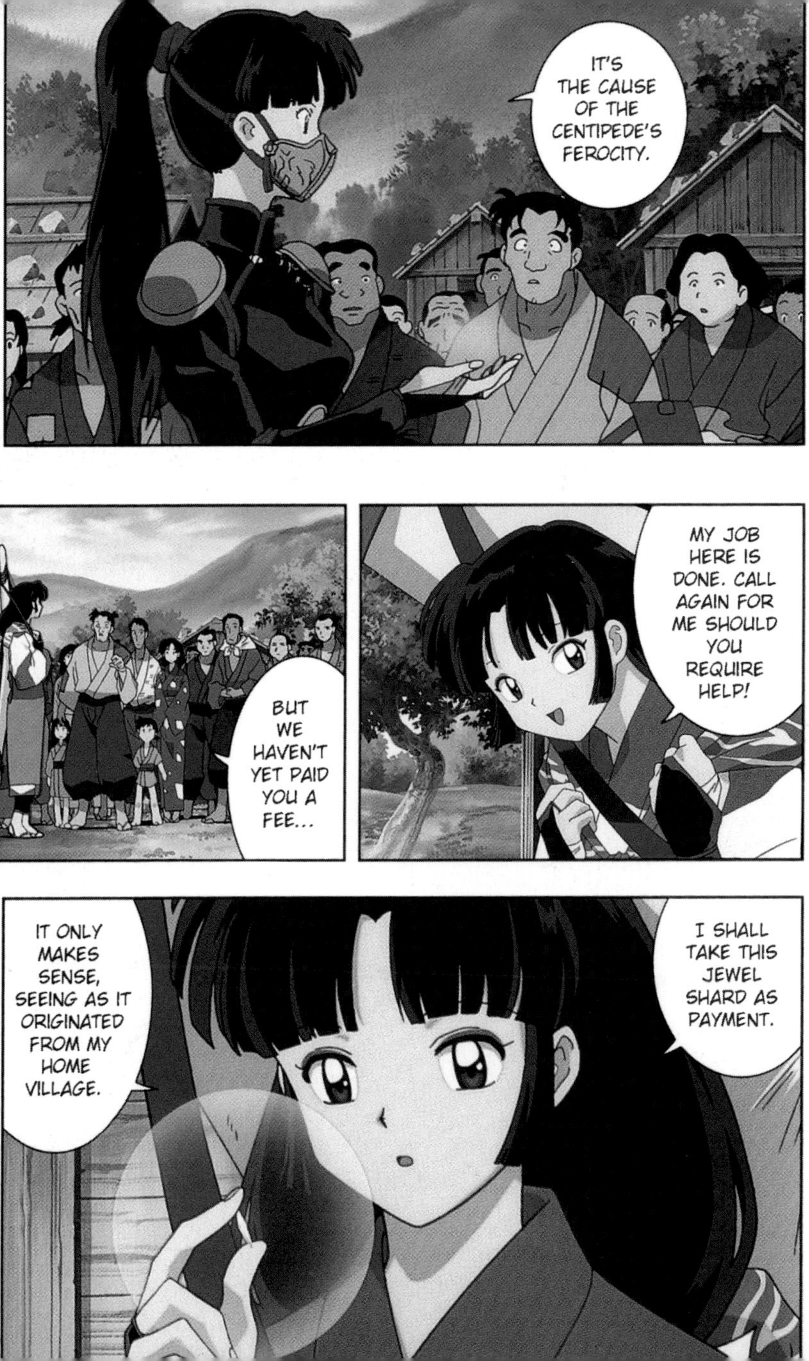
IT'S THE CAUSE OF THE CENTIPEDE'S FEROCITY.
MY JOB HERE IS DONE. CALL AGAIN FOR ME SHOULD YOU REQUIRE HELP!
BUT WE HAVEN'T YET PAID YOU A FEE...
I SHALL TAKE THIS JEWEL SHARD AS PAYMENT.
IT ONLY MAKES SENSE, SEEING AS IT ORIGINATED FROM MY HOME VILLAGE.

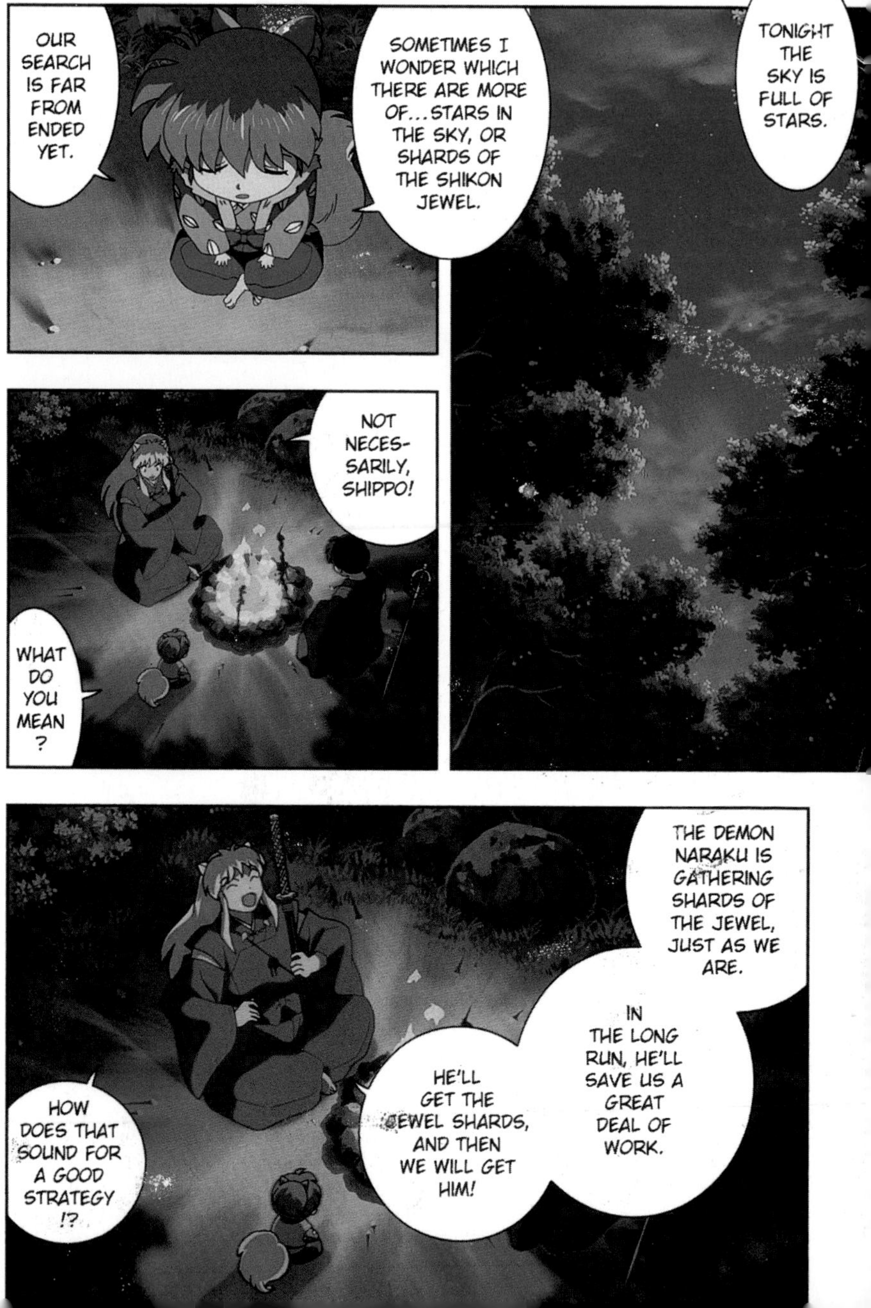
TONIGHT THE SKY IS FULL OF STARS.
SOMETIMES I WONDER WHICH THERE ARE MORE OF... STARS IN THE SKY, OR SHARDS OF THE SHIKON JEWEL.
OUR SEARCH IS FAR FROM ENDED YET.
NOT NECES-SARILY, SHIPPO!
WHAT DO YOU MEAN ?
THE DEMON NARAKU IS GATHERING SHARDS OF THE JEWEL, JUST AS WE ARE.
IN THE LONG RUN, HE'LL SAVE US A GREAT DEAL OF WORK.
HE'LL GET THE JEWEL SHARDS, AND THEN WE WILL GET HIM!
HOW DOES THAT SOUND FOR A GOOD STRATEGY !?

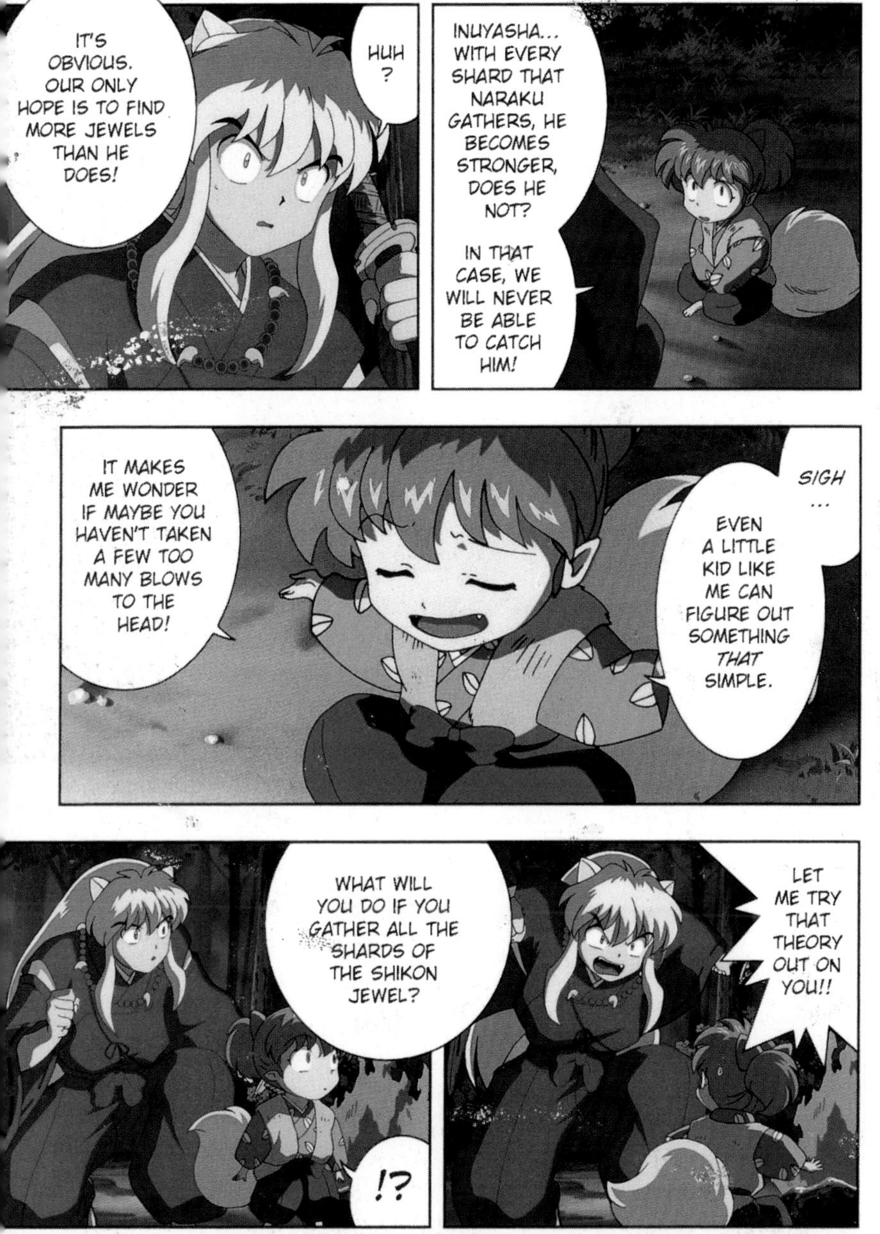
INUYASHA... WITH EVERY SHARD THAT NARAKU GATHERS, HE BECOMES STRONGER, DOES HE NOT?
IN THAT CASE, WE WILL NEVER BE ABLE TO CATCH HIM!
HUH?
IT'S OBVIOUS. OUR ONLY HOPE IS TO FIND MORE JEWELS THAN HE DOES!
SIGH...
EVEN A LITTLE KID LIKE ME CAN FIGURE OUT SOMETHING *THAT* SIMPLE.
IT MAKES ME WONDER IF MAYBE YOU HAVEN'T TAKEN A FEW TOO MANY BLOWS TO THE HEAD!
LET ME TRY THAT THEORY OUT ON YOU!!
WHAT WILL YOU DO IF YOU GATHER ALL THE SHARDS OF THE SHIKON JEWEL?
!?

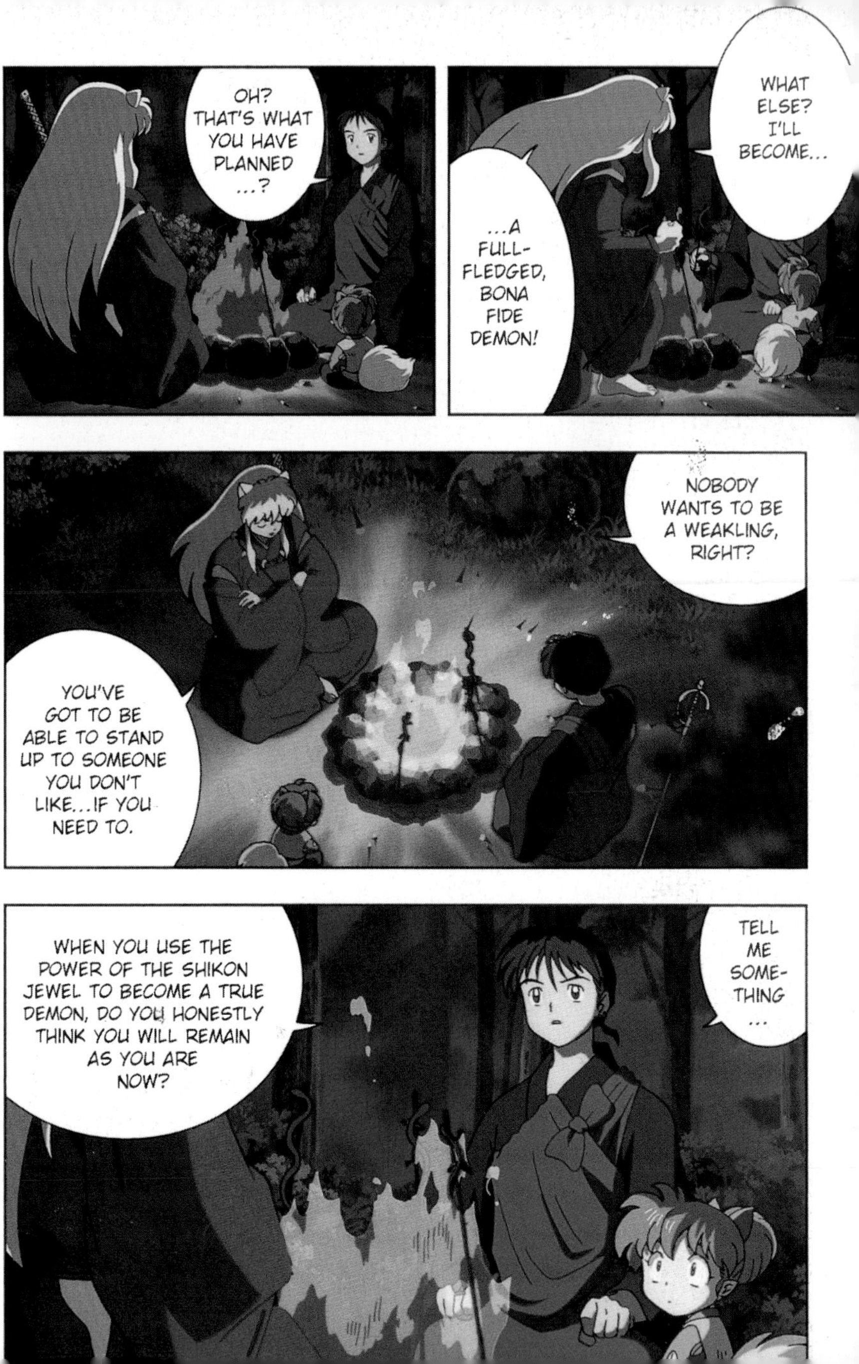
WHAT ELSE? I'LL BECOME...
...A FULL-FLEDGED, BONA FIDE DEMON!
OH? THAT'S WHAT YOU HAVE PLANNED ...?
NOBODY WANTS TO BE A WEAKLING, RIGHT?
YOU'VE GOT TO BE ABLE TO STAND UP TO SOMEONE YOU DON'T LIKE...IF YOU NEED TO.
TELL ME SOME-THING ...
WHEN YOU USE THE POWER OF THE SHIKON JEWEL TO BECOME A TRUE DEMON, DO YOU HONESTLY THINK YOU WILL REMAIN AS YOU ARE NOW?

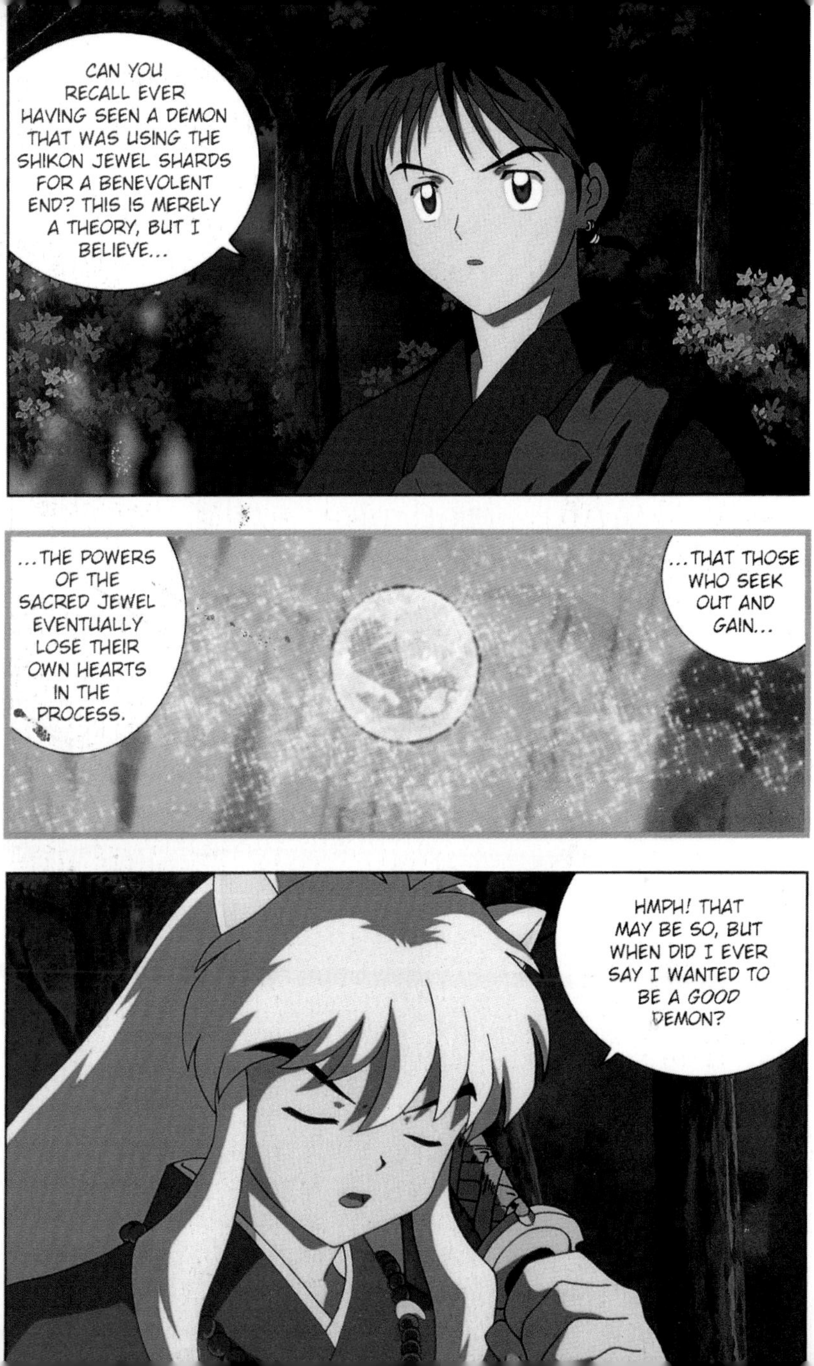
CAN YOU RECALL EVER HAVING SEEN A DEMON THAT WAS USING THE SHIKON JEWEL SHARDS FOR A BENEVOLENT END? THIS IS MERELY A THEORY, BUT I BELIEVE...
...THAT THOSE WHO SEEK OUT AND GAIN...
...THE POWERS OF THE SACRED JEWEL EVENTUALLY LOSE THEIR OWN HEARTS IN THE PROCESS.
HMPH! THAT MAY BE SO, BUT WHEN DID I EVER SAY I WANTED TO BE A *GOOD* DEMON?

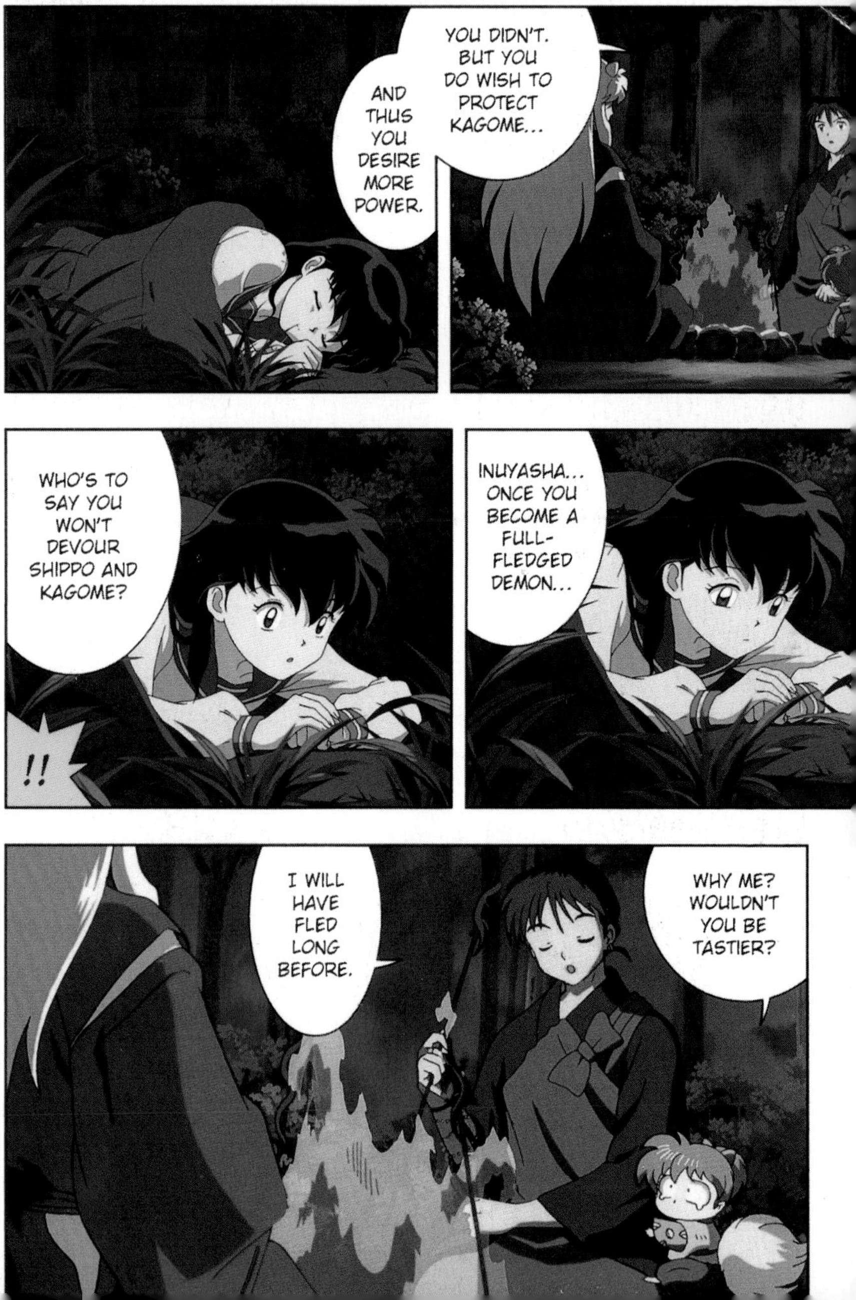
YOU DIDN'T. BUT YOU DO WISH TO PROTECT KAGOME...
AND THUS YOU DESIRE MORE POWER.
INUYASHA... ONCE YOU BECOME A FULL-FLEDGED DEMON...
WHO'S TO SAY YOU WON'T DEVOUR SHIPPO AND KAGOME?
!!
WHY ME? WOULDN'T YOU BE TASTIER?
I WILL HAVE FLED LONG BEFORE.

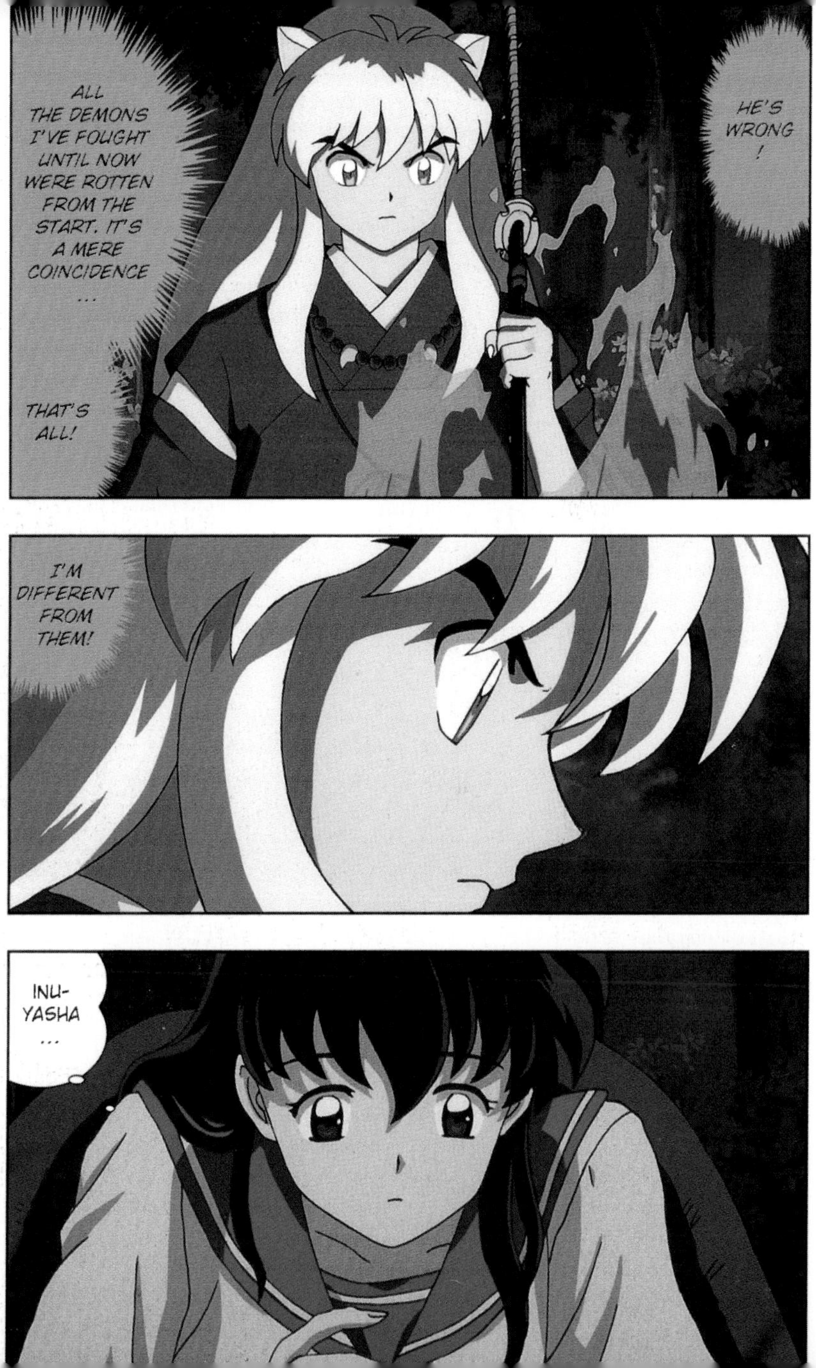
HE'S WRONG!
ALL THE DEMONS I'VE FOUGHT UNTIL NOW WERE ROTTEN FROM THE START. IT'S A MERE COINCIDENCE ...
THAT'S ALL!
I'M DIFFERENT FROM THEM!
INU-YASHA ...

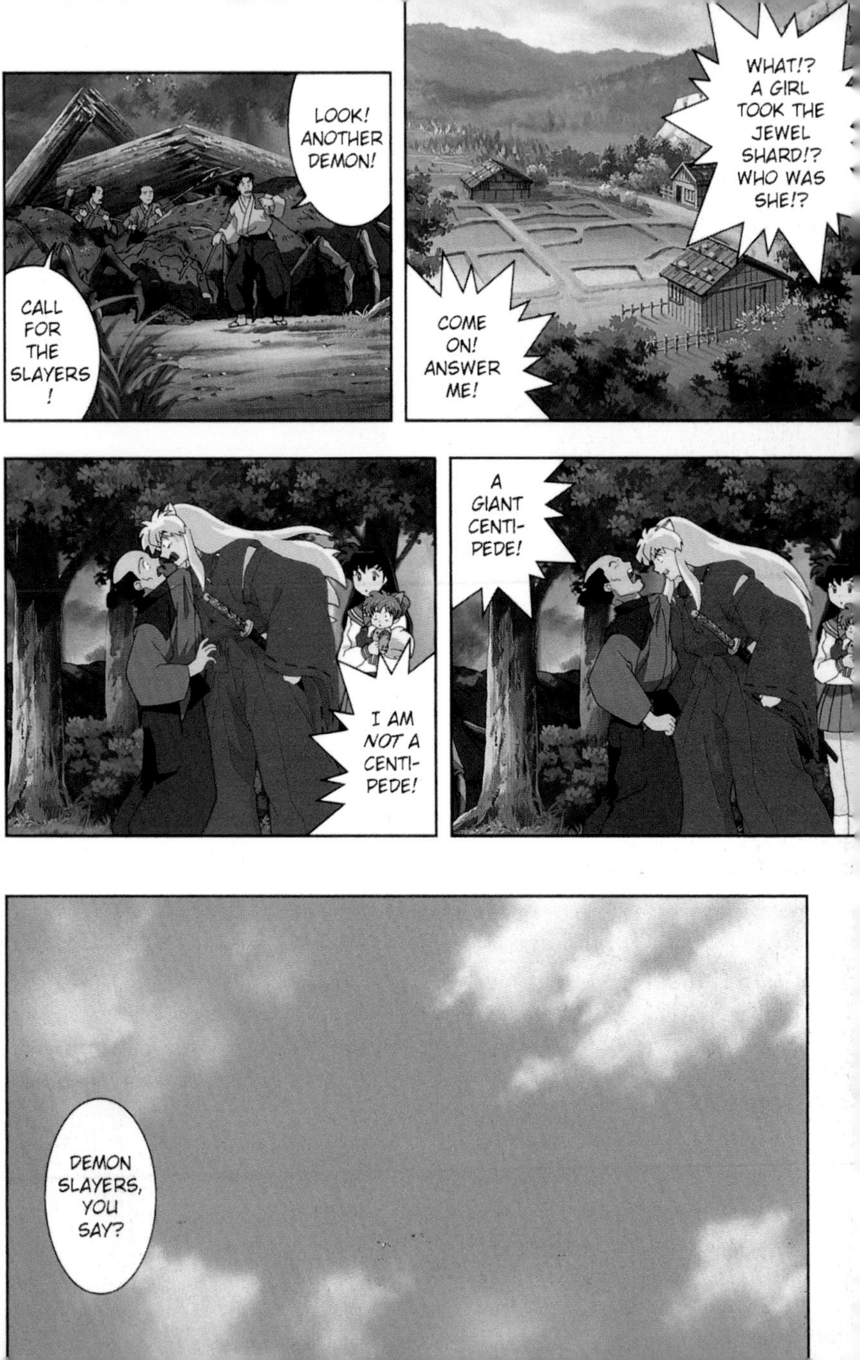
WHAT!? A GIRL TOOK THE JEWEL SHARD!? WHO WAS SHE!?
COME ON! ANSWER ME!
LOOK! ANOTHER DEMON!
CALL FOR THE SLAYERS!
A GIANT CENTIPEDE!
I AM NOT A CENTIPEDE!
DEMON SLAYERS, YOU SAY?

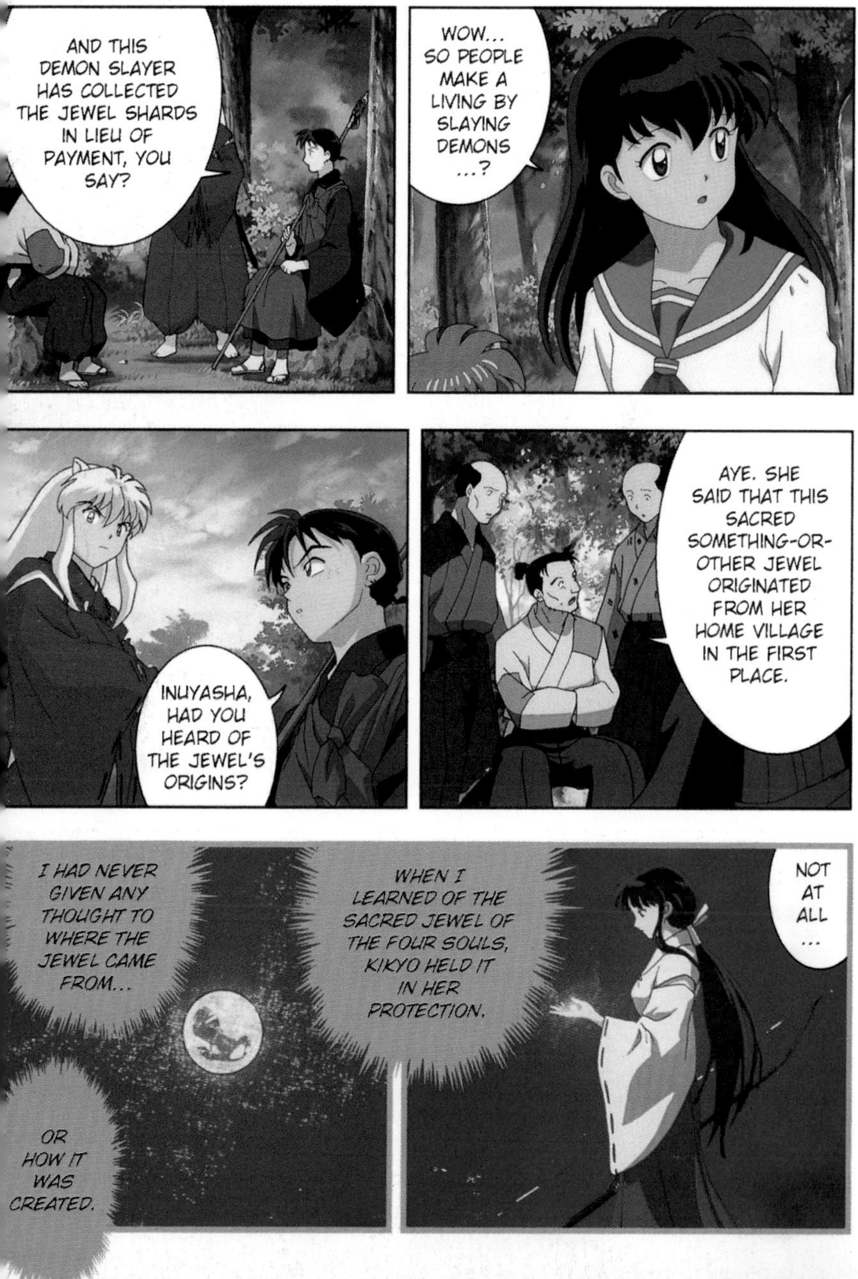
WOW... SO PEOPLE MAKE A LIVING BY SLAYING DEMONS ...?
AND THIS DEMON SLAYER HAS COLLECTED THE JEWEL SHARDS IN LIEU OF PAYMENT, YOU SAY?
AYE. SHE SAID THAT THIS SACRED SOMETHING-OR-OTHER JEWEL ORIGINATED FROM HER HOME VILLAGE IN THE FIRST PLACE.
INUYASHA, HAD YOU HEARD OF THE JEWEL'S ORIGINS?
NOT AT ALL ...
WHEN I LEARNED OF THE SACRED JEWEL OF THE FOUR SOULS, KIKYO HELD IT IN HER PROTECTION.
I HAD NEVER GIVEN ANY THOUGHT TO WHERE THE JEWEL CAME FROM...
OR HOW IT WAS CREATED.

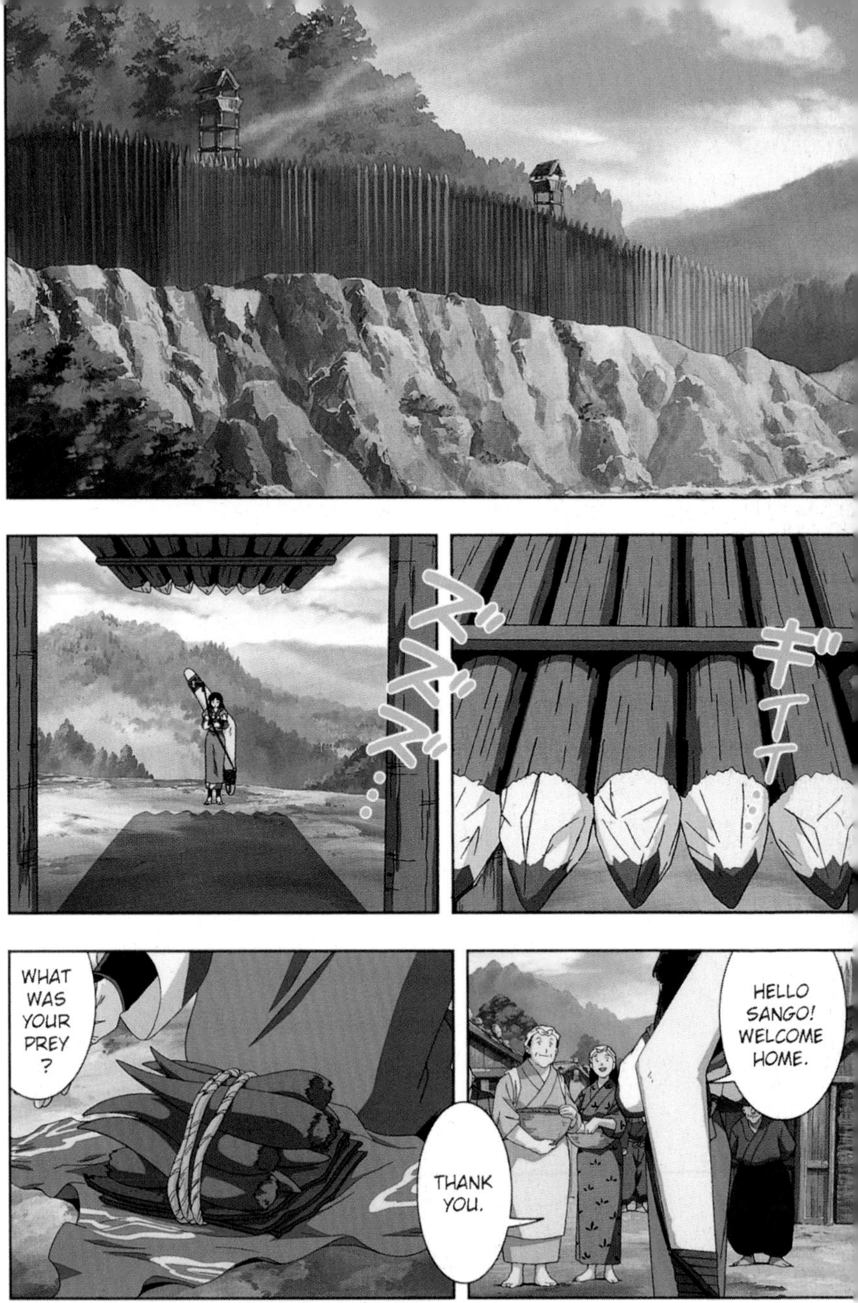

ギイイ
ズズズズ…
HELLO SANGO! WELCOME HOME.
THANK YOU.
WHAT WAS YOUR PREY?

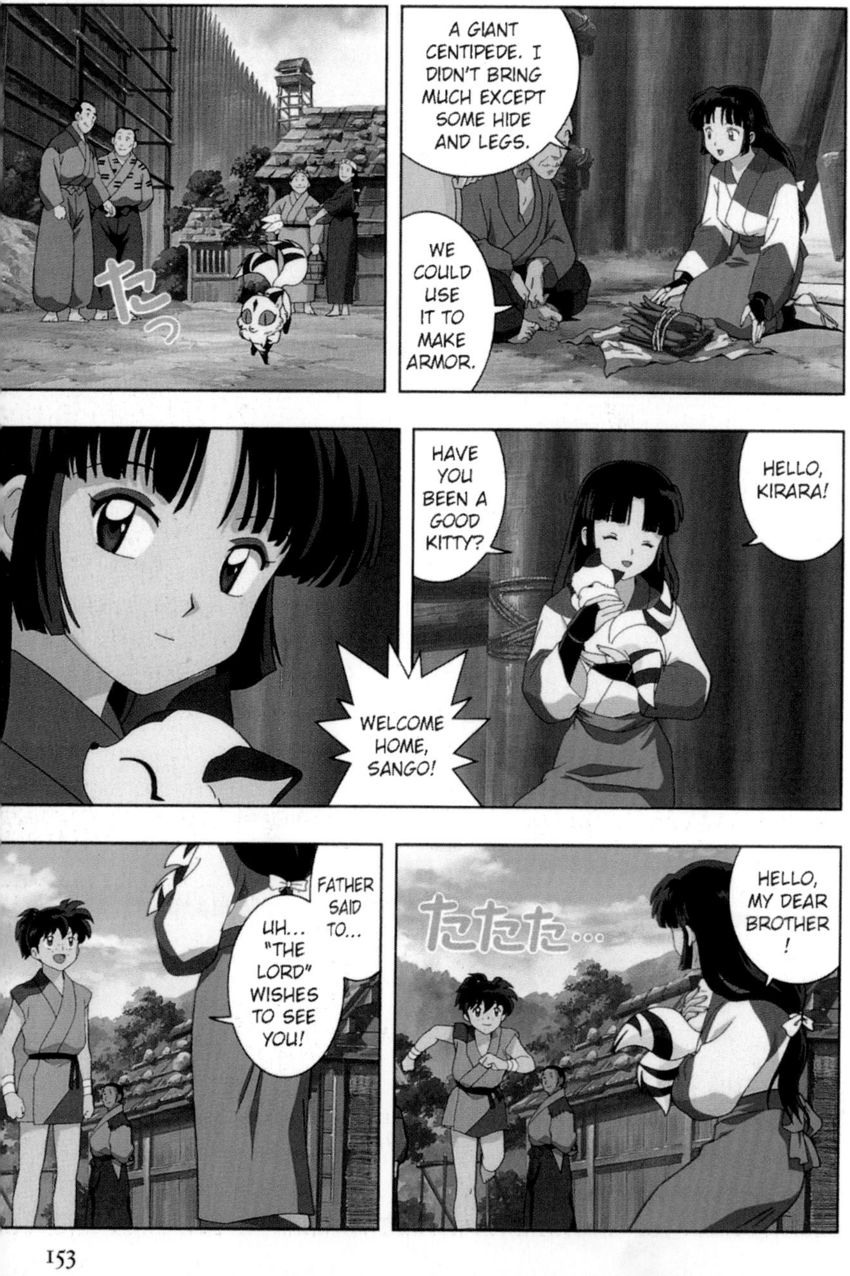
A GIANT CENTIPEDE. I DIDN'T BRING MUCH EXCEPT SOME HIDE AND LEGS.
WE COULD USE IT TO MAKE ARMOR.
たっ
HELLO, KIRARA!
HAVE YOU BEEN A GOOD KITTY?
WELCOME HOME, SANGO!
HELLO, MY DEAR BROTHER!
たたた…
FATHER SAID TO…
UH… "THE LORD" WISHES TO SEE YOU!

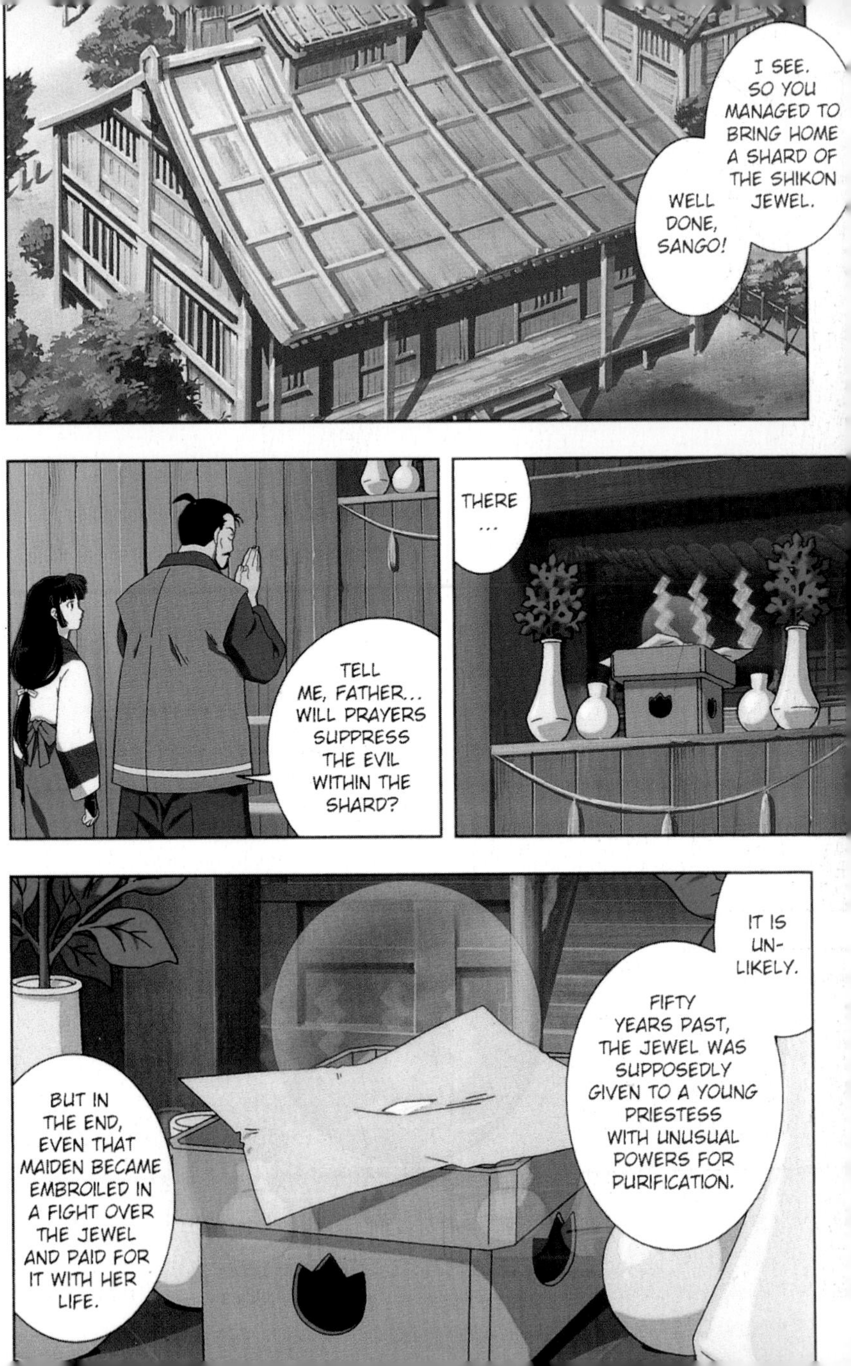
I SEE. SO YOU MANAGED TO BRING HOME A SHARD OF THE SHIKON JEWEL.
WELL DONE, SANGO!
THERE...
TELL ME, FATHER... WILL PRAYERS SUPPRESS THE EVIL WITHIN THE SHARD?
IT IS UN-LIKELY.
FIFTY YEARS PAST, THE JEWEL WAS SUPPOSEDLY GIVEN TO A YOUNG PRIESTESS WITH UNUSUAL POWERS FOR PURIFICATION.
BUT IN THE END, EVEN THAT MAIDEN BECAME EMBROILED IN A FIGHT OVER THE JEWEL AND PAID FOR IT WITH HER LIFE.

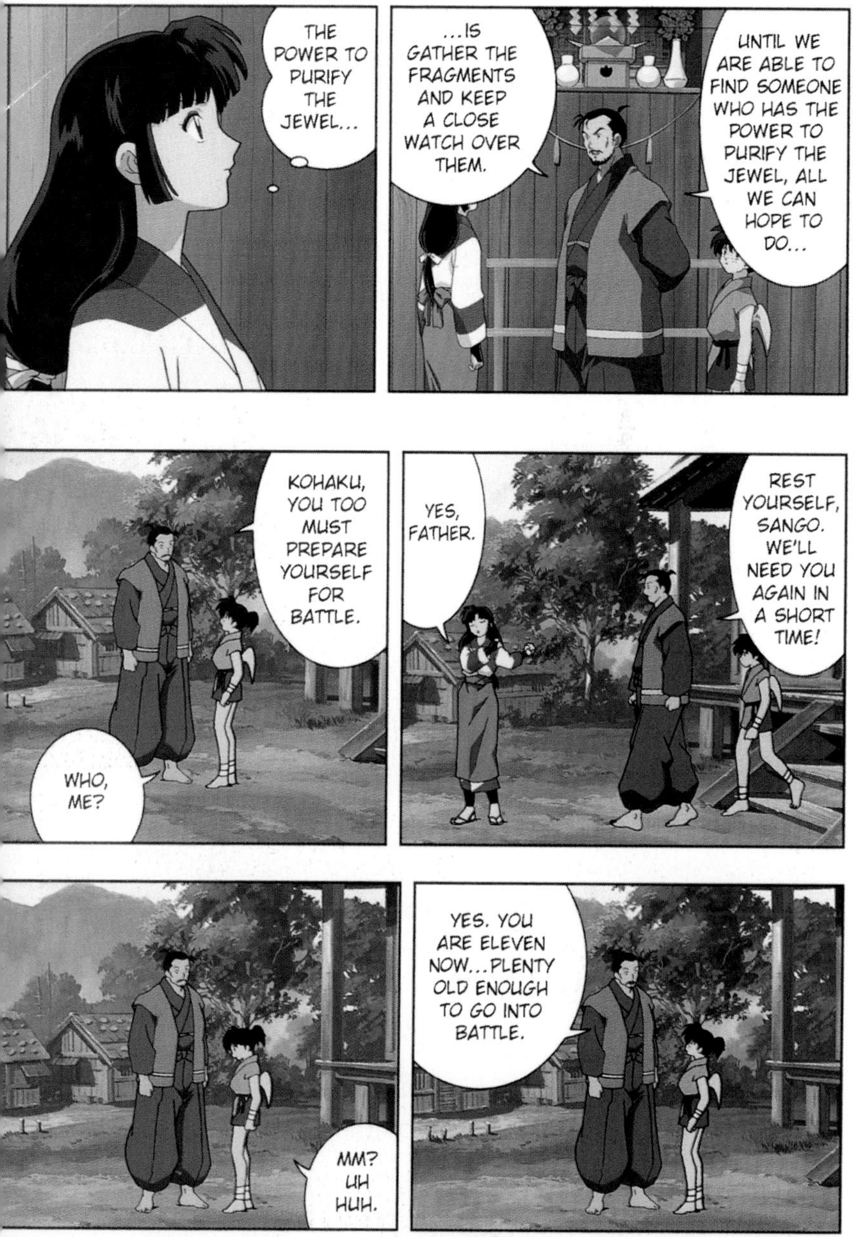
UNTIL WE ARE ABLE TO FIND SOMEONE WHO HAS THE POWER TO PURIFY THE JEWEL, ALL WE CAN HOPE TO DO...
...IS GATHER THE FRAGMENTS AND KEEP A CLOSE WATCH OVER THEM.
THE POWER TO PURIFY THE JEWEL...
REST YOURSELF, SANGO. WE'LL NEED YOU AGAIN IN A SHORT TIME!
YES, FATHER.
KOHAKU, YOU TOO MUST PREPARE YOURSELF FOR BATTLE.
WHO, ME?
YES. YOU ARE ELEVEN NOW...PLENTY OLD ENOUGH TO GO INTO BATTLE.
MM? UH HUH.

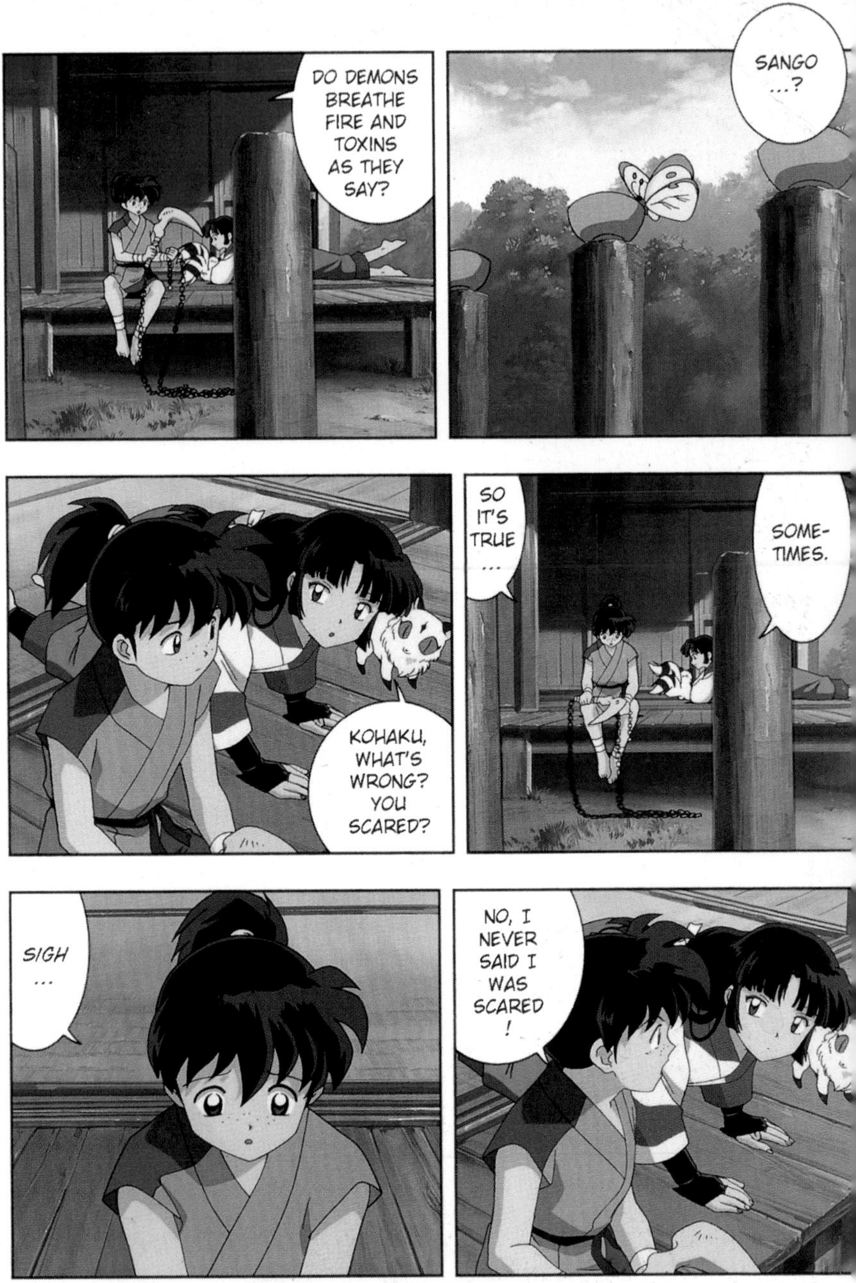
SANGO ...?
DO DEMONS BREATHE FIRE AND TOXINS AS THEY SAY?
SOME-TIMES.
SO IT'S TRUE ...
KOHAKU, WHAT'S WRONG? YOU SCARED?
NO, I NEVER SAID I WAS SCARED!
SIGH ...

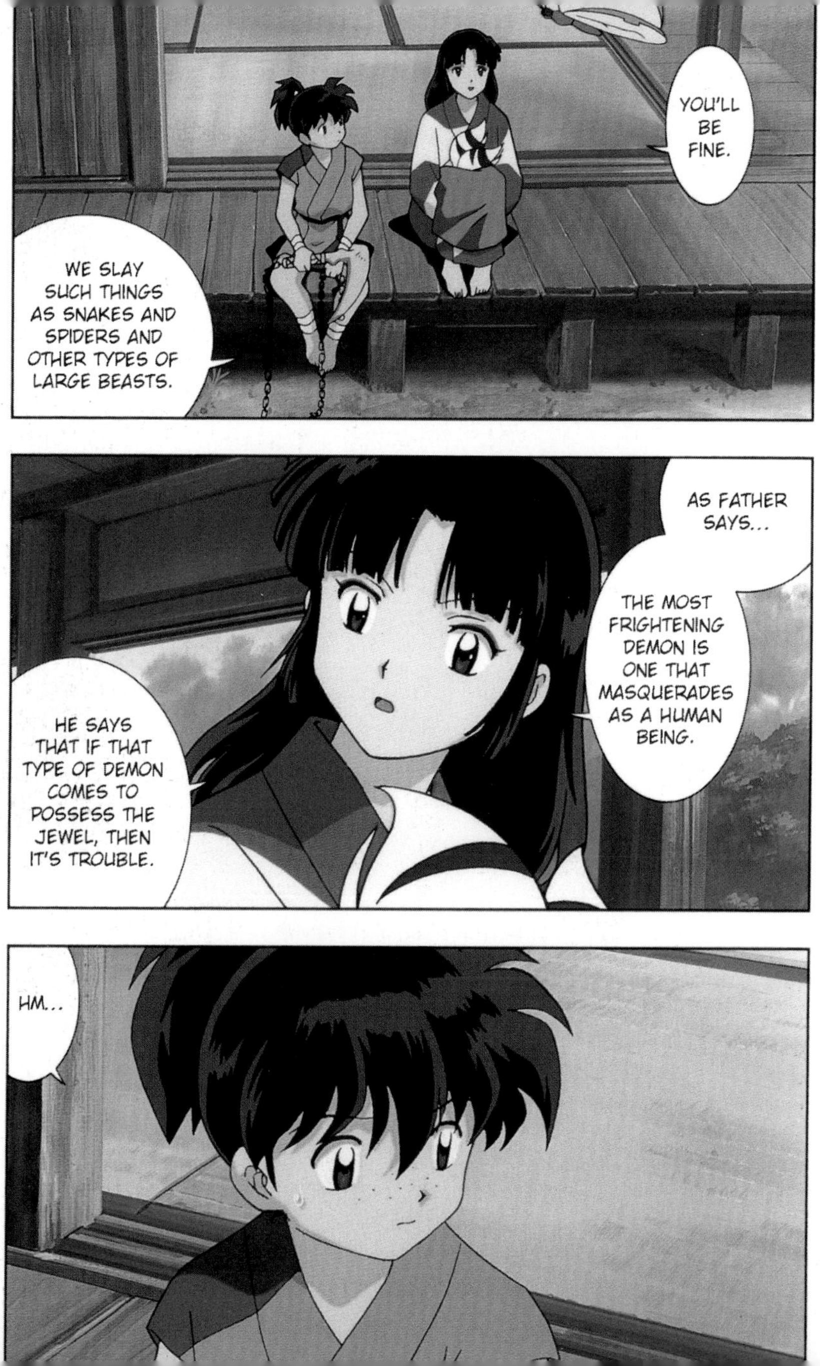
YOU'LL BE FINE.
WE SLAY SUCH THINGS AS SNAKES AND SPIDERS AND OTHER TYPES OF LARGE BEASTS.
AS FATHER SAYS...
THE MOST FRIGHTENING DEMON IS ONE THAT MASQUERADES AS A HUMAN BEING.
HE SAYS THAT IF THAT TYPE OF DEMON COMES TO POSSESS THE JEWEL, THEN IT'S TROUBLE.
HM...

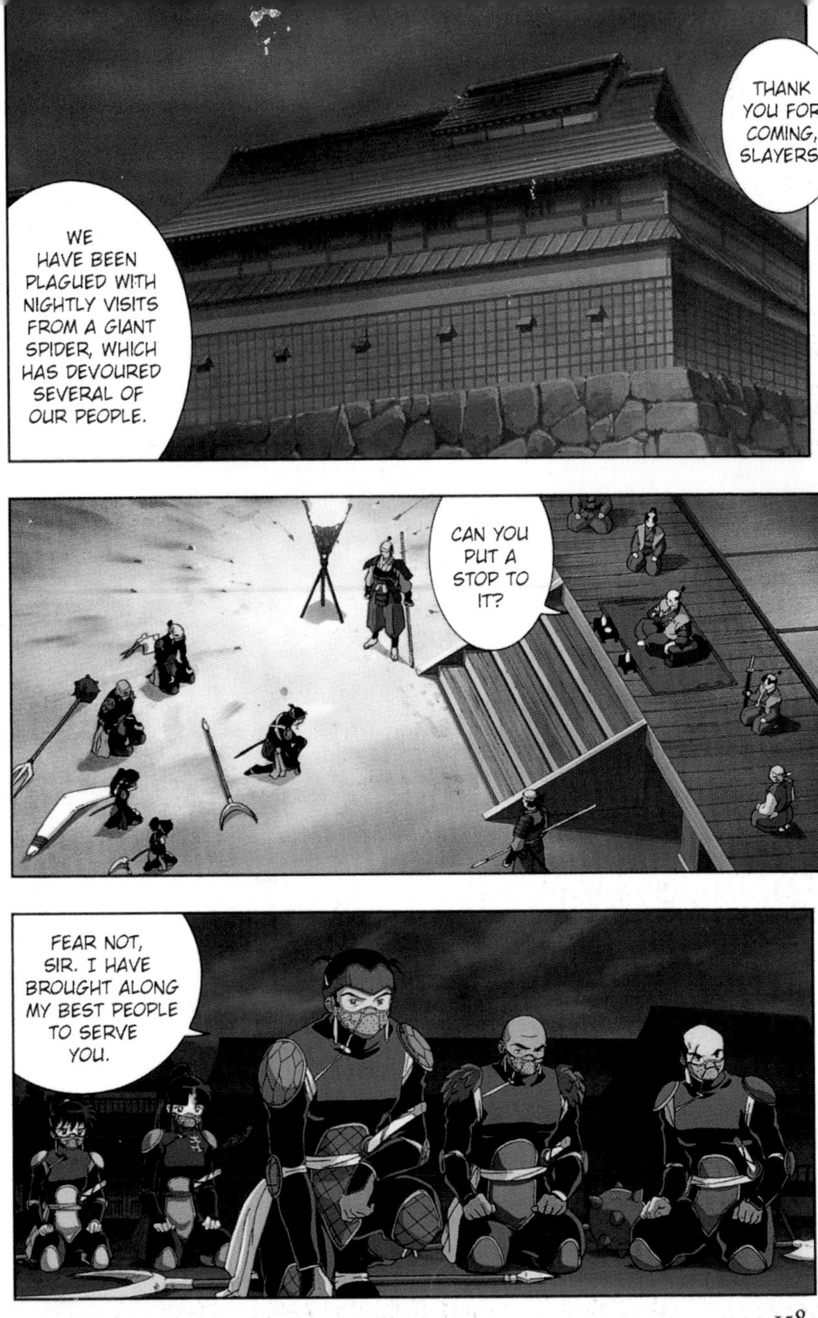
THANK YOU FOR COMING, SLAYERS!
WE HAVE BEEN PLAGUED WITH NIGHTLY VISITS FROM A GIANT SPIDER, WHICH HAS DEVOURED SEVERAL OF OUR PEOPLE.
CAN YOU PUT A STOP TO IT?
FEAR NOT, SIR. I HAVE BROUGHT ALONG MY BEST PEOPLE TO SERVE YOU.

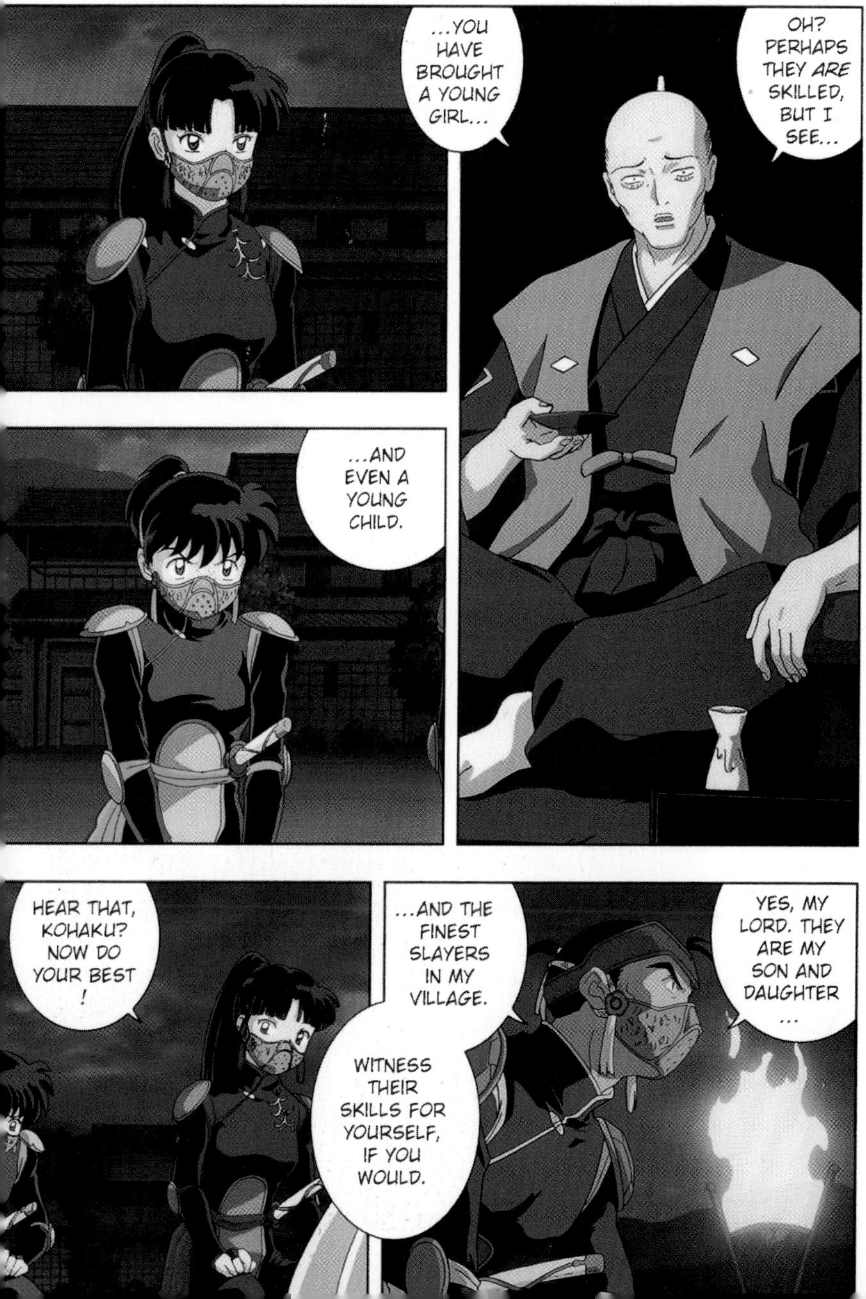
OH? PERHAPS THEY *ARE* SKILLED, BUT I SEE...
...YOU HAVE BROUGHT A YOUNG GIRL...
...AND EVEN A YOUNG CHILD.
YES, MY LORD. THEY ARE MY SON AND DAUGHTER...
...AND THE FINEST SLAYERS IN MY VILLAGE.
WITNESS THEIR SKILLS FOR YOURSELF, IF YOU WOULD.
HEAR THAT, KOHAKU? NOW DO YOUR BEST!

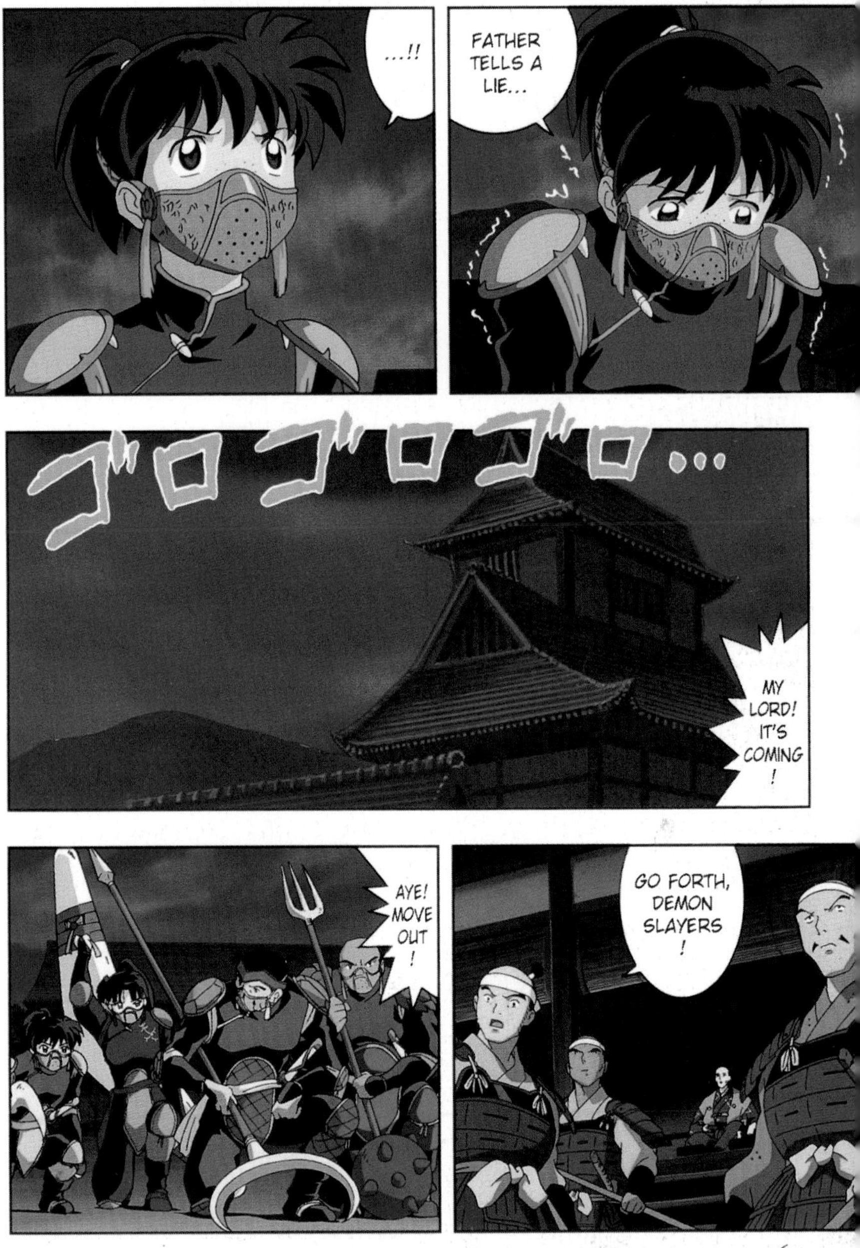
FATHER TELLS A LIE...
...!!
ゴロゴロゴロ...
MY LORD! IT'S COMING!
GO FORTH, DEMON SLAYERS!
AYE! MOVE OUT!

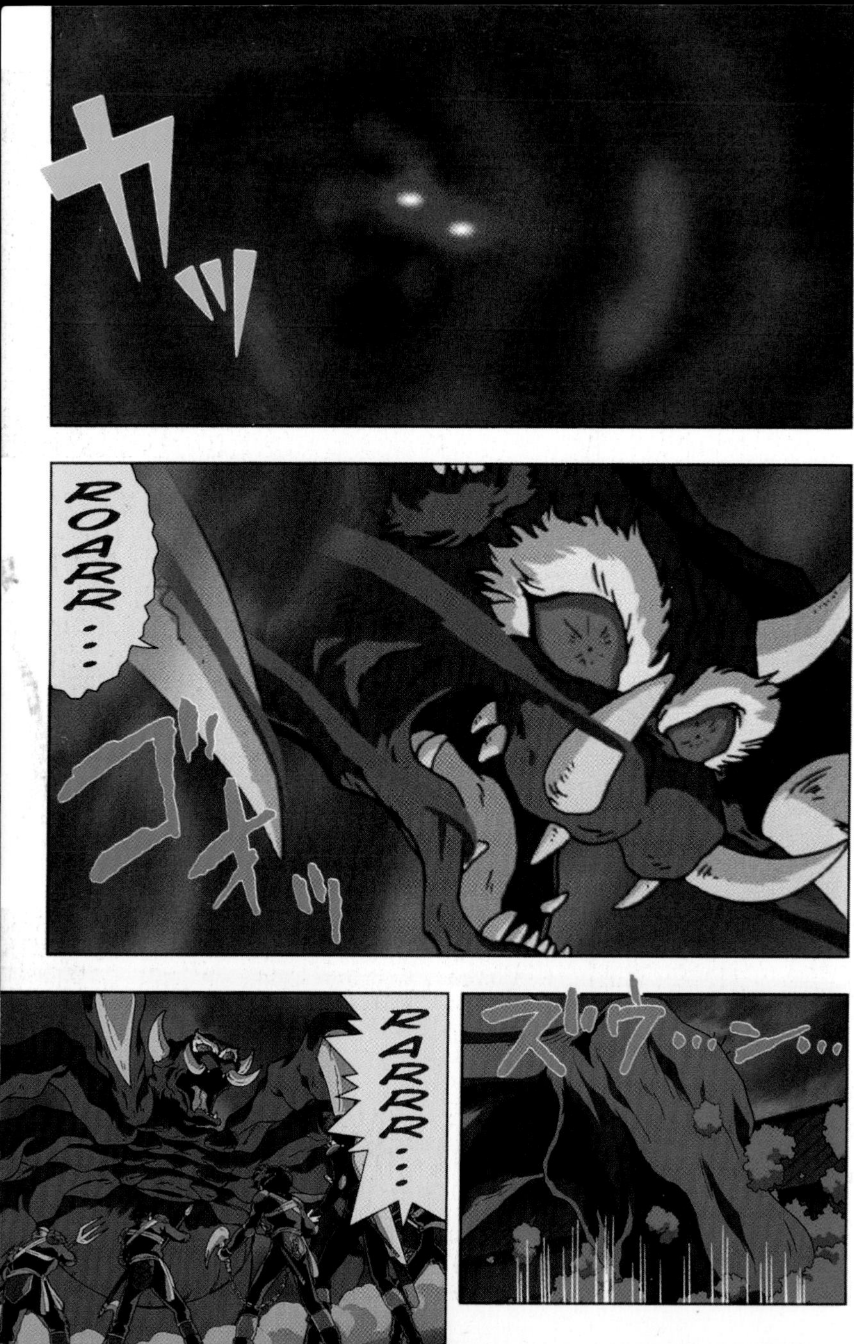
カッ
ROARR...
ゴオッ
ズウ…ン…
RARRR...

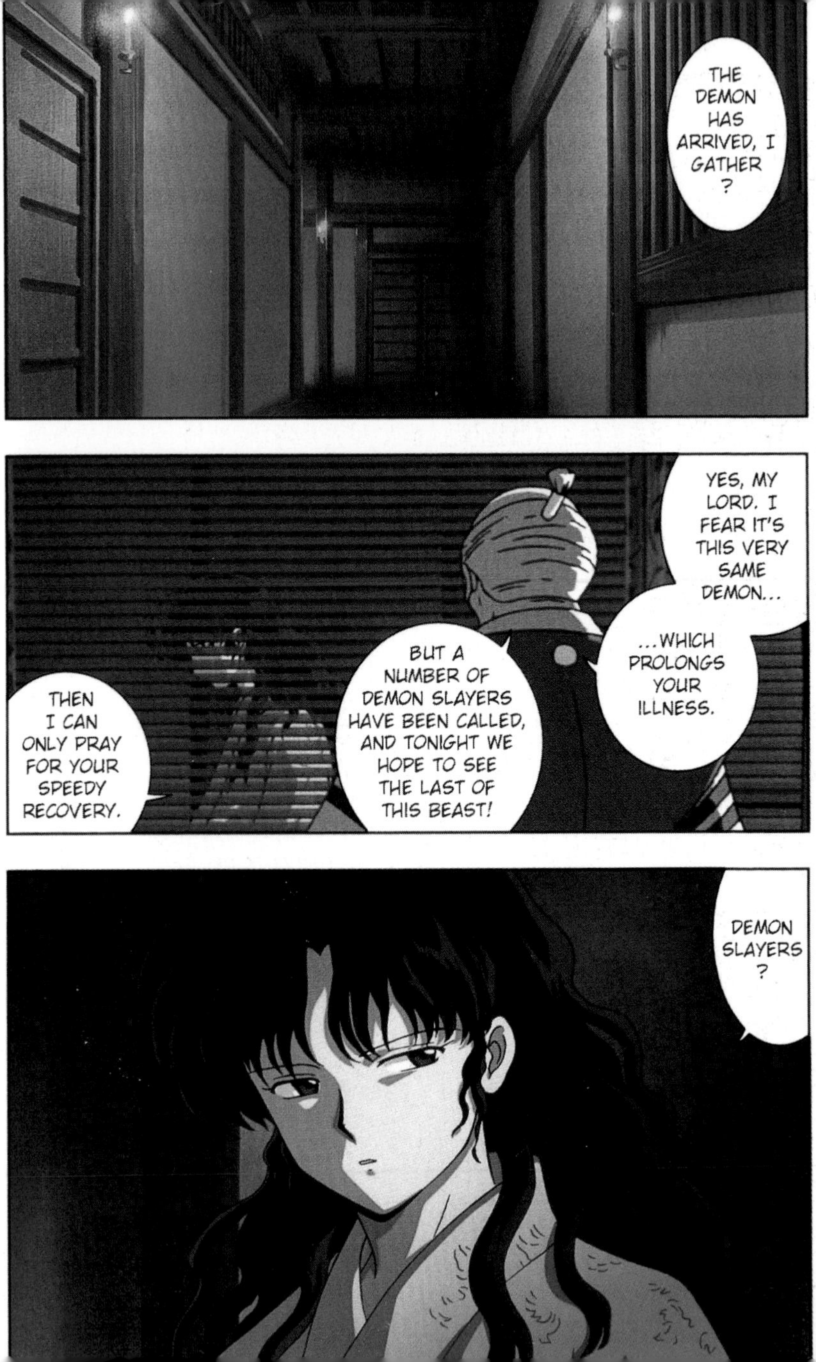
THE DEMON HAS ARRIVED, I GATHER?
YES, MY LORD. I FEAR IT'S THIS VERY SAME DEMON...
...WHICH PROLONGS YOUR ILLNESS.
BUT A NUMBER OF DEMON SLAYERS HAVE BEEN CALLED, AND TONIGHT WE HOPE TO SEE THE LAST OF THIS BEAST!
THEN I CAN ONLY PRAY FOR YOUR SPEEDY RECOVERY.
DEMON SLAYERS?

SUR-
ROUND
IT!

!!

WAAAH!

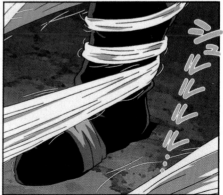

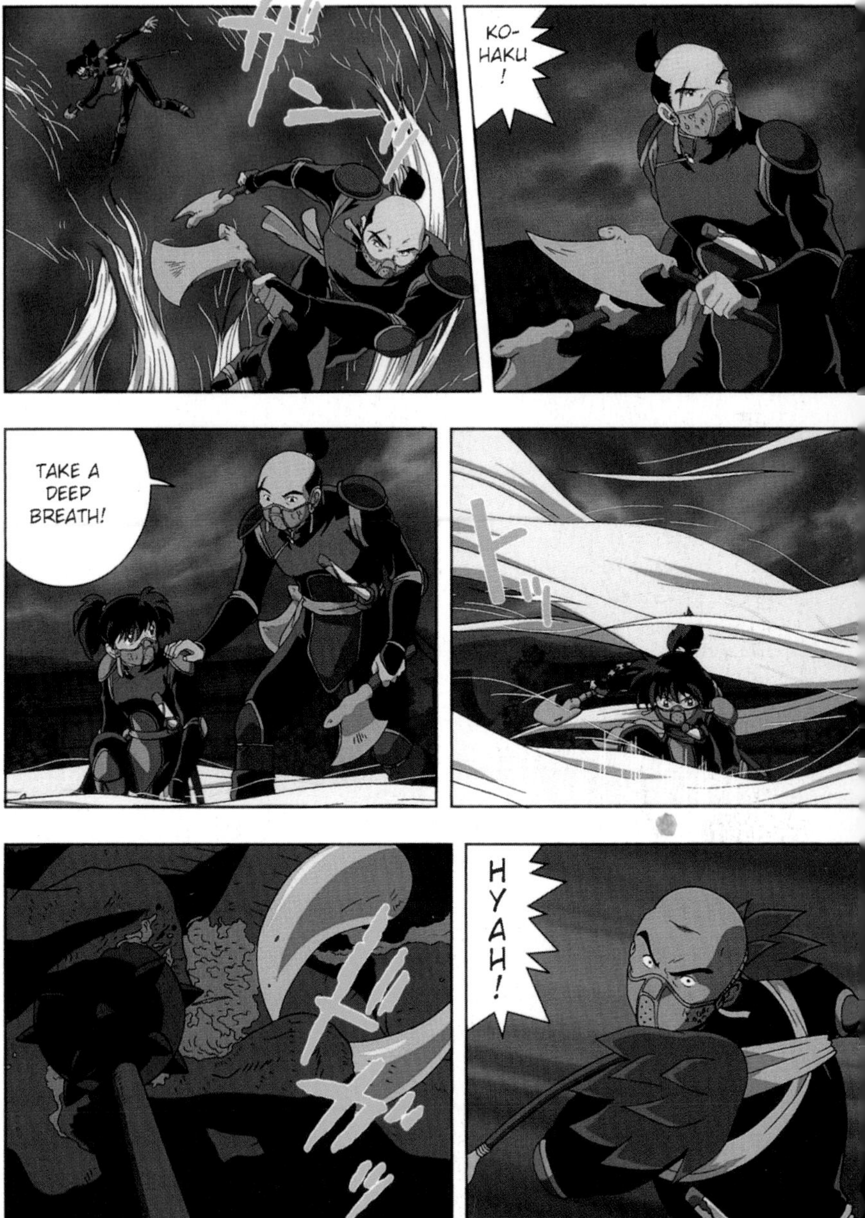
KO-HAKU!
TAKE A DEEP BREATH!
HYAH!

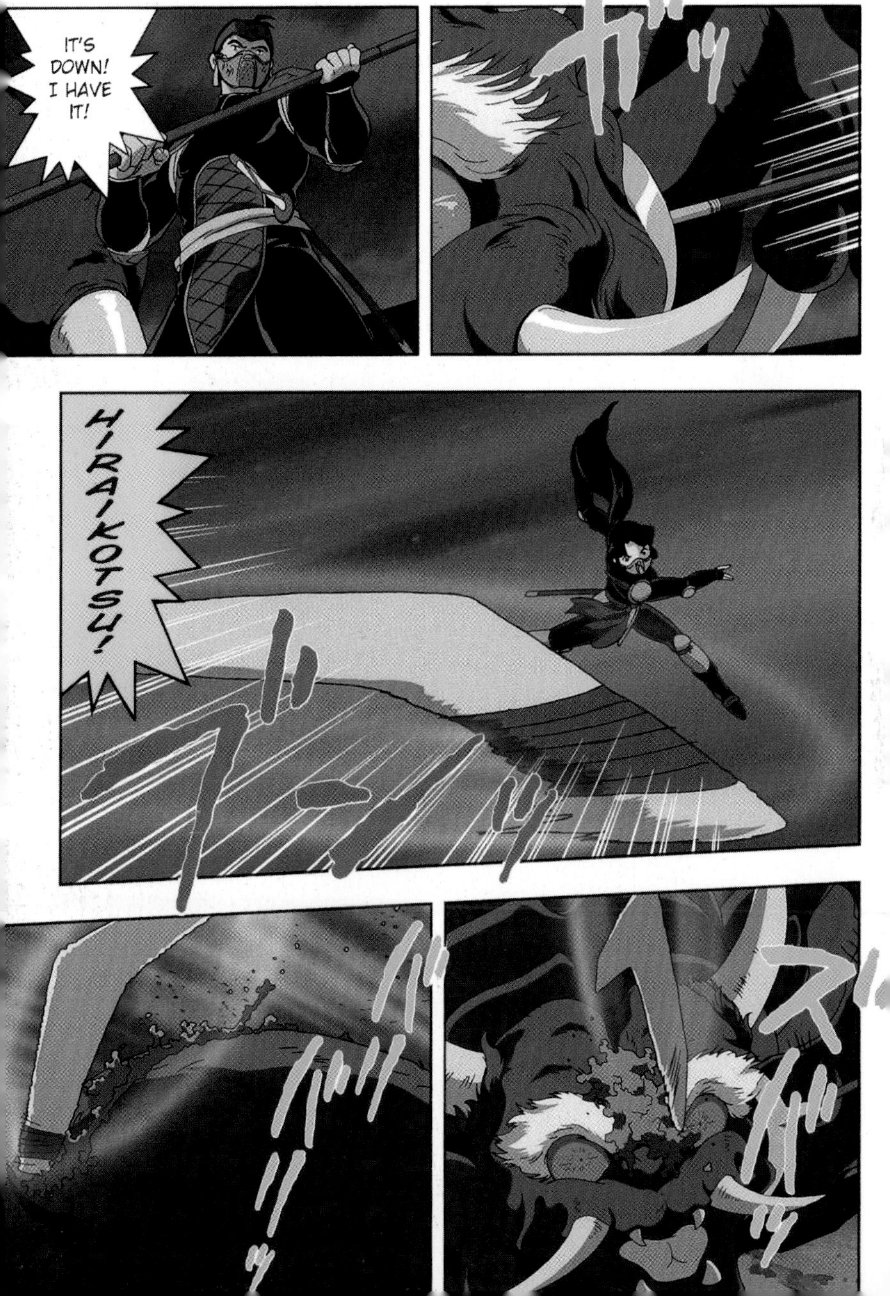
IT'S DOWN! I HAVE IT!
HIRAIKOTSU!

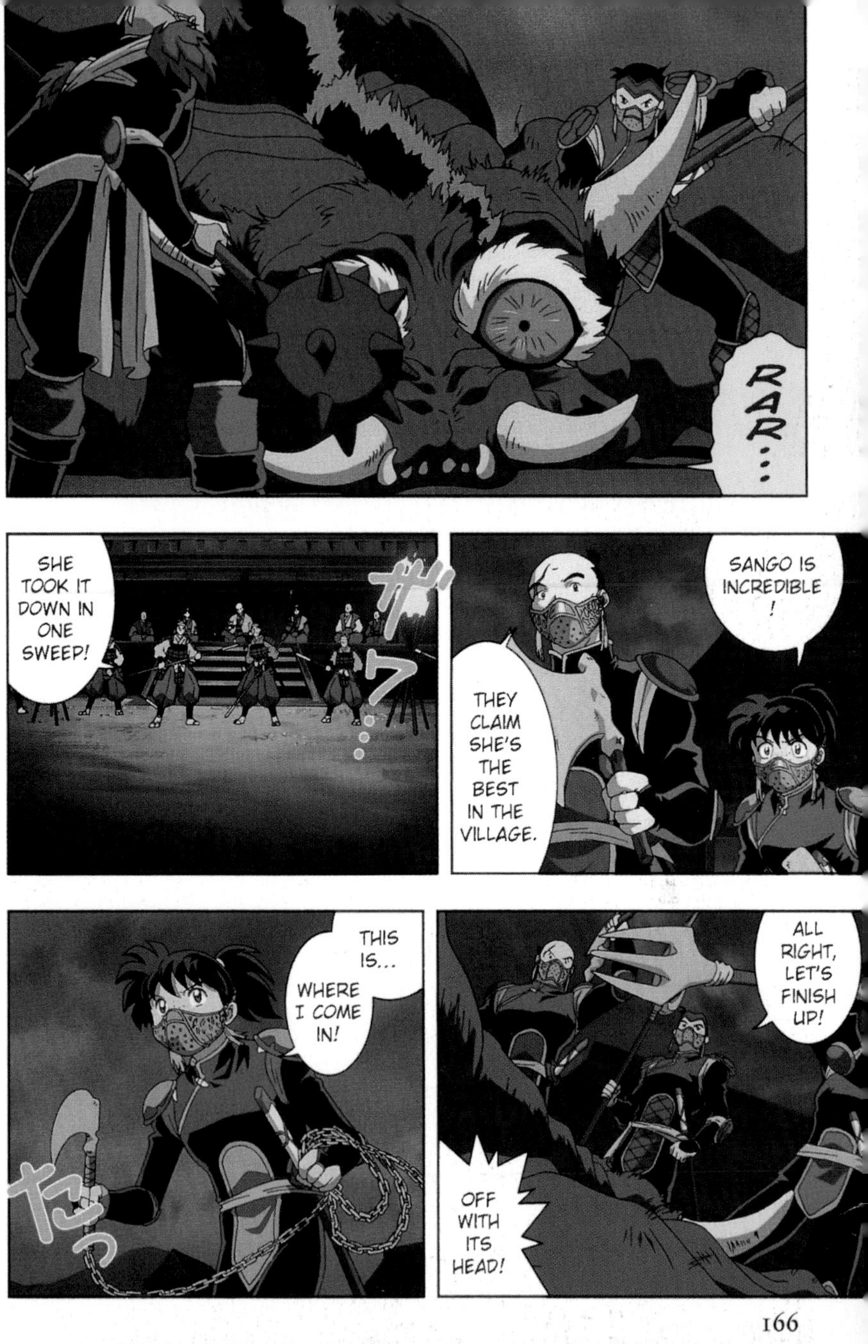
RAR...
SANGO IS INCREDIBLE!
THEY CLAIM SHE'S THE BEST IN THE VILLAGE.
SHE TOOK IT DOWN IN ONE SWEEP!
ザワ
ALL RIGHT, LET'S FINISH UP!
OFF WITH ITS HEAD!
THIS IS... WHERE I COME IN!
たっ

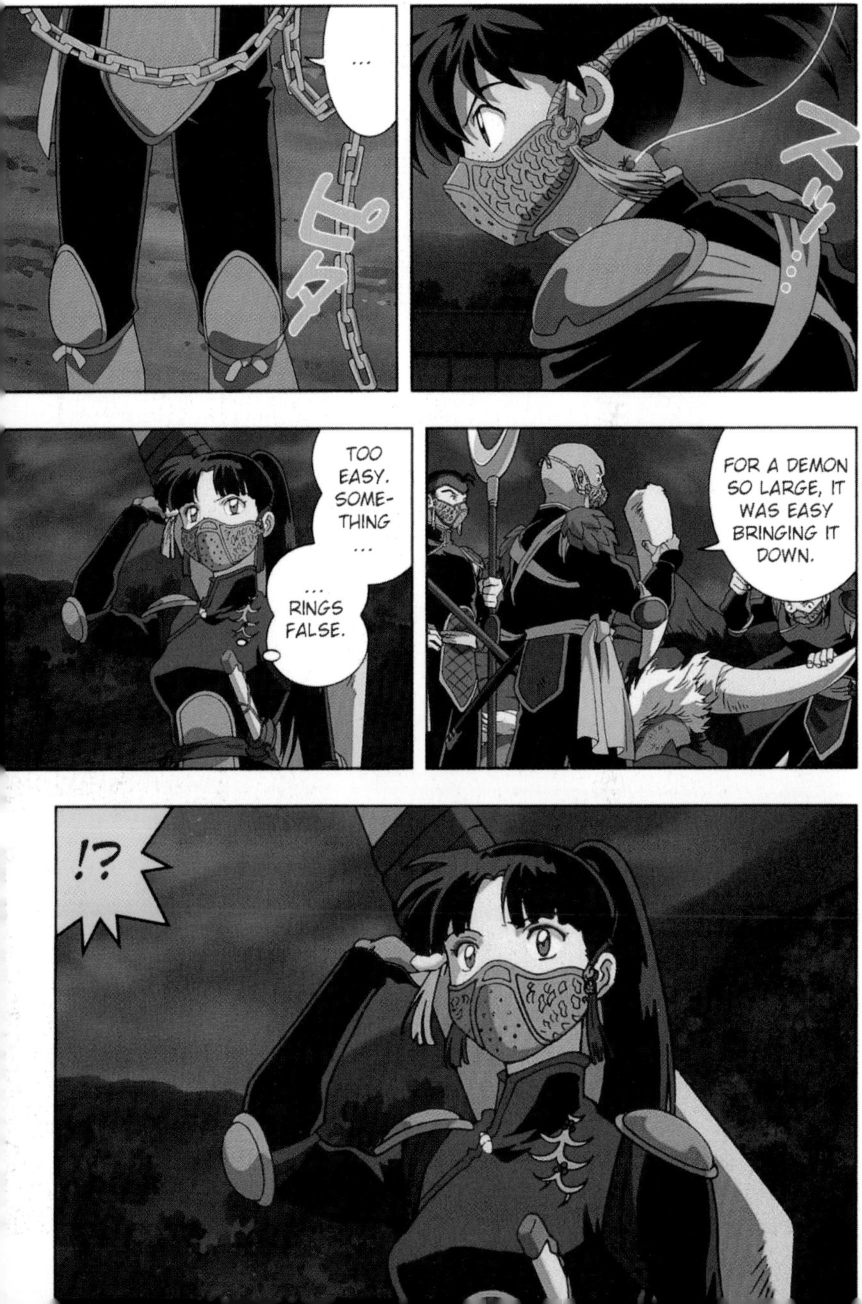
スッ…
…
ピタ
FOR A DEMON SO LARGE, IT WAS EASY BRINGING IT DOWN.
TOO EASY. SOME-THING …
… RINGS FALSE.
!?

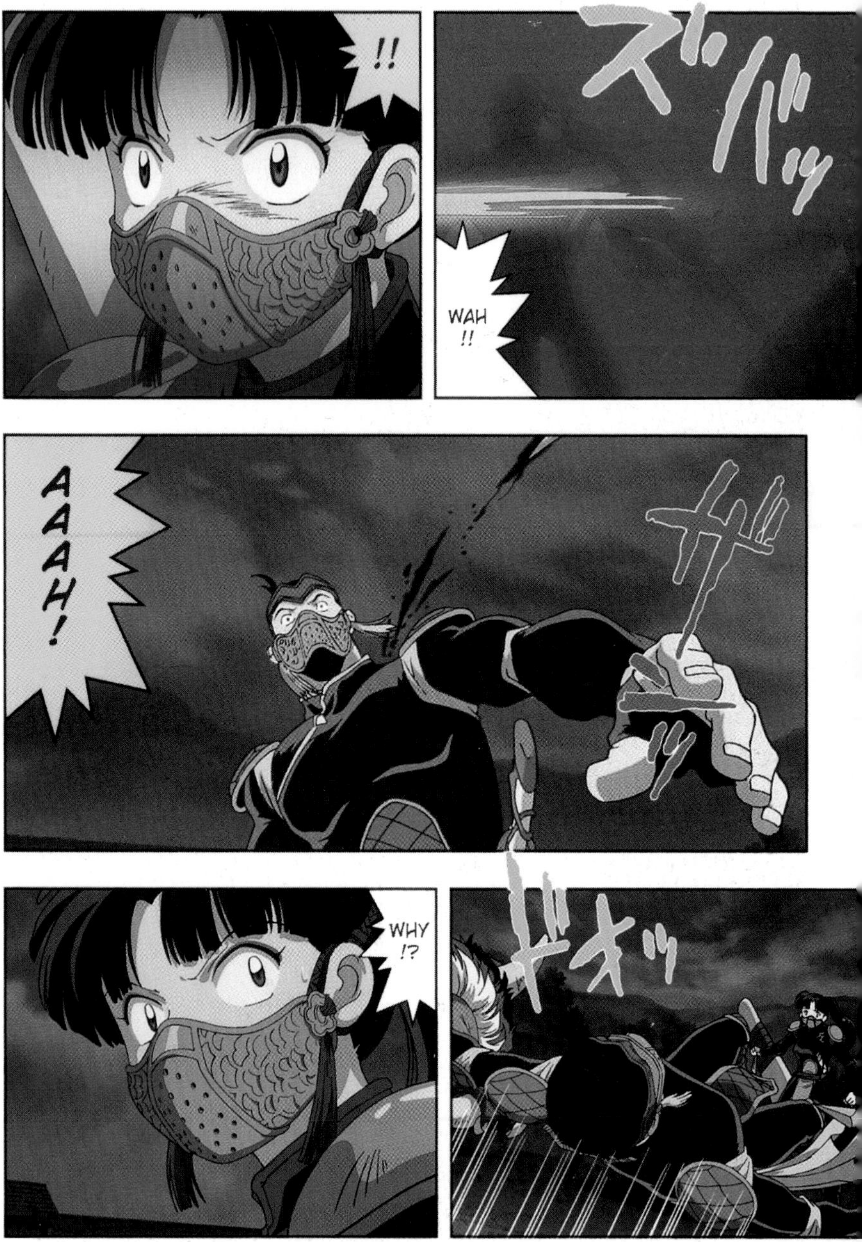
ズバッ
WAH !!
!!
AAAAH!
ドオッ
WHY !?

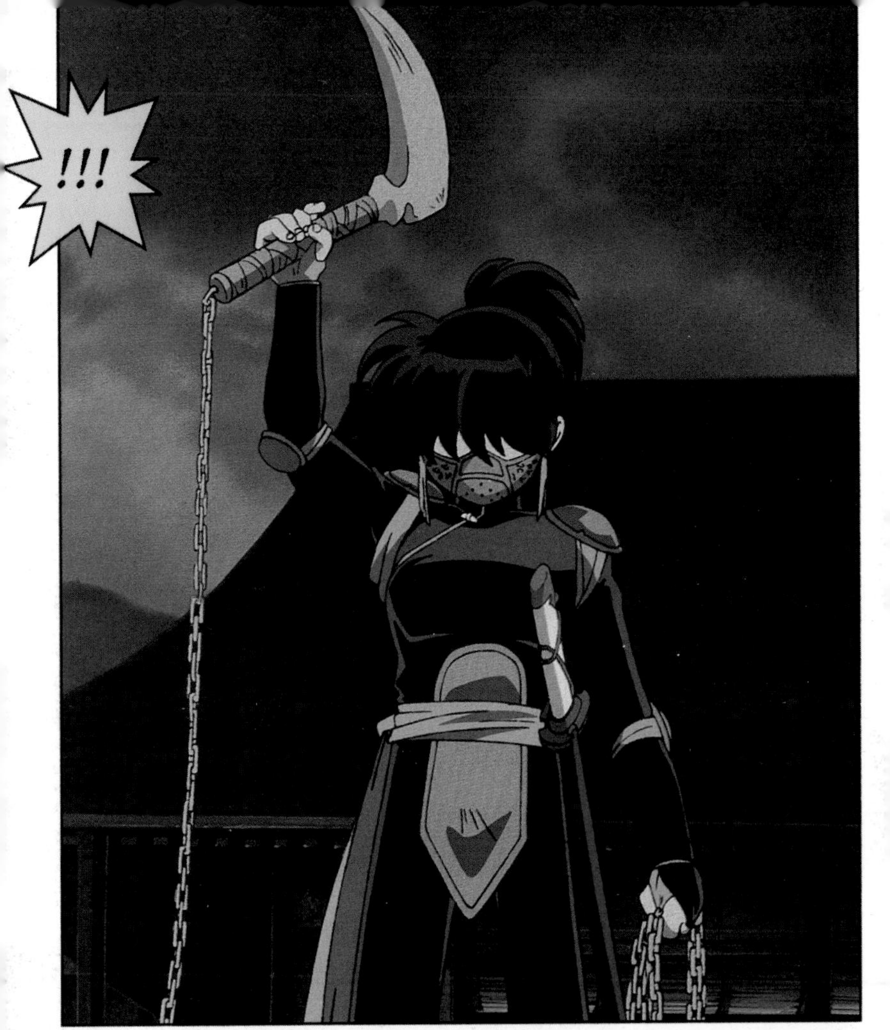
!!!

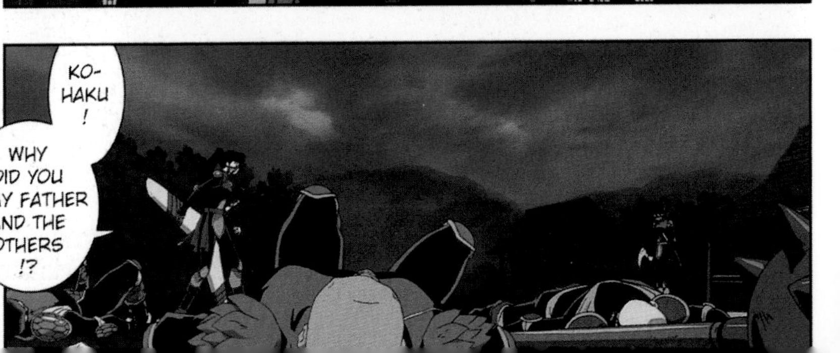
KO-
HAKU
!
WHY
DID YOU
SLAY FATHER
AND THE
OTHERS
!?

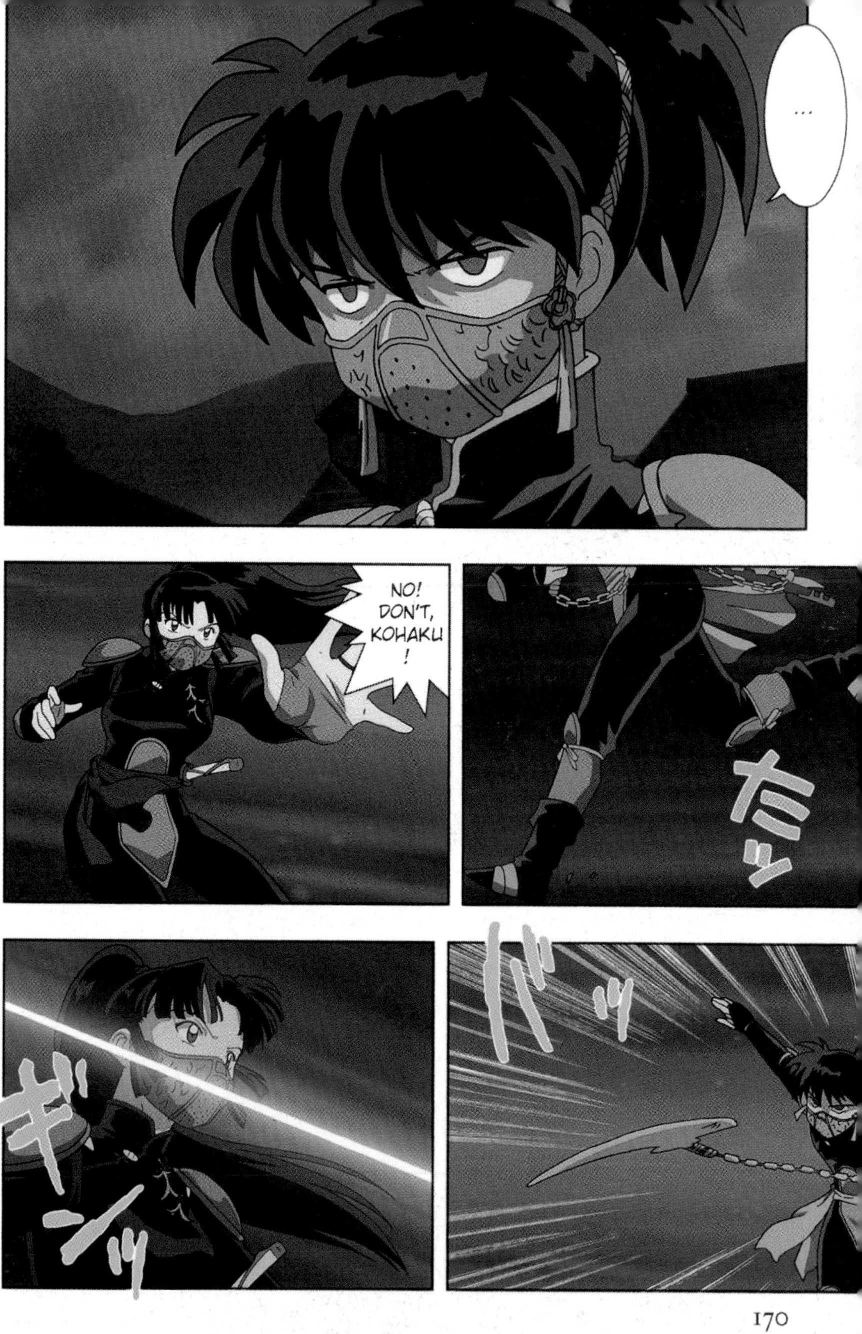
...
タッ
NO! DON'T, KOHAKU!
バッ
ギンッ

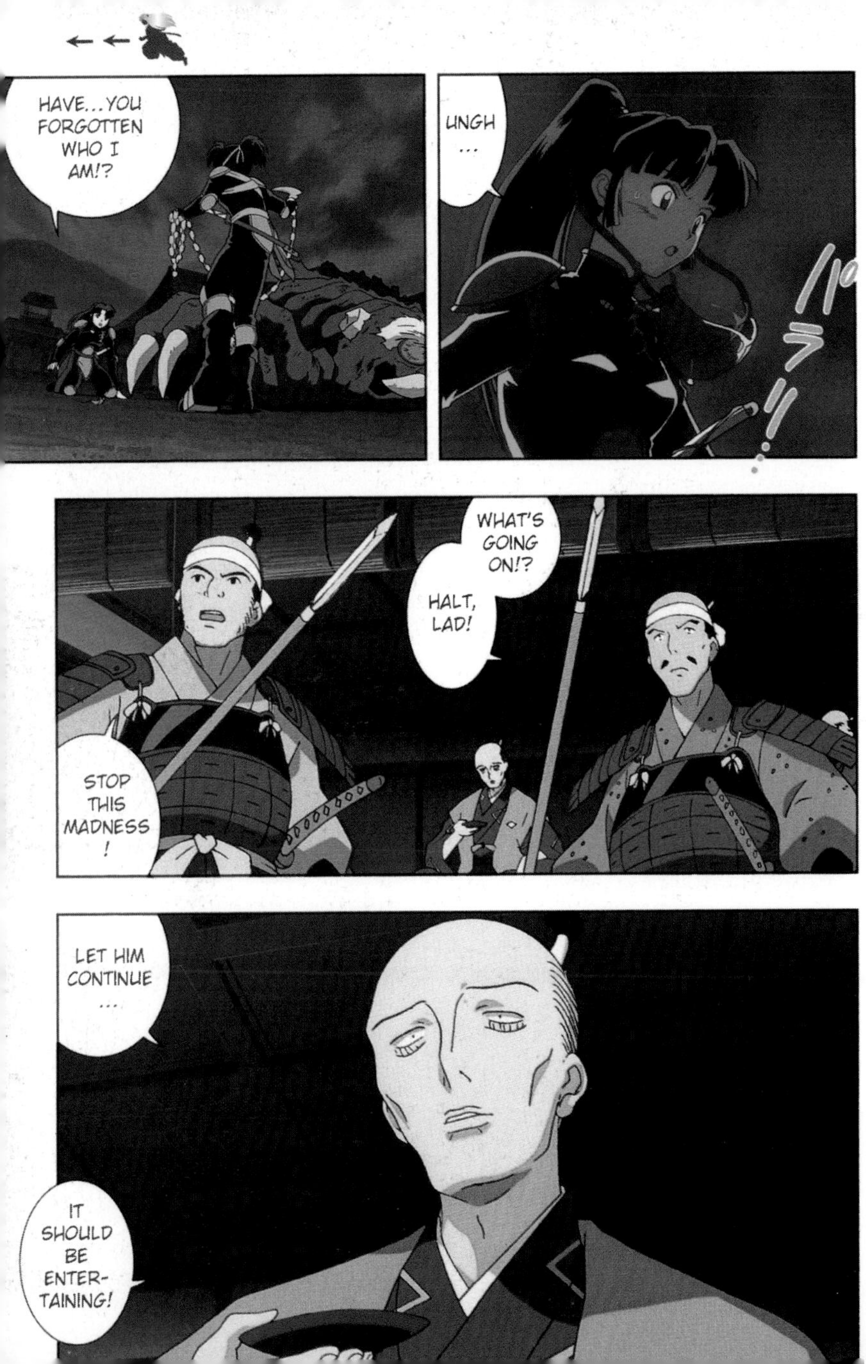
UNGH...
パラリ…
HAVE...YOU FORGOTTEN WHO I AM!?
WHAT'S GOING ON!?
HALT, LAD!
STOP THIS MADNESS!
LET HIM CONTINUE...
IT SHOULD BE ENTER-TAINING!

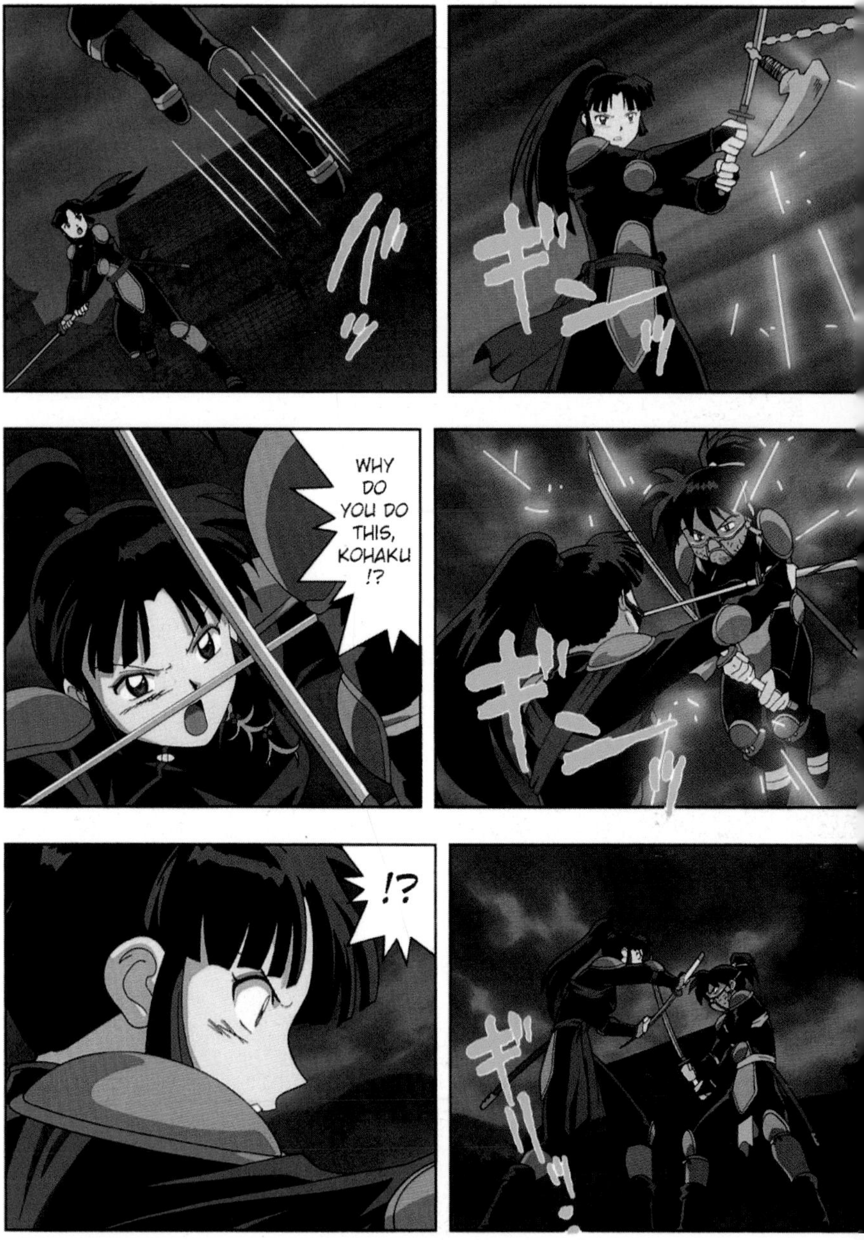
WHY DO YOU DO THIS, KOHAKU!?
!?

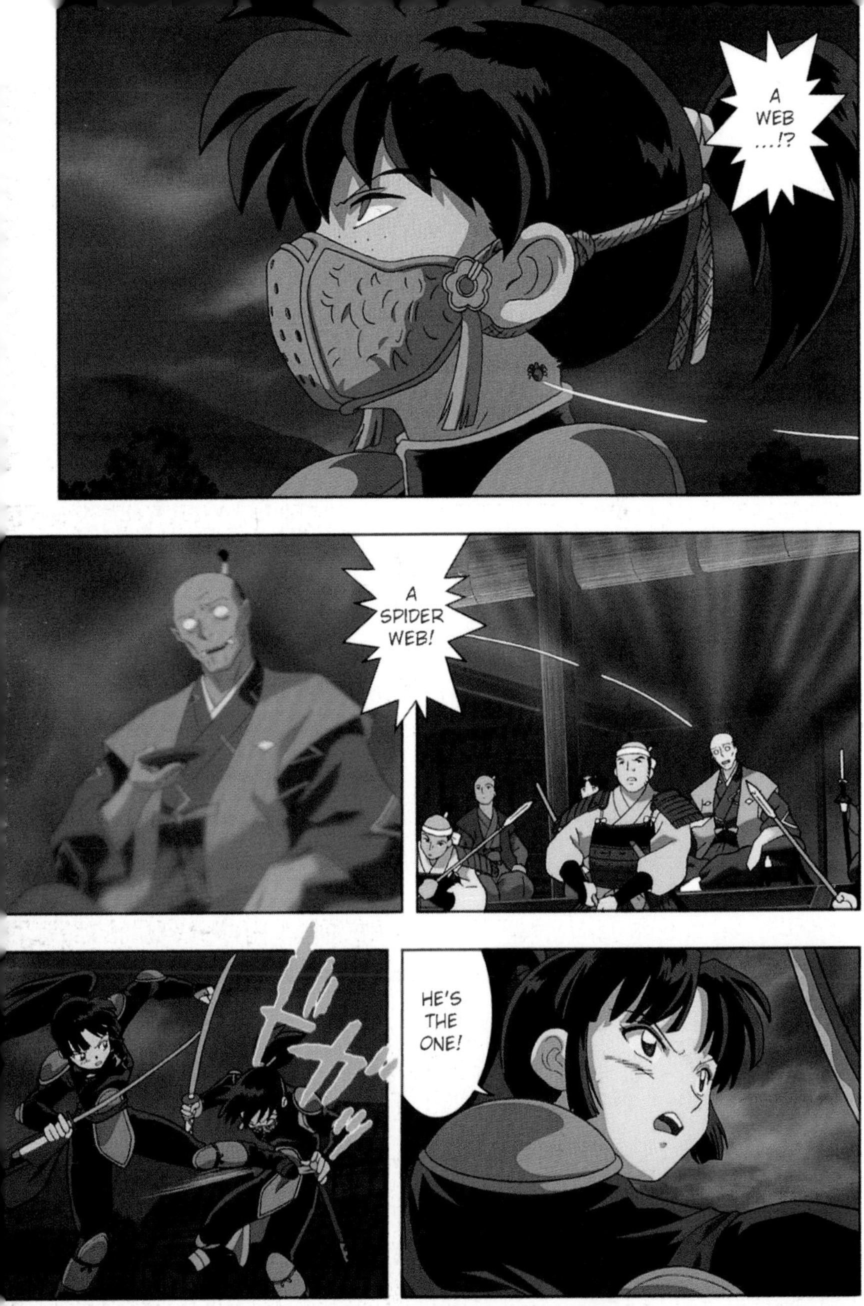
A WEB ...!?
A SPIDER WEB!
HE'S THE ONE!

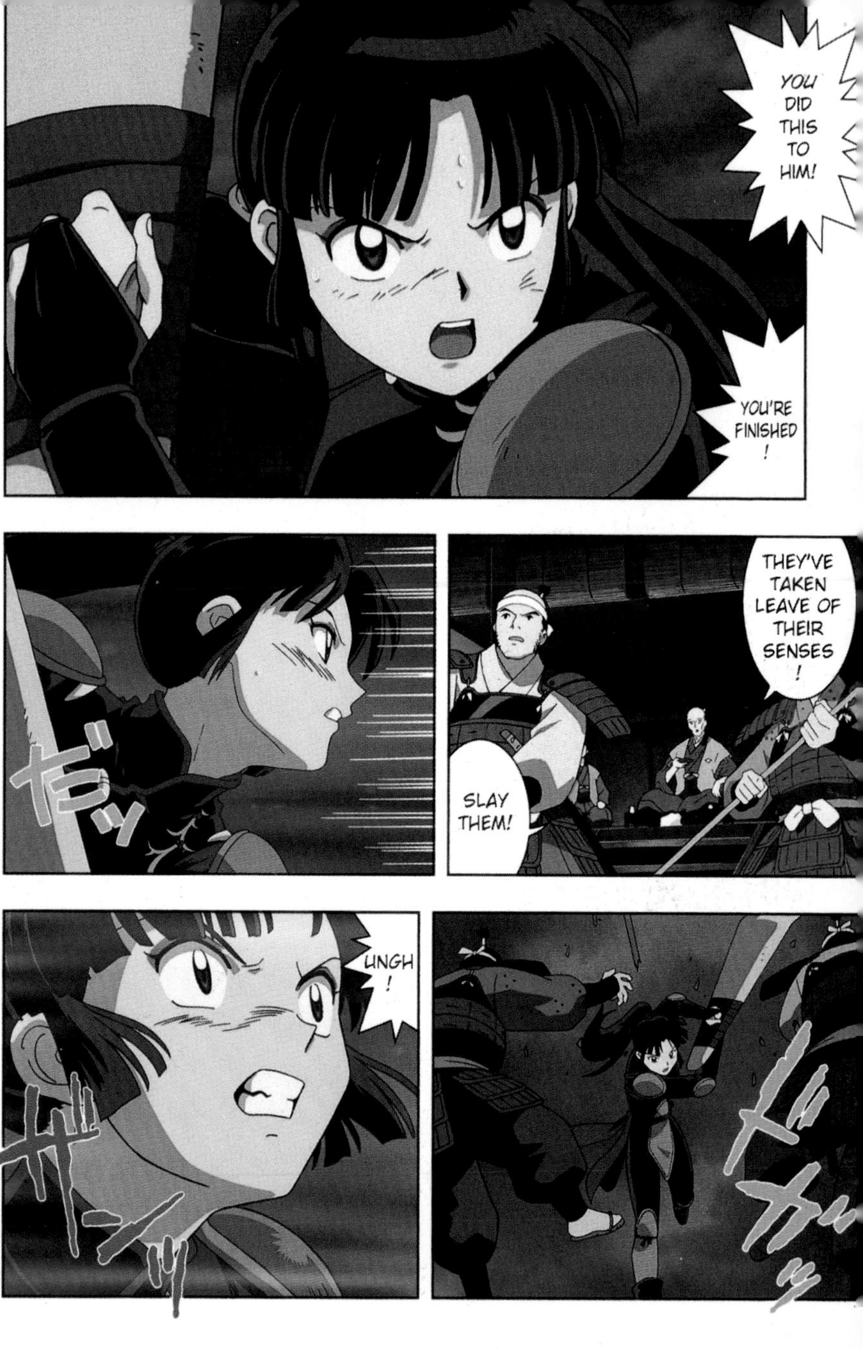
YOU DID THIS TO HIM!
YOU'RE FINISHED!
THEY'VE TAKEN LEAVE OF THEIR SENSES!
SLAY THEM!
UNGH!

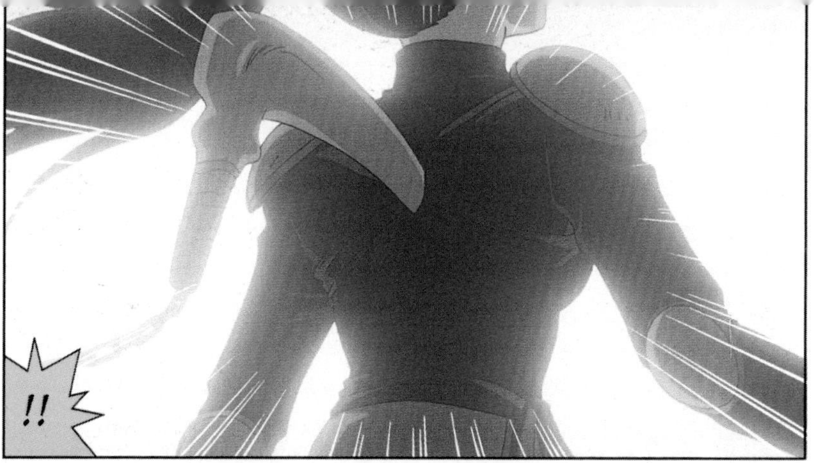
!!

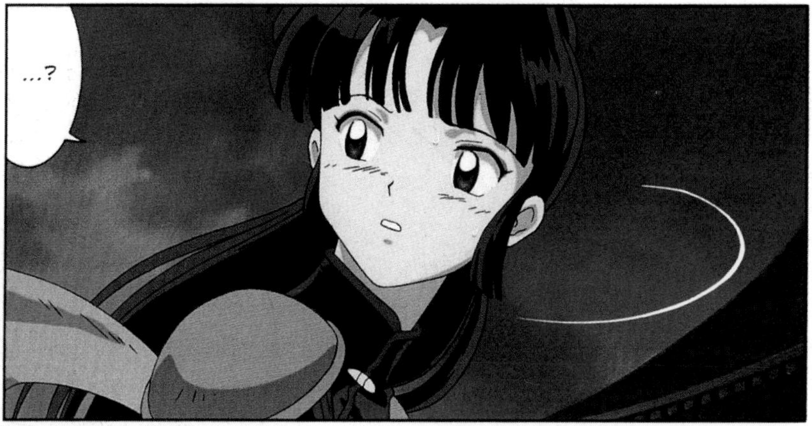
...?

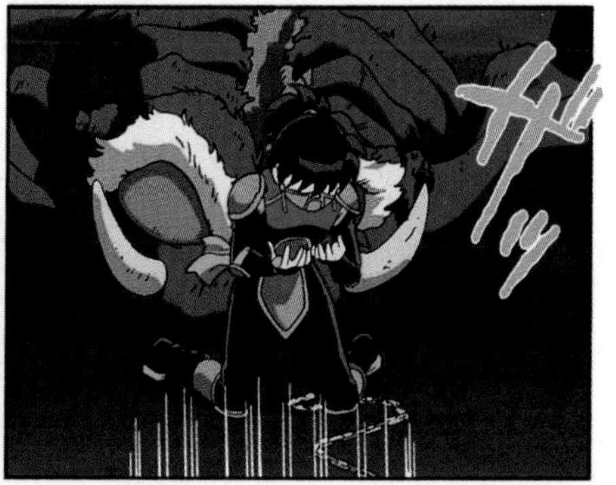

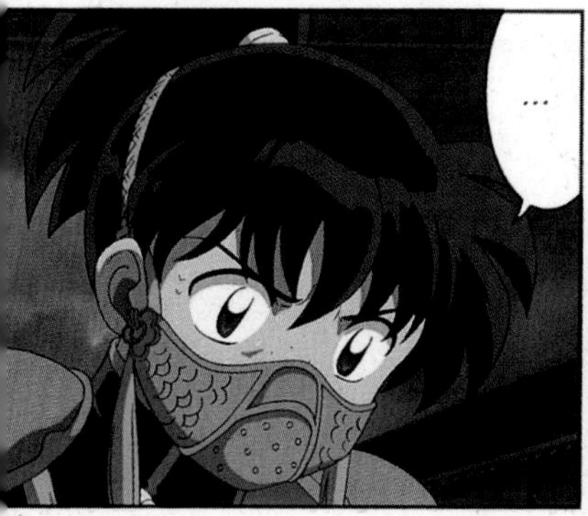
...

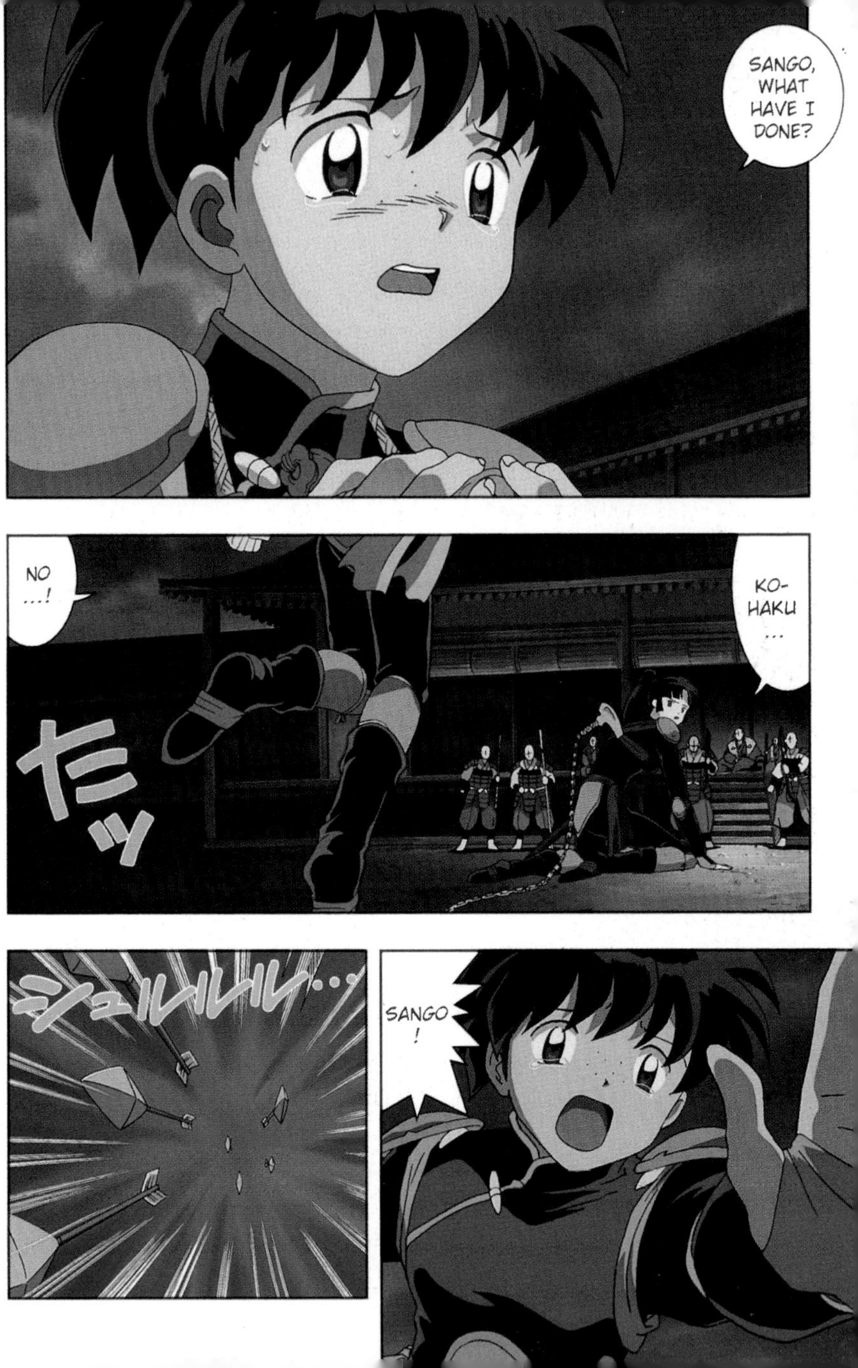
SANGO, WHAT HAVE I DONE?
KO-HAKU ...
NO ...!
SANGO !
シュルルルル…

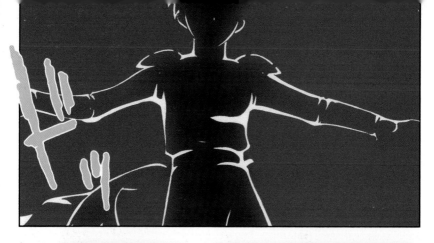

AH!

KOHAKU...

TAKE AIM...

...AT THE CRAZED SIBLINGS!

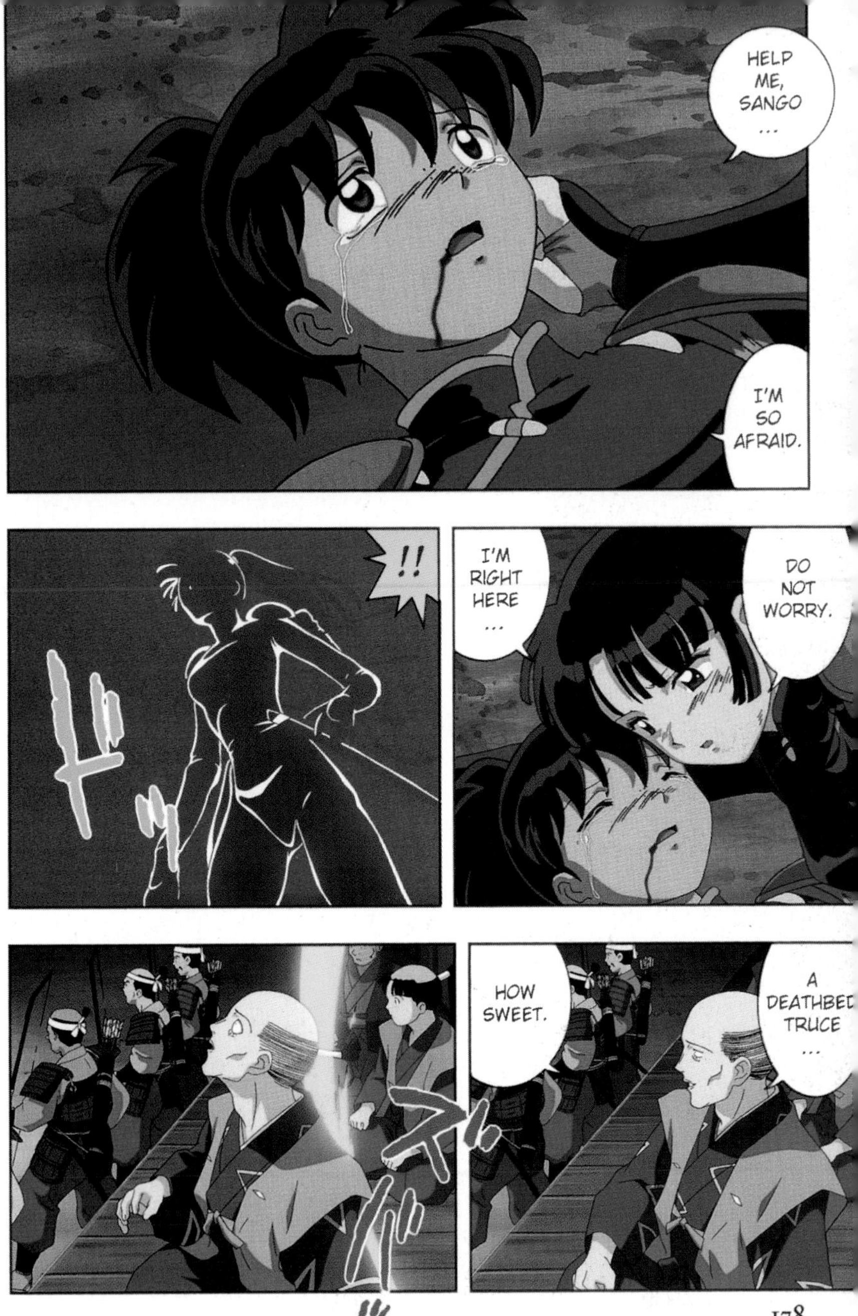
HELP ME, SANGO ...
I'M SO AFRAID.
DO NOT WORRY.
I'M RIGHT HERE ...
!!
A DEATHBED TRUCE ...
HOW SWEET.

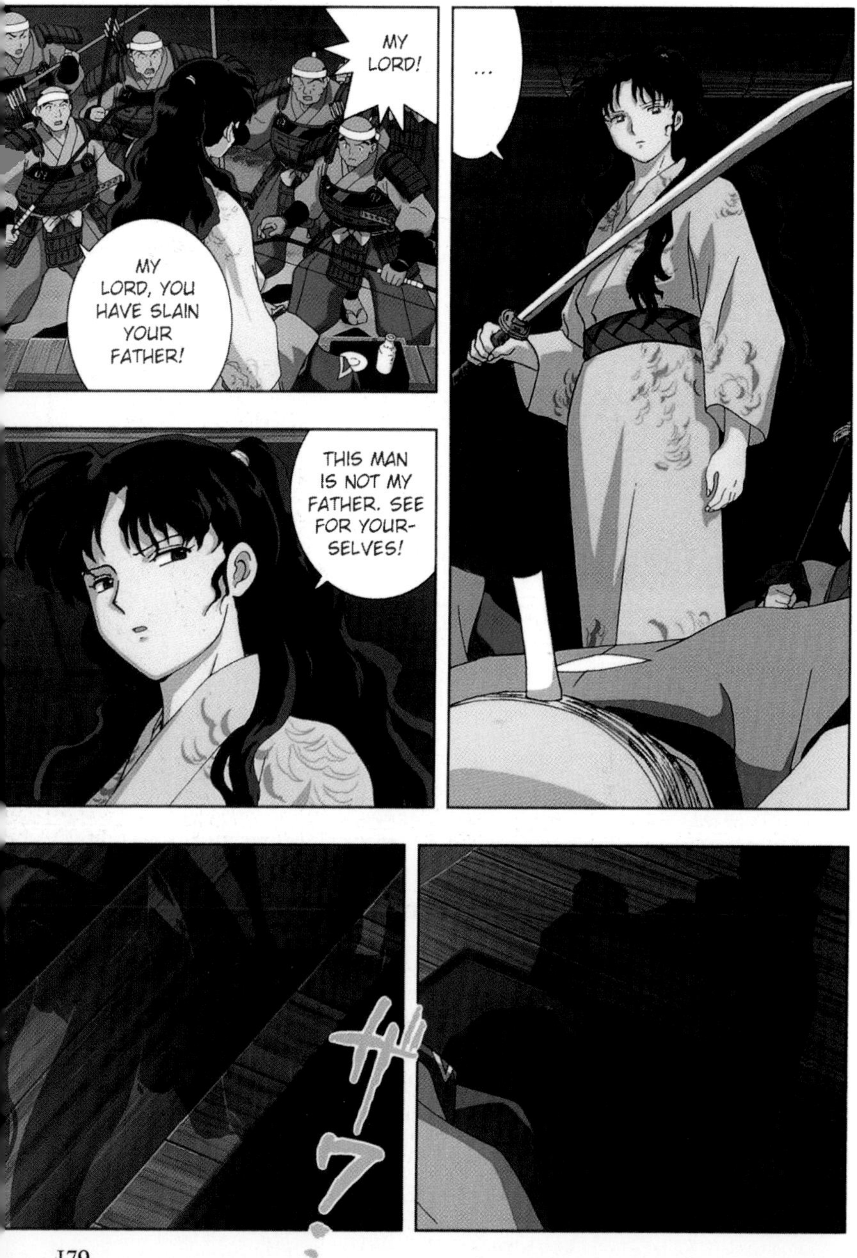
...
MY LORD!
MY LORD, YOU HAVE SLAIN YOUR FATHER!
THIS MAN IS NOT MY FATHER. SEE FOR YOURSELVES!
ザワ

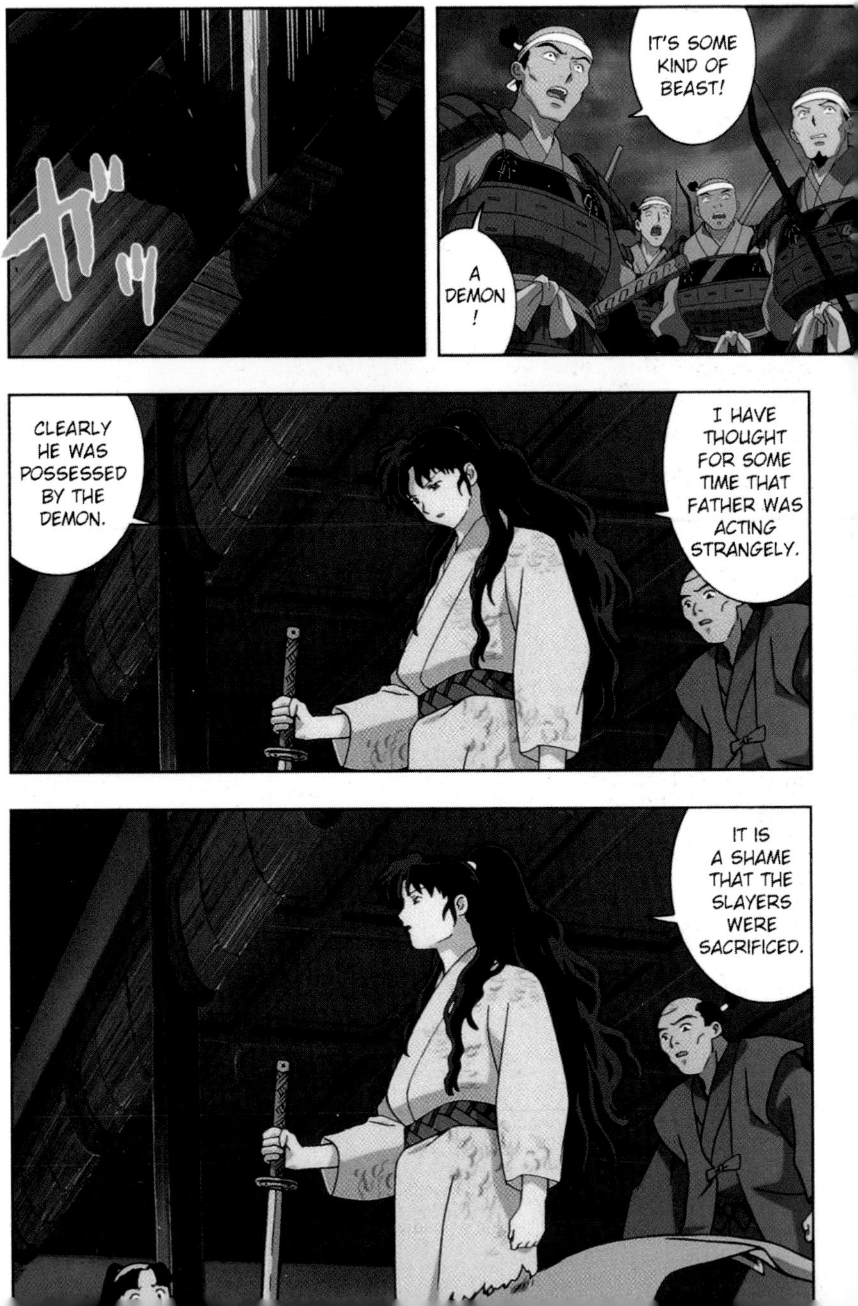
IT'S SOME KIND OF BEAST!
A DEMON!
ガッ
I HAVE THOUGHT FOR SOME TIME THAT FATHER WAS ACTING STRANGELY.
CLEARLY HE WAS POSSESSED BY THE DEMON.
IT IS A SHAME THAT THE SLAYERS WERE SACRIFICED.

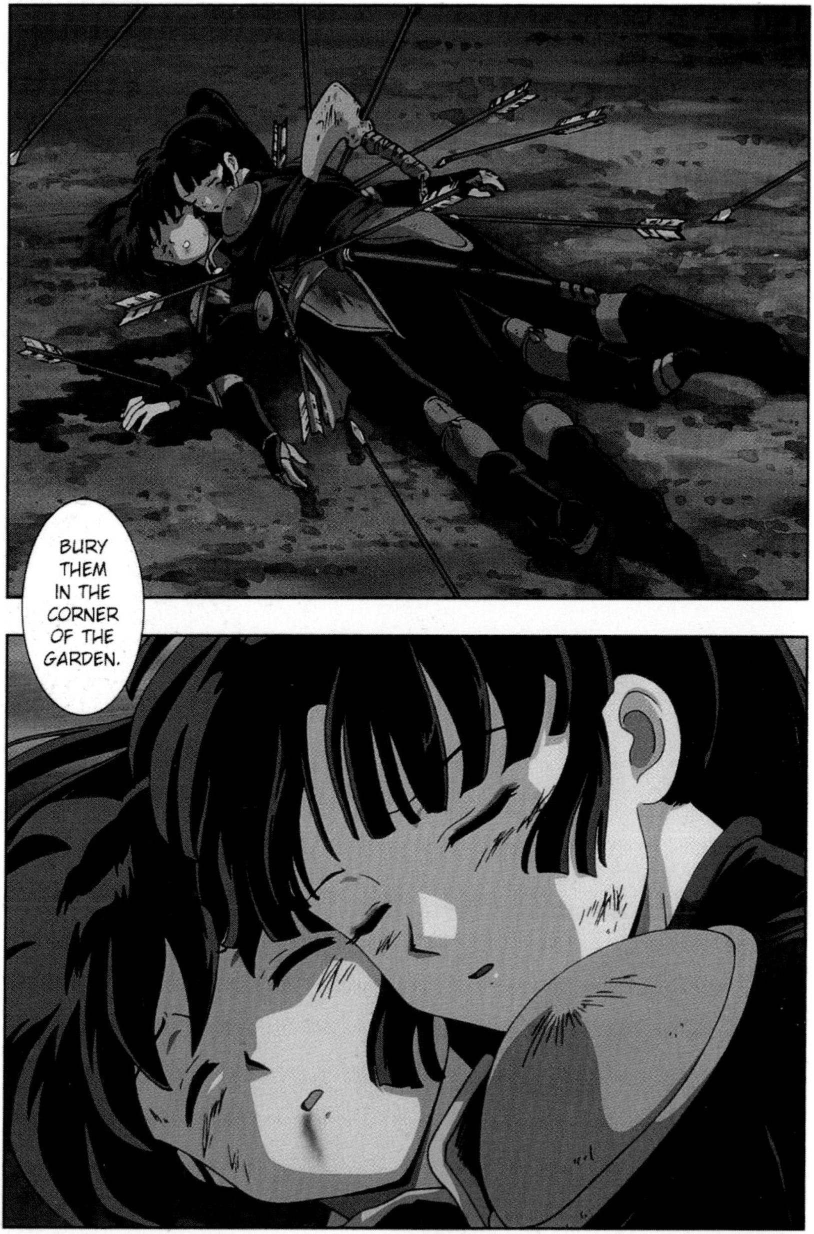
BURY THEM IN THE CORNER OF THE GARDEN.

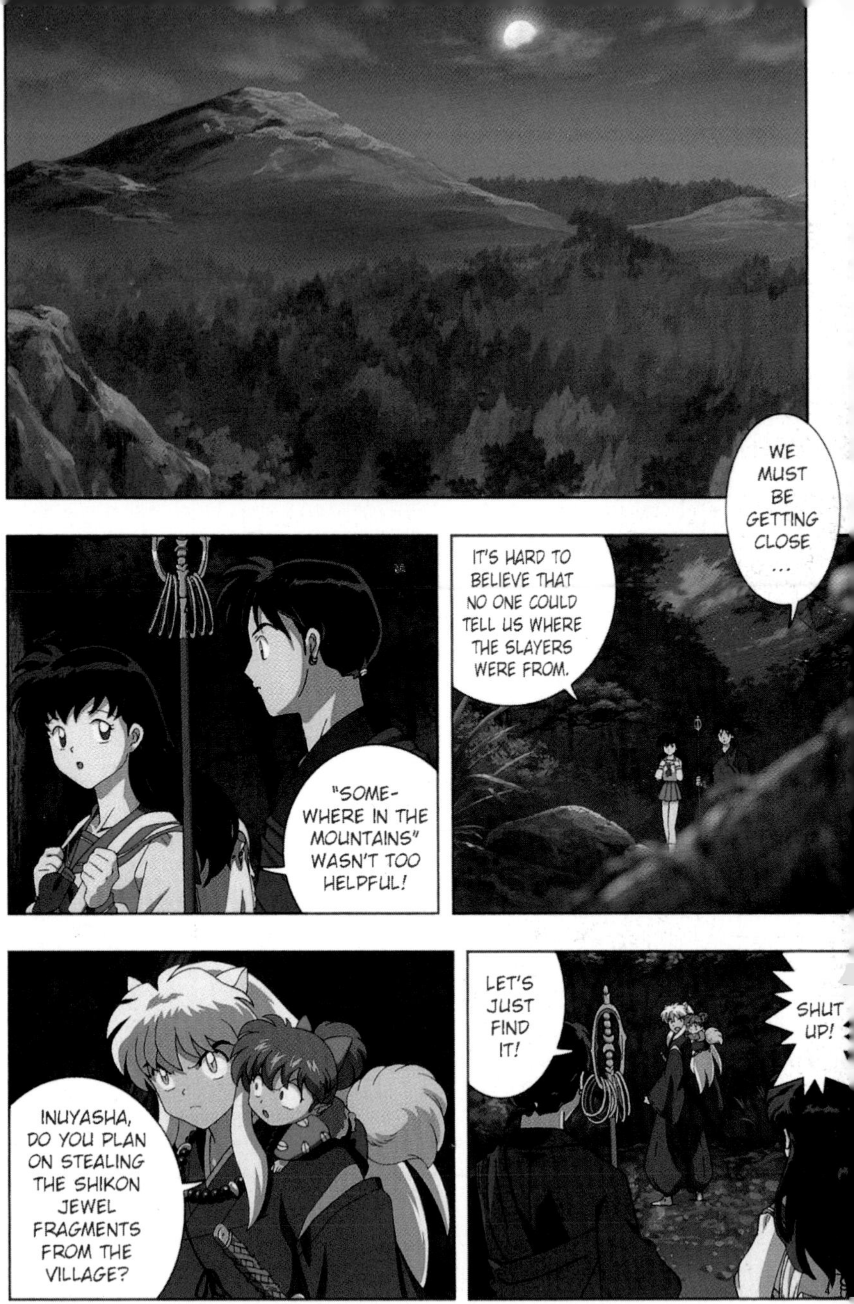
WE MUST BE GETTING CLOSE ...
IT'S HARD TO BELIEVE THAT NO ONE COULD TELL US WHERE THE SLAYERS WERE FROM.
"SOME-WHERE IN THE MOUNTAINS" WASN'T TOO HELPFUL!
SHUT UP!
LET'S JUST FIND IT!
INUYASHA, DO YOU PLAN ON STEALING THE SHIKON JEWEL FRAGMENTS FROM THE VILLAGE?

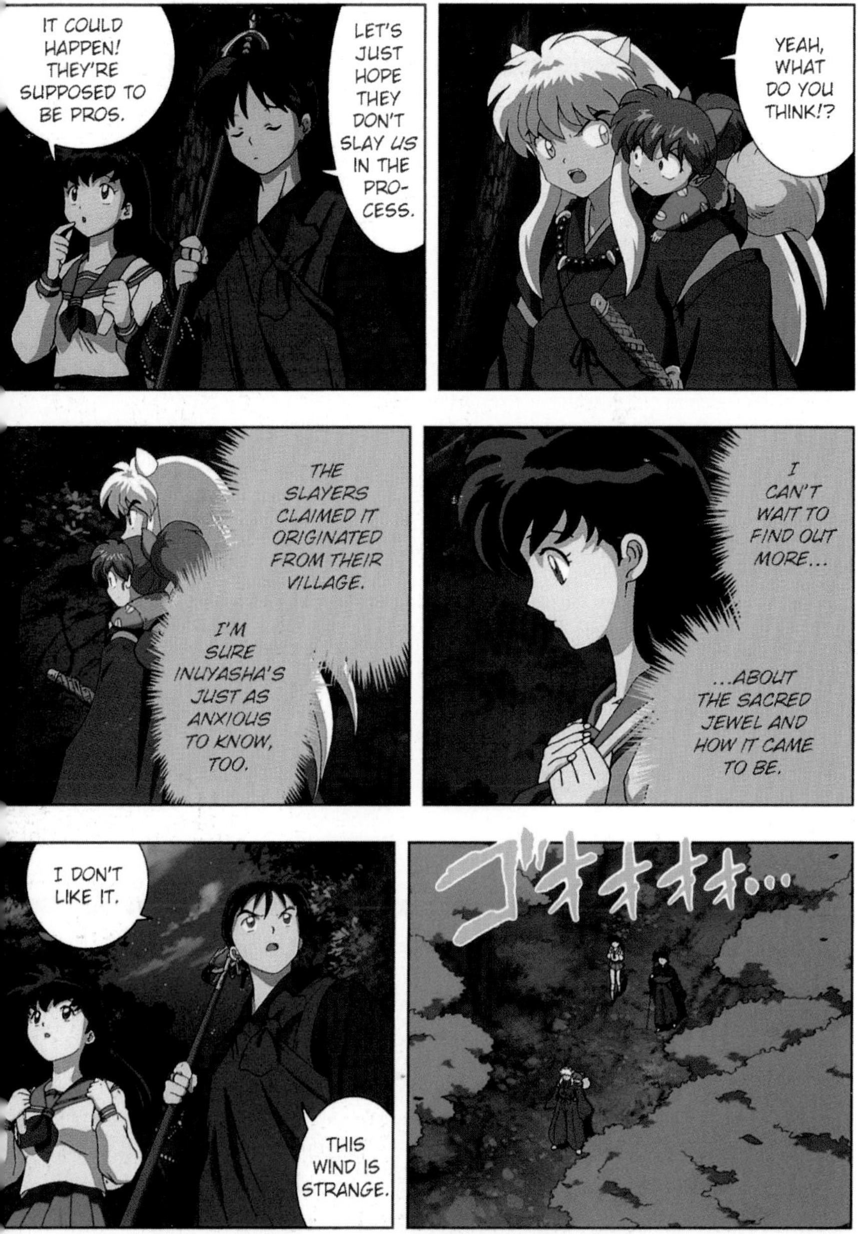
YEAH, WHAT DO YOU THINK!?
LET'S JUST HOPE THEY DON'T SLAY *US* IN THE PRO-CESS.
IT COULD HAPPEN! THEY'RE SUPPOSED TO BE PROS.
I CAN'T WAIT TO FIND OUT MORE...
...ABOUT THE SACRED JEWEL AND HOW IT CAME TO BE.
THE SLAYERS CLAIMED IT ORIGINATED FROM THEIR VILLAGE.
I'M SURE INUYASHA'S JUST AS ANXIOUS TO KNOW, TOO.
ゴオオオオ…
I DON'T LIKE IT.
THIS WIND IS STRANGE.

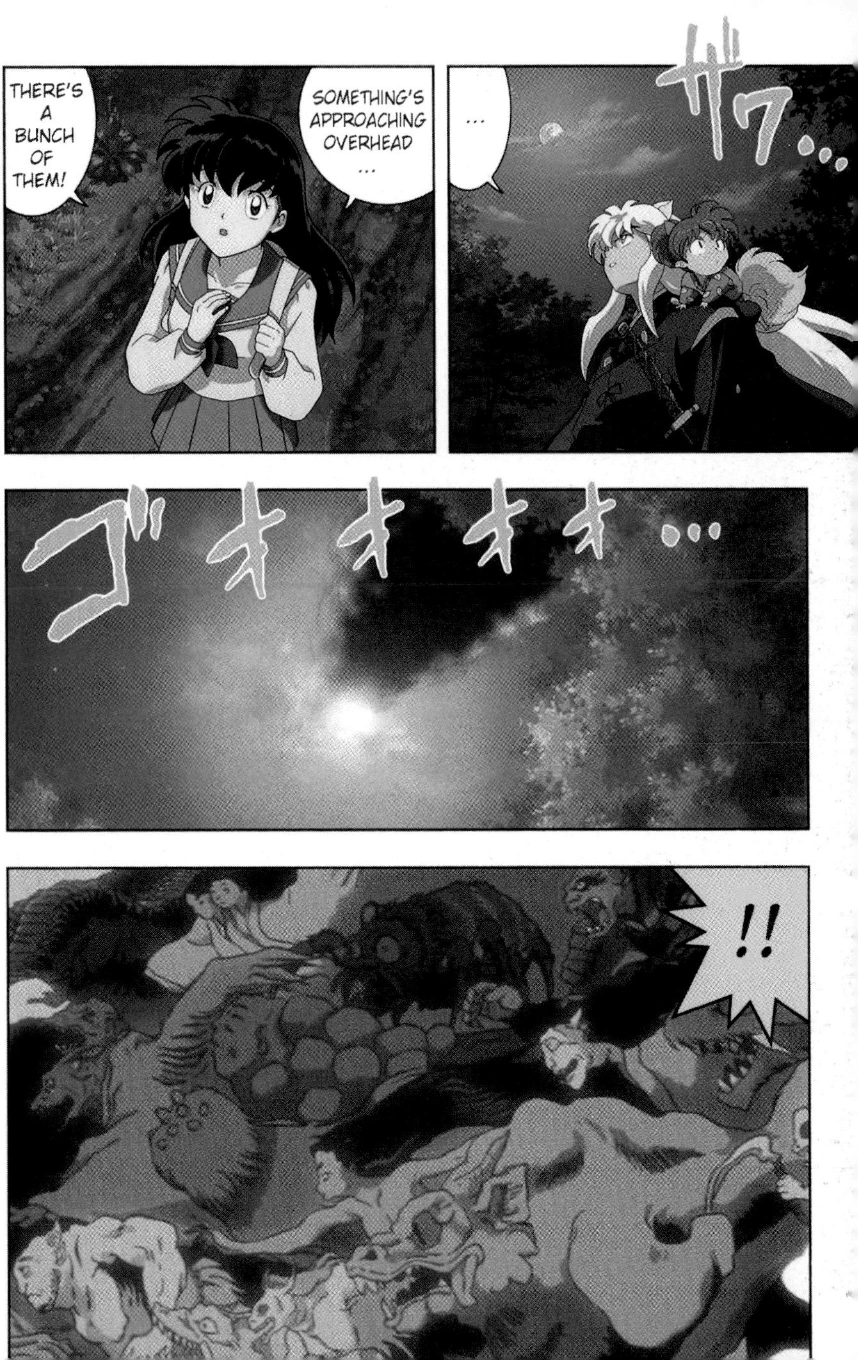
...
ザワ...
SOMETHING'S APPROACHING OVERHEAD ...
THERE'S A BUNCH OF THEM!
ゴォォォォ...
!!

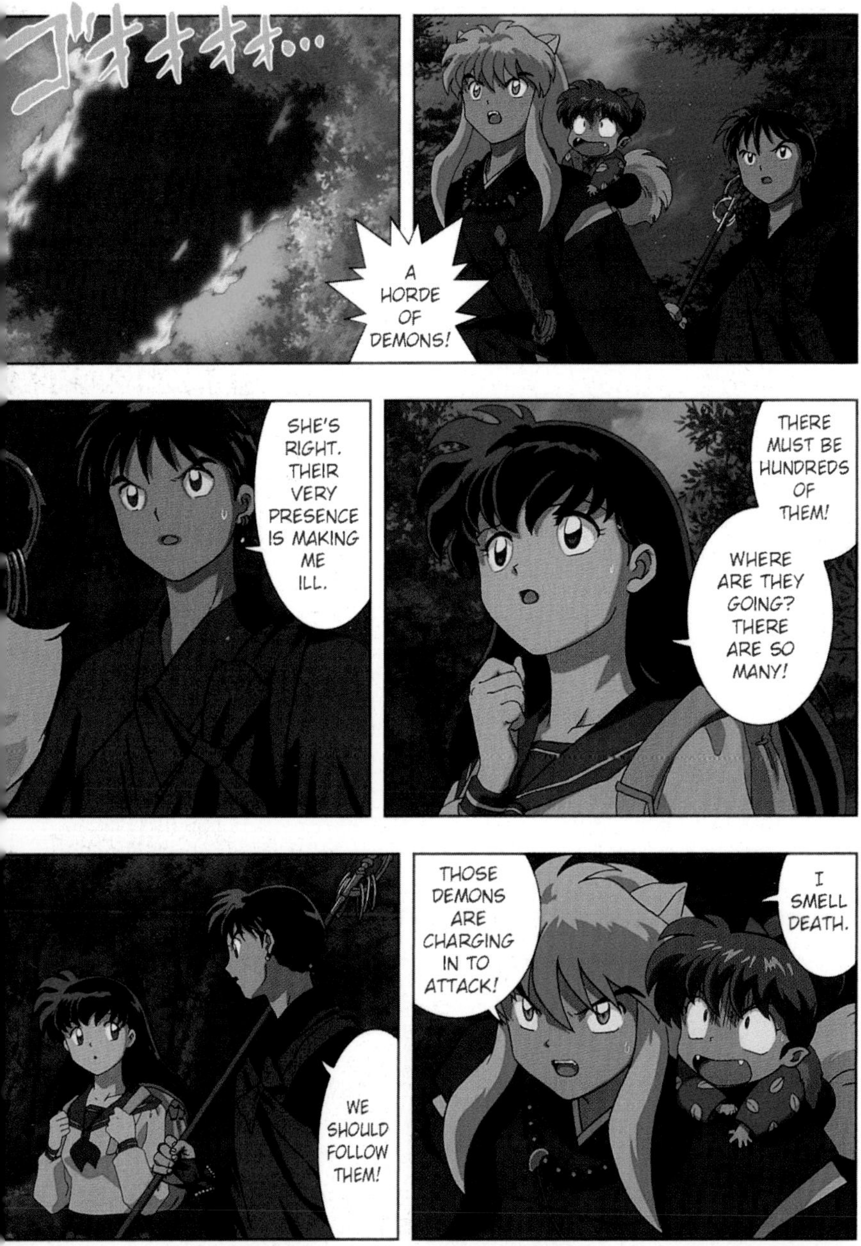
A HORDE OF DEMONS!
ゴオオオオ…
THERE MUST BE HUNDREDS OF THEM!
WHERE ARE THEY GOING? THERE ARE SO MANY!
SHE'S RIGHT. THEIR VERY PRESENCE IS MAKING ME ILL.
I SMELL DEATH.
THOSE DEMONS ARE CHARGING IN TO ATTACK!
WE SHOULD FOLLOW THEM!

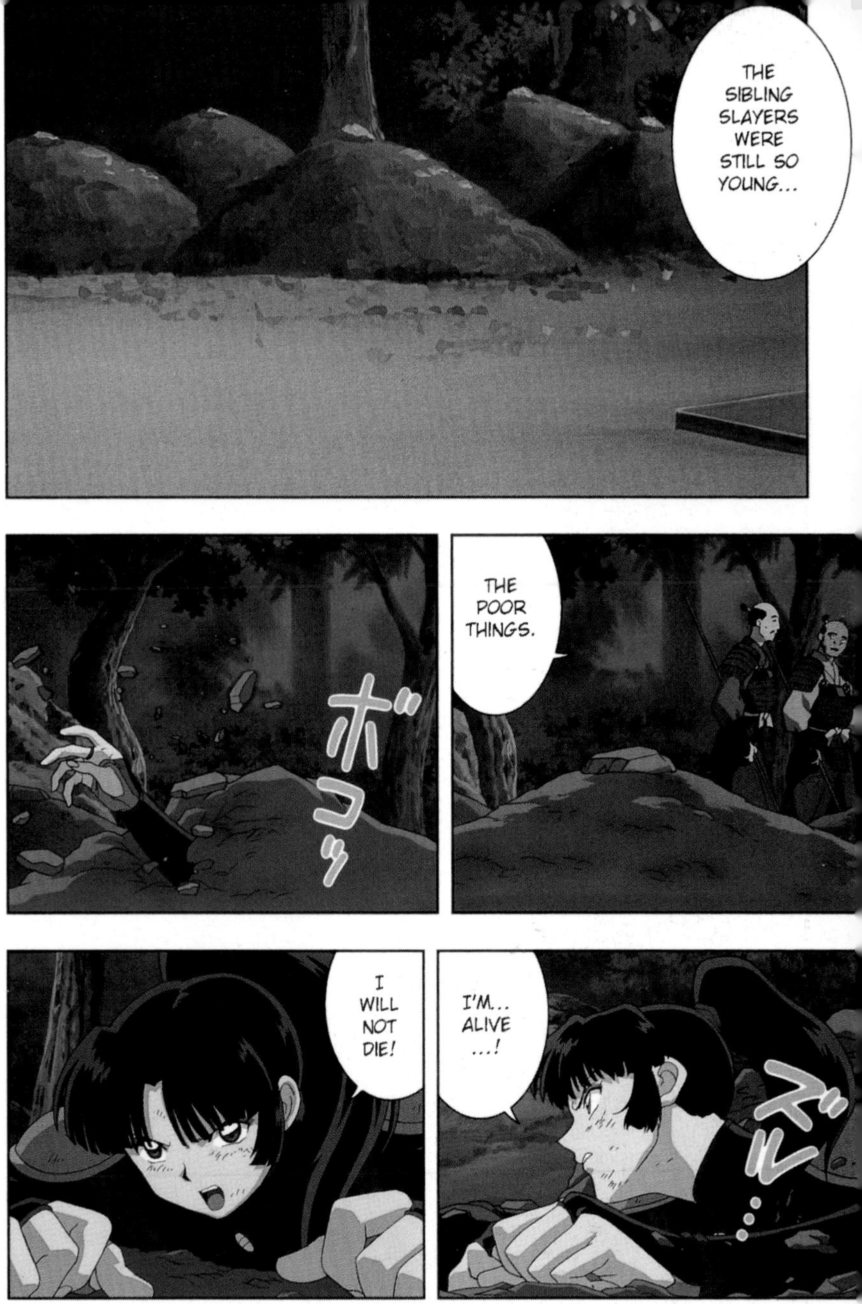
THE SIBLING SLAYERS WERE STILL SO YOUNG...
THE POOR THINGS.
ボコッ
I'M... ALIVE ...!
ズル…
I WILL NOT DIE!

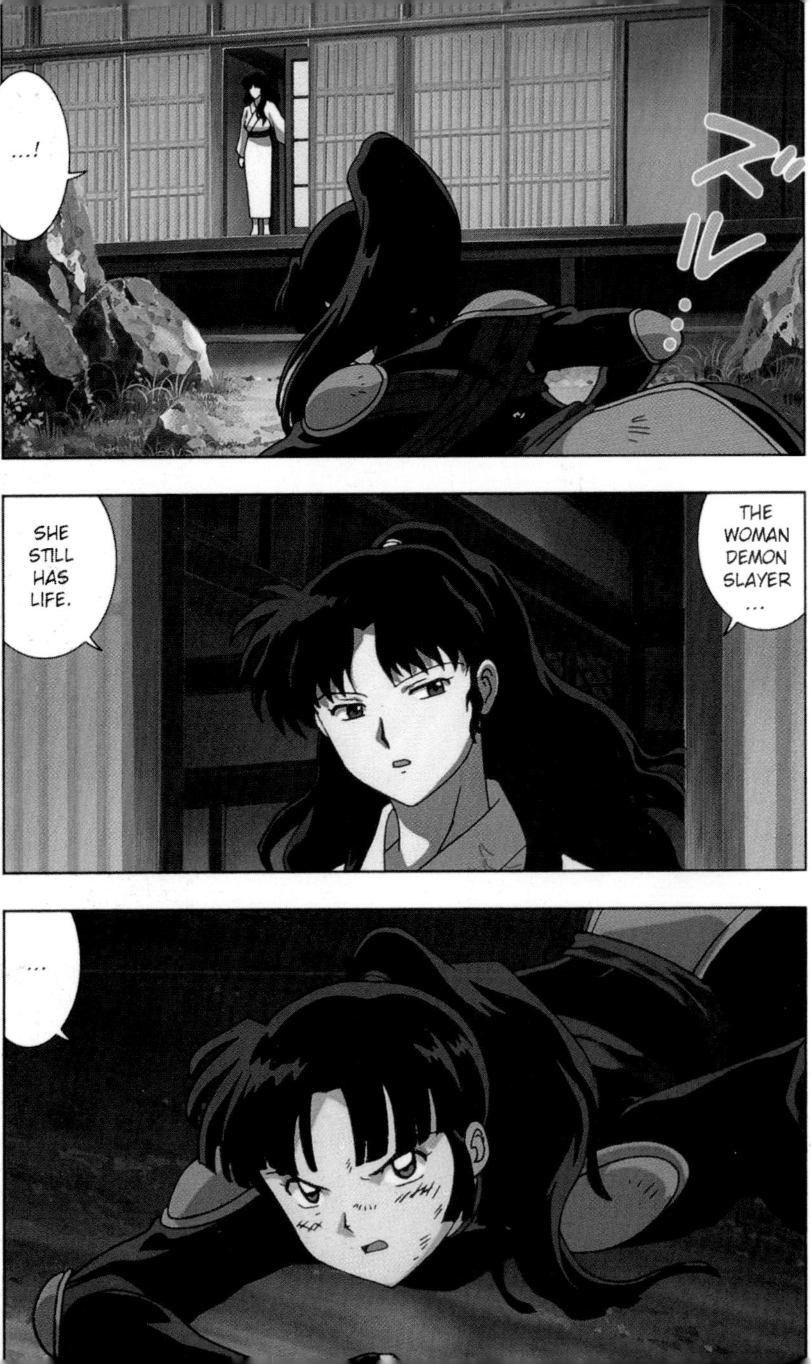
...!
THE WOMAN DEMON SLAYER ...
SHE STILL HAS LIFE.
...

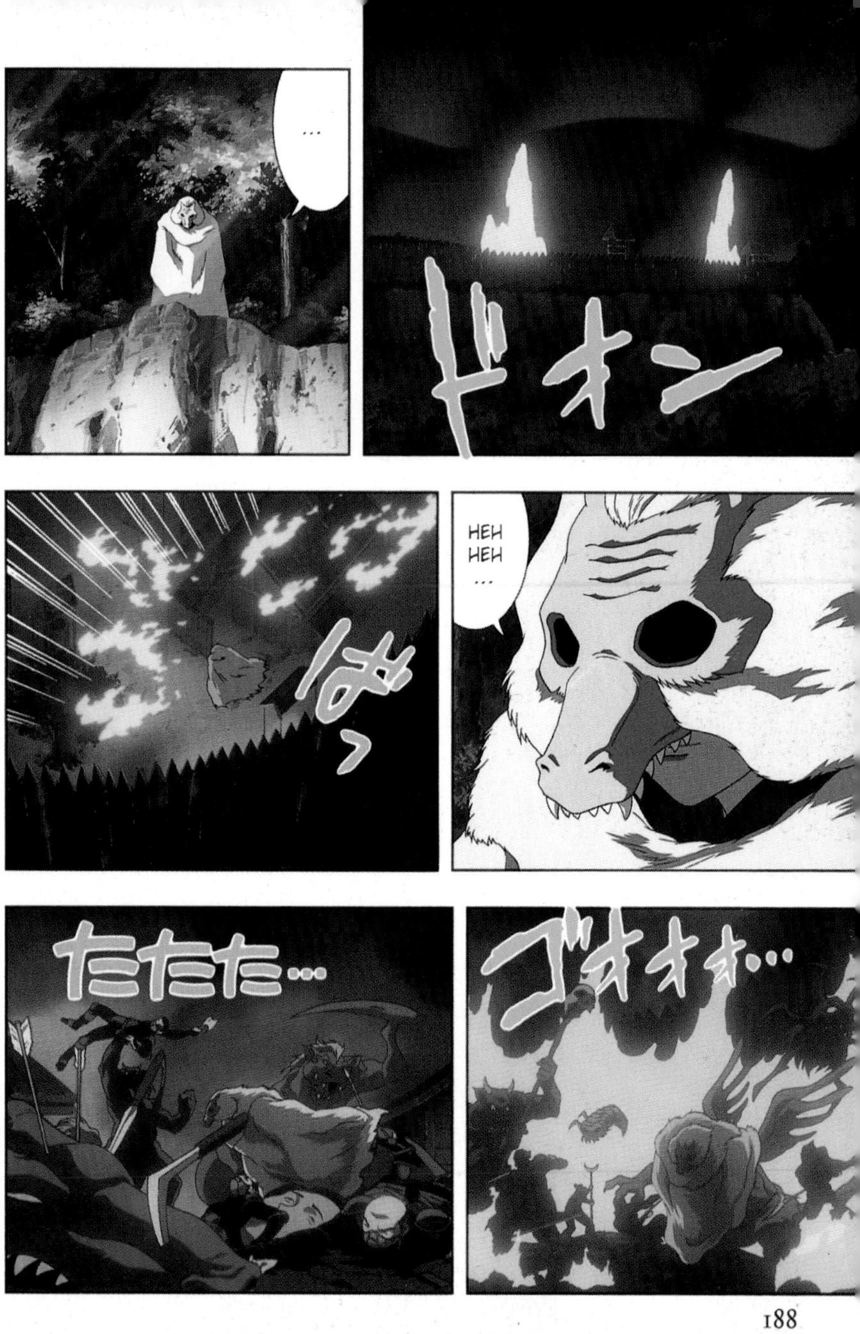
ドオン
...
HEH HEH ...
ばっ
ゴオオオ…
たたた…

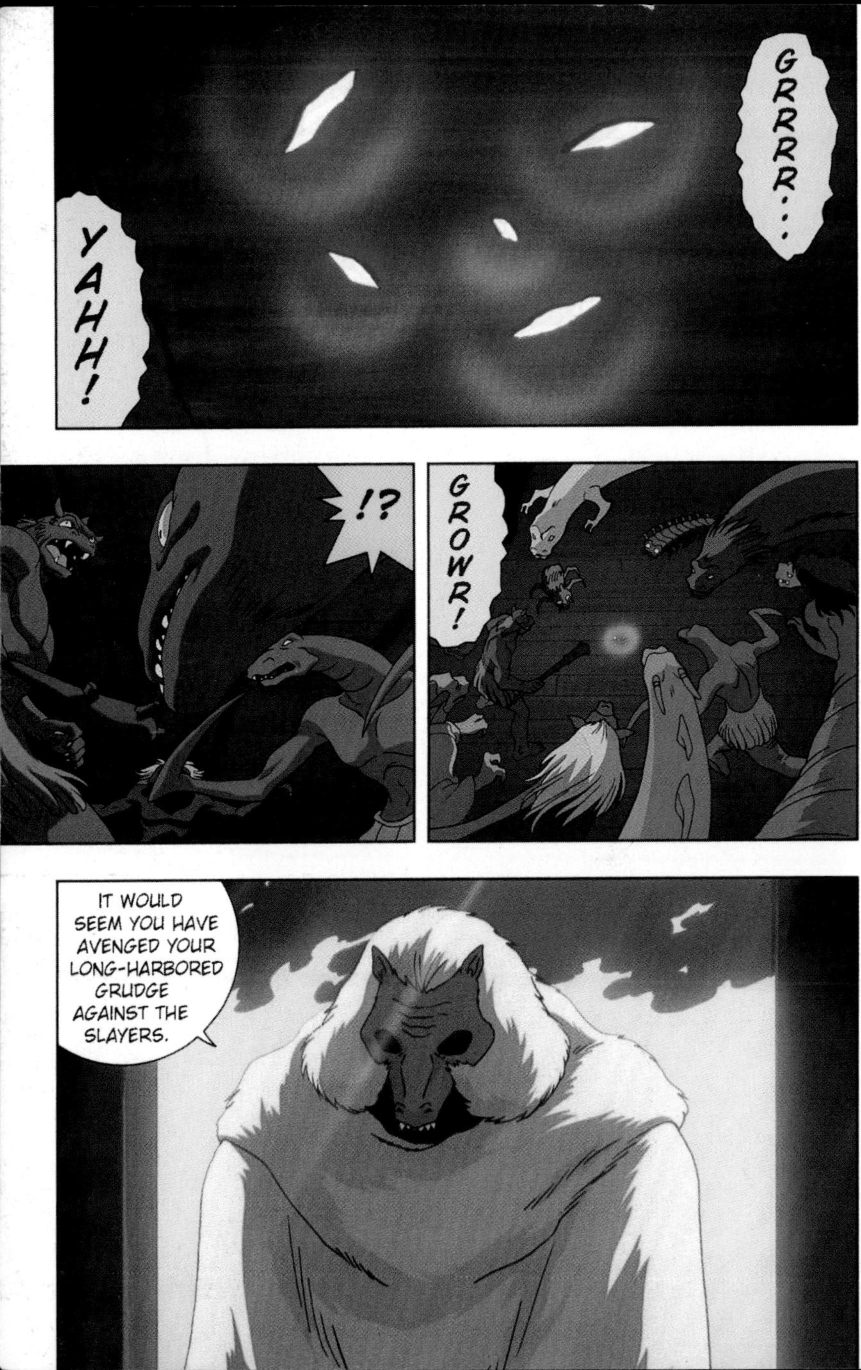
GRRRR...
YAHH!
GROWR!
!?
IT WOULD SEEM YOU HAVE AVENGED YOUR LONG-HARBORED GRUDGE AGAINST THE SLAYERS.

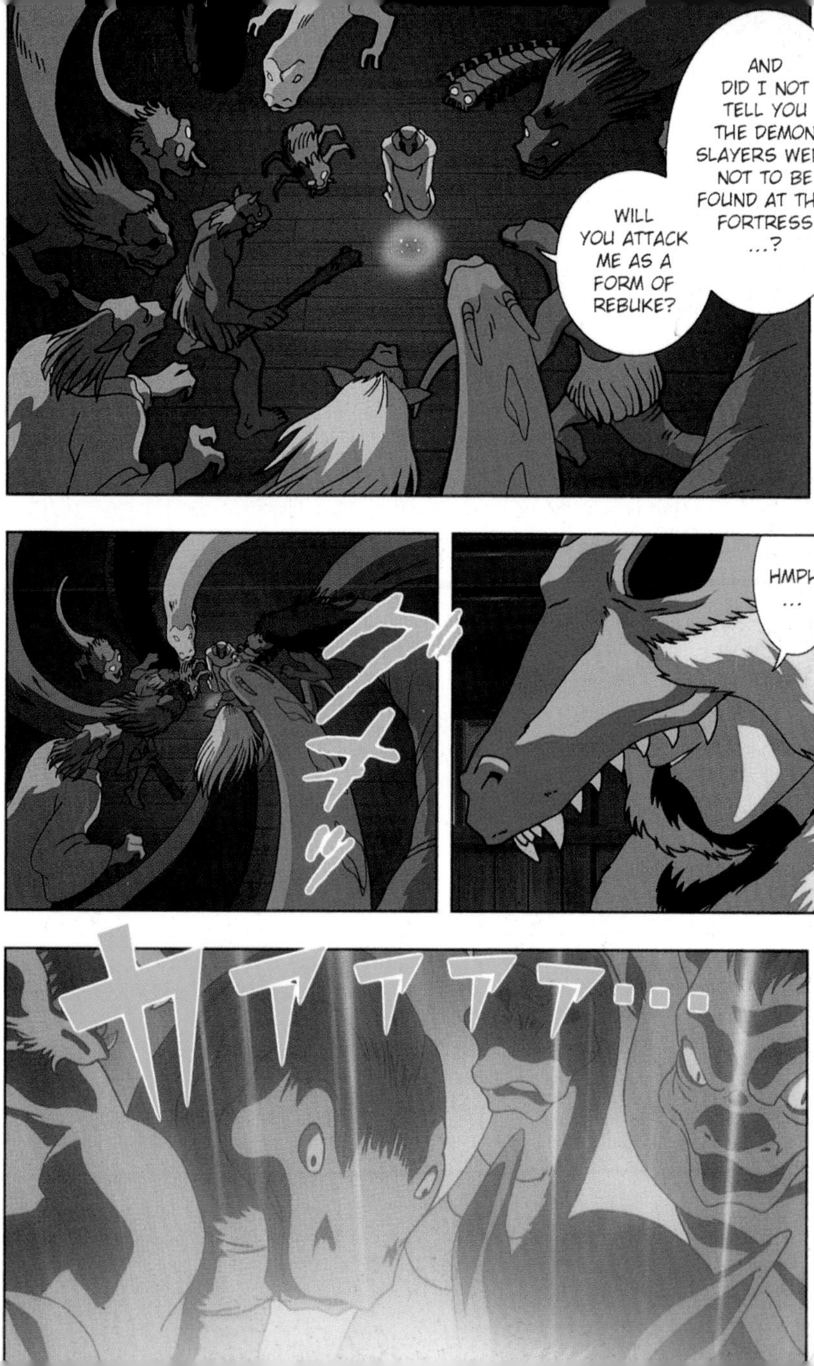
AND DID I NOT TELL YOU THE DEMON SLAYERS WERE NOT TO BE FOUND AT THIS FORTRESS ...?
WILL YOU ATTACK ME AS A FORM OF REBUKE?
HMPH ...
カァァァァ...

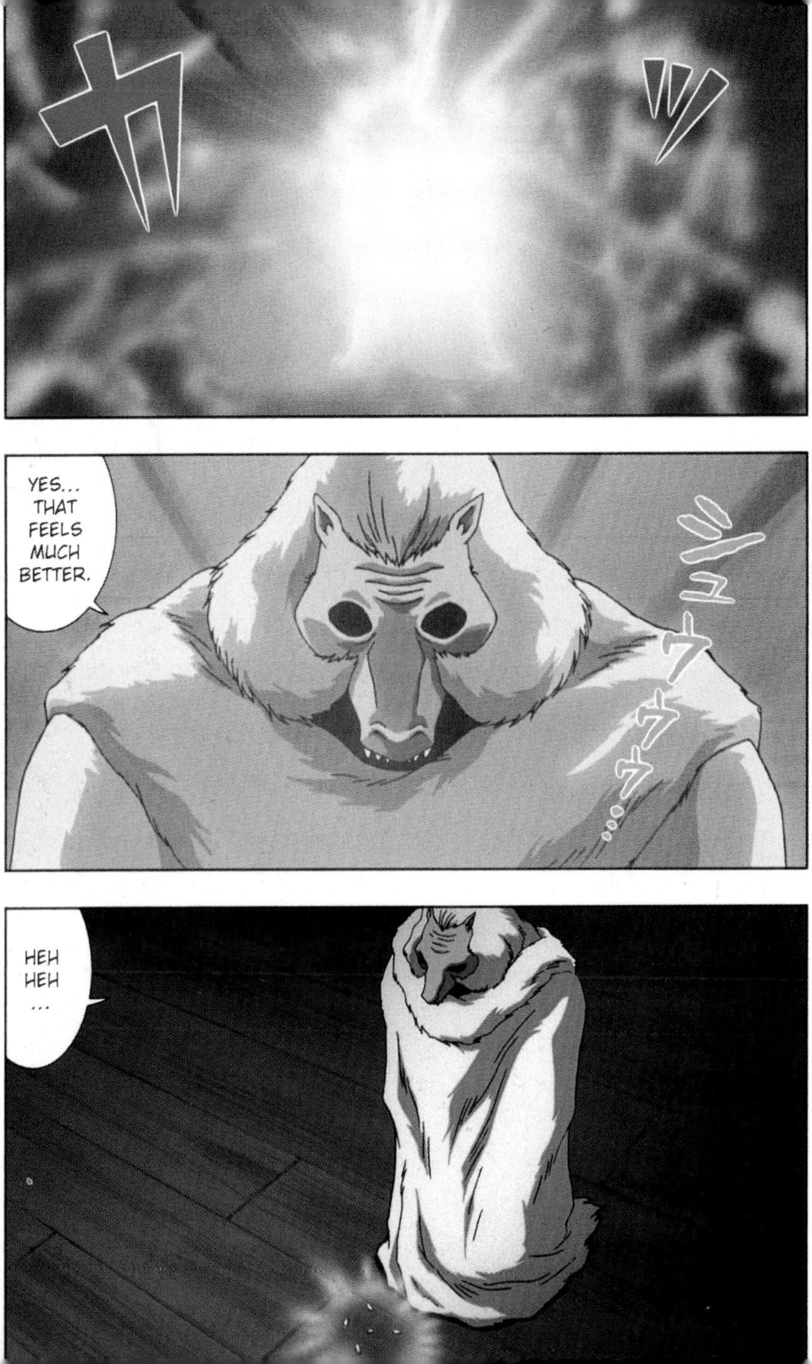
カッ
YES... THAT FEELS MUCH BETTER.
シュウゥゥ…
HEH HEH ...

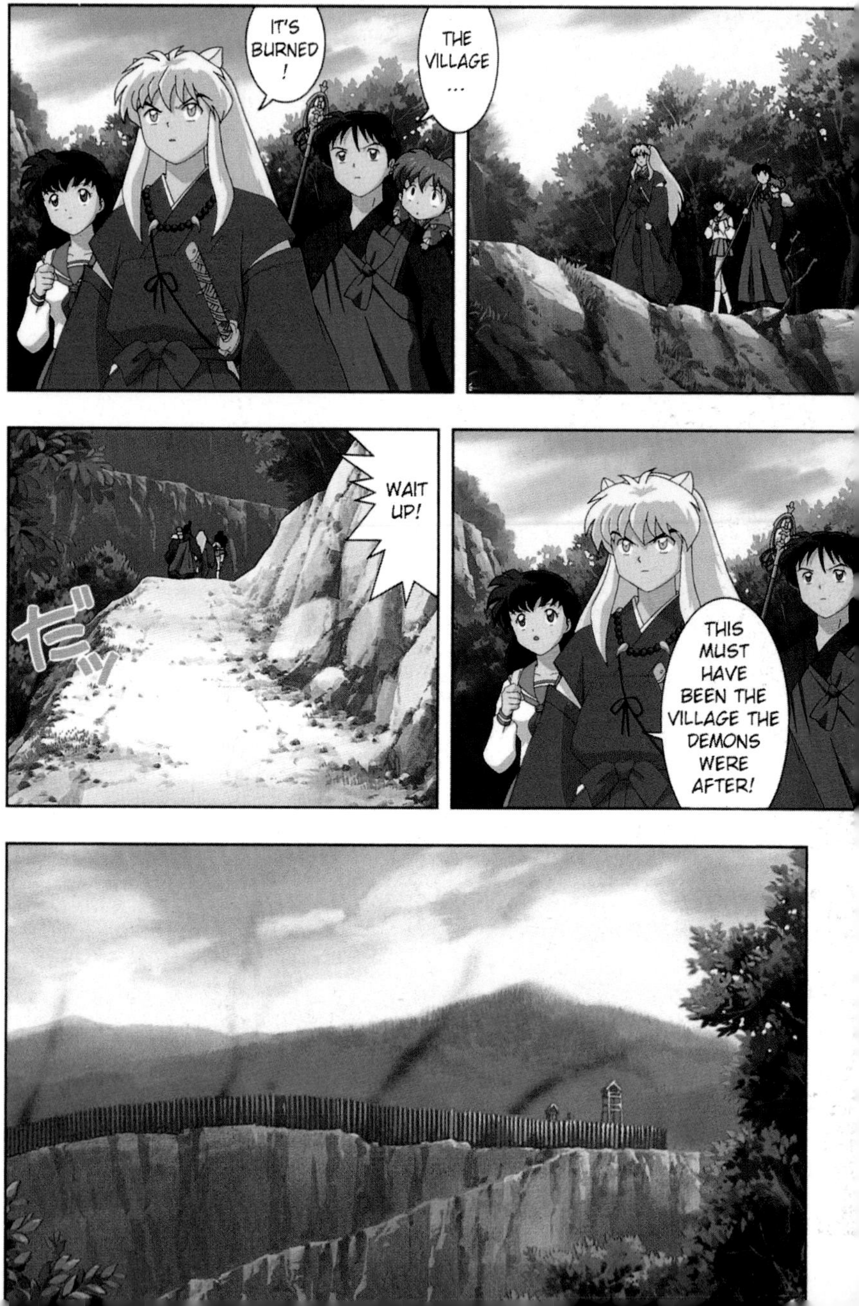
THE VILLAGE ...
IT'S BURNED !
THIS MUST HAVE BEEN THE VILLAGE THE DEMONS WERE AFTER!
WAIT UP!
ダッ

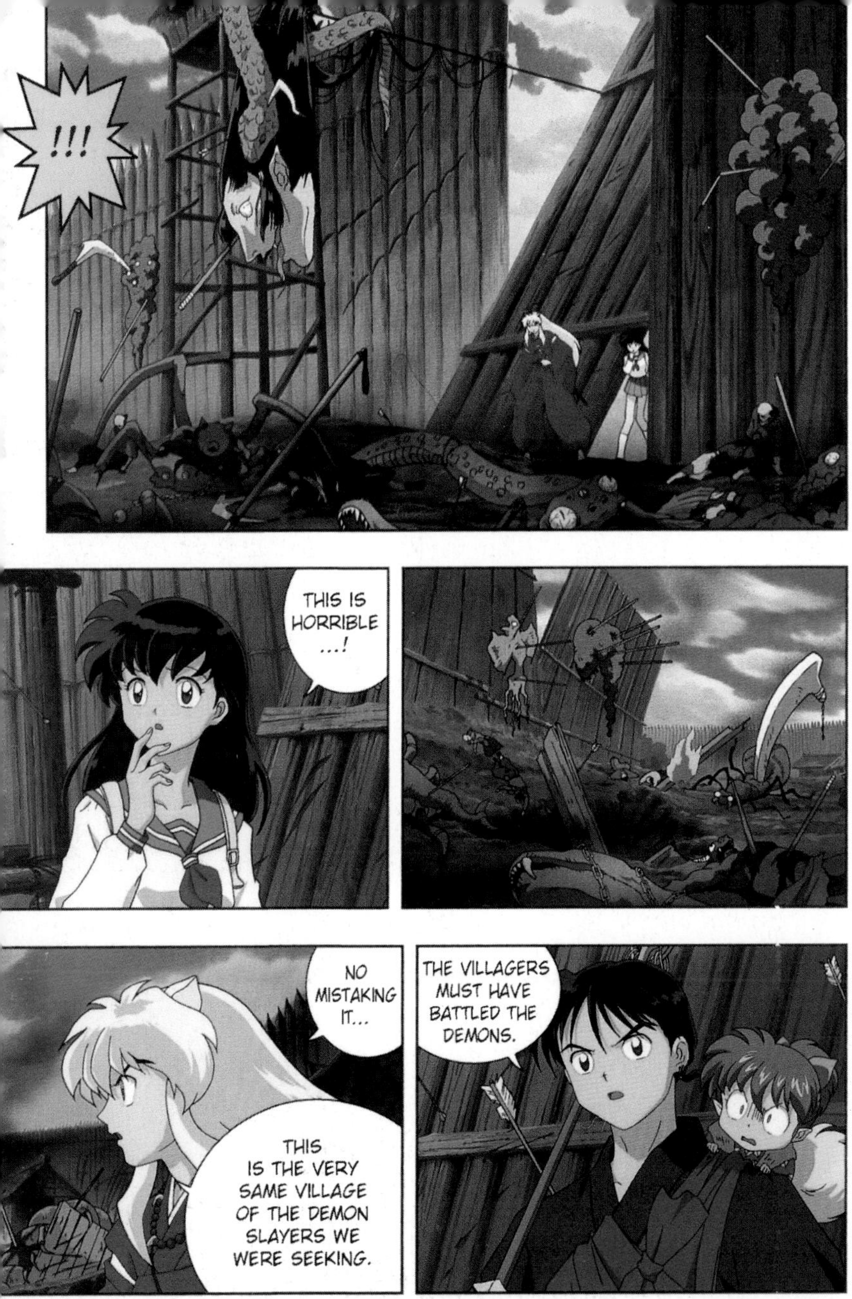
!!!
THIS IS HORRIBLE ...!
THE VILLAGERS MUST HAVE BATTLED THE DEMONS.
NO MISTAKING IT...
THIS IS THE VERY SAME VILLAGE OF THE DEMON SLAYERS WE WERE SEEKING.

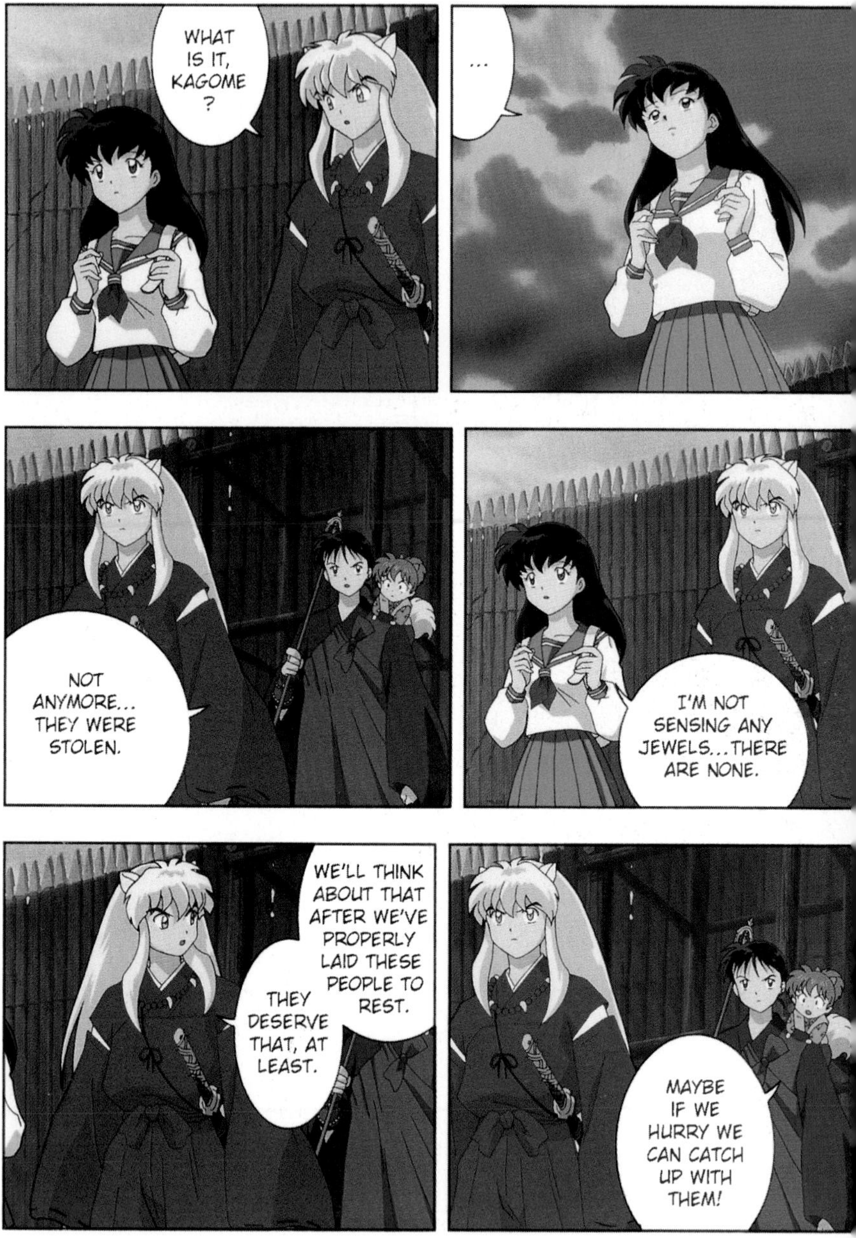
...
WHAT IS IT, KAGOME?
I'M NOT SENSING ANY JEWELS...THERE ARE NONE.
NOT ANYMORE... THEY WERE STOLEN.
MAYBE IF WE HURRY WE CAN CATCH UP WITH THEM!
WE'LL THINK ABOUT THAT AFTER WE'VE PROPERLY LAID THESE PEOPLE TO REST.
THEY DESERVE THAT, AT LEAST.

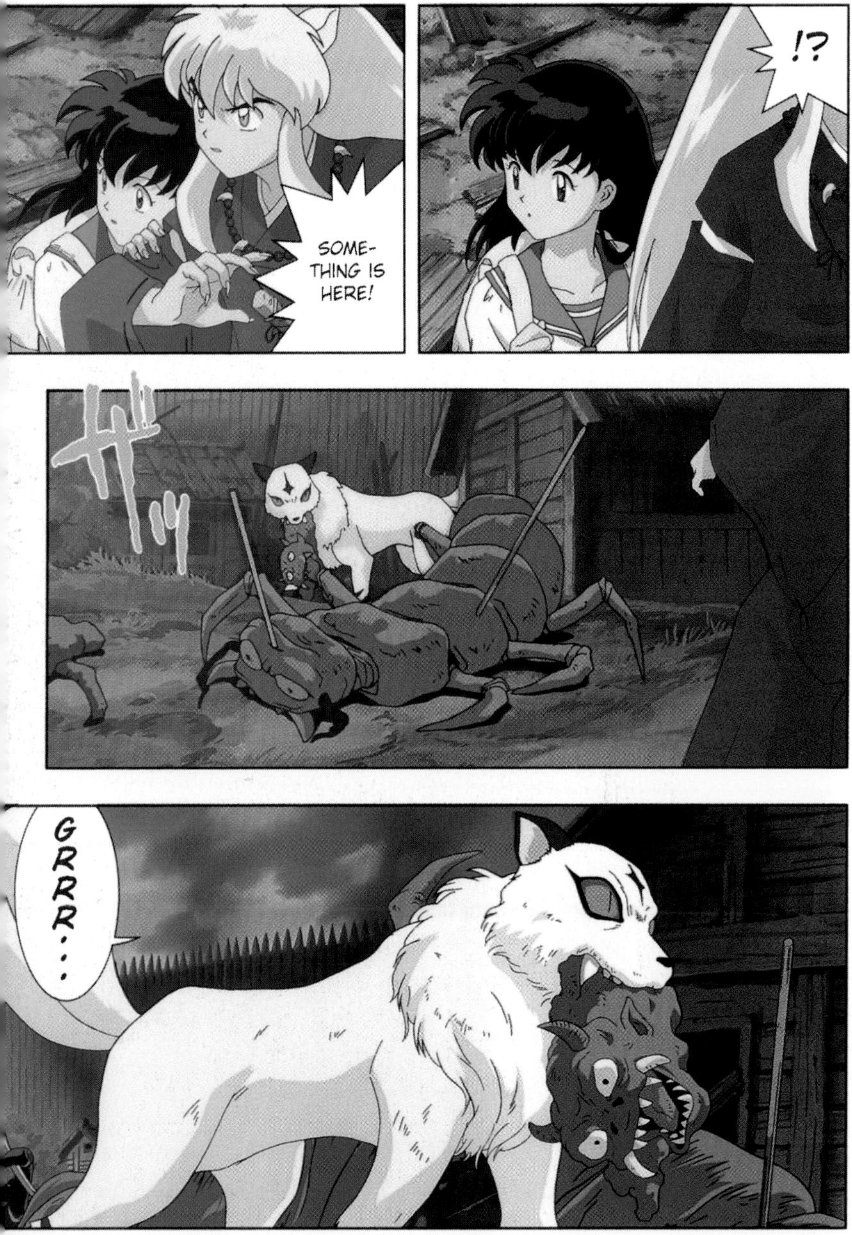
!?
SOME-THING IS HERE!
GRRR...

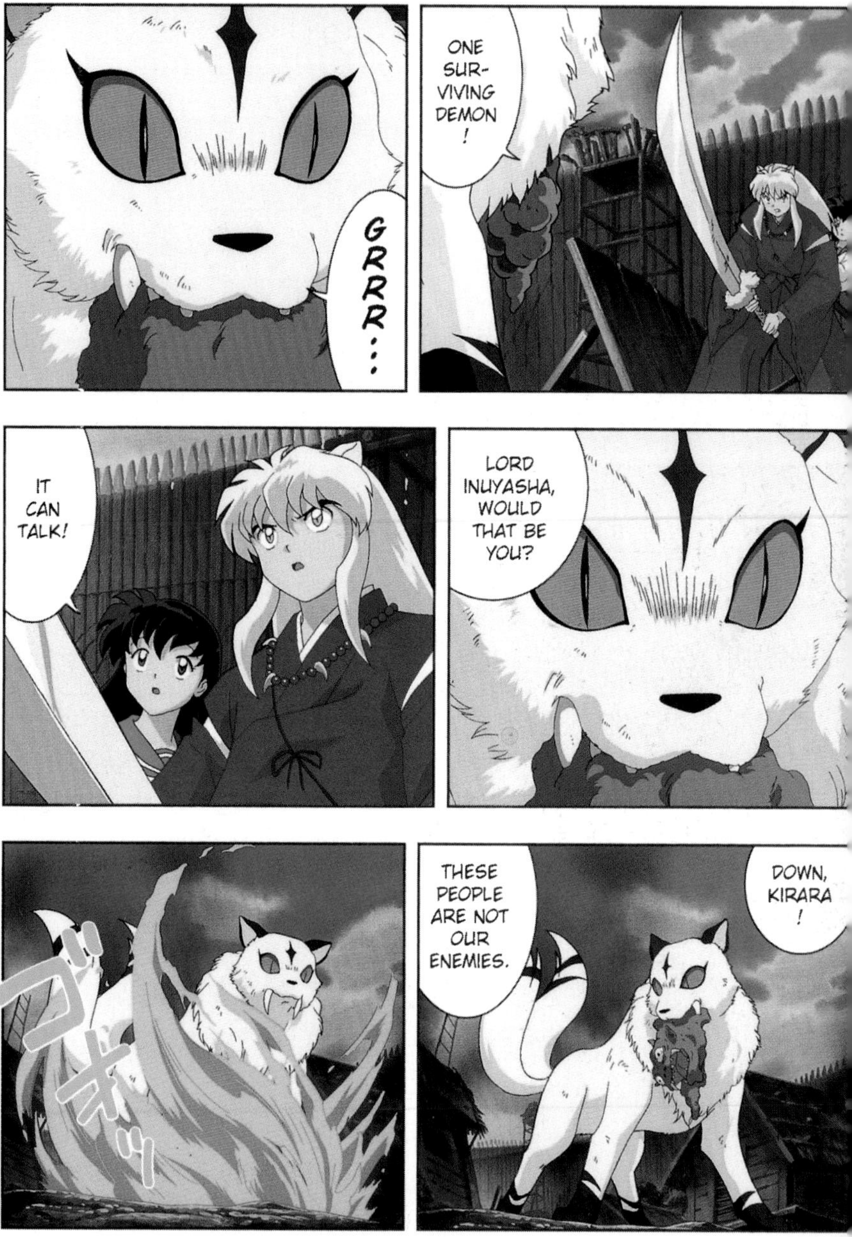
ONE SUR-VIVING DEMON!
GRRR..
LORD INUYASHA, WOULD THAT BE YOU?
IT CAN TALK!
DOWN, KIRARA!
THESE PEOPLE ARE NOT OUR ENEMIES.
ゴォッ

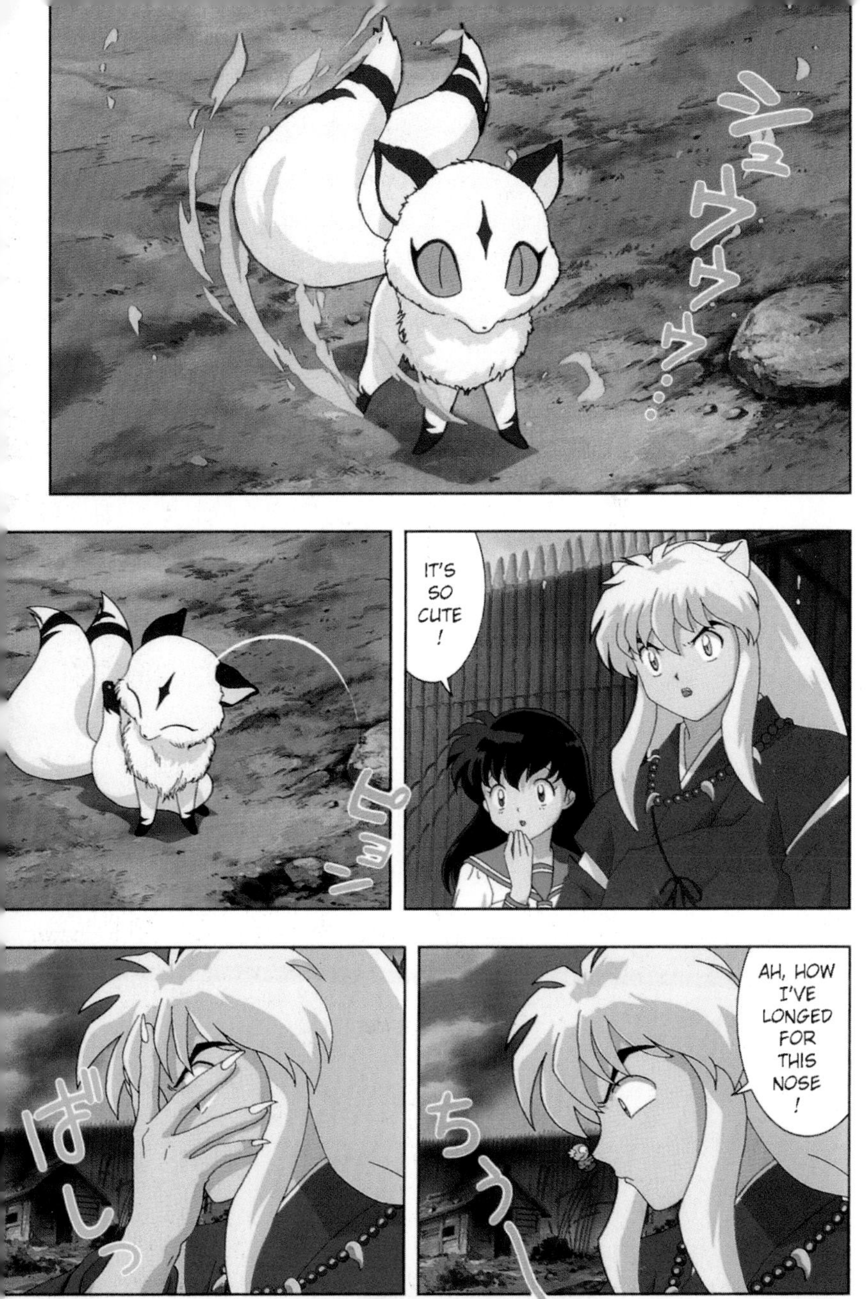
IT'S SO CUTE!
AH, HOW I'VE LONGED FOR THIS NOSE!
ちぅ～
ぱしっ

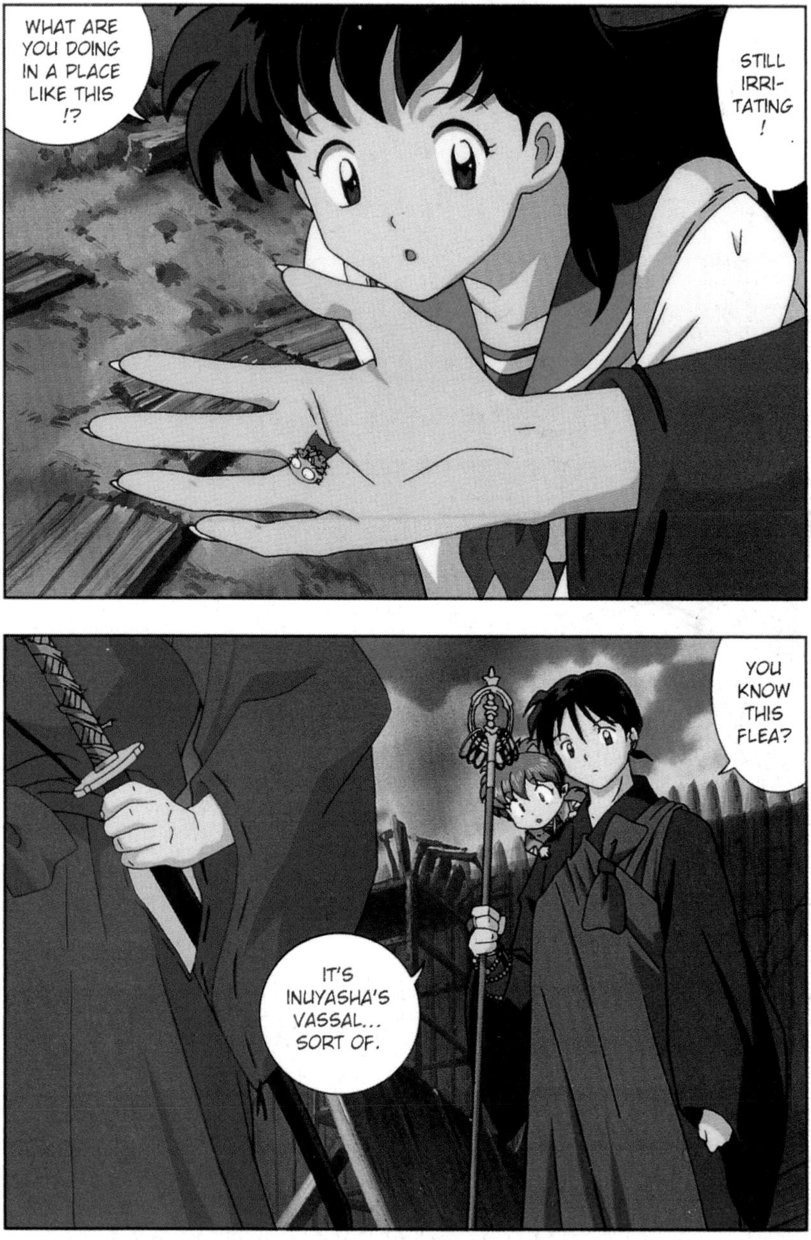
STILL IRRI-TATING!
WHAT ARE YOU DOING IN A PLACE LIKE THIS!?
YOU KNOW THIS FLEA?
IT'S INUYASHA'S VASSAL... SORT OF.

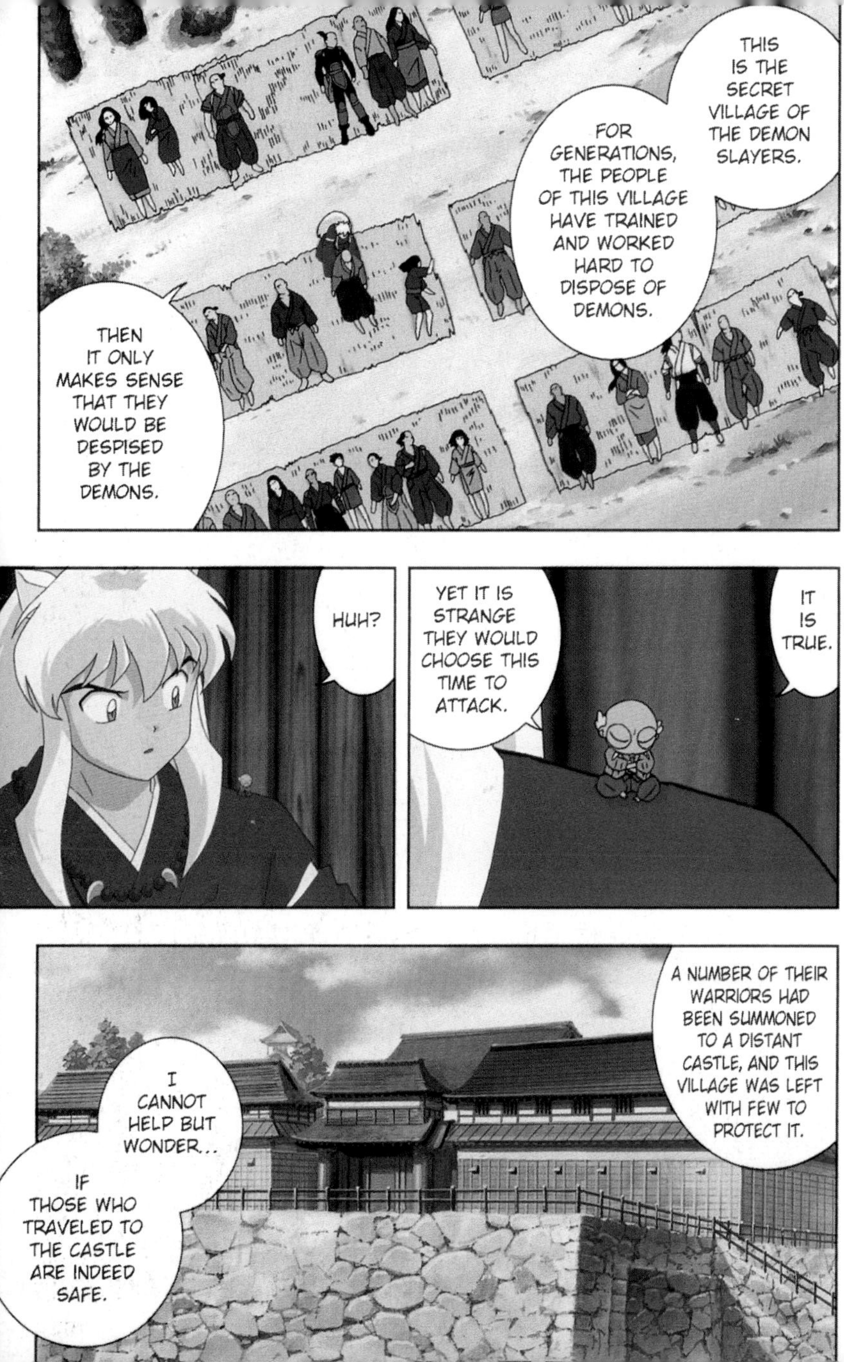
THIS IS THE SECRET VILLAGE OF THE DEMON SLAYERS.
FOR GENERATIONS, THE PEOPLE OF THIS VILLAGE HAVE TRAINED AND WORKED HARD TO DISPOSE OF DEMONS.
THEN IT ONLY MAKES SENSE THAT THEY WOULD BE DESPISED BY THE DEMONS.
IT IS TRUE.
YET IT IS STRANGE THEY WOULD CHOOSE THIS TIME TO ATTACK.
HUH?
A NUMBER OF THEIR WARRIORS HAD BEEN SUMMONED TO A DISTANT CASTLE, AND THIS VILLAGE WAS LEFT WITH FEW TO PROTECT IT.
I CANNOT HELP BUT WONDER...
IF THOSE WHO TRAVELED TO THE CASTLE ARE INDEED SAFE.

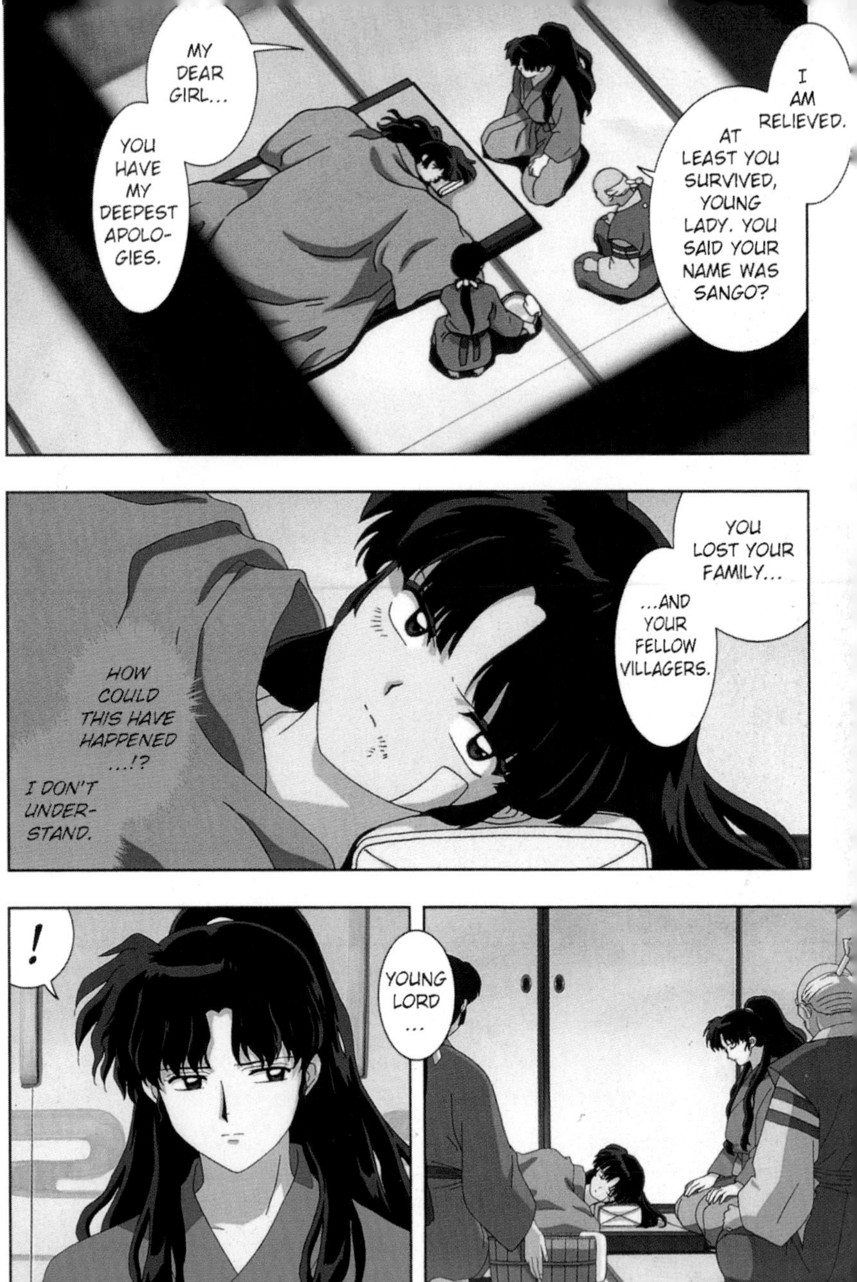
I AM RELIEVED. AT LEAST YOU SURVIVED, YOUNG LADY. YOU SAID YOUR NAME WAS SANGO?
MY DEAR GIRL...
YOU HAVE MY DEEPEST APOLOGIES.
YOU LOST YOUR FAMILY...
...AND YOUR FELLOW VILLAGERS.
HOW COULD THIS HAVE HAPPENED ...!?
I DON'T UNDERSTAND.
YOUNG LORD ...
!

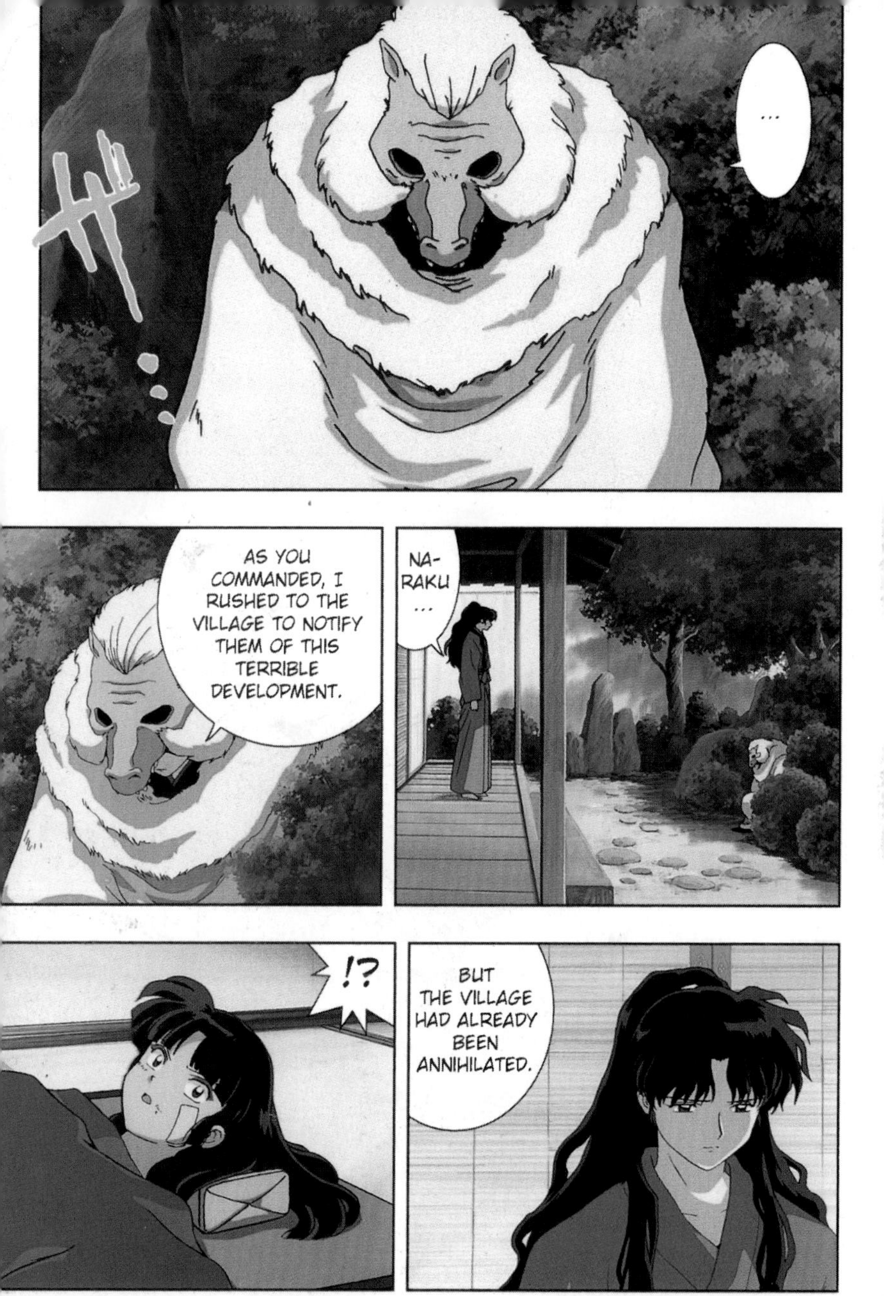
...
NA-RAKU ...
AS YOU COMMANDED, I RUSHED TO THE VILLAGE TO NOTIFY THEM OF THIS TERRIBLE DEVELOPMENT.
BUT THE VILLAGE HAD ALREADY BEEN ANNIHILATED.
!?

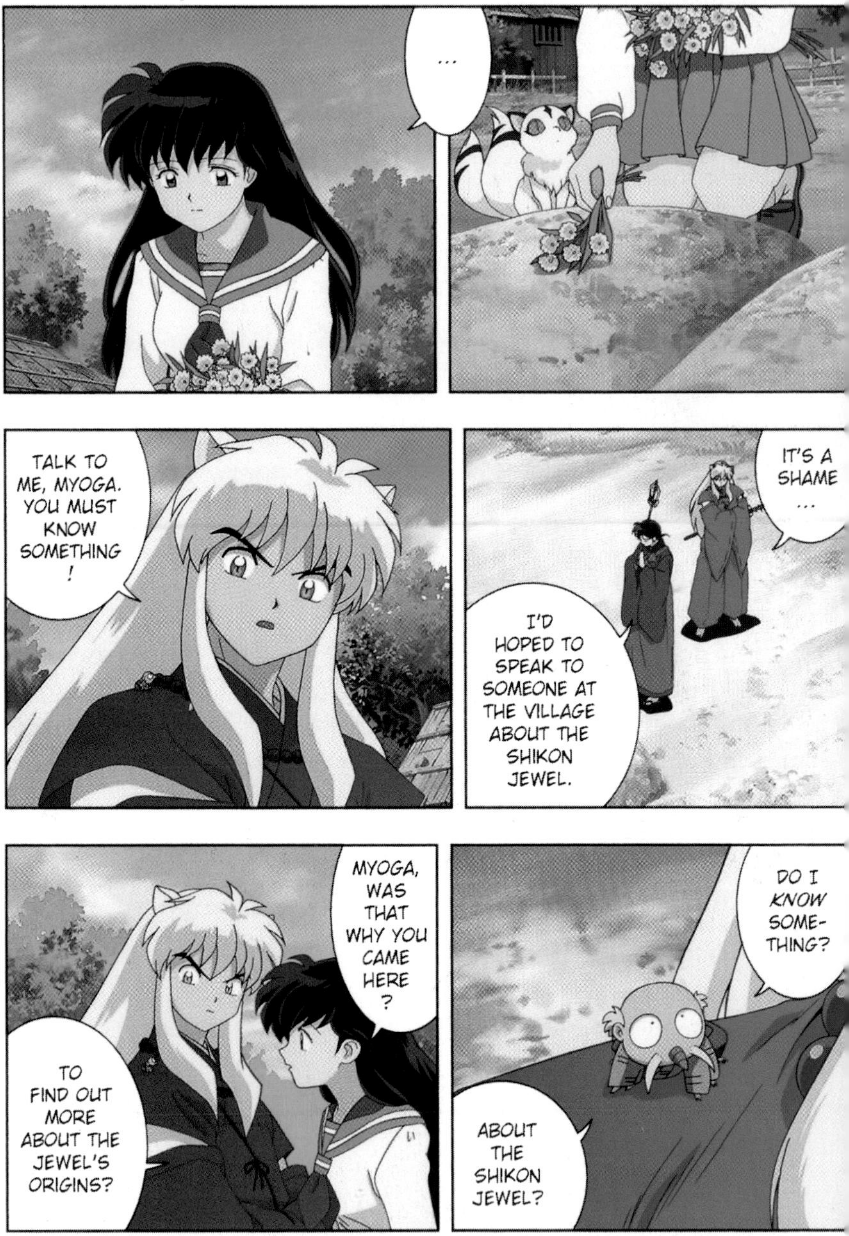
...
IT'S A SHAME ...
I'D HOPED TO SPEAK TO SOMEONE AT THE VILLAGE ABOUT THE SHIKON JEWEL.
TALK TO ME, MYOGA. YOU MUST KNOW SOMETHING!
DO I KNOW SOMETHING?
ABOUT THE SHIKON JEWEL?
MYOGA, WAS THAT WHY YOU CAME HERE?
TO FIND OUT MORE ABOUT THE JEWEL'S ORIGINS?

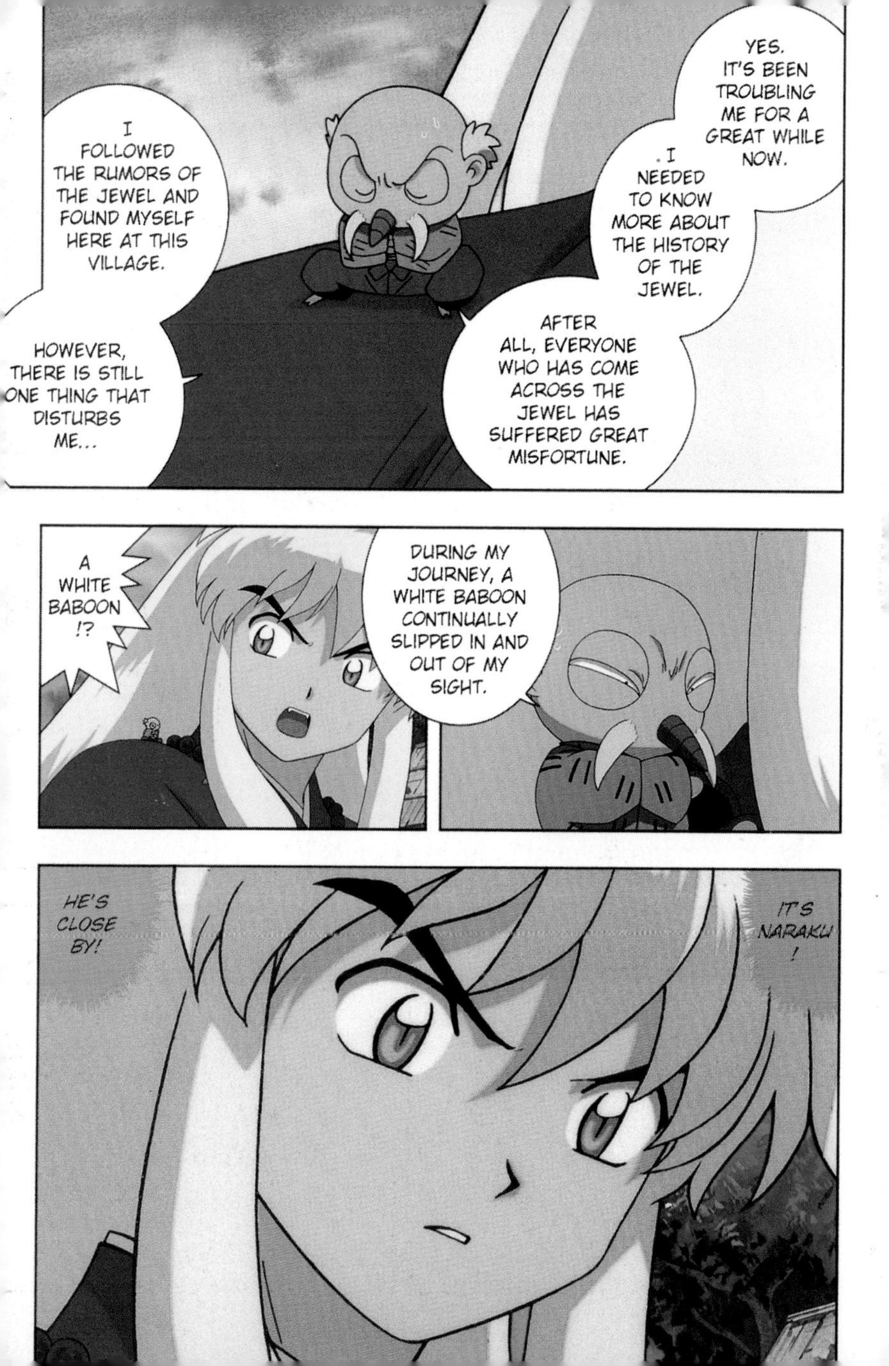
YES. IT'S BEEN TROUBLING ME FOR A GREAT WHILE NOW.
I NEEDED TO KNOW MORE ABOUT THE HISTORY OF THE JEWEL.
I FOLLOWED THE RUMORS OF THE JEWEL AND FOUND MYSELF HERE AT THIS VILLAGE.
AFTER ALL, EVERYONE WHO HAS COME ACROSS THE JEWEL HAS SUFFERED GREAT MISFORTUNE.
HOWEVER, THERE IS STILL ONE THING THAT DISTURBS ME...
DURING MY JOURNEY, A WHITE BABOON CONTINUALLY SLIPPED IN AND OUT OF MY SIGHT.
A WHITE BABOON!?
IT'S NARAKU!
HE'S CLOSE BY!

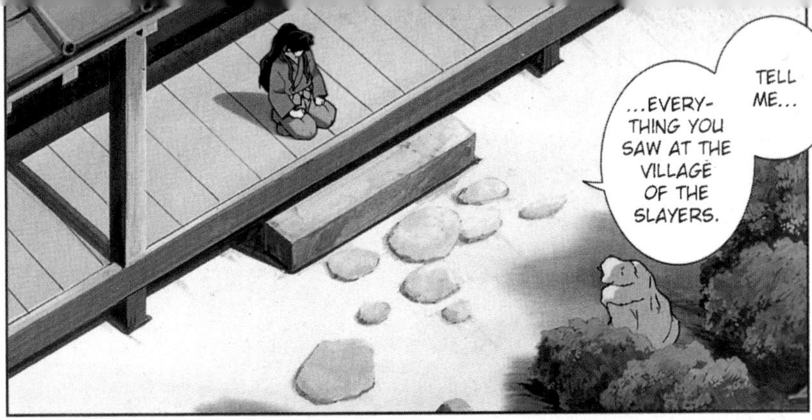
TELL ME...
...EVERYTHING YOU SAW AT THE VILLAGE OF THE SLAYERS.

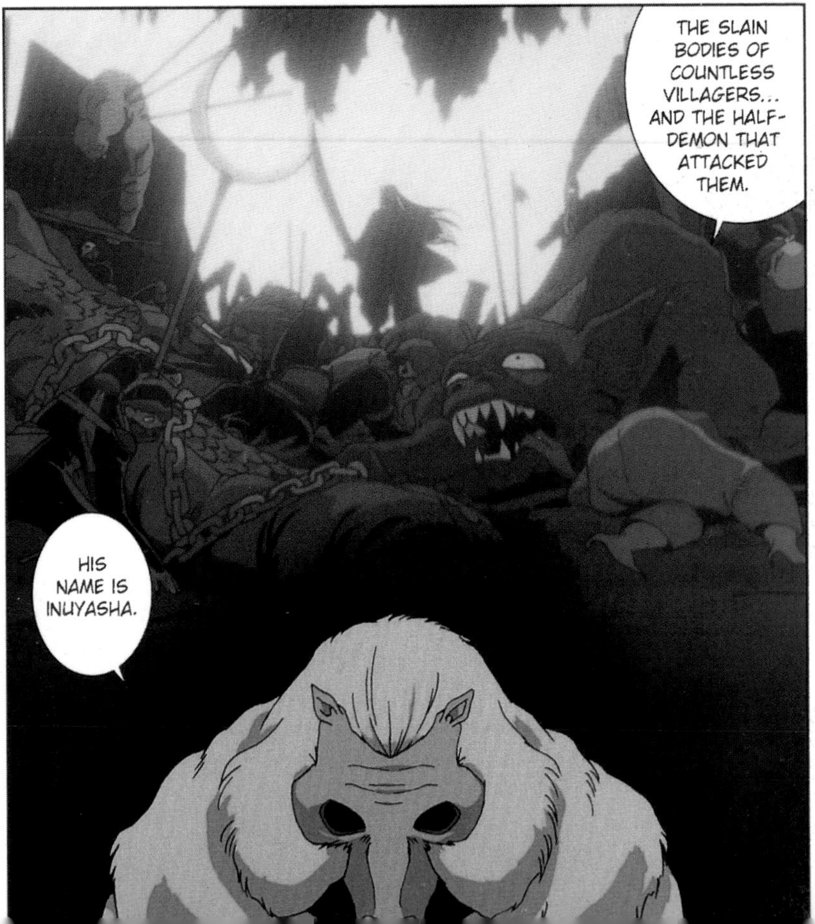
THE SLAIN BODIES OF COUNTLESS VILLAGERS... AND THE HALF-DEMON THAT ATTACKED THEM.
HIS NAME IS INUYASHA.

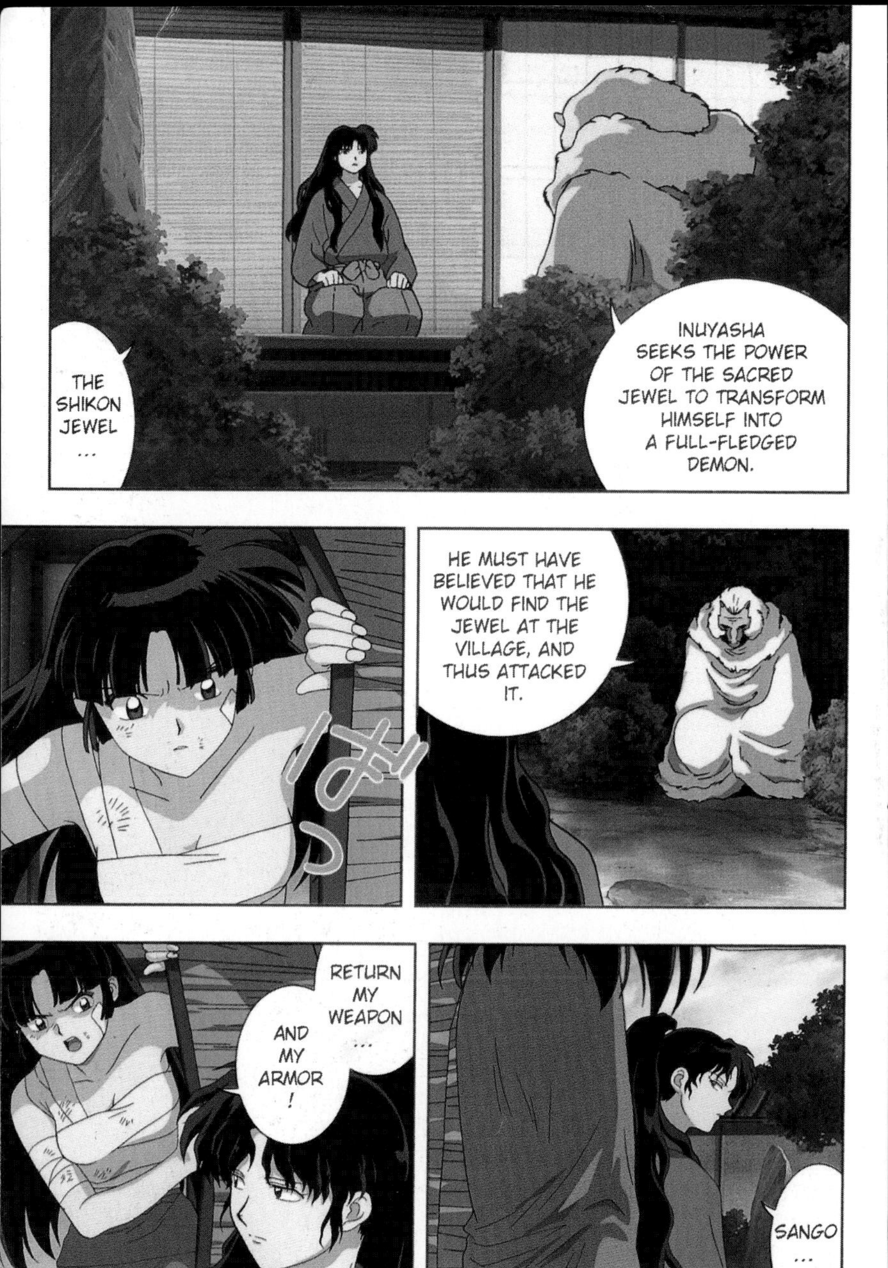
INUYASHA SEEKS THE POWER OF THE SACRED JEWEL TO TRANSFORM HIMSELF INTO A FULL-FLEDGED DEMON.
THE SHIKON JEWEL ...
HE MUST HAVE BELIEVED THAT HE WOULD FIND THE JEWEL AT THE VILLAGE, AND THUS ATTACKED IT.
はっ
SANGO ...
RETURN MY WEAPON ...
AND MY ARMOR !

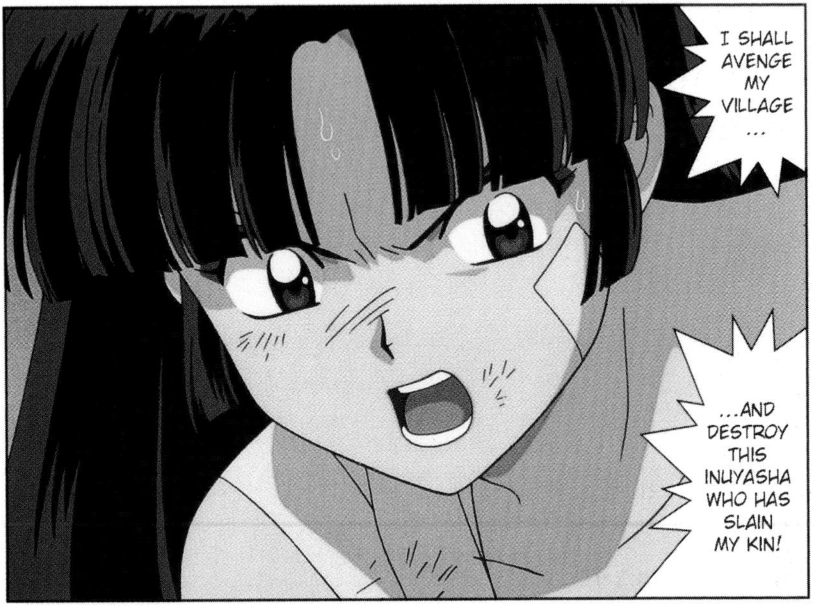
I SHALL AVENGE MY VILLAGE ...
...AND DESTROY THIS INUYASHA WHO HAS SLAIN MY KIN!

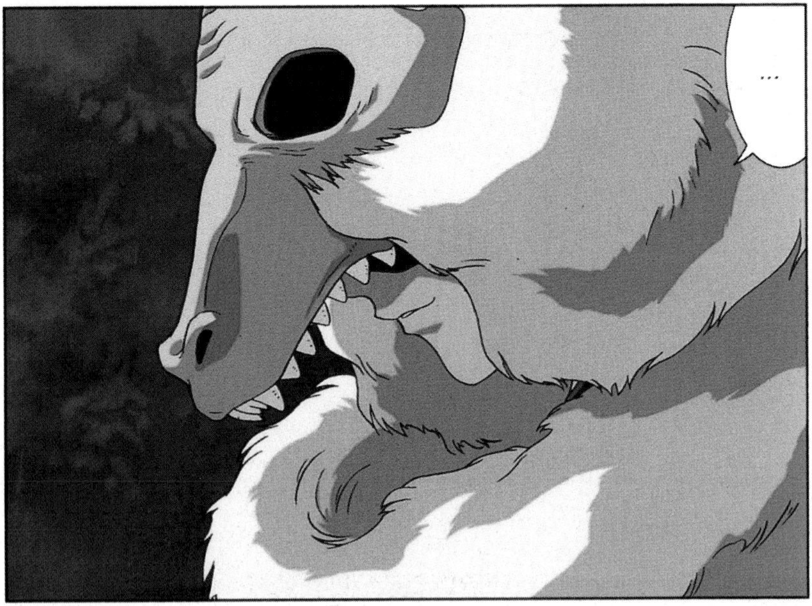
...

TO BE CONTINUED...

Glossary of Sound Effects

Each entry includes: the location, indicated by page number and panel number (so 3.1 means page 3, panel number 1); the phonetic romanization of the original Japanese; and our English "translation"—we offer as close an English equivalent as we can.

34.1 FX: Suu… (dead princess levitates)
34.3 FX: Suu… (body continues to levitate)
34.4 FX: Kaaa… (light shines)
34.5 FX: Gohh (window is broken)

35.1 FX: Gohhh… (whoosh)
35.2 FX: Suu… (soul-stealing demon flying around)
35.4 FX: Fuu… (soul emerging from princess)

36.1 FX: Fuuu… (soul being taken from princess)
36.3 FX: Zuba (slash)
36.5 FX: Fu… (demon turns to smoke)

37.1 FX: Suu… (dead princess's soul sucked back in through mouth)
37.2 FX: Doh (dead princess collapses on pillow)

39.1 FX: Ta (running)
39.5 FX: Gyu… (homely princess squeezes Shippo)

41.3 FX: Su… (Kikyo walking by)

42.3 FX: Suru (Kikyo undoes her hair-band)
42.5 FX: Su… (soul-stealing demons swoop down)

Chapter 22:
A Wicked Smile and Kikyo's Wandering Soul

10.1 FX: Ta ta ta… (running)

13.4 FX: Fura… (monk trips)
13.5 FX: Basa (scroll falls to ground)

16.2 FX: Bachi (crackling)
16.3 FX: Kaa (shining)

20.4 FX: Kaaaa… (shining)

22.1-2 FX: Gohh (roaring)
22.3 FX: Ga (Kikyo grabs Inuyasha)

23.1 FX: Bachi (crackling)
23.2 FX: Ba (Kikyo loses grip)

24.1 FX: Doh doh doh (sound of waterfall)
24.4 FX: Zaaaa… (running water)

31.2 FX: Pito (Kagome snuggles up to Inuyasha)

33.3 FX: Doh (homely princess grabs at Miroku)
33.5 FX: Yura (flames flicker)

43.5 FX: Za (footstep)

45.2 FX: Kaaa… (dragon object shines)
45.5 FX: Ka (dragon object starts to glow)

46.1 FX: Dohhn (beams of light burst out)
46.2 FX: Gohh (whooshing)
46.3 FX: Gohhhh… (whooshing)
46.6 FX: Ga (dragon gets Kikyo by the throat)

47.4 FX: Kaa (dragon object glows)

48.1 FX: Ba (demon-binding dragon explodes)
48.2 FX: Gohh (dragon's dismembered foot heads toward Seikai)
48.3 FX: Ga (foot lands in Seikai's throat)
48.4 FX: Gaku… (Seikai falls to his knees)
48.5 FX: Doh (Seikai drops to the ground)

49.1 FX: Koro… (dragon object rolls)
49.2 FX: Pishi (dragon object cracks)
49.3 FX: Pa—n (dragon object explodes)
49.4 FX: Da (acolyte running away)
49.6 FX: Ga (Seikai grabs Kikyo by the ankle)

50.3 FX: Zuru… (Seikai's grip loosens as he weakens)
50.4 FX: Gaku… (Seikai's head drops as he dies)

52.2 FX: Su… (Kikyo moves hand toward Sayo)
52.3 FX: Biku (she recoils from Kikyo's touch, full of hatred and disgust)

52.5 FX: Su (Kikyo turns away)

56.3 FX: Don (Kagome pushes Inuyasha into river)

59.1 FX: Ga (Inuyasha grabs the acolyte by the robe)

60.1 FX: Doh (Inuyasha lets go of acolyte's robe)
60.5 FX: Ta (Inuyasha touches down)

62.4 FX: Su (Kagome turns away abruptly)

63.2 FX: Gacha (Kagome hops on her bike)

64.5 FX: Fu… (sky darkens)

65.4 FX: Ta ta ta… (running)

66.1 FX: Ta ta ta… (running)
66.2 FX: Su (soul-stealing demon flies)
66.3 FX: Bachi (impact)
66.4 FX: Doh (Shippo and Miroku land smack on ground)
66.5 FX: Pari… (glimmering of spirit shield as Miroku touches it)

67.1 FX: Ta ta ta… (running)
67.2 FX: Za (Kagome slips)

68.2 FX: Zuru… (Kagome slips and falls)
68.4 FX: Zu za za… (Kagome slips down slope)
68.5 FX: Doh (Kagome lands in soft stuff)

110.1-3 FX: Dokun dokun dokun
(heavy thumping heartbeats)
110.4 FX: Kaaaaa… (shining souls escape)

111.4 FX: Zu zu zu…
(Inuyasha and Kikyo sink into hell)

112.4 FX: Ta (Inuyasha leaps)

113.1 FX: Zuba (Inuyasha strikes through demons binding Kagome)
113.2 FX: Ta (Inuyasha lands)

114.3 FX: Gohhhhh…
(whoosh of soul-stealing demons)

116.1 FX: Suu… (Kikyo being borne away by demons)

118.1 FX: Su (Kikyo and demons disappear completely)

122.2 FX: Ta (running)
122.3 FX: Doh (Inuyasha does face plant)

124.1 FX: Zawa…
(clouds parting to expose the moon)
124.3 FX: Za (Kikyo's shadow appears)

127.3 FX: Ka (shining as demons devour Onigumo)

133.2 FX: Ba (Kagome drops into well)

136.1 FX: Suu (Kagome falls into well)
136.2 FX: Toh
(Kagome lands at bottom of well)

Chapter 23:
Kagome's Voice and Kikyo's Kiss

72.1 FX: Zaaaa… (running water)
72.2 FX: Ta (step)

74.1 FX: Bari Bari (crackling)
74.2 FX: Bari (crackling)
74.3 FX: Zuza (Inuyasha sliding)
74.5 FX: Zuru
(Kikyo's hand slips from his grip)

78.5 FX: Su… (sound of magic)

80.1 FX: Ta ta ta… (running)

81.1 FX: Suu… (demons whooshing about)
81.3 FX: Yura… (glimmering of spirit shield)

82.3 FX: Suu… (demon delivers soul)

83.1 FX: Fu… (barrier parts for Inuyasha)

90.4 FX: Za (Inuyasha approaches)

92.1 FX: Za (Inuyasha walks towards Kikyo)

105.1 FX: Gohh (Kikyo starts to sink into hell with Inuyasha)
105.3 FX: Zu zu zu
(Inuyasha and Kikyo going to hell)

108.1 FX: Kaa… (magic gleaming)
108.2 FX: Bachi
(worm demons release Kagome)

163.4 FX: Shururu   ru…
(Kohaku surrounded by web)
163.5 FX: Shururururu… (web wraps around Kohaku's ankle)

164.2 FX: Zan (slayer slashes webs with axe)
164.3 FX: Toh (Kohaku touches down)
164.6 FX: Doga (smash)

165.1 FX: Ga (weapon finds its mark)
165.3 FX: Bun (Sango throws boomerang)
165.4 FX: Zuba (demon whacked in head)
165.5 FX: Bari bari (demon collapses)

166.3 FX: Zawa… (buzz of crowd)
166.5 FX: Ta (clink of chains)

167.1 FX: Su… (spider lands on Kohaku)
167.2 FX: Pita (chains clink)

168.1 FX: Zuba (strike)
168.3 FX: Zan (Sango's father is struck)
168.4 FX: Dosa (Sango's dad collapses)

170.2 FX: Ta (Kohaku runs)
170.4 FX: Ba (Kohaku throws his weapon)
170.5 FX: Gin (blade clangs on Sango's mask)

171.1 FX: Parari
(Sango's mask is knocked off)

172.1 FX: Gin (clang as Sango parries blade on chain)
172.2 FX: Ba (Kohaku leaps)
172.3 FX: Gin (clang of blade on blade)
172.5 FX: Giri (blades pressing against each other)

138.2 FX: Doh (Inuyasha lands in dirt)

Chapter 24:
Enter Sango, the Demon Slayer

140.2 FX: Za za za… (rustling in the forest)
140.4 FX: Za (Sango steps up)

141.1 FX: Doh doh doh
(centipede plows through dirt)
141.2 FX: Gohh (centipede rears up)
141.4 FX: Bun (Sango throws boomerang)
141.5 FX: Zuba (centipede's head slashed from body)

142.1 FX: Zu—n (centipede collapses, dead)
142.2 FX: Kira (jewel shard sparkles)
142.3 FX: Pashi (shard falls into Sango's hand)

152.2 FX: Gii (creak)
152.2-3 FX: Zu zu zu… (gate lifts)

153.2 FX: Ta (Kirara approaches)
153.5 FX: Ta ta ta… (running)

160.3 FX: Goro goro goro…
(rumbling, demons approaching)

161.1 FX: Ka (shining of demon eyes in the darkness)
161.2 FX: Gohh (swoosh)
161.3 FX: Zuu…n…
(sliding thump as demon lands)

163.1 FX: Goh (spider demon spews web)
163.3 FX: Zuba (slash)

173.5 FX: Doga (Sango kicks Kohaku)

174.3 FX: Da (Sango lunges)
174.4 FX: Doga (strike)
174.5 FX: Zan (thunk as Sango is struck in the back)
175.3 FX: Za (Kohaku drops to his knees)

176.2 FX: Ta (running)
176.4 FX: Shururuṛu… (arrows fly through air)

177.1 FX: Doh (arrows thunk into Kohaku's body)

178.3 FX: Doh (Sango falls)
178.5 FX: Zuba (swipe of sword)

179.5 FX: Zawa… (movement of shadow across floor)

180.2 FX: Ga (blade slams into wood)

183.5 FX: Gohhhh… (wind blowing)

184.1 FX: Zawa… (wind)
184.3 FX: Gohhhh… (whoosh of demons passing overhead)

185.2 FX: Gohhh (demons whoosh past)

186.3 FX: Boko (hand pokes out of shallow grave)
186.4 FX: Zuru… (Sango drags herself out of grave)

187.1 FX: Zuru… (Sango dragging herself)

188.1 FX: Dohn (distant explosions as village is sacked)
188.4 FX: Ba (Naraku flies toward village)
188.5 FX: Gohhh… (roar of flames)
188.6 FX: Ta ta ta… (running, battle sound)

190.3 FX: Guoh (whoosh of demons closing in to be absorbed by Naraku)
190.4 FX: Kaaaaa… (shining)

191.1 FX: Ka (explosion of light)
191.2 FX: Shuuuu… (Naraku absorbs strength from the demons)

192.3 FX: Da (they suddenly start running)

195.2 FX: Za (Kirara appears from behind shed)

196.6 FX: Gohh (Kirara bursts into flame)

197.1 FX: Shuuuu… (Kirara shrinks to kitty size)
197.3 FX: Pyon (Myoga springs off)
197.4 FX: Chiuu (slurp)
197.5 FX: Bashi (smack)

201.1 FX: Za… (Naraku appears from out of the bushes)

205.3 FX: Ba (Sango grabs door lintel to drag herself up)

Rated #1 on Cartoon Network's Adult Swim!

In its original, unedited form!

The beloved romantic comedy of errors—a fan favorite!

The zany, wacky study of martial arts at its best!

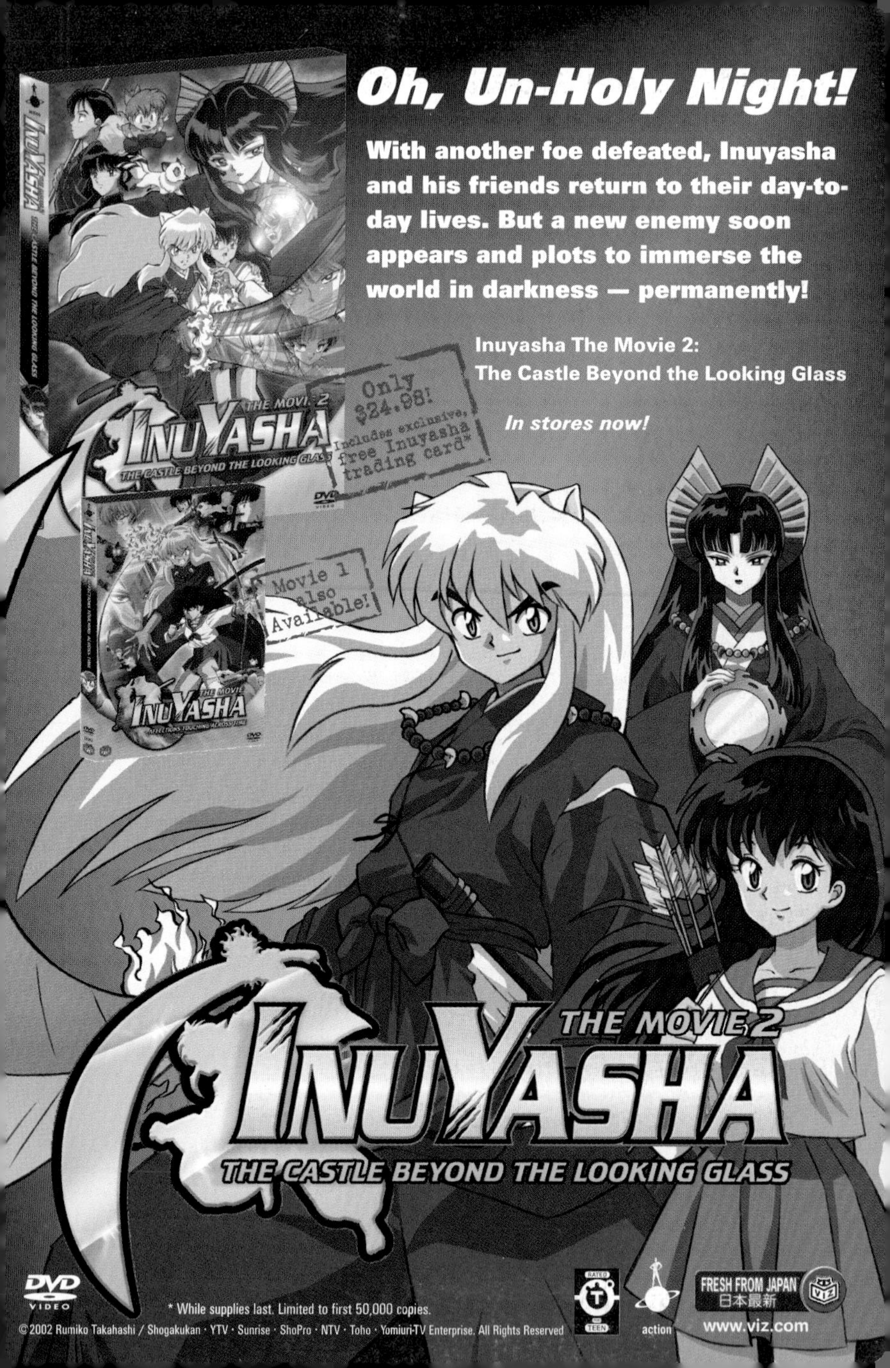

Oh, Un-Holy Night!
With another foe defeated, Inuyasha and his friends return to their day-to-day lives. But a new enemy soon appears and plots to immerse the world in darkness — permanently!
Inuyasha The Movie 2: The Castle Beyond the Looking Glass
In stores now!
Only $24.98! Includes exclusive, free Inuyasha trading card*
Movie 1 also Available!
THE MOVIE 2
INUYASHA
THE CASTLE BEYOND THE LOOKING GLASS
* While supplies last. Limited to first 50,000 copies.
© 2002 Rumiko Takahashi / Shogakukan · YTV · Sunrise · ShoPro · NTV · Toho · Yomiuri-TV Enterprise. All Rights Reserved
DVD VIDEO
RATED T TEEN
action
FRESH FROM JAPAN 日本最新
VIZ
www.viz.com

COMPLETE OUR SURVEY AND LET US KNOW WHAT YOU THINK!

☐ Please do NOT send me information about VIZ products, news and events, special offers, or other information.

☐ Please do NOT send me information from VIZ's trusted business partners.

Name: _____

Address: _____

City: _____ **State:** _____ **Zip:** _____

E-mail: _____

☐ Male ☐ Female **Date of Birth** (mm/dd/yyyy): ___ / ___ / ___ (Under 13? Parental consent required)

What race/ethnicity do you consider yourself? (please check one)

☐ Asian/Pacific Islander ☐ Black/African American ☐ Hispanic/Latino

☐ Native American/Alaskan Native ☐ White/Caucasian ☐ Other: _____

What VIZ product did you purchase? (check all that apply and indicate title purchased)

☐ DVD/VHS _____

☐ Graphic Novel _____

☐ Magazines _____

☐ Merchandise _____

Reason for purchase: (check all that apply)

☐ Special offer ☐ Favorite title ☐ Gift

☐ Recommendation ☐ Other _____

Where did you make your purchase? (please check one)

☐ Comic store ☐ Bookstore ☐ Mass/Grocery Store

☐ Newsstand ☐ Video/Video Game Store ☐ Other: _____

☐ Online (site: _____)

What other VIZ properties have you purchased/own? _____

_____

How many anime and/or manga titles have you purchased in the last year? How many were VIZ titles? (please check one from each column)

ANIME

☐ None
☐ 1-4
☐ 5-10
☐ 11+

MANGA

☐ None
☐ 1-4
☐ 5-10
☐ 11+

VIZ

☐ None
☐ 1-4
☐ 5-10
☐ 11+

I find the pricing of VIZ products to be: (please check one)

☐ Cheap   ☐ Reasonable   ☐ Expensive

What genre of manga and anime would you like to see from VIZ? (please check two)

☐ Adventure   ☐ Comic Strip   ☐ Science Fiction   ☐ Fighting
☐ Horror   ☐ Romance   ☐ Fantasy   ☐ Sports

What do you think of VIZ's new look?

☐ Love It   ☐ It's OK   ☐ Hate It   ☐ Didn't Notice   ☐ No Opinion

Which do you prefer? (please check one)

☐ Reading right-to-left

☐ Reading left-to-right

Which do you prefer? (please check one)

☐ Sound effects in English

☐ Sound effects in Japanese with English captions

☐ Sound effects in Japanese only with a glossary at the back

THANK YOU! Please send the completed form to:

VIZ Survey
42 Catharine St.
Poughkeepsie, NY 12601

All information provided will be used for internal purposes only. We promise not to sell or otherwise divulge your information.